DIGITAL SAT EXAM PREP

"Study is like the light that illuminates the darkness of ignorance, and the knowledge that results is the supreme possession, for it cannot be taken away even by the most skillful of thieves. Study is the weapon that eliminates the enemy which is ignorance. It is also the best friend that guides us through all our difficult moments."

—Dalai lama

CONQUERMINDS PRESS

TABLE OF CONTENTS

DOWNLOAD HERE YOUR FULL-LENGTH SIMULATIONS!

Dear Student,

I'm excited to accompany you on your journey toward conquering the DIGITAL SAT. I understand the effort, dedication, and persistence needed to succeed, and that's why I created this guide—to help you study smarter and more efficiently.

Inside this manual, you'll discover 3 full-length practice exams. Plus, with the included QR code, you can instantly access SEVEN additional tests at no extra cost. I opted for this hybrid format for several key reasons:

- **Cost Savings:** Packing all ten exams into a single printed volume would have increased the weight and price. This way, you get all the content you need without a hefty cost.
- **Instant Updates:** The digital component makes it simple to roll out corrections or new materials promptly, ensuring you always have the most current information.
- **Adaptability:** Whether you prefer printing the tests at home or working on them online, this format adapts to your individual study habits.

My aim is to provide you with a comprehensive, affordable, and user-friendly resource that supports your exam preparation every step of the way. I'm here to help you reach your goals and celebrate your milestones.

Wishing you the very best of luck—happy studying and go ace that exam!

SCAN THE QR CODE!

You will get:

- 7 extra full length exam simulations
- Weekly extra exam bonus

PART I

INTRODUCTION TO THE DIGITAL SAT

CHAPTER 1

WELCOME TO THE NEW SAT

1.1 Understanding the SAT's Role in College Admissions

For many decades, the SAT has served as a standard measure colleges and universities use to assess a student's academic readiness for higher education. While high school grades and extracurricular achievements reflect a broader picture of a student's capabilities, standardized tests like the SAT offer a common benchmark that admissions officers can compare across varying school curricula, grading scales, and regional differences.

To understand its role thoroughly, it helps to consider both the historical context and the current admissions landscape:

- **Historical Context**
  Originally introduced in the early 20th century as the Scholastic Aptitude Test, the SAT was created to broaden access to higher education. Over time, colleges increasingly adopted it (and the similarly purposed ACT) as a tool to gauge critical thinking skills in reading, writing, and math.
- **Admissions Weight**
  Each institution treats the SAT differently. Some universities place a heavier emphasis on it, especially in competitive programs, while others view it as just one of several factors. In today's environment, the SAT can help distinguish applicants in large, competitive pools where admissions officers need an additional metric beyond high school GPAs and personal essays.
- **Test-Optional Movement**
  Over the past decade, many institutions have adopted test-optional or test-flexible policies. These changes give students the choice of submitting SAT scores, recognizing that not all learners demonstrate their strengths best through standardized testing. However, even at test-optional schools, a strong SAT score can help a student stand out or meet certain scholarship criteria.
- **Scholarships and Merit Aid**
  In addition to admissions, SAT scores often influence merit-based financial aid. Many universities and private organizations use a combination of GPA and test scores to award scholarships. A high score may unlock additional funding opportunities, making the SAT not just an admissions requirement but also a financial consideration for families.
- **Global Recognition**
  While widely used in the United States, the SAT also serves as a recognized indicator of academic prowess internationally. For international applicants aiming to study in the U.S., a competitive SAT score can demonstrate readiness to succeed in an American college environment.
- **Complementing Other Application Components**
  It's important to remember that colleges conduct holistic reviews. Admissions committees usually consider essays, recommendation letters, extracurricular involvement, and personal achievements alongside SAT scores. A great SAT performance won't overshadow significant issues elsewhere, but it can reinforce an otherwise strong application.

Despite the evolving debate around standardized testing, the SAT remains a key element in admissions for many institutions, especially for students applying to more competitive schools or seeking certain scholarship opportunities. Understanding its overall purpose helps test-takers recognize why preparation is essential—not simply for a higher score, but for better alignment with college-level work expectations.

1.2 Overview of the Digital Transition

As the landscape of education and technology evolves, the SAT has responded by moving from a traditional paper-and-pencil format to a digital platform. This significant change aims to keep the test more aligned with modern learning tools and streamline the testing experience for students and administrators alike. Understanding the transition's key drivers and benefits helps illustrate why and how the College Board decided to adopt a fully digital model.

- **Reasons Behind the Move**
  - **Technological Advances**: Over the last decade, digital devices—such as laptops and tablets—have become widely accessible. These tools make it possible to deliver a secure, uniform testing experience to a diverse range of students.
  - **Efficiency and Speed**: By offering an online test, the College Board has been able to shorten administration times and expedite score reporting. Digital scoring technology allows for rapid processing once a student completes the exam.
  - **Adaptive Testing Capabilities**: Traditional paper tests can't easily tailor question difficulty to the test-taker's performance. The digital format supports adaptive modules, enabling the SAT to measure skills more precisely while using fewer questions overall.
- **Key Phases of Implementation**
  1. **Pilot Programs**: Early on, select groups of students were invited to test digital prototypes. Feedback from these sessions guided improvements in layout, navigation, and security.
  2. **International Rollout**: Beginning in 2023, international test centers transitioned to the digital version, phasing out paper in most locations outside the United States.
  3. **Nationwide Adoption**: In 2024, schools in the U.S. gradually adopted the digital SAT. By 2025, nearly all official test administrations were offered exclusively through the digital platform.
- **Benefits for Students**
  - **User-Friendly Interface**: The digital SAT includes on-screen tools, like a built-in Desmos calculator, highlighting/annotating features, and timed sections displayed prominently on the interface.
  - **Faster Results**: Because scoring is automated, students often see results quicker, reducing the waiting period and helping them manage admissions timelines more effectively.
  - **Reduced Testing Time**: The adaptive test design is more efficient, allowing the entire SAT to be administered in a shorter window without compromising the depth of skill assessment.
- **Considerations and Challenges**
  - **Device and Connectivity**: Students must have reliable access to an approved device. For those lacking such resources, test centers typically provide school-owned devices to ensure equitable participation.
  - **Learning Curve**: Some test-takers and educators have needed time to familiarize themselves with the testing app, though official practice materials and tutorials aim to smooth this transition.
  - **Test Security**: The digital platform adopts sophisticated security features, but consistent protocols—such as locked-down browsers and ID checks—remain crucial to maintain fairness and integrity.

The digital transition has been a multi-year endeavor marked by continuous updates and refinements. Although it represents a departure from the longstanding paper-based tradition, the College Board views the move as a necessary step to modernize the SAT and provide a more personalized, efficient, and relevant assessment experience.

1.3 Key Differences Between Paper and Digital Versions

As the SAT moves away from pencil-and-paper, the fundamental content remains the same—students are still tested on critical reading, writing, and math skills. However, a number of structural and experiential differences set the digital exam apart. Below is a concise comparison chart highlighting these key changes:

Aspect	Paper-based SAT	Digital SAT
Format & Administration	- Pencil-and-paper test with scantron sheets for answers. - Proctors distribute physical test booklets.	- Computer- or tablet-based test taken via secure testing software. - Digital interface with on-screen questions and answer submission.
Question Delivery	- Static set of questions in one fixed order.	- Adaptive modules that adjust question difficulty based on performance in the first part of each section.

Timing & Length	- Approx. 3 hours total. - Separate Reading, Writing, and Math sections with optional essay.	- Slightly shorter at around 2 hours 14 minutes. - Combined Reading & Writing section and a separate Math section; essay typically not offered.
Tools & Calculators	- Students must bring their own College Board–approved calculator for the designated Math section.	- Built-in Desmos-style graphing calculator available for the entire Math section. - Students can still bring an approved physical calculator if they wish.
Scratch Work	- Students write notes and calculations in the test booklet.	- Physical scratch paper generally provided; digital notes/annotations are also possible in some testing interfaces.
Scoring & Result Turnaround	- Scores available in about 2–3 weeks.	- Faster score reporting, often within a week or two, thanks to automated scoring of digital responses.
Security & Fairness	- Must ensure no external materials are brought in.	- Secure lockdown browser technology with limited functionality to prevent cheating. - Inflexible once the test starts; no internet access.
Adaptability	- No adaptation; all students face the same set of questions.	- Section-level adaptive structure offers more precise measurement of skill level with fewer items overall.

With these differences, the **Digital SAT** often feels more streamlined, letting students engage with questions in an interface similar to digital tools they use daily. At the same time, adopting a new format can require additional preparation—students should practice navigating the adaptive modules, utilizing the on-screen calculator, and ensuring comfort with reading passages on screen.

CHAPTER 2

EXAM STRUCTURE & FORMAT

2.1 Section-by-Section Breakdown (Reading & Writing, Math)

The Digital SAT is divided into two primary sections: **Reading & Writing** and **Math**. Each section is split into two modules, and each module adapts to a student's performance, presenting questions that best gauge their skill level. Though these sections collectively measure your critical thinking, reading comprehension, writing proficiency, and mathematical aptitude, each has its own unique structure and types of questions.

Reading & Writing Section

1. **Combined Format**
    - The Digital SAT merges what were previously the separate Reading Test and Writing & Language Test into a single **Reading & Writing** section.
    - You will see two adaptive modules, each containing short passages followed by individual questions.
2. **Passage Types and Topics**
    - Passages typically span **literature**, **historical documents**, **social sciences**, and **science**-related fields.
    - Each passage is concise—often just a few paragraphs—and each question targets a specific reading or writing skill.
3. **Question Categories**
    - **Reading Comprehension**: Main ideas, details, inferences, author's tone, and purpose.
    - **Vocabulary in Context**: Determining the meaning of words or phrases based on how they are used.
    - **Grammar and Usage**: Subject-verb agreement, pronoun clarity, verb tense, parallel structure, and sentence boundaries.
    - **Rhetorical Skills**: Organization, clarity, conciseness, and effective use of transitions.
4. **Question Formats**
    - **Multiple Choice Only**: Each question has four possible answers.
    - Each question is linked directly to a single short passage or passage excerpt.
5. **Timing and Structure**
    - Overall, expect **two modules** of Reading & Writing. Each module generally contains around **27 questions** and runs about **32 minutes**, for a total of **54 questions** and **64 minutes** in this section.
    - The difficulty of the second module is determined by your performance on the first.
6. **Scoring**
    - Performance in the Reading & Writing section yields a scaled score from **200 to 800**.
    - Adaptive modules mean that strong performance in the first module can lead to more challenging items in the second, potentially offering a higher scoring range.

Math Section

1. **Two Adaptive Modules**
    - Like Reading & Writing, the Math section is split into **two modules** that adjust based on your initial performance.
    - The first module covers a broad mix of difficulty levels, and the second module tailors the difficulty to best assess your skill level.
2. **Content Domains**
    - **Algebra**: Linear equations, systems of equations, and function notation.
    - **Advanced Math**: Polynomials, quadratic equations, exponential functions, and other higher-level concepts.
    - **Problem Solving & Data Analysis**: Ratios, percentages, interpreting graphs, and basic probability/statistics.
    - **Geometry & Trigonometry**: Circles, triangles, angles, right-triangle trigonometry, and other geometric relationships.
3. **Question Types**

- **Multiple Choice**: About three-quarters of the Math items have four answer choices.
- **Student-Produced Responses (Grid-Ins)**: The remaining items require you to enter numerical answers without provided choices.
- A built-in **Desmos-style** graphing calculator is available **throughout the Math section**. You may also bring your own approved calculator.

4. **Timing and Structure**
   - Total Math time is approximately **70 minutes**, with each module spanning about **35 minutes**.
   - Expect around **44 questions** in total, split roughly equally between the two modules.
5. **Scoring**
   - Your Math score ranges from **200 to 800**.
   - As with Reading & Writing, the adaptive format can present more advanced questions if you do well on the first module, enabling a fuller display of your capabilities.

Key Takeaways

- **Two Main Sections**: Rather than three separate segments (Reading, Writing, Math), the Digital SAT consolidates Reading & Writing into one combined section plus a single Math section.
- **Adaptive Modules**: Each section has two modules that adapt in difficulty based on your performance, allowing a more efficient assessment of skill while reducing total testing time.
- **Timing**: Plan for around **64 minutes** on Reading & Writing and **70 minutes** on Math, plus a short break in between.
- **Calculator Integration**: The built-in graphing calculator in the Math section simplifies computational tasks, but familiarity with its functions beforehand is crucial.

This streamlined structure aims to reduce fatigue, emphasize essential college-readiness skills, and allow for a faster score turnaround. Understanding the mechanics of each section and how the adaptive modules work will help you prepare effectively and manage time on test day.

2.2 Adaptive Testing Explained

Adaptive testing is a defining feature of the Digital SAT. Unlike the traditional, static paper format, where every student sees the same questions in the same order, the digital exam tailors part of its content based on a test taker's performance in the first module of each section. This approach aims to evaluate each student's capabilities more efficiently and accurately. Below are key points about how adaptive testing works and why it matters:

How Adaptive Testing Works

1. **Two Modules per Section**
   - Each section (Reading & Writing, Math) is split into **Module 1** and **Module 2**.
   - Module 1 includes a range of question difficulties—easy, medium, and hard—designed to gauge your overall skill level.
2. **Performance-Based Adjustment**
   - After you complete Module 1, the test's algorithm quickly analyzes your responses.
   - Based on your performance, Module 2 can present a set of questions at a difficulty level that aligns with the skills you demonstrated.
3. **Efficient Assessment**
   - By focusing on questions at or near your skill level, the adaptive format measures your true proficiency more precisely.
   - It also **reduces total testing time**, since the test doesn't need to present a full range of easy through hard questions to every student.

Benefits of Adaptive Testing

- **Shorter Overall Exam**: The Digital SAT is about 45 minutes shorter than the old paper-based version, offering a less grueling experience without sacrificing assessment depth.
- **Targeted Measurement**: Stronger students are challenged with more advanced questions, while those needing more foundational practice won't get bogged down in overly complex problems.
- **Faster Score Reporting**: With digital scoring and adaptive algorithms, results can be processed and returned more rapidly, helping you make quicker decisions about retesting or college applications.

Strategies for Tackling Adaptive Modules

1. **Maintain Consistency**

   - Aim for accuracy in Module 1 to access higher-difficulty questions in Module 2 (if your goal is a top score).
   - Don't rush; errors in the first module can result in a second module that limits your upper scoring range.
2. **Handle Early Questions Carefully**
   - Each question in Module 1 can influence the difficulty level assigned later.
   - Stay focused from the start, and avoid guesswork until you're sure you can't determine the correct answer.
3. **Use Time Wisely**
   - Each module has a set number of minutes. If you find a question difficult, mark it and return after addressing other items.
   - This ensures you don't miss easier points and can revisit the more challenging questions if time allows.
4. **Stay Confident**
   - Getting a challenging second module indicates you did well in the first. Keep calm and use your skills, even if you see tougher questions.
   - If the second module remains moderate in difficulty, focus on getting those correct rather than worrying about what might have happened in the first module.

Adaptive testing transforms the SAT from a one-size-fits-all exam into a more nuanced measure of your reading, writing, and math abilities. Understanding its mechanics allows you to approach each module strategically, balancing speed and accuracy to showcase your best performance.

2.3 Timing, Question Count, and Navigation Features

One of the most noticeable changes in the Digital SAT is how the test organizes questions and manages timing. The adaptive format influences both the pace and order in which students tackle the exam. Below is an overview of how timing works, how many questions to expect, and the key navigation tools available during the test.

Overall Timing

- **Reading & Writing Section**
  - Divided into **two modules** of approximately **32 minutes each**, totaling around **64 minutes**.
  - Each module typically contains **27 questions**, for a total of **54** Reading & Writing questions.
- **Math Section**
  - Divided into **two modules** of about **35 minutes each**, totaling around **70 minutes**.
  - Each module generally features **22 questions**, for a total of **44** Math questions.
  - Includes a built-in **Desmos-style** calculator throughout, plus the option to use a personal approved calculator if preferred.
- **Breaks**
  - After finishing the Reading & Writing section, you usually get a **10-minute break** before beginning the Math section.
  - Some test centers may provide additional short breaks, but the standard schedule typically includes one main break.

Question Count and Distribution

- **Reading & Writing**
  - Each module consists of short passages, each followed by a single question.
  - The **distribution of passage topics** (literature, historical documents, social sciences, science) is similar between modules, though Module 2's difficulty may adjust based on prior performance.
- **Math**
  - Around **75%** of the questions are **multiple choice** with **four options**, while the remaining 25% are **student-produced responses** (grid-ins).
  - The range of topics (Algebra, Advanced Math, Geometry/Trigonometry, Problem Solving & Data Analysis) appears in both modules, but Module 2 may present more challenging items if you excel in Module 1.

On-Screen Navigation Features

1. **Question List & Progress Bar**

    - The testing interface typically provides a clear list or progress bar indicating how many questions are in the current module and which question you are currently answering.
    - You can see how many items remain, which helps with pacing.
2. **Flagging or Marking Questions**
    - A **flag** or **mark for review** option allows you to note questions you'd like to revisit if time permits. This feature is especially useful in managing tricky items without losing your overall pace.
3. **Timer Display**
    - A **countdown timer** is usually visible on the screen. It may turn yellow or red during the final minutes of a section to alert you that time is running short.
    - Once the time for a module expires, you can no longer return to those questions.
4. **Navigation Buttons**
    - **Next** and **Previous** buttons let you move among questions within the same module. You typically cannot go back to a previous module once you've submitted it.
    - The interface may offer a "Review" screen showing which items are answered, unanswered, or flagged.
5. **Built-In Tools**
    - **Calculator** for Math: Available directly on the screen at all times in the Math section.
    - **Annotate/Highlight**: Many digital tests allow you to highlight text in Reading & Writing passages.
    - **Scratch Paper**: Physical scratch paper is still provided in testing centers for additional calculations or notes.

Time-management tips

- **Pace Yourself**: Be aware of the timer and the number of questions. Having a rough idea of how many minutes to allocate per item helps prevent rushing at the end.
- **Use Flags Wisely**: If a question seems especially tough, flag it, move on, and return later if you have time.
- **Check Before Submitting**: In each module, try to revisit flagged items or questions you were unsure about before time runs out.
- **Stay Aware of Module Changes**: Once you submit Module 1, you proceed to Module 2. You cannot revisit Module 1 questions once you've moved on.

Mastering these timing and navigation features is crucial to performing your best on the Digital SAT. By planning how to allocate your time, getting comfortable with the on-screen tools, and practicing a systematic approach to answering and reviewing, you can boost both speed and accuracy under real exam conditions.

CHAPTER 3

REGISTRATION AND TEST DAY LOGISTICS

3.1 How to Register (Domestic and International)

Registering for the **Digital SAT** is a straightforward process, but students must pay close attention to deadlines, test dates, and testing locations to ensure a smooth experience. Below is a step-by-step guide to registering for the SAT, both in the **United States** and for **international test-takers**.

Step 1: Create a College Board Account

All SAT registrations go through the **College Board website**. If you haven't already, you'll need to create an account:

1. Visit **collegeboard.org**.
2. Click on "Sign Up" and enter your **name, date of birth, email address, and other personal details**.
3. Create a **username and password** that you'll use to manage test registrations and scores.
4. Complete your **student profile**, including academic interests and planned college majors (this is optional but can help match you with colleges and scholarship programs).

Important: Ensure that the **name** you use exactly matches your government-issued ID, as mismatched names can lead to test-day issues.

Step 2: Choose Your Test Date and Location

A. SAT Test Dates and Deadlines

The SAT is offered **multiple times per year**, typically in **March, May, June, August, October, November, and December**.

- Registration deadlines are usually **about a month before the test date**.
- **Late registration** is available for an additional fee, typically up to 10–14 days before the test date.

Where to Find Dates: Visit the official College Board website's SAT schedule page to see the **most updated list of test dates**.

B. Domestic Test Centers (U.S.)

Students in the U.S. can choose from a wide range of **testing centers**, including:

- High schools
- Community colleges
- Official testing centers

Tip: Select a test center early—popular locations fill up quickly, especially for fall test dates when college applications are due.

C. International Test Centers

For students outside the U.S., the **Digital SAT is available in most countries**, though availability may vary based on region.

- International students must often take the SAT on specific **international test dates**, which may differ from U.S. test dates.
- Some locations **do not** offer the SAT due to local regulations or limited testing capacity.
- Countries with high demand may have limited seating, so register early to secure your spot.

Where to Register: International students can register the same way as U.S. students—through the College Board website.

D. School-Based Testing (SAT School Day)

Many high schools in the U.S. now **offer the SAT during a school day** (called **SAT School Day**).

- If your school participates, you do **not** need to register individually—your school will handle the process.
- Ask your **school counselor** if your school offers this option.

Step 3: Select Testing Accommodations (If Needed)

Students who need accommodations for disabilities should **request approval early** (see section 3.4 for details).

- Accommodations such as **extra time, a separate testing room, or assistive technology** require documentation and College Board approval.
- Requests should be made **months in advance** (at least 2–3 months before your test date).

Step 4: Pay the Registration Fee

A. SAT Registration Costs

- **U.S. Students**: $60
- **International Students**: Additional regional fees may apply
- **Late Registration Fee**: Usually around **$30 extra**
- **Score Reports**: First **4 score reports are free**, but additional reports cost **$12 each**.

B. Fee Waivers

Students from low-income families **may qualify for fee waivers**, which cover:

- **Two** SAT test registrations
- **Unlimited** score reports to colleges
- Free access to some college application fee waivers

To check eligibility, visit the College Board website or ask your **high school counselor**.

Step 5: Confirmation and Test Prep

Once you complete your registration:
✓ You'll receive a **confirmation email** with your test details.
✓ Log into your **College Board account** to verify all information.
✓ Download **SAT practice tests** and review study materials to begin preparing.

Key Registration Deadlines & Considerations

Action	Typical Deadline
Standard Registration	~1 month before test date
Late Registration	~10–14 days before test date (extra fee applies)
Test Date Changes	Allowed up to **5 days before** the exam (fees apply)
Accommodation Requests	At least **2–3 months before** test date

Final Registration Tips

✓ **Register early**—test centers can fill up quickly.
✓ **Double-check your information**—your name must match your official ID.
✓ **Print your admission ticket** before test day—you won't be admitted without it.
✓ **Confirm location details**—know where your test center is and how long it takes to get there.

By following these steps carefully, you can ensure a smooth registration process and avoid last-minute stress leading up to test day.

3.2 Device Requirements and College Board Testing App

The **Digital SAT** is administered on a secure digital platform, requiring students to use an approved device and the official **College Board Bluebook™ app**. To ensure a smooth testing experience, students must **check their device compatibility, install the testing software, and complete necessary system checks before test day**.

Below is a detailed guide to understanding the device requirements and the functionality of the College Board testing app.

Device Requirements

To take the Digital SAT, students must use one of the following **approved devices**:

Device Type	Allowed?	Notes
Windows Laptop	✅Yes	Must have Windows 10 or later. No virtual machines allowed.
Mac Laptop	✅Yes	Must have macOS 10.13 or later.
Chromebook	✅Yes	School-managed or personal Chromebooks must have Chrome OS 89 or later.
iPad (School-Owned)	✅Yes	Must have iPadOS 13.4 or later. Personal iPads **are not** allowed.
Desktop Computer	❌No	Not permitted (students must use a portable device).
Phones/Tablets (Personal)	❌No	Only school-managed iPads are allowed. Personal Android/iOS tablets are not supported.

Minimum Device Specifications

To ensure smooth functionality, your device should meet these **minimum technical requirements**:

- **Battery Life**: Must last at least **3 hours**. If your battery is weak, bring a charger (availability of outlets depends on the test center).
- **Storage**: At least **250 MB of free space** for downloading and running the **Bluebook™ app**.
- **Internet Connection**: Required to start the exam, but the test continues even if the connection drops mid-test.
- **Screen Size**: A minimum of **10.1 inches** recommended for readability and comfort.
- **External Devices**: External keyboards/mice are allowed but must be **wired (no Bluetooth devices allowed).**

TIP: If you don't have an appropriate device, request one from your school or test center **at least 30 days before the test**.

The College Board Bluebook™ App

All students must use **Bluebook™**, the official College Board testing application, to take the SAT. This app ensures a **secure testing environment** while providing built-in tools to assist with the exam.

How to Download and Install Bluebook™

1. **Visit the Official Website**: Go to bluebook.collegeboard.org.
2. **Download the App**: Select the correct version for your **Windows, macOS, Chromebook, or school-issued iPad**.
3. **Install the Software**: Follow on-screen instructions to complete installation.
4. **Log in**: Use your **College Board account** credentials to access your test settings.
5. **Run System Check**: Ensure your device passes compatibility tests **at least a week before test day**.

Features of the Bluebook™ App

The Bluebook™ app is designed to provide **a user-friendly testing experience** while ensuring test security. Below are some key features:

Feature	Function
Built-in Timer	Displays remaining time for each section. Warnings appear when time is running low.

Navigation Buttons	Move between questions within a module (but you **cannot return to a previous module**).
Annotation & Flagging	Highlight text, take digital notes, and mark questions to review later.
Desmos Calculator	Fully functional **graphing calculator** available for the entire Math section.
Scratch Paper Allowed	Though digital annotation is available, students are also provided **physical scratch paper**.
Auto-Save Feature	The test saves automatically every few seconds. If your device restarts or crashes, you can resume without losing progress.

Pre-Test Preparation Checklist

To avoid technical issues on test day, complete the following steps **well in advance**:

- **Install and test the Bluebook™ app** at least **one week before** the exam.
- **Check your login credentials**—confirm your College Board account is active.
- **Run a system check** through the Bluebook™ app to verify compatibility.
- **Fully charge your device** the night before the test.
- **Ensure software is updated**—install any required updates ahead of time.

IMPORTANT: If your device **fails the system check**, immediately contact the College Board or your school to arrange a loaner device.

Test Day Troubleshooting

If you experience technical difficulties on test day, follow these solutions:

Issue	Possible Fix
Bluebook won't launch	Restart your device and try again. If it still doesn't work, inform your proctor.
App crashes mid-test	The test auto-saves. Restart the app, and you should be able to resume where you left off.
Battery running low	Plug in your device if outlets are available. If not, notify your proctor.
Wi-Fi disconnects	The test continues **even if internet drops**; you only need connectivity at the beginning and end.
Frozen screen	Hold the power button to restart your device, then reopen the app and log back in.

Final Tips for a Smooth Digital SAT Experience

✓ **Familiarize yourself with Bluebook™ features** by using official College Board practice tests in the app.
✓ **Bring a fully charged device and a charger**, just in case.
✓ **Arrive early**—test centers may require extra time for device check-in and troubleshooting.
✓ **Use the built-in tools effectively**—highlighting, flagging, and calculator functions can improve efficiency.
✓ **Stay calm if issues arise**—proctors are trained to assist with common technical problems.

Mastering the **device requirements and Bluebook™ app features** will ensure you're fully prepared for test day. By setting up your software ahead of time, practicing within the app, and following troubleshooting strategies, you can approach the Digital SAT with confidence and focus entirely on your performance rather than technical concerns.

3.3 Day-of-Test Checklist (What to Bring, Rules, and Procedures)

The **Digital SAT** requires students to prepare carefully for test day, ensuring they have the correct materials, understand the rules, and follow the procedures to avoid any issues. Arriving prepared can make a significant difference in reducing stress and ensuring a smooth testing experience.

What to Bring on Test Day

To avoid last-minute complications, students must bring only permitted items to the test center. The following are essential:

Required Items

1. **Admission Ticket**
    - Available through your College Board account after registration.
    - Must be printed or displayed on an electronic device (depending on test center policies).
2. **Acceptable Photo ID**
    - The name on your ID must exactly match the name on your admission ticket.
    - Acceptable forms of ID include:
        - Government-issued driver's license or passport
        - Official school ID (with a photo)
        - SAT Student ID Form (if no government or school ID is available)
    - Expired IDs or digital copies are **not allowed**.
3. **Approved Testing Device**
    - A fully charged **Windows laptop, Mac laptop, school-managed Chromebook, or approved school iPad**.
    - The **Bluebook™ testing app** must be installed and ready to use.
    - If your battery is unreliable, bring a **power adapter** as well. Availability of power outlets may vary by test center.
4. **Acceptable Calculator** (Optional)
    - A **graphing calculator** is available within the **Bluebook™ app** for the entire Math section.
    - If preferred, students may bring an approved **physical calculator**, such as:
        - TI-84 Plus series
        - Casio fx-9750GII
        - Other models listed on the College Board website.
    - **No calculator apps on mobile devices are allowed.**
5. **Pencils or Pens for Scratch Work**
    - Though the test is digital, students will receive **scratch paper** for the Math section.

Recommended Items

While not mandatory, the following can be helpful:

- **Charger or Power Bank** (for long test sessions, if outlets are available)
- **Water and Snacks** (only allowed during breaks)
- **Extra Approved ID** (if unsure about primary ID acceptance)
- **Sweater or Jacket** (test centers may have varying temperatures)

Prohibited Items

Certain items are **strictly forbidden** in the testing area. Bringing any of these may result in dismissal and score cancellation:

- **Mobile Phones, Smartwatches, or Wearable Technology**
    - If a phone is brought, it must be **turned off and stored away** per proctor instructions.
    - Smartwatches, fitness trackers, and Bluetooth headphones are also prohibited.

- **Books, Study Notes, or Papers**
    - No printed materials or scratch paper from home are allowed.
- **External Keyboards or Mice**
    - Wireless or Bluetooth accessories are not permitted. Only **wired keyboards/mice** may be used if required.
- **Cameras or Recording Devices**
    - Any attempts to photograph or record test content will result in score cancellation.
- **Other Electronic Devices**
    - Tablets, e-readers, and other non-approved devices cannot be used during the test.

Check-In and Test Procedures

Arrival and Check-In Process

- **Arrival Time**: Arrive **at least 30 minutes before** the scheduled test start time. Late arrivals may not be admitted.
- **Security Check**: Proctors will verify IDs and admission tickets.
- **Device Inspection**:
    - Test administrators may check devices to ensure the Bluebook™ app is installed and functioning.
    - Personal devices must be placed in airplane mode and connected to the testing network (if applicable).

Test Format and Timing

The Digital SAT follows a structured timeline:

Section	Number of Questions	Time per Section	Breaks
Reading & Writing (Module 1)	~27 questions	32 minutes	None
Reading & Writing (Module 2)	~27 questions	32 minutes	10-minute break
Math (Module 1)	~22 questions	35 minutes	None
Math (Module 2)	~22 questions	35 minutes	End of test

After submitting each module, students cannot return to previous questions.

During the Test

- **Monitor the Timer**: A countdown clock is available on the screen for each section.
- **Use On-Screen Tools**: Features such as **flagging questions, highlighting text, and using the built-in calculator** are available in the Bluebook™ app.
- **Follow Proctor Instructions**: Any unauthorized behavior (such as speaking with other test-takers or using a phone) may result in dismissal.

Break Rules

- A **10-minute break** occurs between the **Reading & Writing** section and the **Math** section.
- Snacks and drinks can be **consumed only during breaks**, not during testing.
- Restroom use is allowed only during breaks.
- Devices **must remain closed** during breaks.

What Happens After the Test?

- **Submit the Exam**: At the end of the final section, the Bluebook™ app will prompt you to submit your test.
- **Device Collection (if using school-owned devices)**: School-issued Chromebooks or iPads may need to be returned immediately.
- **Score Release Timeline**: Digital SAT scores are typically available **within 10 days** after the test.

Final Checklist for Test Day Preparation

Task	Completed? (✓)
Printed admission ticket	
Valid photo ID	
Fully charged laptop/approved device	
Installed Bluebook™ app and ran system check	
Physical calculator (optional)	
Scratch paper (provided at test center)	
Pencils/pens	
Arranged transportation to test center	

3.4 Accommodations for Students with Disabilities

The **College Board** provides accommodations for students with documented disabilities to ensure they have an equal opportunity to succeed on the Digital SAT. Accommodations must be **requested and approved in advance** through the College Board's **Services for Students with Disabilities (SSD)**. Below is a detailed breakdown of the accommodation process, eligibility requirements, and available support options.

Eligibility for Accommodations

Students who require accommodations typically have a documented disability that affects their ability to take standardized tests under normal conditions. Common eligibility categories include:

- **Learning Disabilities (Dyslexia, Dyscalculia, etc.)**
- **ADHD and Executive Function Disorders**
- **Physical Disabilities (Cerebral Palsy, Muscular Dystrophy, etc.)**
- **Visual Impairments (Legally Blind, Low Vision)**
- **Hearing Impairments (Deaf, Hard of Hearing)**
- **Medical Conditions (Diabetes, Epilepsy, etc.)**
- **Psychiatric Disorders (Anxiety, Depression, etc.)**

Students must provide documentation from a **licensed medical professional or school disability coordinator** verifying their condition and explaining why accommodations are necessary.

How to Apply for Accommodations

Step 1: Work with Your School's SSD Coordinator

Most students request accommodations through their **high school's SSD coordinator**. This person helps submit the request to the College Board and ensures all documentation is in place.

Step 2: Submit an Online or Paper Application

Requests for accommodations must be submitted via the **College Board SSD Portal**.

- **School-Submitted Requests**: Your SSD coordinator can submit the request online.
- **Student-Submitted Requests**: If applying without school support, students must complete a **Student Eligibility Form** and mail it to the College Board.

Step 3: Provide Required Documentation

Students must submit medical or psychoeducational evaluations demonstrating how their disability impacts testing. Acceptable documentation includes:

- A recent **Individualized Education Program (IEP)** or **504 Plan** (for U.S. students).

- A **doctor's report** or **psychological evaluation** explaining how the disability affects standardized testing.
- Evidence of receiving similar accommodations in school settings.

Step 4: Wait for Approval

The College Board **typically reviews requests within 7-8 weeks**. Approved students receive an **SSD Eligibility Letter**, which outlines their approved accommodations and provides an **SSD Number** to use when registering for the SAT.

Deadlines: Accommodations should be requested **at least three months** before the SAT test date to allow sufficient processing time.

Available Accommodations for the Digital SAT

The **Digital SAT** offers a range of accommodations depending on the student's needs. These fall into three main categories:

1. Extended Time Accommodations

Accommodation	**Description**
Time and a Half (50% Extra Time)	Total test time increases to approx. **3 hours 21 minutes**.
Double Time (100% Extra Time)	Total test time increases to approx. **4 hours 28 minutes**.
More Than Double Time	Typically reserved for students with severe cognitive or physical disabilities.

- Extended time applies to **both modules of a section** (Reading & Writing or Math).
- If a student qualifies for **extra break time**, it is added between modules.

2. Assistive Technology and Accessibility Support

Accommodation	**Description**
Screen Reader & Text-to-Speech (TTS)	Allows visually impaired students to have questions read aloud.
Magnification Software	Enlarges text on screen for students with low vision.
Braille and Tactile Graphics	Provided for students with visual impairments who require braille text.
Large Print (Increased Font Size)	Enlarged text options for students needing larger fonts.

- The **Bluebook™ app** includes **built-in screen magnification and contrast options** for visually impaired students.
- Students using **screen readers** must test in a setting where they can use their assistive technology **without distractions to other test-takers**.

3. Physical and Medical Accommodations

Accommodation	**Description**
Additional Breaks	Students may take breaks **between** and **during** test sections as needed.
Breaks as Needed	No time limit on breaks; often used for medical conditions requiring frequent rest.

Permission for Food/Medication	Students with diabetes, epilepsy, or similar conditions may bring food, drinks, or medicine.
Wheelchair-Accessible Testing Space	Ensures access to test centers for students using wheelchairs.
Preferential Seating	Allows seating near proctors or in low-distraction areas.

- Students requiring **special seating or movement accommodations** should notify their test center in advance to ensure proper arrangements.
- **Breaks as Needed** are reserved for severe medical conditions and must be supported by strong medical documentation.

Testing at Home and Alternate Test Formats

For students with severe disabilities who **cannot test at a center**, the College Board allows **at-home testing** under certain conditions.

- This is rare and **only granted in extreme medical cases**.
- Requires extensive documentation and approval.

Additionally, some students may take a **paper-based SAT** instead of the digital format if their disability prevents computer use. This is only available for **approved cases**.

Accommodations on Test Day: What to Expect

- **Check-in procedures** remain the same as for all students, but students using assistive technology may need extra time for setup.
- If you receive **extended time**, your test day will be longer, and you may need **lunch or additional snacks**.
- Proctors will have a **list of approved accommodations** for each student and will follow official SAT guidelines to ensure fairness.

How to Check Your Accommodations Status

Students who have already received College Board accommodations (for the PSAT, AP exams, etc.) do **not** need to reapply unless requesting **new or additional accommodations**.

- Log in to the **SSD Online Portal** to confirm your accommodations before the SAT.
- If you believe your accommodations were **not properly applied** to your SAT registration, contact the **College Board SSD Office** immediately.

□ **College Board SSD Customer Service**:

- **Phone (U.S.)**: 844-255-7728
- **International**: +1-212-713-8333

Final Reminders for Students Requesting Accommodations

✓ **Apply early**—requests can take up to **eight weeks** to process.
✓ **Use school resources**—work with your school's SSD coordinator for assistance.
✓ **Double-check your approval**—log in to your College Board account to confirm accommodations are assigned.
✓ **Bring necessary medical items**—if approved for food, medicine, or assistive devices, ensure you have them packed for test day.
✓ **Communicate with the test center**—if you have complex accommodations (like a separate testing room), verify logistics ahead of time.

Accommodations are designed to create an equal testing environment for all students. By securing approval early and preparing for test day logistics, students with disabilities can focus on achieving their best SAT performance.

CHAPTER 4

SCORING AND SCORE REPORT

4.1 Score Scale: From 400 to 1600

The **Digital SAT** follows the same scoring system as its previous versions, using a **400 to 1600 scale**. This total score is derived from two main section scores:

- **Reading & Writing Section Score (200–800)**
- **Math Section Score (200–800)**

These two section scores are then combined to produce a **total SAT score ranging from 400 to 1600**. Unlike some other standardized tests, the SAT does not deduct points for incorrect answers, meaning students should attempt every question.

How the SAT is Scored

Each section of the Digital SAT is scored based on a process that involves several steps:

1. **Raw Score Calculation**
   - The raw score is simply the number of correct answers. There are **no penalties for incorrect responses**.
   - Every question carries equal weight, meaning there is no partial credit.
2. **Adaptive Testing Adjustment**
   - Since the Digital SAT uses an **adaptive format**, the difficulty of Module 2 in both the Reading & Writing and Math sections is based on performance in Module 1.
   - If a student performs well in Module 1, they receive a more challenging set of questions in Module 2, potentially allowing them to earn a higher scaled score.
3. **Raw Score to Scaled Score Conversion**
   - The raw scores are converted into **scaled scores** (ranging from 200 to 800 per section).
   - The College Board uses a process called **equating** to ensure that scores are comparable across different test administrations.

Section Scores Breakdown

Section	Score Range	Number of Questions	Time Allotted
Reading & Writing	200–800	54	64 minutes
Math	200–800	44	70 minutes
Total Score	400–1600	98 total	2 hours 14 minutes

Each section contributes equally to the total score, meaning that neither the Reading & Writing nor the Math section is weighted more heavily.

What Constitutes a Good SAT Score?

A "good" SAT score depends on a student's college goals and the competitiveness of the institutions they are applying to. The following are approximate SAT score percentiles based on recent data:

SAT Score	Percentile Rank	Performance Category
1500–1600	98th–99th percentile	Excellent (Highly Competitive)
1300–1490	85th–97th percentile	Very Good (Competitive)

1100–1290	65th–84th percentile	Above Average (Good)
900–1090	40th–64th percentile	Average (Moderate Selectivity)
700–890	10th–39th percentile	Below Average
400–690	Below 10th percentile	Needs Improvement

Many **top-tier universities** (such as Ivy League schools) look for scores in the **1400+ range**, while **state universities** often accept students with scores in the **1100–1300 range**.

How SAT Scores Are Used in College Admissions

1. **Admissions Decisions**
    - Colleges use SAT scores as one of many factors in evaluating an applicant's academic abilities.
    - Some schools have **minimum SAT score requirements**, while others consider scores holistically alongside GPA, extracurricular activities, and essays.
2. **Scholarships and Financial Aid**
    - Many universities and private organizations award **merit-based scholarships** to students with high SAT scores.
    - Some **state scholarship programs** automatically qualify students based on their SAT scores.
3. **Course Placement**
    - Certain schools use SAT scores to determine **placement in college courses**, such as math or writing classes.
    - High scores may allow students to bypass **introductory courses**.
4. **Test-Optional Policies**
    - Many colleges have adopted **test-optional policies**, allowing students to submit SAT scores only if they believe they strengthen their application.
    - However, high SAT scores can still enhance a student's application, especially when applying to competitive programs.

Key Takeaways

- The **Digital SAT is scored on a 400–1600 scale**, with **two section scores** ranging from **200 to 800**.
- Scores are calculated based on **raw scores, adaptive difficulty adjustments, and scaled conversions**.
- A **good SAT score** varies by college, with competitive institutions often looking for **1400+ scores**.
- SAT scores are used for **admissions, scholarships, and course placement**, but many schools now offer **test-optional** policies.
- Since **there is no penalty for wrong answers**, students should **always answer every question**.

Understanding the SAT scoring system helps students **set realistic score goals, develop effective study strategies, and maximize their college admission potential**.

4.2 Raw Score to Scaled Score Conversion

The **Digital SAT** does not report raw scores directly; instead, raw scores are converted into **scaled scores** ranging from **200 to 800 per section** (for a total score of **400 to 1600**). This conversion process ensures that different versions of the test are **fair and comparable**, even if some test forms are slightly harder or easier than others. Below is a detailed explanation of how raw scores are calculated and converted into final SAT scores.

Understanding Raw Scores

A **raw score** is simply the total number of **correct answers** a student gets on each section. The Digital SAT follows a **no-penalty scoring** system, meaning:

- **Correct answers = +1 point**
- **Incorrect or unanswered questions = 0 points (no deductions)**

Each section (Reading & Writing and Math) has a separate raw score. Since the total number of questions differs between sections, the maximum raw score varies:

Section	Number of Questions	Max Raw Score
Reading & Writing	54	54
Math	44	44

How Raw Scores Convert to Scaled Scores

Once a student's raw score is determined, it is **converted into a scaled score (200–800 per section)** through a process called **equating**. This accounts for minor variations in test difficulty across different SAT administrations.

Equating Process

- The College Board **does not use a fixed conversion table** because difficulty levels of tests can vary slightly.
- Instead, an **equating formula** is applied, ensuring that a student who takes a slightly harder version of the SAT is **not unfairly penalized**, and a student who takes an easier version is **not unfairly rewarded**.
- This means that **two students with the same raw score on different test dates may receive slightly different scaled scores**.

Estimated Raw-to-Scaled Score Conversion Table

The exact raw-to-scaled conversion varies with each SAT administration, but below is an **approximate conversion chart** based on historical SAT score trends:

Raw Score	Reading & Writing Scaled Score (Estimated)	Math Scaled Score (Estimated)
54	800	—
50	750–770	800
45	690–720	740–770
40	620–650	680–710
35	540–570	600–640
30	470–500	530–570
25	400–440	460–500
20	350–390	390–440
15	300–340	320–380
10	250–290	270–320
5	200–230	200–250

Important Notes:

- A **perfect score of 800** in a section **does not necessarily require a perfect raw score**. In some cases, a few incorrect answers might still result in an 800 due to equating.
- **Higher difficulty tests** may allow a slightly lower raw score to achieve the same scaled score.
- The **Math section usually has a more predictable conversion**, whereas **Reading & Writing may vary more significantly** due to differences in passage difficulty.

Why the SAT Uses Equating

Equating ensures that scores are fair and **comparable across different test dates**. If a test in **March** is slightly harder than one in **May**, equating **adjusts for difficulty differences** so that students are not unfairly penalized or rewarded.

Key Impacts of Equating

1. **Consistency**: A student scoring **45 raw points** in Math in **March** should have the same scaled score as a student who scored **45 raw points** in Math in **June**, regardless of slight difficulty variations.
2. **Eliminates Advantage**: Students cannot predict an "easier" test date to gain an unfair advantage.
3. **Ensures Fairness**: Colleges trust SAT scores to be **consistent across all test administrations**.

How to Use This Information for SAT Prep

1. Focus on Accuracy, Not Just Completion

- Because **incorrect answers do not reduce your score**, students should attempt every question.
- Rather than **rushing through all questions**, focus on **answering as many as possible correctly**.

2. Understand That Every Question Matters

- Due to the **relatively small number of questions**, **each correct answer makes a big difference** in the scaled score.
- Improving just **3–5 correct answers** can **boost a score by 50+ points**.

3. Aim for Module 2 Difficulty Adjustment

- Since the Digital SAT is **adaptive**, performing well in **Module 1** increases the likelihood of accessing **higher-scoring opportunities** in **Module 2**.
- If the second module is noticeably harder, **it means you performed well in Module 1**—which is an advantage when reaching higher score levels.

Final Key Takeaways

- **Raw Score = Number of Correct Answers** (No penalty for wrong answers).
- Raw scores are converted into **scaled scores (200–800 per section)** using **equating**.
- The **final SAT score is a combination of Reading & Writing and Math scores**, ranging from **400 to 1600**.
- There is **no fixed conversion chart**—the scaling process adjusts based on test difficulty.
- Improving even a few extra correct answers **can significantly boost your final SAT score**.
- Since the Digital SAT is **adaptive**, success in **Module 1** can lead to **higher-scoring potential in Module 2**.

Understanding **how raw scores convert to scaled scores** helps students **set realistic score goals, optimize their test-taking strategies, and track progress effectively during SAT preparation**.

4.3 Subscores and Cross-Test Scores

In addition to the **total score (400–1600)** and **section scores (200–800 per section)**, the Digital SAT provides **subscores** and **cross-test scores** that offer **detailed insights into a student's performance**. These additional scoring categories help students and educators understand strengths and weaknesses in specific skill areas. Below is a comprehensive breakdown of **how subscores and cross-test scores work, what they measure, and how they can be used for SAT preparation.**

Understanding SAT Subscores

Subscores provide a **more detailed breakdown** of performance within the Reading & Writing and Math sections. Each subscore ranges from **1 to 15**, with **higher scores indicating stronger performance** in a specific skill area.

Reading & Writing Subscores (1–15 Scale)

In the Digital SAT, the Reading & Writing section **merges reading comprehension and language skills**, so subscores reflect both **reading ability** and **writing proficiency**:

Subscore	What It Measures
Craft & Structure	Understanding passage organization, tone, and purpose; recognizing rhetorical strategies.

Information & Ideas	Identifying main ideas, supporting details, inferences, and relationships between ideas.
Standard English Conventions	Mastery of grammar, sentence structure, punctuation, and usage rules.
Expression of Ideas	Improving clarity, conciseness, word choice, logical flow, and transitions in writing.

Each of these subscores is based on **performance in multiple-choice questions** throughout the Reading & Writing section. A high score in "Craft & Structure" suggests strong reading comprehension, while a low score in "Standard English Conventions" might indicate a need to review grammar rules.

Math Subscores (1–15 Scale)

The Math section assesses **both foundational and advanced mathematical skills**. The two math subscores provide a closer look at strengths and areas for improvement:

Subscore	**What It Measures**
Algebra	Solving equations, inequalities, systems of equations, and understanding functions.
Advanced Math	Working with polynomials, exponential functions, rational expressions, and complex numbers.

A student who scores **high in Algebra but low in Advanced Math** might need to focus on more complex topics like quadratic equations or function transformations.

Understanding Cross-Test Scores

Cross-test scores evaluate skills that apply across **both the Reading & Writing and Math sections**, particularly in **science and history/social studies contexts**. These scores range from **10 to 40** and highlight a student's ability to **analyze data, interpret evidence, and apply reasoning skills in multiple subjects**.

Cross-Test Score	**What It Measures**
Analysis in History/Social Studies	Ability to read, analyze, and interpret historical documents, arguments, and quantitative data in a social studies context.
Analysis in Science	Understanding and evaluating scientific data, hypotheses, experiments, and research-based conclusions.

These scores are based on questions embedded **throughout the test**, including **historical and scientific reading passages** in the Reading & Writing section and **data interpretation questions** in the Math section.

How Subscores and Cross-Test Scores Are Used

1. **Identifying Strengths and Weaknesses**
    - If a student **excels in Craft & Structure** but struggles with **Standard English Conventions**, they should focus on grammar rules.
    - If a student **performs well in Algebra** but has a **low Advanced Math subscore**, they may need additional practice with quadratics and exponential functions.
2. **College Admissions Insights**
    - Some colleges **consider subscores** when reviewing applications, particularly if students apply for specific majors.
    - Engineering programs may look at **Advanced Math subscores**, while humanities programs might focus on **Craft & Structure** or **Analysis in History/Social Studies**.
3. **Scholarships and Placement Decisions**

    - Certain **STEM scholarships** may require strong cross-test scores in **Analysis in Science**.
    - Some universities use **subscores** to determine **course placement**, especially in English and Math classes.
4. **Guiding Test Prep Strategy**
    - Students preparing for an SAT retake can use their **subscores and cross-test scores** to focus study efforts on weaker areas.
    - SAT tutors and educators often analyze these detailed scores to create **personalized study plans**.

Key Takeaways

- **Subscores (1–15) measure performance in specific skill areas** (Algebra, Advanced Math, Grammar, Reading Comprehension).
- **Cross-test scores (10–40) assess science and social studies reasoning skills across all sections.**
- These detailed scores help **students understand strengths and weaknesses, guide study strategies, and may be considered by colleges and scholarships.**
- **Focusing on improving weak subscore areas can lead to significant score gains in future SAT attempts.**

By using subscores and cross-test scores effectively, students can **target their SAT preparation efficiently, enhance their college applications, and boost their overall performance** on the Digital SAT.

4.4 Sending Scores and Superscoring

Once students receive their SAT scores, the next step is deciding **how and when to send scores to colleges**. The College Board offers multiple score-reporting options, including **automatic free reports, additional paid reports, score choice, and superscoring**. Understanding these options is essential to maximize the impact of SAT scores in the college admissions process.

How to Send SAT Scores

1. Free Score Reports (First Four Reports)

- Each SAT registration includes the option to send **four free score reports** to colleges.
- These reports must be selected **before** the test date or within **nine days after taking the SAT**.
- Once sent, **these scores cannot be canceled or changed**.
- Free reports can be sent to **colleges, scholarship organizations, and NCAA eligibility programs**.

2. Additional Score Reports (After Test Day)

- If students need to send scores after the **nine-day window**, they must order additional reports.
- Cost: **$12 per report** (waived for students with an SAT fee waiver).
- These reports can be sent at any time, allowing students to wait until all SAT test attempts are completed.

3. Rush Reporting (Faster Processing)

- **Rush score reports** deliver SAT scores to colleges within **1–4 business days** (instead of the standard timeline of **one to two weeks**).
- Cost: **$31 per rushed report** (in addition to the standard $12 fee per report).
- Rush reports can be useful for students applying close to college deadlines.

4. Score Choice (Sending Only Your Best Scores)

- **Score Choice™** allows students to **choose which SAT test dates** to send to colleges.
- Colleges **only receive the selected test scores**, not all SAT attempts.
- Some colleges, however, require students to send **all SAT scores from every test date**, so students should check each college's SAT score policy before using Score Choice.

What is SAT Superscoring?

Many colleges **superscore the SAT**, meaning they take the **highest section scores** from multiple test dates to create the best possible combined score.

How Superscoring Works

A superscore is calculated by combining the **highest Reading & Writing section score** and the **highest Math section score** across multiple SAT attempts.

Test Date	Reading & Writing Score	Math Score	Total Score
SAT Taken in March	**650**	720	1370
SAT Taken in May	630	**750**	1380
Superscored SAT	**650**	**750**	**1400**

In this example, rather than considering the total score from a single SAT attempt, the **superscore (1400)** reflects the best performance in each section.

Colleges That Accept Superscores

- Many universities **accept superscoring**, allowing students to improve their overall score by retaking only one section.
- Some **do not superscore** and only consider the highest composite SAT score from a single test date.
- Students should check the admissions policies of each target college to determine if superscoring is available.

When to Send SAT Scores

1. Early Decision and Early Action Applicants

- Students applying for **early decision (ED) or early action (EA)** must ensure their scores arrive before the **college's early deadline** (often **November 1** or **November 15**).
- If an SAT test is scheduled close to the deadline, students may need to use **rush reporting**.

2. Regular Decision Applicants

- Most **regular decision deadlines** fall between **January 1 and February 1**, allowing students to send scores from fall and early winter test dates.

3. Scholarship and NCAA Eligibility

- Some scholarships and NCAA athletic eligibility programs require **official SAT scores**.
- Deadlines vary, so students should verify submission requirements **well in advance**.

Fee Waivers for Score Reports

- Students eligible for SAT **fee waivers** receive **unlimited free score reports**.
- Waivers apply to both the **initial four free reports** and any additional score reports requested later.
- This benefit is especially valuable for students applying to multiple colleges.

Final Key Takeaways

- **Students can send four free SAT score reports** within **nine days of test day**.
- **Additional reports** cost **$12 per college**, and **rush reporting** is available for an extra fee.
- **Score Choice™ lets students choose which SAT test dates** to send, but some colleges require all scores.
- **Superscoring allows colleges to combine a student's highest section scores** from multiple test dates.
- **Deadlines vary by college**, so students should check submission policies carefully.

By **strategically sending SAT scores**, taking advantage of **superscoring**, and planning around deadlines, students can **maximize their chances of admission and scholarships**.

CHAPTER 5

TESTING MINDSET AND STUDY PLANNING

5.1 Setting Goals and Designing a Study Schedule

A well-structured study plan is key to **maximizing SAT performance** and ensuring steady progress without burnout. Effective SAT preparation starts with **setting clear goals**, **understanding personal strengths and weaknesses**, and **designing a study schedule** that balances content review, practice tests, and strategic skill-building.

Step 1: Define Your SAT Goal Score

Before creating a study schedule, students should determine their **target SAT score** based on their college and scholarship goals.

How to Set a Target Score

1. **Research College SAT Requirements**
   - Look at the **middle 50% SAT range** of your target schools. This represents the **25th to 75th percentile SAT scores** of admitted students.
   - If a college has an SAT middle 50% range of **1250–1400**, students should aim for at least a **1400** to be competitive.
2. **Consider Scholarship Thresholds**
   - Many universities and private organizations offer **merit scholarships** for students who achieve specific SAT scores.
   - For example, a **1350+ score** might qualify for partial scholarships, while a **1450+ score** could open opportunities for full tuition assistance.
3. **Baseline Your Current Ability**
   - If you have taken the SAT before, use your previous score as a starting point.
   - If you haven't, take an **official full-length SAT practice test** to gauge your current level.

Sample Target Score Strategy

Current Score	Target Score	Study Plan Duration
Below 1000	1200+	3–4 months
1100–1200	1350+	2–3 months
1250+	1450+	6–8 weeks
1400+	1500+	4–6 weeks

Step 2: Assess Strengths and Weaknesses

Use a Diagnostic Test

- A **full-length practice test** (from the College Board's Bluebook™ app or Khan Academy) helps identify **which sections and question types need improvement**.
- Students should analyze **which types of mistakes** they make:
  - **Content Errors** (lack of knowledge, such as forgetting geometry formulas).
  - **Strategy Errors** (poor time management, second-guessing correct answers).
  - **Careless Mistakes** (misreading a question, simple miscalculations).

Create a Strength & Weakness Table

Section	Strengths	Weaknesses

Reading & Writing	Strong in main idea questions	Struggles with vocabulary in context
Math	Confident in algebra	Weak in trigonometry

This table helps **prioritize study focus areas** rather than spending equal time on all content.

Step 3: Design a Study Schedule

An effective SAT study plan should be **realistic, structured, and adjustable**. It should include:

- **Content Review**: Strengthening weaker topics.
- **Practice Questions**: Daily drills on targeted skills.
- **Full-Length Practice Tests**: Simulating real test conditions.
- **Strategy Work**: Pacing, elimination tactics, and adaptive test navigation.

How Many Hours Should You Study?

Weeks Until Test	Study Time Per Week	Total Study Hours
12 Weeks	4–6 hours	50+ hours
8 Weeks	6–8 hours	50–60 hours
4 Weeks	10–12 hours	40+ hours
2 Weeks	15–20 hours	30–40 hours

Sample 8-Week Study Plan

Week	Focus Area
Week 1	Take a full-length **diagnostic test**. Identify strengths and weaknesses. Review SAT format and timing.
Week 2	Review fundamental **Algebra & Advanced Math**. Practice **Grammar & Rhetorical Skills** in Writing.
Week 3	Focus on **Problem Solving & Data Analysis** in Math. Work on **Reading Comprehension strategies**.
Week 4	Take a **full-length timed practice test**. Analyze mistakes and adjust focus areas.
Week 5	Strengthen **trigonometry & geometry** concepts. Review **vocabulary and transitions** for Writing.
Week 6	Practice with **adaptive modules** and simulated conditions. Improve **time management**.
Week 7	Take another **full-length practice test**. Review weak points and fine-tune strategies.
Week 8	Final review of major concepts. Focus on **test-day strategies and confidence-building**.

Step 4: Adjust Your Study Plan as Needed

- **Track Your Progress**: After every full-length practice test, **analyze mistakes** and shift focus accordingly.
- **Increase Study Time in Weak Areas**: If geometry is consistently weak, **dedicate extra sessions** to reviewing formulas and solving related problems.
- **Stay Flexible**: Some topics may need more practice than others. Adjust time allocation as needed.

Final Key Takeaways

- **Set a target SAT score** based on college admissions and scholarship goals.
- **Take a diagnostic test** to identify strengths and weaknesses.
- **Design a study schedule** that includes content review, practice drills, and full-length practice tests.

- **Track progress and adjust strategies** to focus on areas that need improvement.
- **Consistency is key**—regular, focused study sessions over weeks or months will lead to better performance than last-minute cramming.

By setting **realistic goals and following a structured study plan**, students can **improve their SAT scores efficiently** and approach test day with confidence.

5.2 Overcoming Test Anxiety

Test anxiety is a common challenge for SAT test-takers, often leading to **nervousness, self-doubt, and decreased performance**. While some level of stress can be beneficial in keeping students alert and focused, excessive anxiety can interfere with concentration and decision-making. The good news is that **test anxiety can be managed with the right strategies**, allowing students to perform at their best on test day.

Understanding Test Anxiety: Causes and Symptoms

Common Causes of Test Anxiety

1. **Fear of Failure** – Worrying about how a low SAT score may affect college admissions or scholarships.
2. **Lack of Preparation** – Feeling unready due to insufficient study time or ineffective study strategies.
3. **High Expectations** – Pressure from parents, teachers, or personal goals.
4. **Negative Experiences** – Past struggles with standardized tests or previous poor SAT performance.
5. **Perfectionism** – Feeling the need to answer every question perfectly, leading to overthinking.

Symptoms of Test Anxiety

Test anxiety can manifest both physically and mentally. Recognizing these symptoms early can help students implement strategies to reduce stress.

Type	Symptoms
Physical	Rapid heartbeat, sweating, nausea, dizziness, headaches, muscle tension.
Emotional	Fear, panic, frustration, irritability, self-doubt.
Cognitive	Racing thoughts, difficulty focusing, trouble recalling information, blanking out on questions.
Behavioral	Procrastination, avoidance of studying, excessive review of the same material, rushing through the test.

Proven Strategies to Reduce Test Anxiety

1. Prepare Thoroughly in Advance

- One of the best ways to **reduce test anxiety** is to **study consistently** over several weeks or months.
- **Use a structured study plan** (see section 5.1) to cover all test areas.
- Take **at least 3–4 full-length practice tests** to get comfortable with timing and question styles.

2. Simulate Test Conditions

- Take **practice tests in a quiet room** without distractions, using only allowed materials.
- Use a **timer** to simulate the SAT's timing structure.
- Familiarity with the format builds confidence and reduces fear of the unknown.

3. Develop a Pre-Test Routine

- **The night before the test**, gather all necessary materials (ID, admission ticket, calculator, fully charged device).
- **Get a full night's sleep**—at least **7–8 hours**—to stay mentally sharp.
- **Eat a balanced breakfast** on test day to maintain focus and energy levels.

4. Use Relaxation Techniques

- **Deep Breathing Exercise:**
    - Inhale deeply for **4 seconds**, hold for **4 seconds**, and exhale slowly for **4 seconds**. Repeat **3–5 times** to calm the nervous system.

- **Progressive Muscle Relaxation:**
  - Tense and relax different muscle groups (shoulders, hands, legs) to relieve physical tension.
- **Visualization:**
  - Picture yourself **walking into the test center confidently**, answering questions easily, and finishing the test feeling accomplished.

5. Reframe Negative Thoughts

- Replace **self-doubt** with **positive affirmations**:
  - Instead of "I'm terrible at math," say: **"I have prepared well, and I am improving."**
  - Instead of "I always mess up on tests," say: **"I can manage my time and perform my best."**
- **Stay realistic**: A single test **does not define your intelligence or future success**.

6. Manage Time Effectively During the Test

- **Don't rush** through questions, but also **don't dwell too long** on difficult ones.
- **Use the flagging feature** in the Digital SAT to return to hard questions later.
- **If you feel overwhelmed, pause for 10 seconds**, take a deep breath, and reset your focus.

7. Keep Perspective: The SAT is Just One Part of College Admissions

- Colleges **consider many factors**, including GPA, extracurricular activities, essays, and letters of recommendation.
- A **lower-than-expected score is not the end of the world**—students can retake the SAT if necessary.

On Test Day: Quick Anxiety-Reduction Checklist

✓ **Arrive early** to avoid last-minute stress.
✓ **Take deep breaths before starting** each section.
✓ **Read each question carefully**—don't rush due to nerves.
✓ **Skip and return** to difficult questions to stay confident.
✓ **Use positive self-talk** to maintain focus.
✓ **Stay hydrated and take breaks** when allowed.

Final Key Takeaways

- **Anxiety is normal**, but preparation and **mental strategies** can keep it under control.
- **Simulating test conditions** with practice tests builds familiarity and confidence.
- **Relaxation techniques**, such as **deep breathing and visualization**, help calm nerves.
- **Reframing negative thoughts** with positive affirmations improves focus.
- **Managing time wisely during the test** prevents stress from escalating.
- The SAT is **just one part of college admissions**, and **retaking is always an option**.

By implementing these techniques, students can **approach the SAT with confidence**, stay calm under pressure, and **achieve their best possible performance**.

5.3 Maintaining Motivation and Consistency

Preparing for the **Digital SAT** requires sustained effort over weeks or months. However, many students struggle with **motivation dips, burnout, or procrastination**, making it difficult to follow through with their study plans. To achieve **consistent progress**, students need effective strategies to stay motivated, track improvements, and maintain focus.

Understanding Motivation and Consistency

Motivation is what **drives** a student to study, while consistency is what **keeps** them going even when motivation fades. Successful SAT preparation requires both.

- **Motivation** is often strongest at the start but can decrease over time.
- **Consistency** ensures that students continue making progress **even when motivation is low**.

Students who rely **only on motivation** often struggle to complete their study plans. The key is to build habits that make studying a **daily or weekly routine** rather than something based purely on mood or inspiration.

Step 1: Define a Strong "Why" for Taking the SAT

Students who connect SAT preparation to a **meaningful goal** are more likely to stay motivated. Ask:

- **What is my reason for taking the SAT?**
  - To get into a dream college?
  - To qualify for a scholarship?
  - To feel more confident in test-taking?
- **What will an improved SAT score allow me to do?**
  - Increase college options?
  - Avoid remedial classes?
  - Reduce stress in the admissions process?

Writing down a clear **"why" statement** and keeping it visible (on a desk, phone wallpaper, or study planner) can **serve as a daily reminder** of the bigger picture.

Step 2: Create a Realistic and Enjoyable Study Routine

A study plan should be **manageable, not overwhelming**. The best schedules balance **structured study sessions** with **breaks to prevent burnout**.

Best Practices for a Consistent Study Routine

✓ **Set specific study times**—make SAT prep part of a **weekly schedule**, just like school or extracurricular activities.
✓ **Use a dedicated study space**—avoid distractions by studying in the same place each time.
✓ **Combine different study methods**—mixing practice questions, timed tests, and concept review helps prevent boredom.
✓ **Start small**—even **30 minutes per day** is better than cramming once a week.
✓ **Make studying rewarding**—set up **a reward system** (e.g., 2 hours of focused study = 30 minutes of free time).

Sample Weekly SAT Study Plan (Balanced Approach)

Day	Study Focus	Time Commitment
Monday	Algebra & Problem Solving Drills	1 hour
Tuesday	Reading Comprehension Practice	45 minutes
Wednesday	Full Writing Section Practice	1 hour
Thursday	Math (Geometry & Trigonometry)	45 minutes
Friday	Review Mistakes from Past Tests	30 minutes
Saturday	Full-Length Practice Test	3 hours
Sunday	Rest or Light Review	Optional

This structure ensures **regular practice** while preventing **burnout**.

Step 3: Track Progress and Celebrate Improvements

Tracking progress is a powerful motivator because it shows **visible improvement** over time.

Ways to Track SAT Progress

✓ **Score Tracking** – Record scores from full-length practice tests to see improvements.
✓ **Error Log** – Keep a list of mistakes and review them weekly.
✓ **Study Journal** – Write down **what was learned**, what was difficult, and what to improve next.

Example SAT Progress Tracker (Math Section)

Practice Test Date	Raw Score	Scaled Score	Mistake Type	Next Steps
Week 1	22/44	550	Algebra Errors	Review quadratic equations
Week 3	28/44	600	Timing Issues	Work on pacing strategies
Week 6	35/44	680	Small Miscalculations	Double-check work
Week 8	40/44	750	Few Minor Errors	Maintain accuracy

Seeing **small but steady improvements** can increase confidence and motivation.

Step 4: Find Ways to Stay Engaged and Avoid Burnout

Even with a strong study routine, students may experience **periods of fatigue**. These strategies help prevent burnout:

1. Change Up Study Methods

- Use a **mix of resources**: textbooks, online videos, practice apps, and group discussions.
- Try **teaching concepts** to a friend or family member—this reinforces understanding.
- Use **gamification**—apps like Khan Academy and Quizlet offer interactive SAT challenges.

2. Take Breaks and Rest

- Overstudying can lead to **mental exhaustion**.
- Use the **Pomodoro Technique** (25 minutes study, 5 minutes break) for focused sessions.
- Ensure **at least one rest day per week** to recharge.

3. Join a Study Group or Get a Study Partner

- A study partner can provide **accountability and motivation**.
- Teaching each other material can **improve retention**.

Step 5: Stay Positive and Adjust as Needed

SAT preparation is a **marathon, not a sprint**. Setbacks are part of the process, but how students respond to them determines success.

Handling Setbacks

- If practice test scores **drop unexpectedly**, analyze **what changed** in strategy or focus.
- If struggling with consistency, **adjust the study plan** to fit real-life commitments.
- If feeling unmotivated, **revisit personal goals** and **remind yourself why the SAT matters**.

Mindset Shift: View Challenges as Growth Opportunities

✓ Instead of: **"I'm bad at math."** → Say: **"I haven't mastered math yet, but I can improve."**
✓ Instead of: **"I keep making mistakes."** → Say: **"Each mistake helps me learn something new."**

Final Key Takeaways

- **Motivation starts the process, but consistency leads to success**.
- **Set a clear goal** (college admissions, scholarships) to stay focused.
- **Create a realistic study schedule** that fits into daily life.
- **Track progress regularly** to see improvement and stay motivated.
- **Prevent burnout** by using different study methods, taking breaks, and staying flexible.
- **Adjust when needed**—if a routine isn't working, modify it.

By **staying disciplined, tracking improvement, and keeping a positive mindset**, students can **maintain motivation and consistency throughout their SAT preparation journey** and achieve their target scores.

PART II

READING & WRITING SECTION (THEORY AND PRACTICE)

CHAPTER 6

UNDERSTANDING THE READING & WRITING SECTION

6.1 New Combined R&W Structure: Two Adaptive Modules

The **Digital SAT** introduces a significant change to the **Reading & Writing (R&W) section**, which now features a **combined format** instead of separate Reading and Writing sections. This streamlined structure **assesses reading comprehension, grammar, and rhetorical skills together**, offering a more integrated approach to verbal reasoning. Additionally, the **section is adaptive**, meaning question difficulty **adjusts based on performance** as students progress through the exam.

Overview of the Digital SAT Reading & Writing Structure

Feature	Digital SAT Reading & Writing
Total Time	64 minutes
Number of Modules	2 (adaptive)
Total Questions	54
Time per Module	32 minutes
Question Format	Multiple-choice (4 answer choices)
Passage Length	Short (25–150 words per passage)
Topics Covered	Literature, History, Social Sciences, Science, Humanities
Scoring Range	200–800

Each question is linked to a **brief passage or passage excerpt**, and students answer **one question per passage**, unlike the old format, which featured multiple questions per longer passage.

Adaptive Module Structure in the R&W Section

The Reading & Writing section is **divided into two modules**, each containing **27 questions**. The difficulty of **Module 2** is determined by the student's performance in **Module 1**.

How the Adaptive System Works

1. **Module 1 (Standard Mix of Questions)**
   - The first module contains a mix of **easy, medium, and hard** questions.
   - The **computer algorithm evaluates performance** in real-time as students answer.
2. **Module 2 (Adjusted Difficulty)**
   - If a student performs **well in Module 1**, they receive a **more challenging Module 2** with harder questions.
   - If a student struggles in Module 1, they receive a **moderate or easier Module 2** with questions of similar or slightly lower difficulty.

Key Effects of the Adaptive System

- **Higher-scoring students are given more complex and advanced questions**, allowing them to demonstrate a broader range of verbal skills.
- **Lower-scoring students receive a section better suited to their current skill level**, making the test fairer and reducing frustration.

- **Final scores are determined by both performance and question difficulty**, so students who enter the harder Module 2 may have a greater chance at a higher score.

Types of Questions in the R&W Section

The **Reading & Writing section integrates different question types**, evaluating students' comprehension and writing abilities simultaneously. Each question falls into one of four key categories:

Category	Skills Tested
Craft & Structure	Understanding vocabulary in context, identifying main ideas, analyzing rhetorical techniques.
Information & Ideas	Making inferences, identifying supporting evidence, summarizing passages.
Standard English Conventions	Grammar, punctuation, sentence structure, verb usage.
Expression of Ideas	Improving clarity, conciseness, logical organization, and transitions.

Instead of large, multi-paragraph passages followed by multiple questions, **each question is linked to a short text excerpt**, requiring precise and efficient reading.

Example Questions that Mirror the Digital SAT

The following examples **reflect the new short-passage, single-question format** of the Digital SAT Reading & Writing section.

Example 1: Vocabulary in Context (Craft & Structure)

Passage:
The scientist's discovery was a **watershed** moment in the field, leading to a complete revision of established theories.

Question:
In the passage, the word **watershed** most nearly means:

A) catastrophic
B) significant
C) predictable
D) mysterious

Correct Answer: B) significant
(The passage describes an important moment in science, so "significant" fits best.)

Example 2: Sentence Structure (Standard English Conventions)

Sentence:
The committee, which **meet** once a month, is responsible for approving new policies.

Question:
Which revision corrects the grammatical error in the sentence?

A) (No change)
B) The committee, which **meets** once a month, is responsible for approving new policies.
C) The committee, which meeting once a month, is responsible for approving new policies.
D) The committee, which have met once a month, is responsible for approving new policies.

Correct Answer: B) The committee, which meets once a month, is responsible for approving new policies.
("Committee" is singular, so the verb should be "meets" instead of "meet.")

Example 3: Main Idea & Supporting Evidence (Information & Ideas)

Passage:
The introduction of high-speed rail has transformed travel between major cities, reducing commute times and

increasing economic growth in connected regions. Studies show that in countries with well-developed rail networks, there has been a measurable increase in commerce and tourism.

Question:

Which choice best summarizes the main idea of the passage?

A) High-speed rail has contributed to economic benefits and faster travel.

B) Some cities rely more on trains than on cars for transportation.

C) The construction of rail networks has decreased air travel.

D) Rail systems are more efficient than bus systems for daily commutes.

Correct Answer: A) High-speed rail has contributed to economic benefits and faster travel.
(The passage discusses both economic growth and reduced travel times, making A the best choice.)

Example 4: Logical Transitions (Expression of Ideas)

Sentence:

Many experts argue that artificial intelligence will revolutionize industries like healthcare and finance. _____, others remain skeptical about its long-term impact.

Question:

Which transition best completes the sentence?

A) As a result

B) However

C) Similarly

D) Consequently

Correct Answer: B) However

(The sentence presents a contrast between experts who support AI and those who are skeptical.)

Strategies for Success in the Digital SAT R&W Section

1. **Read with Precision**
   - Since passages are short, **focus on every word** to grasp meaning quickly.
   - Expect **concise but complex sentence structures** that require precise understanding.
2. **Anticipate the Question Type**
   - If the passage is **informational**, expect questions about main ideas or supporting evidence.
   - If it includes a **bolded word**, it's likely a **vocabulary-in-context** question.
   - If a sentence has **underlined text**, expect **grammar or structure** questions.
3. **Master Time Management**
   - Each module is **32 minutes long** for **27 questions**, so aim to answer **one question per minute**.
   - **Don't linger on tough questions**—flag them and return if time allows.
4. **Familiarize Yourself with Adaptive Testing**
   - **Performing well in Module 1** increases the difficulty of Module 2, potentially leading to a **higher score**.
   - If Module 2 feels harder, **this is a good sign**—it means you're in the top score range.

Final Key Takeaways

- **The Reading & Writing section is now combined** into **two adaptive modules** with **54 total questions**.
- **Each question is linked to a short passage**, with **one question per passage** instead of long multi-question sets.
- **Questions cover four major skills:** Vocabulary, Reading Comprehension, Grammar, and Writing Clarity.
- **The test is adaptive**, meaning performance in **Module 1 affects the difficulty of Module 2**.
- **Success requires both reading comprehension and strong grammar skills.**

By mastering **precision reading, efficient time management, and adaptive strategies**, students can **maximize their Digital SAT Reading & Writing score** and confidently tackle this section on test day.

6.2 Passage Types (Literary, Informational, Scientific, etc.)

The **Reading & Writing section** of the **Digital SAT** contains passages drawn from **a variety of subject areas**, testing a student's ability to comprehend and analyze different types of texts. Each passage is **short (25–150 words)** and is followed by a **single multiple-choice question**. Understanding the **types of passages** that appear on the test and how to approach them is essential for success.

Overview of Passage Types

The Digital SAT categorizes passages into four main types:

Passage Type	Source Material	Skills Tested
Literary Passages	Fiction, novels, short stories	Narrative comprehension, character relationships, tone, style
Informational Passages	Nonfiction, essays, speeches	Main ideas, supporting details, structure, author's purpose
Historical/Social Science Passages	U.S. and world history, economics, sociology, psychology	Argument analysis, historical context, claims and evidence
Scientific Passages	Biology, chemistry, physics, environmental science	Data interpretation, hypothesis evaluation, research summaries

Each passage requires students to **quickly extract key information, analyze arguments, and apply reading comprehension strategies**.

1. Literary Passages

What to Expect

- Excerpts from **novels, short stories, or plays**, often from **classic or modern literature**.
- The passages describe **characters, settings, or dramatic situations**, testing how well students **interpret narrative structure and tone**.
- These passages **do not test literary analysis like AP Literature**; instead, they focus on **basic comprehension and meaning.**

Example Literary Passage and Question

Passage:

Julia sat by the window, watching the streetlights flicker as the rain drummed softly on the glass. She held the letter tightly, her fingers pressing into the folds. The words were clear, yet her mind resisted them, unwilling to accept what they meant.

Question:

What does the passage suggest about Julia's emotional state?

A) She is relieved to receive the letter.
B) She is hesitant to open the letter.
C) She is deeply affected by the letter's contents.
D) She is distracted by the rain outside.

Correct Answer: C) She is deeply affected by the letter's contents.

(The passage describes Julia's hesitation and resistance to accepting the letter's meaning, implying an emotional response.)

Strategies for Literary Passages

✓ **Identify character emotions** and relationships.
✓ **Look for descriptive words** that reveal tone (e.g., "softly" and "unwilling to accept" signal an emotional response).
✓ **Pay attention to figurative language** that may indicate deeper meaning.

2. Informational Passages

What to Expect

- **Nonfiction texts**, including **essays, opinion pieces, and speeches**.
- Often involve **persuasive arguments**, requiring students to **determine main ideas and evaluate supporting evidence**.
- May include **comparisons, cause-and-effect relationships, or problem-solving discussions**.

Example Informational Passage and Question

Passage:

In recent years, urban gardens have become an increasingly popular solution to food insecurity. By transforming vacant lots into productive green spaces, communities can cultivate fresh produce while also strengthening neighborhood ties. Studies show that access to locally grown fruits and vegetables not only improves dietary health but also fosters a sense of environmental responsibility.

Question:

What is the main purpose of the passage?

A) To criticize urban gardening as an ineffective trend.
B) To explain the benefits of urban gardening.
C) To describe how urban gardening negatively affects local businesses.
D) To argue for stricter regulations on urban gardening.

Correct Answer: B) To explain the benefits of urban gardening.

(The passage presents a positive perspective on urban gardening and its benefits.)

Strategies for Informational Passages

✓ **Identify the central argument or message** in the first sentence or last sentence.
✓ **Pay attention to key transition words** (e.g., "therefore," "as a result," "however") to understand the passage's structure.
✓ **Look for supporting evidence** that reinforces the main idea.

3. Historical/Social Science Passages

What to Expect

- Excerpts from **historical documents, sociology studies, economics discussions, and political writings**.
- These passages test a student's ability to **analyze arguments, understand claims, and evaluate evidence**.
- May include perspectives on **government, human behavior, civil rights, and historical events**.

Example Historical/Social Science Passage and Question

Passage:

In his speech on March 4, 1865, President Abraham Lincoln urged reconciliation between the North and South. He famously stated, "With malice toward none, with charity for all," emphasizing that the country's unity depended on compassion rather than vengeance. Despite the devastation of the Civil War, Lincoln's vision aimed to heal the nation rather than deepen its divisions.

Question:

What is the main idea of the passage?

A) Lincoln sought to punish the South for the Civil War.
B) Lincoln believed compassion was necessary for national unity.
C) Lincoln wanted to encourage more conflict between the North and South.
D) Lincoln's speech signaled his resignation from office.

Correct Answer: B) Lincoln believed compassion was necessary for national unity.

(The passage describes Lincoln's emphasis on reconciliation rather than punishment.)

Strategies for Historical/Social Science Passages

✓ **Understand the context**—historical passages often reference key figures or events.
✓ **Identify the author's claim**—these passages usually present **arguments or political viewpoints**.
✓ **Recognize persuasive language**—watch for emotional appeals, rhetorical devices, and supporting evidence.

4. Scientific Passages

What to Expect

- Excerpts from **scientific research papers, studies, and data-driven articles**.
- These passages do **not** require prior knowledge of science but test a student's ability to **interpret and analyze scientific reasoning**.
- May include **hypotheses, experimental results, or discussions of technological advancements**.

Example Scientific Passage and Question

Passage:

Researchers studying migratory birds have found that magnetic fields play a crucial role in navigation. By tracking the movement of birds fitted with GPS devices, scientists observed that disruptions in Earth's magnetic field corresponded with changes in migration patterns. These findings suggest that birds rely on geomagnetic cues in addition to visual landmarks.

Question:

Which conclusion is best supported by the passage?

A) Birds migrate randomly without any guiding factors.
B) Magnetic fields influence bird migration patterns.
C) Scientists have proven that all birds use the same migration route.
D) GPS tracking is ineffective for studying bird behavior.

Correct Answer: B) Magnetic fields influence bird migration patterns.

(The passage provides direct evidence linking magnetic fields to bird navigation.)

Strategies for Scientific Passages

✓ **Identify the research focus**—scientific passages often describe studies or experiments.
✓ **Look for cause-and-effect relationships**—what factors influence results?
✓ **Recognize the passage's conclusion**—the last sentence often contains the main takeaway.

Final Key Takeaways

- The Digital SAT **features a variety of passage types**, including **literary, informational, historical, and scientific texts**.
- **Each passage is short (25–150 words) and paired with one multiple-choice question.**
- **Reading comprehension strategies vary by passage type**—narrative passages require tone analysis, while scientific passages emphasize data interpretation.
- **Understanding the structure of different passages can improve accuracy and efficiency** during the test.

By **practicing each passage type and using effective reading strategies**, students can **boost their SAT Reading & Writing scores and approach the exam with confidence**.

6.3 Question Format: Short Passages, Single Question per Passage

The **Digital SAT Reading & Writing section** introduces a streamlined approach to verbal reasoning, featuring **short passages**, each paired with **a single multiple-choice question**. This format differs significantly from the traditional SAT, which used longer passages followed by multiple questions. Understanding how this new format works and developing **efficient reading strategies** is key to success.

Overview of the New Question Format

Feature	Digital SAT Format
Passage Length	25–150 words

Questions Per Passage	1 question per passage
Total Questions	54 (across two adaptive modules)
Time Per Module	32 minutes
Question Types	Reading comprehension, vocabulary, grammar, rhetoric
Answer Choices	4 options (A, B, C, D)
Adaptive Nature	Performance in Module 1 determines difficulty of Module 2

Each question is directly tied to **a single short passage**, eliminating **multi-question passage sets** seen in previous versions of the SAT. This structure requires students to **quickly interpret text, identify key information, and select the best answer in under a minute**.

Key Types of Questions in the Digital SAT R&W Section

Each short passage is designed to assess **one specific reading or writing skill**. Below is a breakdown of the **four main question types** and examples that mimic the real exam.

Question Type	What It Tests
Craft & Structure	Vocabulary in context, sentence meaning, rhetorical purpose
Information & Ideas	Main ideas, supporting details, inference
Standard English Conventions	Grammar, punctuation, sentence structure
Expression of Ideas	Clarity, conciseness, logical flow, transitions

Each passage presents **a single challenge**, so students must **read efficiently and answer accurately within limited time constraints**.

Example Questions That Mirror the Digital SAT

1. Craft & Structure: Vocabulary in Context

Passage:

The scientist's hypothesis was initially dismissed as **untenable**, but later experiments proved its validity.

Question:

What does the word **untenable** most nearly mean in the passage?

A) Unproven

B) Indefensible

C) Revolutionary

D) Complicated

Correct Answer: B) Indefensible

(The passage suggests that the hypothesis was first rejected, meaning "untenable" must mean something like "unable to be supported.")

Strategy Tip:

✓ Identify **context clues**—look for surrounding words that indicate the **tone or meaning** of the term.

✓ Substitute each answer choice into the sentence to see which one makes the most sense.

2. Information & Ideas: Main Idea and Supporting Evidence

Passage:

Urban beekeeping has gained popularity as a sustainable practice. By cultivating hives in city spaces, beekeepers help pollinate local plants, support declining bee populations, and contribute to biodiversity efforts.

Question:

Which choice best summarizes the main idea of the passage?

A) Urban beekeeping is an effective method for promoting environmental sustainability.
B) Bee populations have been increasing in urban environments.
C) Local gardens benefit more from beekeeping than rural farms.
D) Beekeeping is an outdated agricultural practice.
Correct Answer: A) Urban beekeeping is an effective method for promoting environmental sustainability.
(The passage emphasizes how urban beekeeping supports biodiversity and sustainability, making A the best choice.)
Strategy Tip:
✓ Focus on the **first and last sentence**, as they often state the main idea.
✓ Eliminate answers that **introduce new information** not supported by the passage.

3. Standard English Conventions: Grammar and Punctuation

Sentence:
Neither the students nor the teacher **were** aware that the assembly had been canceled.
Question:
Which choice correctly revises the sentence?
A) (No change)
B) Neither the students nor the teacher **was** aware that the assembly had been canceled.
C) Neither the students nor the teacher **are** aware that the assembly had been canceled.
D) Neither the students nor the teacher **were being** aware that the assembly had been canceled.
Correct Answer: B) Neither the students nor the teacher was aware that the assembly had been canceled.
(The subject is "the teacher," which is singular, so the verb should be "was" instead of "were.")
Strategy Tip:
✓ Pay attention to **subject-verb agreement**, especially with tricky structures like "neither… nor."
✓ Identify the **true subject** of the sentence before selecting the verb.

4. Expression of Ideas: Logical Transitions

Sentence:
The study found that exposure to natural light improved students' ability to focus. _____, researchers recommended adjusting classroom lighting to maximize natural sunlight.
Question:
Which transition best completes the sentence?
A) However
B) Consequently
C) Nevertheless
D) In contrast
Correct Answer: B) Consequently
(The second sentence presents a recommendation based on a study's findings, making "consequently" the logical transition.)
Strategy Tip:
✓ Identify whether the **second sentence supports or contradicts** the first.
✓ Use **cause-and-effect transitions** for explanations and **contrast transitions** for opposing ideas.

Strategies for Answering Short-Passage, Single-Question Format

1. Read the Question First

Before reading the passage, **glance at the question** to know what to focus on. This saves time and prevents unnecessary rereading.

2. Identify the Purpose of the Passage

Since each passage tests **a single skill**, determine if it's assessing **meaning, structure, or correctness** before answering.

3. Use Process of Elimination

- Eliminate answer choices that are **too extreme, off-topic, or unrelated** to the passage.
- For vocabulary questions, eliminate **synonyms that don't match the sentence's tone**.

4. Manage Time Effectively

- The section includes **54 questions in 64 minutes**, meaning **you have about 1 minute per question**.
- If stuck on a question, **flag it and move on**—don't let one tough item derail your pacing.

Final Key Takeaways

- **The Digital SAT features short passages (25–150 words), with one question per passage.**
- **Question types include vocabulary, main idea, grammar, and logical transitions.**
- **Each question targets a single skill, making precision and efficiency essential.**
- **Effective strategies include reading the question first, eliminating wrong answers, and managing time wisely.**

By **practicing with short, focused reading exercises** and developing **efficient question-solving techniques**, students can confidently tackle the **Reading & Writing section of the Digital SAT** and improve their overall performance.

CHAPTER 7

READING SKILLS

7.1 Identifying Main Ideas and Themes

The ability to **identify the main idea or theme** of a passage is a fundamental reading skill tested on the **Digital SAT Reading & Writing section**. Every passage—whether **literary, informational, historical, or scientific**—presents a central message, and students must determine **what the passage is primarily about** and how its details support that idea.

Understanding **main ideas** and **themes** helps students **quickly comprehend short passages**, answer questions accurately, and improve **reading efficiency** under timed conditions.

What is a Main Idea?

The **main idea** of a passage is its **central message or argument**—the key point the author is trying to communicate. It is often found in **one or two sentences** and answers the question:

"What is the passage about?"

- The **main idea is not a small detail**; it **summarizes the passage as a whole**.
- It should be **broad enough to cover the entire passage** but **not too vague**.
- It is often found in the **first or last sentence**, but in some cases, it must be inferred.

What is a Theme? (For Literary Passages)

In **fiction or narrative texts**, the **theme** refers to **the deeper message or lesson** the author conveys. Unlike the main idea, which is **specific to one passage**, themes are often **universal ideas** that apply beyond the text.

Common literary themes include:

- **Perseverance in adversity**
- **The struggle for freedom**
- **The impact of technology on society**
- **The dangers of unchecked ambition**

A theme **does not summarize plot details**; instead, it focuses on **what the story reveals about human nature or society**.

Recognizing Main Ideas in Different Passage Types

Passage Type	How to Identify the Main Idea
Informational Passages	Look for the **thesis statement**, often in the first or last sentence.
Historical/Social Science	Identify the **argument or claim** being made about history or society.
Scientific Passages	Focus on the **research question or hypothesis** the passage explores.
Literary Passages	Determine the **central event, character struggle, or message** of the excerpt.

Example Questions That Mirror the Digital SAT

Example 1: Informational Passage (Main Idea Identification)

Passage:

Over the last decade, researchers have examined the impact of social media on mental health. Some studies indicate a strong correlation between excessive screen time and increased anxiety levels among adolescents. However, other research suggests that social media can provide valuable social connections, especially for individuals who feel isolated. The debate continues as scientists work to determine whether the benefits outweigh the risks.

Question:

Which choice best states the main idea of the passage?

A) Social media has only negative effects on mental health.

B) Researchers are debating the effects of social media on mental health.

C) Excessive screen time always causes anxiety in teenagers.

D) Scientists agree that social media benefits isolated individuals.

Correct Answer: B) Researchers are debating the effects of social media on mental health.

(The passage presents both positive and negative viewpoints, showing an ongoing debate.)

Strategy for Informational Passages

✓ Look for **words signaling argument or contrast** (e.g., "however," "while," "some studies suggest").

✓ Identify the **overall takeaway** rather than focusing on one side of the argument.

Example 2: Historical Passage (Main Idea Identification)

Passage:

The Seneca Falls Convention of 1848 marked a turning point in the American women's rights movement. Organized by Elizabeth Cady Stanton and Lucretia Mott, the convention produced the Declaration of Sentiments, a document that called for gender equality in law and society. Though progress was slow, this event laid the groundwork for future suffrage movements, ultimately leading to the passage of the 19th Amendment in 1920.

Question:

Which statement best captures the main idea of the passage?

A) The Seneca Falls Convention was the first political gathering in American history.

B) The women's rights movement began in 1920 with the passage of the 19th Amendment.

C) The Seneca Falls Convention played a key role in the early women's rights movement.

D) Elizabeth Cady Stanton and Lucretia Mott opposed women's suffrage.

Correct Answer: C) The Seneca Falls Convention played a key role in the early women's rights movement.

(The passage highlights the convention's significance in shaping the movement.)

Strategy for Historical Passages

✓ Focus on **why the event is important**, not just what happened.

✓ Identify key historical figures and their contributions.

Example 3: Scientific Passage (Main Idea Identification)

Passage:

Scientists have long studied the migratory behavior of monarch butterflies. Recent research suggests that these butterflies use Earth's magnetic field to navigate their journey across thousands of miles. Experiments indicate that when the magnetic field is disrupted, monarchs struggle to maintain their flight path. This discovery has led scientists to rethink how various species migrate.

Question:

Which choice best states the main idea of the passage?

A) Monarch butterflies rely on the Earth's magnetic field to migrate.

B) Butterfly migration is less predictable than previously thought.

C) Scientists have fully mapped butterfly migration routes.

D) Experiments have shown that butterflies cannot complete migration without human intervention.

Correct Answer: A) Monarch butterflies rely on the Earth's magnetic field to migrate.

(The passage focuses on how monarchs use magnetism to navigate.)

Strategy for Scientific Passages

✓ Identify **cause-and-effect relationships** (e.g., "when disrupted, monarchs struggle").

✓ Look for **new discoveries or research findings**.

Example 4: Literary Passage (Theme Identification)
Passage:
Elena stood at the edge of the track, her heart pounding. The starting pistol fired, and she launched forward, pushing herself harder than ever before. She thought about the years of early morning training, the sacrifices, and the setbacks. With one final surge, she crossed the finish line, not knowing if she had won—but knowing that she had given everything she had.
Question:
Which theme is best reflected in the passage?
A) The importance of perseverance and determination.
B) The challenges of working with a team.
C) The impact of technology on modern sports.
D) The dangers of pushing oneself too hard.
Correct Answer: A) The importance of perseverance and determination.
*(Elena's efforts and dedication reflect a **theme of perseverance**.)*

Strategy for Literary Passages

✓ Identify the **main conflict or emotional struggle**.
✓ Look for **universal lessons or messages**.

Strategies for Identifying Main Ideas and Themes

1. **Focus on the First and Last Sentence**
   - The **main idea** is often introduced at the beginning or summarized at the end.
2. **Ask: "What is this passage mostly about?"**
   - If a passage describes **different viewpoints**, the main idea might highlight **the debate itself**.
   - If a passage presents **a scientific study**, the main idea will likely focus on **the study's purpose or findings**.
3. **Avoid Traps: Don't Focus Only on One Detail**
   - Wrong answer choices often **overemphasize minor details** instead of summarizing the passage as a whole.
4. **Identify Transition Words That Signal the Main Idea**
   - **Contrast words** ("however," "although") introduce different viewpoints.
   - **Cause-and-effect words** ("therefore," "as a result") often signal **conclusions**.

Final Key Takeaways

- **The main idea is the central message of a passage**—it **summarizes the text as a whole**, not just a single detail.
- **Themes in literary passages** focus on **universal lessons**, such as perseverance or the struggle for freedom.
- **Each passage on the Digital SAT presents only one question**, so students must **quickly identify key information**.
- **Practice recognizing the main idea efficiently** using first and last sentences, key transitions, and summaries.

By mastering **main ideas and themes**, students can **answer questions faster, improve accuracy, and maximize their SAT Reading & Writing score.**

7.2 Finding Supporting Details and Making Inferences

The **Digital SAT Reading & Writing section** frequently tests a student's ability to identify **supporting details** and make **inferences** based on short passages. These skills are essential for understanding **how authors present evidence, develop arguments, and imply meanings beyond what is directly stated**.

Understanding Supporting Details

Supporting details are **pieces of evidence or examples** that strengthen a passage's **main idea**. They often answer the question:

"How does the author support their argument or claim?"

Common Types of Supporting Details

Type	Example
Facts & Statistics	"A recent study found that students who study in 25-minute intervals retain 30% more information."
Examples	"Many great inventors, such as Thomas Edison and Nikola Tesla, failed multiple times before succeeding."
Quotations	"As Dr. Thompson states, 'Renewable energy is the key to reducing carbon emissions.'"
Historical References	"The Great Depression of the 1930s serves as an example of how financial instability can impact global economies."

Identifying supporting details **requires careful reading** to determine how specific pieces of information **connect to the overall argument or main idea**.

Example Question: Supporting Details

Passage:

Exercise has been linked to improved cognitive function in adolescents. A recent study found that students who engaged in regular physical activity scored higher on problem-solving tasks than those who did not. Researchers believe that increased blood flow to the brain enhances focus and memory, leading to better academic performance.

Question:

Which sentence provides the best evidence for the claim that exercise benefits cognitive function?

A) Researchers believe that blood flow to the brain enhances focus and memory.
B) A recent study found that students who exercised scored higher on problem-solving tasks.
C) Many students enjoy playing sports in their free time.
D) Schools often promote physical education programs.

Correct Answer: B) A recent study found that students who exercised scored higher on problem-solving tasks.

*(This sentence provides **concrete evidence**—a study that directly supports the claim.)*

Understanding Inferences

An **inference** is a conclusion that is **not directly stated in the passage but can be logically drawn from the given information**. Inference questions require students to **read between the lines** and recognize **implied meanings**.

"What can be reasonably concluded from this passage?"

Common Inference Types

Type of Inference	Example Question
Author's Attitude	"How does the author feel about renewable energy policies?"
Predicting Outcomes	"Based on the passage, what is the most likely consequence of deforestation?"
Drawing Logical Conclusions	"What can be inferred about the relationship between nutrition and mental health?"

To answer inference questions, **look for clues** in the passage that suggest **implied information**.

Example Question: Making Inferences

Passage:

Despite the growing popularity of remote work, some employers remain skeptical about its long-term effects on productivity. A recent survey found that while many employees appreciate the flexibility, managers report difficulty in maintaining team collaboration and accountability.

Question:

What can be inferred from the passage?

A) All employees prefer remote work over in-office jobs.
B) Some employers worry that remote work may reduce productivity.
C) Most businesses have completely eliminated in-person work.
D) Companies with remote work policies always struggle with collaboration.

Correct Answer: B) Some employers worry that remote work may reduce productivity.
(The passage states that "some employers remain skeptical," supporting this inference.)

Key Strategies for Answering Supporting Detail and Inference Questions

1. Read the Question First

- **If the question asks for supporting details**, look for **direct evidence** in the passage.
- **If the question asks for an inference**, read for **implied meanings rather than stated facts**.

2. Look for Keywords and Context

- Identify **words that indicate evidence**, such as **"studies show," "research suggests," "for example,"** and **"according to experts."**
- For inference questions, focus on **tone, word choice, and context clues**.

3. Use Process of Elimination

- Remove answers that are **too extreme, contradict the passage, or introduce unrelated information**.

4. Verify the Answer with the Passage

- Ensure the correct answer **is supported by information in the text**, even if it's not stated outright.

Final Key Takeaways

- **Supporting details directly back up the main idea**, often through **facts, statistics, examples, or expert opinions**.
- **Inference questions require logical reasoning** based on the passage's tone, language, and context.
- **Effective reading strategies include identifying keywords, looking for cause-and-effect relationships, and eliminating incorrect choices**.
- **Every answer must be supported by information in the passage**—even in inference questions, which rely on implied meanings rather than direct statements.

By **practicing supporting detail and inference questions**, students can develop stronger **reading comprehension skills** and improve accuracy on the **Digital SAT Reading & Writing section**.

7.3 Understanding Vocabulary in Context

The **Digital SAT Reading & Writing section** frequently tests students on **vocabulary in context**, assessing their ability to determine the **meaning of a word or phrase based on how it is used in a passage**. Unlike traditional vocabulary tests that require memorization of definitions, these questions focus on **interpreting meaning within the passage's context**—often with words that have **multiple meanings** depending on usage.

What Does "Vocabulary in Context" Mean?

Vocabulary in context questions ask:

"What does this word or phrase most nearly mean in the passage?"

- The same word can have **different meanings** depending on how it is used.
- **Context clues** in the sentence help determine the **intended definition**.
- The correct answer is often **not the most common meaning of the word**.

Common Types of Vocabulary in Context Questions

Question Type	Example
Multiple-Meaning Words	"What does 'novel' most nearly mean in the passage?" (Could mean "new" or "a book")
Figurative Language	"What does the phrase 'a storm of emotions' suggest?"
Context-Dependent Meanings	"What does 'critical' mean in the sentence: 'She played a critical role in the project'?" (Could mean 'important' or 'harsh')

Example Vocabulary-in-Context Questions That Mirror the Digital SAT

Example 1: Multiple-Meaning Words

Passage:
The scientist's discovery was considered **novel**, challenging long-standing theories in the field.
Question:
What does the word **"novel"** most nearly mean in the passage?
A) Fictional
B) Traditional
C) Innovative
D) Unimportant
Correct Answer: C) Innovative
(The passage suggests that the discovery challenged old theories, meaning it was something new or groundbreaking.)
Strategy:
✓ Identify **how the word is used**—does it describe a person, object, or idea?
✓ Eliminate **common meanings** that don't fit (e.g., "novel" as a book).

Example 2: Context-Dependent Meanings

Passage:
The teacher's **critical** feedback helped the students refine their essays, allowing them to improve their arguments.
Question:
What does the word **"critical"** most nearly mean in the passage?
A) Harsh
B) Necessary
C) Judgmental
D) Scientific
Correct Answer: B) Necessary
(In this case, "critical" means "important" or "necessary," not "harsh.")
Strategy:
✓ Consider **whether the word has a positive or negative tone**.
✓ Replace the word with the answer choices to see which fits best.

Example 3: Figurative Language

Passage:
As the deadline approached, a **storm of emotions** overtook the students, filling the room with nervous energy.

Question:
What does the phrase **"a storm of emotions"** most nearly mean?
A) A sudden outburst of feelings
B) A discussion about the weather
C) A peaceful moment of reflection
D) A lack of emotional response
Correct Answer: A) A sudden outburst of feelings
(The phrase "storm of emotions" suggests an overwhelming or intense feeling, not an actual storm.)

Strategy:

✓ Identify **figurative language**—phrases that are not literal (e.g., "storm of emotions" = strong feelings).
✓ Look at **tone and imagery**—does the phrase suggest **energy, intensity, confusion, or peace**?

Effective Strategies for Answering Vocabulary in Context Questions

1. Read the Sentence Before and After the Word

- **Surrounding sentences provide context** for the word's meaning.
- Pay attention to **cause-and-effect relationships** or **contrasts** (e.g., "but," "although," "therefore").

2. Try Replacing the Word with Each Answer Choice

- Substitute each answer choice in the sentence and see **which one makes sense**.
- **If two choices seem possible, re-read the entire passage** for clarity.

3. Watch Out for Common Meanings That Don't Fit

- The **most common definition of a word is often a trap answer**.
- If a word has multiple meanings, consider **how it fits within the specific sentence**.

4. Identify Signal Words That Change Meaning

- **Contrast words**: "however," "but," "although" suggest an **opposite meaning**.
- **Cause-and-effect words**: "because," "therefore," "as a result" help define meaning.

Final Key Takeaways

- **Vocabulary-in-context questions test understanding of words as they are used in a passage, not just dictionary definitions.**
- **The correct meaning depends on the context, not the most common definition.**
- **Use surrounding sentences to determine meaning, especially for multiple-meaning words and figurative language.**
- **Practice substituting answer choices into the passage to see which makes sense.**

By **mastering vocabulary in context**, students can improve their **accuracy on the Digital SAT Reading & Writing section** and better interpret **complex texts in college-level reading.**

7.4 Tone, Style, and Author's Purpose

The **Digital SAT Reading & Writing section** frequently assesses a student's ability to recognize **tone, style, and author's purpose**. These elements are crucial for understanding **why** a passage was written and **how** the author conveys their message. Mastering these concepts allows students to interpret **both the literal and implied meanings** of texts, improving both accuracy and speed on the exam.

Understanding Tone

Tone refers to the **author's attitude toward the subject** or audience. It is **revealed through word choice, phrasing, and sentence structure**. Recognizing tone helps determine whether an author is being **informative, persuasive, critical, humorous, or neutral**.

Common Tones Found on the SAT

Tone Category	Examples
Positive	Enthusiastic, optimistic, respectful, admiring
Negative	Critical, sarcastic, skeptical, disappointed
Neutral/Objective	Informative, factual, formal, analytical
Emotional/Strong	Passionate, urgent, outraged, hopeful
Humorous/Satirical	Playful, ironic, sarcastic, witty

How to Identify Tone:

✓ **Look at word choice**—are words neutral, emotional, or persuasive?

✓ **Check for exaggeration, irony, or sarcasm**—these suggest a **non-literal meaning**.

✓ **Observe punctuation and structure**—exclamation points, short sentences, or rhetorical questions often indicate **strong emotion or persuasion**.

Example Question: Identifying Tone

Passage:

The newly discovered exoplanet orbits its star at an astonishing speed, completing a full revolution in just 12 hours. This remarkable finding challenges previous astronomical models and opens new avenues for understanding planetary formation.

Question:

Which best describes the tone of the passage?

A) Skeptical

B) Objective

C) Humorous

D) Nostalgic

Correct Answer: B) Objective

(The passage presents scientific information in a factual, neutral tone.)

Strategy:

✓ **Avoid extreme answers unless the passage has strong emotional language.**

✓ **If the passage presents facts, the tone is likely neutral or analytical.**

Understanding Style

Style refers to the way an author presents information. It includes **sentence structure, vocabulary, and rhetorical devices** that shape the passage's readability and impact.

Common Writing Styles on the SAT

Style Type	Characteristics
Formal	Complex sentences, sophisticated vocabulary, objective tone
Informal	Conversational, casual phrasing, contractions, first-person perspective
Persuasive	Emotional appeals, rhetorical questions, strong language
Descriptive	Vivid imagery, figurative language, sensory details
Expository	Clear, structured explanations, definitions, and examples

Example Question: Identifying Style

Passage:

Unlike traditional maps that rely on human-drawn boundaries, digital mapping technology uses satellite imagery to provide precise, real-time updates. This innovation enhances accuracy and efficiency in navigation, disaster response, and environmental monitoring.

Question:

Which best describes the style of the passage?

A) Poetic and abstract

B) Persuasive and emotional

C) Informative and analytical

D) Informal and conversational

Correct Answer: C) Informative and analytical

(The passage explains a concept using factual information and a neutral tone.)

Strategy:

✓ **Look at sentence structure**—formal writing has longer, more structured sentences.

✓ **Check for emotional words**—if absent, the style is likely **neutral or analytical**.

Understanding Author's Purpose

The **author's purpose** is the **reason** they wrote the passage. On the SAT, common purposes include:

Purpose	Common Clues
To Inform	Presents facts, data, or unbiased explanations
To Persuade	Uses emotional language, rhetorical questions, strong claims
To Entertain	Engages the reader with humor, storytelling, or suspense
To Explain a Concept	Uses definitions, structured explanations, step-by-step descriptions
To Argue a Point	Presents and defends a position on a controversial topic

Example Question: Identifying Author's Purpose

Passage:

Climate change is causing noticeable shifts in global weather patterns. According to recent studies, rising temperatures have led to increased storm intensity and changing rainfall patterns. If left unaddressed, these trends could have devastating effects on ecosystems and human populations.

Question:

What is the primary purpose of the passage?

A) To entertain readers with an engaging story

B) To argue for urgent action against climate change

C) To criticize scientists who study climate change

D) To provide an objective analysis of climate change patterns

Correct Answer: D) To provide an objective analysis of climate change patterns.

(The passage presents factual information rather than a strong argument or emotional appeal.)

Strategy:

✓ **Identify whether the passage presents facts or opinions**—factual passages are often **informative**, while opinionated passages are **persuasive or argumentative**.

✓ **Look for key phrases that signal persuasion**, such as **"we must," "it is necessary," "this proves"**—these suggest the author is trying to convince the reader.

Strategies for Answering Tone, Style, and Author's Purpose Questions

1. Identify Emotion and Word Choice

- **Strong emotional words** suggest a **persuasive or passionate tone**.
- **Neutral, fact-based writing** suggests **an informative or analytical tone**.

2. Look for Rhetorical Devices

- **Persuasive passages** often use **rhetorical questions, emotional appeals, or repetition**.
- **Descriptive passages** use **vivid imagery and figurative language**.

3. Check for Clues in the First and Last Sentence

- The **first sentence** often introduces the **main idea and tone**.
- The **last sentence** often summarizes the **author's purpose**.

Final Key Takeaways

- **Tone** reflects the **author's attitude** and can be **positive, negative, neutral, or emotional**.
- **Style** includes **word choice, sentence structure, and rhetorical techniques** to shape the passage's presentation.
- **Author's purpose** explains **why the text was written**—to inform, persuade, explain, or entertain.
- **Recognizing key words and sentence structure** can help determine whether a passage is **factual, opinion-based, formal, or informal**.

By mastering **tone, style, and author's purpose**, students can **improve reading comprehension, answer SAT questions with confidence, and efficiently interpret complex texts.**

CHAPTER 8

WRITING AND LANGUAGE SKILLS

8.1 Grammar Essentials (Subject-Verb Agreement, Pronouns, etc.)

The **Digital SAT Writing & Language section** assesses a student's ability to apply proper **grammar rules, sentence structure, and writing mechanics**. Mastering **subject-verb agreement, pronoun usage, and other grammar essentials** is crucial for answering multiple-choice questions accurately.

This section will cover:
✓ **Subject-Verb Agreement**
✓ **Pronoun Clarity and Agreement**
✓ **Verb Tense Consistency**
✓ **Modifiers and Word Order**

1. Subject-Verb Agreement

Definition:
A singular subject requires a **singular verb**, and a plural subject requires a **plural verb**.

Basic Rules:

Subject Type	Example
Singular subject + Singular verb	The student **writes** an essay.
Plural subject + Plural verb	The students **write** essays.
Compound subject (joined by 'and')	Sarah and Tom **are** studying.
Subjects joined by 'or' or 'nor'	Neither Sarah nor Tom **is** late.
Collective nouns (team, group, class, etc.)	The team **is** practicing.

Example Question: Subject-Verb Agreement
Sentence:
The committee **decide** on the budget every year.
Question:
Which revision corrects the grammatical error?
A) The committee **decide** on the budget every year.
B) The committee **decides** on the budget every year.
C) The committee **were deciding** on the budget every year.
D) The committee **are deciding** on the budget every year.
Correct Answer: B) The committee decides on the budget every year.
("Committee" is a collective noun, treated as singular, so the verb should be "decides.")

Strategy Tip:
✓ **Identify the true subject**—avoid being misled by words between the subject and verb.
✓ **Watch for collective nouns**—they are singular unless referring to individual members acting separately.

2. Pronoun Clarity and Agreement

Definition:
A pronoun must **clearly refer to a noun** (called the antecedent) and **match in number and gender**.

Common Pronoun Errors:

Error Type	Incorrect Example	Corrected Sentence

Unclear Antecedent	When Sarah and Lisa arrived, **she** was late.	When Sarah and Lisa arrived, **Lisa** was late.
Singular/Plural Mismatch	Each of the students brought **their** notebook.	Each of the students brought **his or her** notebook.
Pronoun Shift	If one studies hard, **you** will succeed.	If one studies hard, **one** will succeed.

Example Question: Pronoun Clarity and Agreement
Sentence:
If a student wants to improve **their** writing, they should practice daily.
Question:
Which revision best corrects the pronoun error?
A) If a student wants to improve **their** writing, they should practice daily.
B) If a student wants to improve **his or her** writing, he or she should practice daily.
C) If students want to improve **his or her** writing, he or she should practice daily.
D) If a student wants to improve **their** writing, one should practice daily.
Correct Answer: B) If a student wants to improve his or her writing, he or she should practice daily.
("Student" is singular, so the pronoun must also be singular: "his or her.")

Strategy Tip:
✓ **Check that pronouns match in number and gender** with the noun they refer to.
✓ **Avoid unclear pronouns** that could refer to multiple subjects.

3. Verb Tense Consistency

Definition:
Verb tenses should remain **consistent within a sentence or passage**, unless a change in time is clearly indicated.

Common Verb Tense Errors:

Incorrect	Corrected
She **studies** every night but **forgot** her book today.	She **studies** every night but **forgets** her book today.
When I **was** a child, I **play** outside every day.	When I **was** a child, I **played** outside every day.
By the time they arrived, the party **ended**.	By the time they arrived, the party **had ended**.

Example Question: Verb Tense Consistency
Sentence:
The scientist **discovered** a new element and **is publishing** her findings next week.
Question:
Which revision corrects the verb tense inconsistency?
A) The scientist **discovered** a new element and **is publishing** her findings next week.
B) The scientist **discovers** a new element and **is publishing** her findings next week.
C) The scientist **discovered** a new element and **will publish** her findings next week.
D) The scientist **had discovered** a new element and **published** her findings next week.
Correct Answer: C) The scientist discovered a new element and will publish her findings next week.
(Past tense "discovered" must be followed by future tense "will publish" for consistency.)

Strategy Tip:
✓ **Ensure all verbs match the timeframe** indicated in the sentence.
✓ **Use past perfect ("had done") for actions completed before another past event**.

4. Modifiers and Word Order

Definition:

A modifier **describes or clarifies another part of the sentence**. Misplaced or dangling modifiers **create confusion**.

Common Modifier Errors:

Incorrect	Corrected
Running late, the bus was missed by Sarah.	Running late, Sarah missed the bus.
Covered in frosting, the baker admired the cake.	The baker admired the cake covered in frosting.

Example Question: Misplaced Modifier

Sentence:

Walking to school, the backpack felt heavy on James's shoulders.

Question:

Which revision corrects the misplaced modifier?

A) Walking to school, the backpack felt heavy on James's shoulders.
B) The backpack felt heavy on James's shoulders walking to school.
C) Walking to school, James felt the backpack heavy on his shoulders.
D) James, walking to school, felt the backpack heavy on his shoulders.

Correct Answer: C) Walking to school, James felt the backpack heavy on his shoulders.
(James, not the backpack, is the one walking to school.)

Strategy Tip:

✓ **Make sure the modifying phrase is next to the noun it describes.**
✓ **If the sentence sounds awkward or unclear, check for misplaced modifiers.**

Final Key Takeaways

- **Subject-verb agreement**: Singular subjects take singular verbs; plural subjects take plural verbs.
- **Pronoun clarity and agreement**: Ensure pronouns clearly refer to the correct noun and match in number and gender.
- **Verb tense consistency**: Keep verb tenses aligned unless a time change is explicitly stated.
- **Modifiers and word order**: Modifiers must be **placed next to the words they describe** to avoid confusion.

By mastering **these grammar essentials**, students can **significantly improve accuracy in the SAT Writing & Language section** and develop stronger **sentence structure skills** for both the test and academic writing.

8.2 Syntax and Sentence Structure

The **Digital SAT Writing & Language section** assesses a student's ability to recognize **correct sentence structure** and **improve sentence clarity**. Understanding **syntax**—the arrangement of words and phrases to create well-formed sentences—is crucial for achieving **concise, logical, and grammatically sound writing**.

This section will cover:

✓ **Sentence Structure Basics**
✓ **Common Sentence Errors (Run-ons, Fragments, and Comma Splices)**
✓ **Parallel Structure**
✓ **Sentence Combining and Clarity**

1. Sentence Structure Basics

A well-structured sentence contains:

- **A subject** (who or what the sentence is about)
- **A verb** (the action or state of being)
- **A complete thought**

Types of Sentences

Sentence Type	Definition	Example
Simple Sentence	Contains one independent clause.	The dog **barked** loudly.
Compound Sentence	Contains two independent clauses joined by a conjunction.	The dog **barked**, but the cat **remained calm**.
Complex Sentence	Contains one independent clause and at least one dependent clause.	Because the dog **barked**, the cat **ran away**.
Compound-Complex Sentence	Contains at least two independent clauses and one dependent clause.	Because the dog **barked**, the cat **ran away**, and the owner **looked outside**.

Why This Matters on the SAT:

- **Simple sentences** provide clarity but can sound choppy if overused.
- **Complex and compound sentences** allow for more sophisticated writing when used correctly.

2. Common Sentence Errors (Run-ons, Fragments, and Comma Splices)

A. Run-On Sentences

Definition: Two or more independent clauses joined **without correct punctuation or a conjunction**.

Incorrect:
The weather was perfect we decided to go for a hike.

Corrected Versions:

- The weather was perfect, **so** we decided to go for a hike. (**Using a conjunction**)
- The weather was perfect; we decided to go for a hike. (**Using a semicolon**)
- The weather was perfect. We decided to go for a hike. (**Splitting into two sentences**)

B. Sentence Fragments

Definition: A **dependent clause or phrase** that is **missing a subject, verb, or complete thought**.

Incorrect:
Because the students worked late into the night.

Corrected Version:
Because the students worked late into the night, **they were exhausted the next morning**.

C. Comma Splices

Definition: Two independent clauses joined **only by a comma**, which is grammatically incorrect.

Incorrect:
The experiment was a success, the results were surprising.

Corrected Versions:
✓ **Using a conjunction:** The experiment was a success, **and** the results were surprising.
✓ **Using a semicolon:** The experiment was a success; the results were surprising.
✓ **Splitting into two sentences:** The experiment was a success. The results were surprising.

Example Question: Run-On Sentences
Sentence:
The artist painted all afternoon the new mural was nearly finished by evening.
Question:
Which revision best corrects the sentence?
A) The artist painted all afternoon; the new mural was nearly finished by evening.
B) The artist painted all afternoon, the new mural was nearly finished by evening.
C) The artist painted all afternoon the new mural, which was nearly finished by evening.
D) The artist painting all afternoon, the new mural was nearly finished by evening.
Correct Answer: A) The artist painted all afternoon; the new mural was nearly finished by evening.
(A semicolon correctly joins two independent clauses.)

Strategy Tip:
✓ **Check for two independent clauses**—if they are incorrectly joined, fix them with a conjunction, semicolon, or period.

3. Parallel Structure

Definition:

Parallel structure ensures that **items in a list or paired ideas follow the same grammatical format**.

Incorrect Sentence	Corrected Version
She enjoys **reading, writing, and to paint**.	She enjoys **reading, writing, and painting**.
The proposal was both **logical and it was persuasive**.	The proposal was both **logical and persuasive**.

Example Question: Parallel Structure
Sentence:
The teacher emphasized that students should **complete their homework, reviewing their notes, and to study for tests**.
Question:
Which revision best corrects the sentence?
A) The teacher emphasized that students should **complete their homework, review their notes, and study for tests**.
B) The teacher emphasized that students should **complete their homework, reviewing their notes, and to study for tests**.
C) The teacher emphasized that students should **complete their homework, and review their notes and to study for tests**.
D) The teacher emphasized that students should **complete their homework, reviewed their notes, and studied for tests**.
Correct Answer: A) The teacher emphasized that students should complete their homework, review their notes, and study for tests.
(All verbs are now in the same form: ***"complete," "review," "study."****)*

Strategy Tip:
✓ **Check lists and paired ideas**—they should follow the **same grammatical pattern**.

4. Sentence Combining and Clarity

On the SAT, some questions require students to **combine two sentences smoothly** while maintaining clarity and logical flow.

Techniques for Sentence Combining:

✓ **Use a semicolon for closely related independent clauses.**
✓ **Use a relative clause (who, which, that) to avoid redundancy.**
✓ **Use concise transitions (although, because, while) to connect ideas.**

Example Question: Sentence Combining
Sentences:
The scientist won an award. She made a breakthrough in cancer research.
Question:
Which choice best combines the two sentences?
A) The scientist, who made a breakthrough in cancer research, won an award.
B) The scientist made a breakthrough in cancer research, and she won an award.
C) The scientist won an award, making a breakthrough in cancer research.
D) The scientist made a breakthrough in cancer research; an award was won.
Correct Answer: A) The scientist, who made a breakthrough in cancer research, won an award.
(This version correctly combines the sentences using a ***relative clause*** *for conciseness and clarity.)*

Strategy Tip:
✓ **Choose the most concise, clear option** that maintains **all essential information**.

Final Key Takeaways

- **Avoid run-ons, fragments, and comma splices**—sentences must have **proper punctuation** between independent clauses.
- **Use parallel structure in lists and paired ideas** to maintain grammatical consistency.
- **Sentence combining should be logical, clear, and concise.**
- **Check word order** to avoid misplaced modifiers and awkward phrasing.

By mastering **sentence structure and syntax**, students can **improve clarity, readability, and accuracy on the Digital SAT Writing & Language section**, ensuring they avoid common errors and communicate ideas effectively.

8.3 Punctuation, Parallelism, and Other Common Pitfalls

The **Digital SAT Writing & Language section** assesses a student's ability to apply proper **punctuation rules, maintain parallel structure, and avoid common grammatical pitfalls**. Mastering these areas ensures clarity, conciseness, and accuracy in writing.

This section will cover:
✓ **Punctuation Rules (Commas, Semicolons, Colons, Dashes, Apostrophes, etc.)**
✓ **Parallelism in Sentences**
✓ **Other Common Pitfalls (Misplaced Modifiers, Wordiness, Redundancy)**

1. Punctuation Rules on the SAT

Punctuation plays a critical role in sentence structure. The SAT frequently tests the correct use of **commas, semicolons, colons, dashes, and apostrophes**.

A. Comma Usage (,)

✓ **Separating Items in a List**

- **Correct:** The conference covered **leadership, teamwork, and communication skills**.
  ✓ **After an Introductory Phrase**
- **Correct:** After a long day, **she decided to go for a run**.
  ✓ **Before a Conjunction (FANBOYS) When Joining Two Independent Clauses**
- **Correct:** He wanted to stay home, **but** his friends convinced him to go out.
  ✓ **Setting Off Non-Essential Information**

- **Correct:** The Eiffel Tower, **which was built in 1889**, remains a global icon.

✓ Common Comma Error: Comma Splice (Incorrectly Joining Two Independent Clauses with a Comma)

- **Incorrect:** The storm was intense, the streets flooded quickly.
- **Correct:** The storm was intense, **so** the streets flooded quickly.

B. Semicolon Usage (;)

✓ Joining Two Related Independent Clauses Without a Conjunction

- **Correct:** The test was difficult; many students struggled with the last section.

  ✓ Separating Complex List Items (When Items Contain Commas)
- **Correct:** The speakers included John Smith, the CEO; Sarah Brown, the CFO; and Michael Lee, the head of marketing.

✓ Common Semicolon Error: Using a Semicolon Instead of a Comma with FANBOYS

- **Incorrect:** The dog was tired; but he kept running.
- **Correct:** The dog was tired, **but** he kept running.

C. Colon Usage (:)

✓ Introducing a List, Explanation, or Example

- **Correct:** She packed everything for the trip: sunscreen, snacks, and extra clothes.

  ✓ Before an Explanation or Clarification
- **Correct:** There was only one rule: never be late.

✓ Common Colon Error: Using a Colon After a Verb or Preposition

- **Incorrect:** The ingredients include: flour, sugar, and eggs.
- **Correct:** The ingredients include flour, sugar, and eggs.

D. Dash Usage (—)

✓ Replacing Parentheses or Commas for Additional Information

- **Correct:** The museum's newest exhibit—an interactive VR experience—was a hit among visitors.

  ✓ Indicating an Abrupt Shift or Emphasis
- **Correct:** She had one goal—to win the championship.

✓ Common Dash Error: Mixing Dashes and Other Punctuation Incorrectly

- **Incorrect:** The best players (Tom, Sarah, and Luis—were chosen for the team.
- **Correct:** The best players—Tom, Sarah, and Luis—were chosen for the team.

E. Apostrophe Usage (')

✓ Indicating Possession

- **Singular:** The dog's leash (belongs to one dog).
- **Plural:** The dogs' park (belongs to multiple dogs).

  ✓ Forming Contractions
- **Correct:** It's (it is) a great day.

✓ Common Apostrophe Error: Confusing It's vs. Its

- **Incorrect:** The cat licked it's paws.
- **Correct:** The cat licked **its** paws.

2. Parallelism in Sentences

Definition:

Parallel structure ensures that **lists, comparisons, and paired ideas follow the same grammatical format**.

Common Parallelism Errors

Incorrect	Corrected
She enjoys **reading, writing, and to paint**.	She enjoys **reading, writing, and painting**.

The proposal was both **logical and it was persuasive**.	The proposal was both **logical and persuasive**.

✓ **Check for consistency in verb forms** (e.g., all gerunds or all infinitives).

✓ **Ensure comparisons use the same structure**.

Example Question: Parallelism

Sentence:

The program emphasized the importance of **communication, problem-solving, and to work as a team**.

Question:

Which revision best corrects the sentence?

A) The program emphasized the importance of **communication, problem-solving, and to work as a team**.

B) The program emphasized the importance of **communication, problem-solving, and teamwork**.

C) The program emphasized the importance of **communicating, problem-solving, and to work as a team**.

D) The program emphasized the importance of **communication, problem-solving, and working as a team**.

Correct Answer: D) The program emphasized the importance of communication, problem-solving, and working as a team.

(All elements now follow the same grammatical pattern.)

3. Other Common Pitfalls

A. Misplaced Modifiers

✓ Modifiers should be **placed next to the word they describe** to avoid confusion.

Incorrect: Walking down the street, the trees looked beautiful.

(Implies that the trees were walking down the street.)

Correct: Walking down the street, **I admired the beautiful trees**.

B. Wordiness & Redundancy

✓ SAT favors **concise writing**—eliminate **unnecessary words**.

Incorrect: The reason why she left early was because she had an appointment.

Correct: She left early because she had an appointment.

✓ Avoid phrases that repeat the same idea.

Wordy	Concise
In my personal opinion	In my opinion
At this point in time	Now
The reason is because	The reason is

Example Question: Conciseness and Clarity

Sentence:

The company's new policy is a policy that will improve efficiency.

Question:

Which revision best improves clarity?

A) The company's new policy is a policy that will improve efficiency.

B) The company's new policy is improving efficiency.

C) The company's new policy will improve efficiency.

D) The company's new policy is an improvement for efficiency.

Correct Answer: C) The company's new policy will improve efficiency.

*(This version is **concise** and eliminates redundancy.)*

Final Key Takeaways

✓ **Master punctuation rules**—commas, semicolons, colons, dashes, and apostrophes are frequently tested.
✓ **Use parallel structure** in lists, comparisons, and verb forms.
✓ **Avoid misplaced modifiers** by placing descriptions next to the words they modify.
✓ **Eliminate wordiness and redundancy** to make sentences more concise and clear.

By **practicing these skills**, students can **avoid common pitfalls and improve accuracy on the Digital SAT Writing & Language section**, ensuring they write with **precision and clarity**.

8.4 Rhetorical Skills: Clarity, Cohesion, and Transitions

The **Digital SAT Writing & Language section** evaluates students' ability to **enhance clarity, improve cohesion, and use effective transitions** in writing. These rhetorical skills are crucial for constructing well-organized, logically connected, and easy-to-read sentences.

This section will cover:
✓ **Clarity – Choosing precise and effective wording**
✓ **Cohesion – Structuring ideas logically**
✓ **Transitions – Connecting sentences and paragraphs smoothly**

1. Clarity: Choosing Precise and Effective Wording

Definition:

Clarity ensures that writing is **direct, unambiguous, and concise**. SAT questions often ask students to revise sentences to remove **wordiness, redundancy, and vague phrasing**.

Common Clarity Errors & Fixes

Error Type	Incorrect	Corrected
Wordiness	Due to the fact that	Because
Redundancy	Unexpected surprise	Surprise
Vague Pronoun Reference	They say that exercise is good.	Experts say that exercise is good.
Imprecise Language	She was somewhat angry.	She was frustrated.

Example Question: Clarity

Sentence:
In order to improve **his writing, he needs to practice consistently on a regular basis**.
Question:
Which revision best improves clarity?
A) In order to improve his writing, he needs to practice consistently on a regular basis.
B) To improve his writing, he needs to practice regularly.
C) He needs to practice to improve his writing in a way that is consistent.
D) His writing can be improved by practicing regularly in a consistent manner.
Correct Answer: B) To improve his writing, he needs to practice regularly.
(Removes unnecessary words while maintaining meaning.)

Strategy Tip:
✓ **Eliminate wordy phrases and redundant expressions**.
✓ **Replace vague words with specific, precise alternatives**.

2. Cohesion: Structuring Ideas Logically

Definition:

Cohesion ensures that ideas within a sentence or paragraph are **logically arranged** so that the text flows smoothly.

Common Cohesion Errors & Fixes

Error Type	Incorrect	Corrected
Ideas presented in the wrong order	I went home after my workout, which was intense.	After my intense workout, I went home.
Repetitive phrasing	He studies hard every day. He reviews his notes daily.	He studies hard and reviews his notes daily.
Weak or unclear connections	The research supports the theory, but additional evidence is required.	While the research supports the theory, additional evidence is required.

Example Question: Cohesion

Sentence:

The book provides a historical overview of the Renaissance. It also explains how art and culture evolved during that time. The printing press played a crucial role in spreading new ideas.

Question:

Where should the sentence about the printing press be placed for the best logical flow?

A) Before the first sentence
B) After the second sentence
C) At the end of the paragraph
D) It is best where it is

Correct Answer: B) After the second sentence.

(The sentence about the printing press logically follows the discussion about how art and culture evolved, as the printing press contributed to that evolution.)

Strategy Tip:

✓ **Identify logical progression**—does the order of information make sense?
✓ **Look for pronouns like "this" or "it"**—they should clearly refer to a previously mentioned idea.

3. Transitions: Connecting Sentences and Paragraphs Smoothly

Definition:

Transitions **help connect ideas within and between sentences or paragraphs**, ensuring that writing flows logically.

Types of Transitions on the SAT

Transition Type	Purpose	Examples
Addition	Adds more information	Furthermore, in addition, also
Contrast	Shows opposing ideas	However, on the other hand, conversely
Cause & Effect	Shows a relationship between actions	As a result, therefore, consequently
Example or Clarification	Provides examples or explanations	For instance, such as, in other words

Example Question: Transitions

Sentence:

The study revealed that students who read daily score higher on vocabulary tests. _______, researchers recommend incorporating reading into academic curriculums.

Question:

Which transition best completes the sentence?

A) However
B) Consequently
C) In contrast
D) For example
Correct Answer: B) Consequently.
(The second sentence presents a logical result of the first, making "consequently" the best choice.)

Strategy Tip:
✓ **Identify the relationship between sentences**—is it cause and effect, contrast, or continuation?
✓ **Eliminate choices that create illogical connections**.

Final Key Takeaways

- **Clarity**: Use precise and concise wording. **Avoid wordiness, redundancy, and vague phrasing**.
- **Cohesion**: Ensure **logical sentence structure** and **avoid misplaced or disorganized ideas**.
- **Transitions**: Choose the correct transition type to **connect sentences logically**.

By **mastering rhetorical skills**, students can improve **writing effectiveness and accuracy**, ensuring they **score higher on the SAT Writing & Language section**.

CHAPTER 9

STRATEGIES FOR R&W SUCCESS

9.1 Time Management and Module-Adaptive Tactics

The **Digital SAT Reading & Writing section** consists of two adaptive modules, each with **27 questions in 32 minutes**, totaling **54 questions in 64 minutes**. This structure requires **strong time management skills** to ensure students complete all questions efficiently while maintaining accuracy. Additionally, since the test is **adaptive**, performance in **Module 1 determines the difficulty of Module 2**, making strategic pacing even more critical.

This section will cover:
✓ **Understanding Time Constraints**
✓ **Pacing Strategies for Each Module**
✓ **Module-Adaptive Tactics**
✓ **When to Skip, Flag, and Return to Questions**

1. Understanding Time Constraints

Each **Reading & Writing module** has:

- **27 questions**
- **32 minutes to complete**
- **1 minute and 11 seconds per question (on average)**

Module	Number of Questions	Time Per Module	Time Per Question
Module 1	27	32 min	~1 min 11 sec
Module 2	27	32 min	~1 min 11 sec

Key Challenge: Since some questions are easier and others are harder, **spending too much time on one question can cost valuable time needed for others**.

2. Pacing Strategies for Each Module

A. The First 10 Minutes: Build Momentum
✓ Aim to complete **the first 10–12 questions in about 10 minutes**.
✓ Answer **easier questions quickly**, ensuring enough time for difficult ones later.

B. The Next 15 Minutes: Manage Mid-Test Fatigue
✓ Don't slow down too much—stick to **1 minute per question on average**.
✓ Use the **flagging tool** to mark tricky questions for review.

C. The Last 7 Minutes: Review and Complete Remaining Questions
✓ **Return to flagged questions**—but don't spend too much time second-guessing.
✓ If time is running out, **guess strategically rather than leaving questions blank**.

Time Breakdown Strategy

Question Type	Ideal Time to Spend
Vocabulary in Context	~30 seconds
Main Idea/Inference	~45–60 seconds
Grammar & Syntax	~30–45 seconds
Logical Transitions	~30 seconds

Data Interpretation	~45–60 seconds

3. Module-Adaptive Tactics

The **Reading & Writing section is adaptive**, meaning that:

- **Module 1** is the same for all students.
- **Module 2** varies in difficulty based on **Module 1 performance**.
- **Higher difficulty questions in Module 2 can boost the scoring potential.**

How to Use Adaptive Testing to Your Advantage

✓ **Maximize Accuracy in Module 1:**

- Answer easier questions **confidently and quickly**.
- Avoid careless mistakes—every point matters in determining the next module's difficulty.

✓ **Prepare for a More Challenging Module 2 (If Performing Well):**

- Expect **longer sentences, denser passages, and more abstract vocabulary**.
- Spend **slightly more time per question**, but maintain overall pacing.

✓ **If Module 2 Feels Easier (Indicating Module 1 Was Weaker):**

- Don't panic—focus on **maximizing accuracy** to improve scoring potential.
- Ensure **no skipped or careless mistakes**.

4. When to Skip, Flag, and Return to Questions

✓ **Skip Immediately if:**

- A question is **taking more than 90 seconds** to answer.
- You don't recognize the vocabulary or structure.

✓ **Flag and Return If:**

- The question seems solvable but needs **a fresh look** after easier ones are completed.
- The passage requires **more context** to understand.

✓ **Make an Educated Guess If:**

- Time is running out, and **skipping is not an option**.
- You can **eliminate at least one or two answer choices**.

Final Key Takeaways

✓ **Time is limited—maintain a steady pace** without overanalyzing easy questions.
✓ **Maximize accuracy in Module 1** to secure a higher-difficulty Module 2.
✓ **Use strategic skipping and flagging**—don't waste time on one tough question.
✓ **Prepare for more challenging Module 2 questions** by expecting **denser text and trickier grammar rules**.

By mastering **time management and adaptive tactics**, students can **approach the Digital SAT Reading & Writing section with confidence and efficiency, ensuring they maximize their score potential.**

9.2 Approaches to Short Passages and Single-Question Readings

The **Digital SAT Reading & Writing section** consists of **short passages**, each followed by a **single multiple-choice question**. Unlike the previous SAT format, where students analyzed **long passages with multiple questions**, the new format requires **quick comprehension and precise reasoning** for each standalone question.

This section will cover:
✓ **Understanding the Short-Passage Format**
✓ **Efficient Reading Techniques**
✓ **Common Question Types and Strategies**

1. Understanding the Short-Passage Format

Each question in the **Digital SAT Reading & Writing section** is tied to a **brief passage (25–150 words)**, followed by **one question**.

Feature	Digital SAT Format
Passage Length	25–150 words
Questions Per Passage	1
Total Questions	54 (across two modules)
Time Per Question	~1 minute 11 seconds
Question Types	Vocabulary, main idea, inference, grammar, transitions

Key Challenge:
Since passages are **short**, students **must extract key information quickly** while ensuring accuracy.

2. Efficient Reading Techniques

Since each passage has **only one question**, students **do not need to read every word carefully**. Instead, use these **strategic reading techniques**:

A. Read the Question First

- **Why?** It helps you **identify what to focus on** while reading.
- **Example:** If the question asks for **the main idea**, you should prioritize **the first and last sentence** of the passage.

B. Skim for Key Information

- **Identify:**
  ✓ Main topic (first and last sentence)
  ✓ Contrasts and shifts (e.g., "however," "although," "but")
  ✓ Supporting evidence (examples, research, statistics)

C. Eliminate Unnecessary Details

- Since each passage has **only one question**, do not spend time **memorizing details** that may not be relevant.

3. Common Question Types and Strategies

Each passage presents **one of four key question types**:

A. Vocabulary in Context

✓ Tests **word meaning based on the passage**
✓ The correct meaning is often **not the most common definition**

Example Question:
Passage:
The scientist's hypothesis was initially dismissed as **untenable**, but later experiments proved its validity.
Question:
What does the word **"untenable"** most nearly mean in the passage?
A) Unproven
B) Indefensible
C) Revolutionary
D) Complicated
Correct Answer: B) Indefensible
(The passage suggests the hypothesis was first rejected, meaning "untenable" must mean something like "unable to be supported.")

✓ **Strategy:**
✓ Look for **context clues** around the word.
✓ Eliminate answers that don't fit the sentence's meaning.

B. Main Idea & Inference Questions

✓ Ask about **the overall meaning or an implied idea** in the passage.

Example Question:
Passage:
Urban beekeeping has gained popularity as a sustainable practice. By transforming vacant lots into productive green spaces, beekeepers help pollinate local plants, support declining bee populations, and contribute to biodiversity efforts.
Question:
What is the main idea of the passage?
A) Urban beekeeping is an effective method for promoting environmental sustainability.
B) Bee populations have been increasing in urban environments.
C) Local gardens benefit more from beekeeping than rural farms.
D) Beekeeping is an outdated agricultural practice.
Correct Answer: A) Urban beekeeping is an effective method for promoting environmental sustainability.

✓ **Strategy:**
✓ Focus on the **first and last sentence** to determine the main idea.
✓ If the question asks for an **inference**, look for **hints rather than direct statements**.

C. Logical Transitions & Sentence Flow

✓ Tests **how ideas connect** within a passage
✓ The correct transition must match the **relationship between ideas**

Example Question:
Sentence:
The study found that exposure to natural light improved students' ability to focus. _____, researchers recommended adjusting classroom lighting to maximize natural sunlight.
Question:
Which transition best completes the sentence?
A) However
B) Consequently
C) In contrast
D) For example
Correct Answer: B) Consequently
(The second sentence presents a logical result of the first, making "consequently" the best choice.)

✓ **Strategy:**
✓ Identify the relationship between sentences (cause-effect, contrast, addition).
✓ Eliminate choices that create **illogical** connections.

D. Grammar & Sentence Structure

✓ Tests **sentence clarity, parallelism, and verb agreement**

Example Question:
Sentence:
The teacher emphasized that students should **complete their homework, reviewing their notes, and to study for tests**.

Question:
Which revision best corrects the sentence?
A) The teacher emphasized that students should **complete their homework, review their notes, and study for tests**.
B) The teacher emphasized that students should **complete their homework, reviewing their notes, and to study for tests**.
C) The teacher emphasized that students should **complete their homework, and review their notes and to study for tests**.
D) The teacher emphasized that students should **complete their homework, reviewed their notes, and studied for tests**.
Correct Answer: A) The teacher emphasized that students should complete their homework, review their notes, and study for tests.

✓ **Strategy:**
✓ Identify **parallel structures**—all elements in a list must follow the same grammatical form.
✓ Look for **misplaced modifiers and awkward phrasing**.

4. Summary of Key Strategies

Strategy	Why It Works
Read the question first	Helps focus on what information matters most
Skim for key ideas	Saves time by identifying essential details quickly
Use context for vocabulary questions	Helps determine meaning based on surrounding words
Identify logical relationships for transitions	Ensures smooth sentence connections
Apply process of elimination	Removes incorrect answers and improves accuracy

Final Key Takeaways

✓ **Each passage is short (25–150 words), so read efficiently.**
✓ **Read the question first** to focus on relevant details.
✓ **Skim for main ideas, key transitions, and essential facts.**
✓ **Use elimination strategies** to improve accuracy.

By mastering **approaches to short passages and single-question readings**, students can **enhance comprehension, improve pacing, and maximize accuracy on the Digital SAT Reading & Writing section**.

9.3 Skimming vs. Close Reading: Balancing Speed and Accuracy

The **Digital SAT Reading & Writing section** requires students to read efficiently while maintaining accuracy. Since each passage is **short (25–150 words) and paired with one question**, balancing **skimming** and **close reading** is essential for **effective time management and comprehension**.

This section will cover:
✓ **When to Skim vs. When to Read Closely**
✓ **Skimming Techniques for Fast Comprehension**
✓ **Close Reading Strategies for Detail-Oriented Questions**
✓ **Applying Skimming and Close Reading in SAT Questions**

1. When to Skim vs. When to Read Closely

Situation	Skimming or Close Reading?	Why?

Identifying the main idea	Skimming	The first and last sentences usually reveal the central idea.
Understanding tone and purpose	Skimming	Word choice and sentence structure provide quick insights.
Vocabulary in context questions	Close Reading	The surrounding sentence clarifies word meaning.
Inference questions	Close Reading	Requires deeper analysis beyond stated facts.
Grammar and sentence structure questions	Close Reading	Details are crucial for accuracy.
Logical transition questions	Skimming	Recognizing contrast, cause-effect, or addition quickly helps.

Key Insight: Not all questions require close reading. Knowing **when to skim** saves time for **harder, detail-focused questions**.

2. Skimming Techniques for Fast Comprehension

Definition:
Skimming is **reading quickly to grasp the overall meaning** without focusing on every word.

How to Skim Efficiently on the SAT

✓ **Read the first and last sentence of the passage**

- The main idea is often introduced in the first sentence and reinforced in the last.

✓ **Look for signal words (contrast, cause-effect, examples)**

- Words like **however, therefore, in contrast, for instance** help identify important points.

✓ **Ignore unnecessary details**

- Skip long descriptions and focus on **key arguments, facts, and transitions**.

Example: Skimming for Main Idea

Passage:
Urban beekeeping is growing in popularity, providing ecological and economic benefits. Beekeepers in major cities report that rooftop hives help sustain pollinator populations, which are declining worldwide. These hives not only contribute to local biodiversity but also produce high-quality honey that supports small businesses. Despite some concerns about space constraints, urban beekeeping offers an innovative solution for sustainable food production in cities.

Question:
Which choice best summarizes the passage?
A) Urban beekeeping is a controversial practice due to space limitations.
B) The rise of urban beekeeping has provided multiple benefits to both nature and local economies.
C) Beekeepers are struggling to maintain pollinator populations due to urban expansion.
D) Most cities are banning rooftop beekeeping due to environmental concerns.
Correct Answer: B) The rise of urban beekeeping has provided multiple benefits to both nature and local economies.
*(Skimming shows that the passage highlights **both ecological and economic benefits** of urban beekeeping.)*

✓ **Why Skimming Works:**
✓ **The first sentence provides the main idea** ("Urban beekeeping is growing in popularity, providing ecological and economic benefits.")

✓ **The last sentence reinforces the takeaway** ("Urban beekeeping offers an innovative solution for sustainable food production in cities.")

3. Close Reading Strategies for Detail-Oriented Questions

Definition:
Close reading involves **analyzing every word in a sentence carefully** to understand specific meanings, relationships, and implications.

When to Use Close Reading on the SAT

✓ **For Vocabulary in Context questions**
✓ **For Inference questions**
✓ **For Grammar and Sentence Structure questions**

Example: Close Reading for Vocabulary in Context

Passage:
Despite early skepticism, the scientist's theory eventually **gained traction**, leading to widespread acceptance in the scientific community.
Question:
What does the phrase **"gained traction"** most nearly mean in the passage?
A) Lost popularity
B) Became widely accepted
C) Was officially rejected
D) Required additional research
Correct Answer: B) Became widely accepted
(Close reading shows that "leading to widespread acceptance" directly supports this answer.)

✓ **Why Close Reading Works:**
✓ The phrase **"leading to widespread acceptance"** provides **a clear context clue** for "gained traction."
✓ **Reading the full sentence** ensures that words are interpreted correctly in context.

Example: Close Reading for Inference Questions

Passage:
While online learning has become more common, some educators argue that in-person instruction remains essential for developing social skills. However, recent studies show that well-designed virtual programs can foster collaboration and communication among students.
Question:
What can be inferred from the passage?
A) Online learning cannot replace in-person instruction.
B) Some virtual programs help students build social skills.
C) Educators unanimously support online education.
D) Most students prefer online learning over in-person classes.
Correct Answer: B) Some virtual programs help students build social skills.
(The phrase "recent studies show that well-designed virtual programs can foster collaboration and communication" supports this inference.)

✓ **Why Close Reading Works:**
✓ The **contrast between opinions** ("some educators argue" vs. "recent studies show") helps clarify the inference.
✓ **Paying attention to "can" vs. "always"** ensures accuracy—choice B correctly uses **"some" instead of "all."**

4. Applying Skimming and Close Reading in SAT Questions

Question Type	Use Skimming or Close Reading?	Why?
Main Idea	Skimming	Focuses on the first and last sentences.
Vocabulary in Context	Close Reading	Requires understanding how a word is used in context.
Logical Transitions	Skimming	Recognizing relationships between ideas is key.
Grammar & Sentence Structure	Close Reading	Small details affect correctness.
Inference	Close Reading	Requires deeper analysis beyond direct statements.

5. Final Key Takeaways

✓ **Use skimming for general meaning, structure, and logical transitions.**
✓ **Use close reading for precise details, vocabulary, and inference questions.**
✓ **Practice switching between both techniques to optimize time and accuracy.**
✓ **Recognize when a question requires deeper analysis vs. quick comprehension.**

By **balancing skimming and close reading effectively**, students can **maximize accuracy while maintaining speed**, leading to **higher performance on the Digital SAT Reading & Writing section.**

9.4 Process of Elimination and Guessing Strategy

The **Digital SAT Reading & Writing section** requires students to answer **54 questions in 64 minutes**, leaving little room for hesitation. **Using the process of elimination (POE) and strategic guessing** is crucial for maximizing accuracy, especially on difficult questions. Since the SAT has **no penalty for incorrect answers**, every question should have an answer, even if it's a guess.

This section will cover:

✓ **Understanding the Process of Elimination (POE)**
✓ **Common Wrong Answer Types and How to Spot Them**
✓ **Strategic Guessing Techniques**
✓ **When to Guess vs. When to Skip and Return**

1. Understanding the Process of Elimination (POE)

The **Process of Elimination (POE)** helps students **narrow down answer choices** by **eliminating incorrect ones first**, rather than looking for the correct answer immediately.

Step-by-Step Approach for POE

✓ **Step 1: Read the Question First**

- Identify **what the question is asking** before reading the passage.
  ✓ **Step 2: Identify Extreme or Illogical Answers**
- Cross out choices that **contradict the passage** or sound exaggerated.
  ✓ **Step 3: Test Remaining Choices**
- Compare the remaining answers **with the passage for accuracy**.
  ✓ **Step 4: Make an Educated Guess If Unsure**
- If two choices seem close, **pick the most neutral or general answer**.

2. Common Wrong Answer Types and How to Spot Them

A. Too Extreme or Absolute

- Words like **always, never, completely, absolutely** are often incorrect unless the passage strongly supports them.
- **Example:**
  - **Passage:** "Most scientists believe climate change is influenced by human activity."
  - **Wrong Answer:** "All scientists believe climate change is entirely caused by humans."
  - **Right Answer:** "Many scientists believe human activity influences climate change."

B. Out of Scope (Not Mentioned in the Passage)

- Some choices introduce **irrelevant information** not discussed in the passage.
- **Example:**
  - **Passage:** Discusses effects of pollution on marine life.
  - **Wrong Answer:** "Pollution has no impact on marine ecosystems."
  - **Right Answer:** "Pollution negatively affects marine life, according to research."

C. Opposite of the Passage

- Some choices directly **contradict** what the passage states.
- **Example:**
  - **Passage:** "The author argues that urban gardening provides environmental benefits."
  - **Wrong Answer:** "The author believes urban gardening has no benefits."

D. Too Specific or Too Broad

- **Too Specific:** Focuses on **a small detail rather than the main idea**.
- **Too Broad:** Overgeneralizes the passage's content.
- **Example:**
  - **Passage:** "Dogs require training and socialization to behave well in public spaces."
  - **Wrong Answer (Too Specific):** "Dogs need socialization only when they are young."
  - **Wrong Answer (Too Broad):** "All animals need training."
  - **Right Answer:** "Training and socialization help dogs behave in public."

3. Strategic Guessing Techniques

Since the **SAT does not penalize incorrect answers**, students should **never leave a question blank**. When unsure, strategic guessing **increases the probability of selecting the correct answer**.

Best Guessing Strategies

✓ Eliminate at Least Two Choices Before Guessing

- Even without knowing the correct answer, removing two wrong choices improves chances from **25% to 50%**.

✓ Pick the Most Neutral or Moderate Answer

- SAT passages tend to avoid extreme claims.
- If stuck between two answers, **choose the one that sounds more balanced or reasonable**.

✓ Stick to One Letter for Random Guesses

- If time is running out and you must fill in multiple guesses, **choose the same letter (A, B, C, or D) consistently**.
- Random guessing across letters **lowers** your odds of getting at least some correct.

4. When to Guess vs. When to Skip and Return

When to Guess Immediately

✓ **You have eliminated at least two answer choices** and are unsure between the last two.
✓ **The question is taking too long** (over 90 seconds).
✓ **Time is running out** and you don't have time to return later.

When to Skip and Return Later

✓ **You are completely unsure and need more time to think.**
✓ **The question involves a passage reference you haven't read yet.**
✓ **You are behind on time and need to complete easier questions first.**

5. Example Questions Using POE and Guessing Strategies

Example 1: Process of Elimination for Main Idea Questions

Passage:
Advances in medical imaging have significantly improved early disease detection. Technologies such as MRI and CT scans allow doctors to diagnose conditions before symptoms appear, leading to better treatment outcomes.
Question:
Which best states the main idea of the passage?
A) Medical imaging has changed little over the years.
B) MRI and CT scans are expensive medical procedures.
C) Medical imaging technologies improve early disease detection.
D) The risks of medical imaging outweigh the benefits.
✓ **Using POE:**
✗**A is incorrect**—The passage states that imaging has "significantly improved," contradicting "changed little."
✗**B is incorrect**—The passage does not mention costs.
✗**D is incorrect**—The passage supports imaging, not its risks.
✓ **Correct Answer: C)**

Example 2: Process of Elimination for Vocabulary in Context

Sentence in Passage:
Despite early skepticism, the scientist's theory eventually **gained traction**, leading to widespread acceptance in the field.
Question:
What does "gained traction" most nearly mean?
A) Lost popularity
B) Became widely accepted
C) Was officially rejected
D) Required additional research
✓ **Using POE:**
✗**A is incorrect**—The phrase "widespread acceptance" contradicts "lost popularity."
✗**C is incorrect**—The theory was **eventually accepted, not rejected**.
✗**D is incorrect**—There is no mention of "additional research."
✓ **Correct Answer: B)**

6. Summary of Key Strategies

Strategy	How It Helps
Process of Elimination (POE)	Narrows down choices, increasing accuracy
Look for Extreme or Opposite Answers	These are often incorrect

Identify Answer Choices That Are Too Specific or Too Broad	The SAT prefers balanced answers
Pick the Most Neutral or Moderate Answer	Avoid overly strong or emotional choices
Never Leave a Question Blank	No penalty for guessing

Final Key Takeaways

✓ Always use POE—cross out at least two answers before guessing.
✓ Be cautious of extreme, opposite, or out-of-scope choices.
✓ If unsure, pick the answer that is the most neutral or moderate.
✓ Use a consistent letter (A, B, C, D) if time is running out.
✓ Skipping should be strategic—mark and return later if possible.

By mastering the **Process of Elimination and Guessing Strategy**, students can **maximize accuracy, improve test efficiency, and boost their Digital SAT scores.**

PART III

MATH SECTION (THEORY AND PRACTICE)

CHAPTER 10

OVERVIEW OF THE MATH SECTION

10.1 Math Format: Two Adaptive Modules

The **Digital SAT Math section** has undergone significant changes, shifting from a traditional fixed-format test to an **adaptive structure** with **two modules**. Understanding how these modules function is essential for **effective test-taking strategies and time management**.

This section will cover:

✓ **Digital SAT Math Section Overview**
✓ **Structure and Timing of the Two Adaptive Modules**
✓ **How Adaptive Testing Works in the Math Section**
✓ **Scoring and Impact of the Adaptive System**

1. Digital SAT Math Section Overview

Feature	**Digital SAT Math**
Total Time	70 minutes
Number of Modules	2 (Adaptive)
Total Questions	44
Time per Module	35 minutes
Question Types	Multiple-choice & grid-in responses
Calculator Usage	Allowed throughout (Desmos built-in)

Key Differences from the Paper SAT:

✓ The **calculator is allowed for all questions** (previously, there was a no-calculator section).
✓ The test is **adaptive**, meaning **Module 2 adjusts based on Module 1 performance**.
✓ Fewer questions than the **paper SAT (58 questions) but same 200–800 scoring range**.

2. Structure and Timing of the Two Adaptive Modules

Each module contains a mix of **algebra, advanced math, problem-solving, data analysis, and geometry/trigonometry questions**.

Module	**Number of Questions**	**Time Per Module**	**Question Types**
Module 1	22	35 minutes	Mix of easy, medium, and hard questions
Module 2	22	35 minutes	Adjusts difficulty based on Module 1 performance

Key Insight:

- The **first module is the same for all students**, with a mix of **easy, medium, and hard** questions.
- The **second module adapts** based on **Module 1 performance**:
  - **Stronger performance in Module 1 → Harder Module 2**
  - **Weaker performance in Module 1 → Easier Module 2**

3. How Adaptive Testing Works in the Math Section

The **adaptive structure** is designed to measure student ability more efficiently than a traditional fixed test.

How It Works

1. **Module 1: Standard Mix of Questions**
   - All students receive a **mix of difficulty levels** (easy, medium, hard).
   - The **computer analyzes performance** to determine Module 2 difficulty.
2. **Module 2: Adaptive Difficulty**
   - If a student **performs well in Module 1**, they receive a **more challenging Module 2** with harder problems.
   - If a student **performs moderately or struggles in Module 1**, they receive a **medium or easier Module 2**.

Why This Matters:

- Students who **reach the harder Module 2** have a higher potential to score in the **600–800 range**.
- Students in the **easier Module 2 are capped at a lower score range**, making accuracy in **Module 1 crucial**.

4. Scoring and Impact of the Adaptive System

The **Digital SAT Math section is scored from 200–800**, with **both accuracy and difficulty level** affecting the final score.

Module 1 Performance	**Module 2 Level Assigned**	**Score Potential**
Strong (High Accuracy)	Harder Module 2	600–800 range
Moderate (Medium Accuracy)	Medium Module 2	450–650 range
Weak (Low Accuracy)	Easier Module 2	Below 500 range

How to Maximize Your Score in the Adaptive Math Section

✓ Prioritize Accuracy in Module 1:

- **Strong performance in Module 1** increases the chance of unlocking a **higher-scoring Module 2**.
- Avoid careless mistakes in early, easy-to-medium questions.

✓ Expect More Complex Questions in Harder Module 2:

- Questions will require **more steps, deeper reasoning, and algebraic manipulation**.
- Stay calm—this means you are **in the highest scoring range**!

✓ Use the Calculator Wisely:

- The **Desmos calculator** is available throughout the test—practice using it efficiently.
- Some problems **may be easier to solve manually**, so don't rely solely on the calculator.

5. Summary of Key Strategies

Strategy	**Why It Works**
Maximize accuracy in Module 1	Ensures access to a higher-scoring Module 2
Use time wisely (35 minutes per module)	Avoid rushing, but don't get stuck on one question
Expect increased difficulty in Module 2	More challenging questions mean you're in the high-scoring tier
Utilize the built-in calculator strategically	Speeds up calculations but isn't always necessary
Double-check key answers in Module 1	Reducing mistakes early can significantly impact score range

Final Key Takeaways

✓ The **Digital SAT Math section consists of two adaptive modules**, each with **22 questions in 35 minutes**.
✓ **Module 1 is the same for all students**, while **Module 2 adjusts based on Module 1 performance**.
✓ **Higher performance in Module 1 unlocks harder Module 2 questions**, allowing access to **higher scores (600–800 range)**.
✓ **Time management, calculator efficiency, and early accuracy are key to maximizing your SAT Math score**.

By mastering **the adaptive format and strategic question approach**, students can **navigate the Digital SAT Math section efficiently and boost their performance.**

10.2 Built-In Desmos Calculator and Calculator Policies

The **Digital SAT Math section** allows **calculator use throughout the entire test**, a significant change from the old SAT format. This section will cover:

✓ **The Built-In Desmos Calculator: Features and Functions**
✓ **Calculator Policies and Approved Physical Calculators**
✓ **When to Use vs. When to Avoid the Calculator**
✓ **Strategies for Efficient Calculator Use on the SAT**

1. The Built-In Desmos Calculator: Features and Functions

The Digital SAT provides a **built-in Desmos graphing calculator**, accessible within the Bluebook™ testing app. This means:

✓ **Every student has access to a graphing calculator, even if they don't bring a physical one.**
✓ **Students should practice using Desmos before test day** to maximize efficiency.
✓ **The calculator remains available for all 44 math questions** (no separate no-calculator section).

Key Features of the Desmos Graphing Calculator

Feature	**How It Helps on the SAT**
Graphing Equations	Allows students to visualize functions, intersections, and slopes.
Solving Equations	Can check algebraic solutions by graphing and identifying x-values.
Table Generation	Converts equations into data tables for quick pattern recognition.
Basic & Advanced Operations	Performs exponents, roots, and fractions efficiently.
Zoom & Trace Functions	Helps analyze function behavior and intersections.

How to Access It on Test Day:

- The **Desmos calculator is embedded into the Digital SAT interface** and can be opened at any time during the Math section.
- Familiarizing yourself with its functions **before test day** is essential for maximizing efficiency.

Example Question Using Desmos on the Digital SAT

Question:

The equation of a line is given as $y = 3x - 7$. What is the x-value when $y = 5$?

✓ **Solving with Desmos:**

1. Enter $y = 3x - 7$ into the Desmos calculator.
2. Adjust settings or use the "trace" function to find when $y = 5$.
3. Identify the corresponding **x-value**.

✓ **Answer:** $x = 4$.

Why Use Desmos?

- Graphing the function visually confirms the correct solution.
- This method is **faster than solving algebraically under time pressure**.

2. Calculator Policies and Approved Physical Calculators

While students have access to **the built-in Desmos calculator**, they **can still bring an approved physical calculator** if they prefer.

Approved Calculator Types

✓ **Graphing Calculators** (Most Recommended)
✓ **Scientific Calculators**
✓ **Four-Function Calculators** (Least Recommended)

Popular Approved Calculators for the SAT

Brand	Models Allowed
Texas Instruments (TI)	TI-84 Plus, TI-83, TI-Nspire (non-CAS)
Casio	fx-9750GII, fx-991EX, ClassWiz series
HP	HP Prime (non-CAS), HP 39gII

□ **Prohibited Calculators:**

- **CAS (Computer Algebra System) calculators**, such as the **TI-89 and TI-Nspire CAS**.
- **Laptops, tablets, mobile phones, or smartwatches**.
- **Calculators with internet connectivity or QWERTY keyboards**.

Recommendation:

- If comfortable with Desmos, **a physical calculator may not be necessary**.
- However, some students **prefer familiarity with their own calculator** for certain operations.

3. When to Use vs. When to Avoid the Calculator

While **having a calculator for all math questions is beneficial**, knowing **when to use it efficiently** is key.

When to Use the Calculator

✓ **Graphing Linear or Quadratic Equations**
✓ **Solving Complex Fractions or Exponents Quickly**
✓ **Finding Function Intersections**
✓ **Checking Work for Algebraic Equations**

When to Avoid the Calculator

□ **Simple Arithmetic or Basic Algebra** (e.g., $6 + 7$ or $2x + 3 = 11$)
□ **Recognizing Algebraic Patterns** (e.g., Factoring $x^2 - 9$ into $(x - 3)(x + 3)$)
□ **Overusing the Graphing Feature** (Some problems are faster with algebraic solving)

Key Insight:
Using a calculator **for every question slows down pacing**—know when mental math or traditional algebra is faster.

4. Strategies for Efficient Calculator Use on the SAT

A. Familiarize Yourself with Desmos Features Before Test Day

✓ Practice **graphing functions, solving equations, and using tables** on Desmos.
✓ Understand **how to trace a graph to find intersections**—this is useful for solving equations visually.

B. Use the Calculator to Double-Check Your Work
✓ After solving algebraically, **verify by graphing the equation and checking key points**.
C. Don't Depend on the Calculator for Every Question
✓ Some problems are **faster to solve manually**—use estimation and mental math when possible.
D. Know When to Use a Physical Calculator vs. Desmos
✓ If bringing a physical calculator, **use it for quick arithmetic** and leave **graphing-heavy tasks to Desmos**.

5. Example Questions to Practice Calculator Use

Example 1: Best Use of the Graphing Calculator

Solve for x:

$$2x^2 - 3x - 5 = 0$$

✓ **Using Desmos:**

1. Enter $y = 2x^2 - 3x - 5$.
2. Identify **where the function crosses the x-axis**.
3. The **x-values of the intercepts are the solutions**.

✓ **Answer:** $x = -1$ or $x = 2.5$.

Example 2: When a Calculator is Not Needed

Simplify: $(3x + 2)(x - 4)$.

□ **Avoid using the calculator—factor manually.**
✓ **Answer:** $3x^2 - 10x - 8$.

Key Takeaway:

- **Using a calculator for simple algebra slows you down.**
- **Only use it when necessary.**

6. Summary of Key Strategies

Strategy	Why It Works
Practice with Desmos before test day	Familiarity speeds up problem-solving
Use Desmos for graphing-heavy questions	Quickly solves equations and intersections
Use a physical calculator for quick arithmetic	Saves time on basic calculations
Avoid overusing the calculator	Some questions are faster to solve manually

Final Key Takeaways

✓ **The Desmos graphing calculator is built into the Digital SAT**—students should **practice using it before test day**.
✓ **Physical calculators are allowed**, but must be from the **approved list**.
✓ **Knowing when to use the calculator vs. solving manually is crucial for time management.**
✓ **Using Desmos for complex equations and function graphing can speed up problem-solving.**

By mastering **calculator use and efficiency**, students can **improve accuracy, solve problems faster, and maximize their SAT Math score**.

10.3 Multiple-Choice vs. Student-Produced Responses (Grid-In)

The **Digital SAT Math section** consists of two types of questions:
✓ **Multiple-Choice Questions (MCQs)** – 75% of the test
✓ **Student-Produced Responses (Grid-In Questions)** – 25% of the test

Understanding the **differences between these question types, how to approach them, and strategies for avoiding common mistakes** is crucial for **maximizing accuracy and efficiency**.

1. Overview of Multiple-Choice vs. Grid-In Questions

Feature	Multiple-Choice Questions (MCQs)	Student-Produced Responses (Grid-In)
Number of Questions	~33 (75% of Math section)	~11 (25% of Math section)
Answer Format	Choose from **4 options (A-D)**	Enter a **numerical answer** manually
Guessing Strategy	Use **Process of Elimination (POE)**	No answer choices—must solve correctly
Answer Type	Whole numbers, fractions, decimals	Whole numbers, fractions, decimals
Difficulty Level	Varies (easy, medium, hard)	Typically **medium to hard**
Calculator Allowed?	Yes (Desmos built-in)	Yes (Desmos built-in)

Key Difference: Grid-in questions require students to solve problems without answer choices, eliminating the option to guess from provided answers.

2. Understanding Multiple-Choice Questions (MCQs)

A. How to Approach Multiple-Choice Questions

✓ **Step 1: Read the Question Carefully**
✓ **Step 2: Solve Before Looking at Answer Choices** (to avoid trap answers)
✓ **Step 3: Use Process of Elimination (POE)**
✓ **Step 4: Plug Answer Choices Back In (If Applicable)**

Example MCQ: Algebraic Equation

Question:
Solve for x in the equation:

$$3x - 5 = 16$$

A) $x = 3$
B) $x = 5$
C) $x = 7$
D) $x = 8$

✓ **Solution:**

1. Add 5 to both sides:

$$3x = 21$$

2. Divide by 3:

$$x = 7$$

✓ **Correct Answer: C)** $x = 7$

Strategy Tip:
✓ If **time is limited**, plug the answer choices back into the equation to check which one works.

3. Understanding Student-Produced Responses (Grid-In Questions)

Grid-In Questions require students to **calculate answers and enter them manually**. Unlike multiple-choice questions, **there are no answer choices to guide you**.

How to Approach Grid-In Questions

✓ **Step 1: Solve the Problem Normally**
✓ **Step 2: Double-Check Calculations**
✓ **Step 3: Write Answer in the Grid Correctly**

Example Grid-In: Solving for a Fraction

Question:
A pizza is divided into 12 equal slices. If Sam eats 5 slices, what fraction of the pizza is left?

✓ **Solution:**

1. Sam eats **5 out of 12 slices**, so **remaining slices** $= 12 - 5 = 7$.
2. The fraction remaining is $\frac{7}{12}$.

✓ **Final Answer:** $\frac{7}{12}$

Key Strategy:
✓ **Enter answers as reduced fractions or decimals** (e.g., $\frac{7}{12}$ **or 0.583** but not $\frac{14}{24}$).

4. Rules for Entering Grid-In Answers

Grid-In Answer Entry Rules:

✓ **No negative numbers** – The grid does not allow negative answers.

✓ **No mixed fractions** – Convert mixed numbers into improper fractions or decimals (e.g., write $5\frac{1}{2}$ as 5.5 **or** $\frac{11}{2}$).
✓ **Decimals must fit within the grid** – If a decimal is too long, round it to the nearest value that fits.
✓ **If more than one correct answer exists, any valid equivalent is accepted**.

Example: Common Grid-In Entry Errors

Correct Answer	Correct Grid Entry	Incorrect Entry
$\frac{2}{5}$	$\frac{2}{5}$ or 0.4	$\frac{4}{10}$ (not in simplest form)
3.75	3.75	3 3/4 (mixed number, not accepted)
$\frac{7}{2}$	$\frac{7}{2}$ or 3.5	3 1/2 (mixed number, not accepted)

Strategy Tip:
✓ **If unsure, enter the decimal form to avoid fraction simplification mistakes**.

5. Strategies for Multiple-Choice vs. Grid-In Questions

Strategy	Why It Works
Use Process of Elimination (POE) for MCQs	Increases chances of selecting the correct answer
Plug answer choices back into equations (MCQs)	Helps verify correct solutions
Double-check calculations for Grid-Ins	No answer choices to rely on, so accuracy is critical

Enter answers in the simplest form (Grid-Ins)	Ensures the answer is recognized as correct
Use Desmos for complex calculations	Speeds up difficult algebra and graphing problems

6. Example: When to Use a Calculator for Grid-In Questions

Question:
Solve for x in the equation:

$$2x^2 - 8x + 6 = 0$$

✓ **Using the Quadratic Formula:**

$$x = \frac{-(-8) \pm \sqrt{(-8)^2 - 4(2)(6)}}{2(2)}$$

✓ **Using the Desmos Calculator:**

1. Enter $y = 2x^2 - 8x + 6$.
2. Find **x-intercepts (where** $y = 0$**).**
3. The calculator shows $x = 1$ **and** $x = 3$.

✓ **Final Answer: 1 or 3** (either answer is correct).

Why Use Desmos?
✓ **Faster than manually solving with the quadratic formula**.

7. Summary of Key Differences and Strategies

Feature	Multiple-Choice (MCQs)	Student-Produced Responses (Grid-In)
Answer Choices	4 options (A-D)	No answer choices
Guessing Strategy	Use POE & plug-in	No guessing option—must solve
Common Mistakes	Picking trap answers	Entering answers incorrectly
Calculator Use	Helpful for complex problems	Essential for large calculations

8. Final Key Takeaways

✓ **Multiple-choice questions offer answer choices—use elimination strategies to increase accuracy.**
✓ **Grid-in questions require students to produce their own answers—there's no guessing option.**
✓ **Use the built-in Desmos calculator for complex math problems, especially graphing and solving quadratics.**
✓ **Grid-in answers must be correctly formatted (simplified fractions or decimals).**
✓ **For grid-in questions, always double-check work—small mistakes can cost points.**

By **understanding the differences between multiple-choice and grid-in questions** and using **strategic approaches for each**, students can improve **accuracy, speed, and overall performance on the SAT Math section**.

CHAPTER 11

ALGEBRA AND LINEAR EQUATIONS

11.1 Solving Linear Equations and Inequalities

The **Digital SAT Math section** frequently tests students on **linear equations and inequalities**, which form the foundation of algebra. These problems assess a student's ability to **manipulate equations, solve for variables, and interpret inequalities in real-world contexts**.

This section will cover:

✓ **Solving One-Variable Linear Equations**
✓ **Solving Linear Inequalities**
✓ **Word Problems Involving Linear Equations and Inequalities**
✓ **Graphing Linear Equations and Inequalities**

1. Solving One-Variable Linear Equations

A **linear equation** is an equation that forms a straight line when graphed. It has the general form:

$$ax + b = c$$

where:

- x is the variable
- a, b, and c are constants

Steps to Solve Linear Equations

1. **Isolate the variable** by undoing addition/subtraction.
2. **Eliminate coefficients** by multiplying or dividing.
3. **Verify your answer** by substituting it back into the equation.

Example 1: Basic Linear Equation

Solve for x:

$$3x - 5 = 10$$

✓ **Solution:**

1. Add 5 to both sides:

$$3x = 15$$

2. Divide by 3:

$$x = 5$$

✓ **Final Answer:** $x = 5$

SAT Strategy:
✓ **Check your answer** by substituting $x = 5$ back into the original equation.

Example 2: Solving an Equation with Fractions

Solve for x:

$$\frac{2x}{3} + 4 = 10$$

✓ **Solution:**

1. Subtract 4 from both sides:

$$\frac{2x}{3} = 6$$

2. Multiply both sides by 3 to eliminate the fraction:

$$2x = 18$$

3. Divide by 2:

$$x = 9$$

✓ **Final Answer:** $x = 9$

SAT Strategy:
✓ Multiply through by the **denominator first** to eliminate fractions early.

2. Solving Linear Inequalities

A **linear inequality** expresses a relationship where two expressions are not necessarily equal.

Types of Inequalities

$$ax + b > c$$

$$ax + b < c$$

$$ax + b \geq c$$

$$ax + b \leq c$$

Key Rules:
✓ **Solving inequalities follows the same steps as solving equations.**
✓ **If you multiply or divide by a negative number, reverse the inequality sign.**

Example 3: Solving a Linear Inequality

Solve for x:

$$5x - 7 > 8$$

✓ **Solution:**

1. Add 7 to both sides:

$$5x > 15$$

2. Divide by 5:

$$x > 3$$

✓ **Final Answer:** $x > 3$

SAT Strategy:
✓ Graphing the inequality on a number line can help visualize the solution set.

Example 4: Reversing the Inequality Sign

Solve for x:

$$-2x + 4 \leq 10$$

✓ **Solution:**

1. Subtract 4 from both sides:

$$-2x \leq 6$$

2. **Divide by -2** (and reverse the inequality sign):

$$x \geq -3$$

✓ **Final Answer:** $x \geq -3$

Key Rule:
✓ **Multiplying or dividing by a negative number flips the inequality sign.**

3. Word Problems Involving Linear Equations and Inequalities

Many SAT questions present **real-world problems** that must be translated into equations or inequalities before solving.

Example 5: Word Problem - Linear Equation

Problem:
Sarah earns 12$perhouratherjob. If sheworks$ h $hoursandearnsatotalof$300, how many hours did she work?

✓ **Equation:**

$$12h = 300$$

✓ **Solving:**

$$h = \frac{300}{12} = 25$$

✓ **Final Answer:** 25 hours

SAT Strategy:
✓ Identify **what the variable represents** before writing the equation.

Example 6: Word Problem - Linear Inequality

Problem:
A school is renting buses for a field trip. Each bus can hold **40 students**, and the school has **at most 320 students** attending. What is the maximum number of buses needed?

✓ **Inequality:**

$$40b \geq 320$$

✓ **Solving:**

$$b \geq \frac{320}{40} = 8$$

✓ **Final Answer:** $b \geq 8$ → The school needs at least **8 buses**.

SAT Strategy:
✓ Pay attention to phrases like **"at most"** (≤) and **"at least"** (≥) to determine the correct inequality sign.

4. Graphing Linear Equations and Inequalities

The **Digital SAT allows calculator use** for graphing linear equations and inequalities. Understanding how to graph can **confirm solutions visually**.

Graphing a Linear Equation

The equation of a line follows:

$$y = mx + b$$

- m = slope (rise/run)
- b = y-intercept (where the line crosses the y-axis)

✓ **Example:** Graphing $y = 2x + 3$

- Start at $y = 3$ (y-intercept).
- Use the slope $2/1$ (rise 2, run 1).
- Plot points and draw the line.

Graphing a Linear Inequality

- **Use a solid line for ≤ or ≥.**
- **Use a dashed line for < or >.**
- **Shade the correct side** of the graph based on the inequality sign.

✓ **Example:** Graph $y \geq 2x - 5$

- Graph $y = 2x - 5$ as a solid line.
- Shade **above** the line (since $y \geq$).

SAT Strategy:
✓ **Use the Desmos calculator** to graph equations and inequalities quickly.

5. Summary of Key Strategies

Concept	Strategy
Solving Linear Equations	Isolate x, balance both sides
Solving Inequalities	Flip the sign when multiplying/dividing by a negative
Word Problems	Define variables, set up an equation or inequality
Graphing	Identify slope and y-intercept, use Desmos for visualization

6. Final Key Takeaways

✓ **Linear equations and inequalities form the foundation of algebra on the SAT.**
✓ **Always isolate the variable when solving equations.**
✓ **Flip the inequality sign when multiplying or dividing by a negative number.**
✓ **Translate word problems into equations before solving.**
✓ **Use the Desmos calculator for graphing and checking solutions.**

By **practicing these algebra skills**, students can **increase accuracy, improve speed, and maximize their SAT Math score.**

11.2 Systems of Equations and Inequalities

The **Digital SAT Math section** frequently tests **systems of equations and inequalities**, assessing a student's ability to **solve for multiple variables, interpret solutions graphically, and apply these concepts to real-world problems**. These questions require a strong understanding of algebraic manipulation, substitution, elimination, and graphing strategies.

This section will cover:
✓ **Solving Systems of Linear Equations (Substitution & Elimination Methods)**
✓ **Graphing Systems of Equations and Finding Solutions**
✓ **Solving Systems of Inequalities**
✓ **Real-World Applications of Systems of Equations and Inequalities**

1. Solving Systems of Linear Equations

A **system of equations** consists of two or more equations with **two or more variables**. The goal is to **find the values of the variables that satisfy all equations simultaneously**.

Solution Types in a System of Equations

Type of System	Graphical Representation	Number of Solutions
Consistent & Independent	Two lines intersect at one point	One unique solution
Consistent & Dependent	Two overlapping lines (same equation)	Infinite solutions
Inconsistent	Two parallel lines (never intersect)	No solution

A. Solving by Substitution Method

The **substitution method** is useful when one equation is **already solved for a variable**.

✓ **Steps for Substitution:**

1. Solve **one equation for one variable**.
2. Substitute into the other equation.
3. Solve for the remaining variable.
4. Plug back to find the second variable.

◆ Example 1: Solving by Substitution

Solve for x and y:

$$y = 3x + 2$$

$$2x + y = 8$$

✓ **Step 1: Substitute $y = 3x + 2$ into the second equation:**

$$2x + (3x + 2) = 8$$

✓ **Step 2: Solve for x:**

$$5x + 2 = 8$$

$$5x = 6$$

$$x = \frac{6}{5}$$

✓ **Step 3: Plug $x = \frac{6}{5}$ into $y = 3x + 2$:**

$$y = 3\left(\frac{6}{5}\right) + 2$$

$$y = \frac{18}{5} + 2 = \frac{28}{5}$$

✓ **Final Answer: $x = \frac{6}{5}, y = \frac{28}{5}$**

□ **SAT Strategy:**
✓ Use substitution when **one equation is already solved for a variable**.

B. Solving by Elimination Method

The **elimination method** is effective when both equations are in standard form (**Ax + By = C**).

✓ **Steps for Elimination:**

1. Multiply equations to align coefficients.

2. Add or subtract equations to eliminate a variable.
3. Solve for the remaining variable.
4. Plug back to find the second variable.

Example 2: Solving by Elimination

Solve for x and y:

$$4x + 3y = 20$$

$$2x - 3y = 4$$

✓ **Step 1: Add the two equations (since $+3y$ and $-3y$ cancel out):**

$$(4x + 3y) + (2x - 3y) = 20 + 4$$

$$6x = 24$$

$$x = 4$$

✓ **Step 2: Plug $x = 4$ into the first equation:**

$$4(4) + 3y = 20$$

$$16 + 3y = 20$$

$$3y = 4$$

$$y = \frac{4}{3}$$

✓ **Final Answer:** $x = 4, y = \frac{4}{3}$

SAT Strategy:
✓ Use elimination when **both equations are in standard form** and can be easily aligned for cancellation.

2. Graphing Systems of Equations and Finding Solutions

How Graphing Helps Solve Systems of Equations

✓ The solution to a system is **the point where the two lines intersect**.
✓ If **no intersection**, the system has **no solution** (parallel lines).
✓ If the lines **overlap**, the system has **infinite solutions**.

Example 3: Graphing a System of Equations

Solve for x and y:

$$y = 2x + 3$$

$$y = -x + 1$$

✓ **Graph both equations and find their intersection.**
✓ The two lines intersect at $(-2, -1)$.

✓ **Final Answer:** $x = -2, y = -1$

SAT Strategy:
✓ Use the **Desmos calculator** to quickly graph both equations and locate the intersection.

3. Solving Systems of Inequalities

A **system of inequalities** represents regions of the coordinate plane instead of specific points.

✓ **Steps to Solve:**

1. **Graph each inequality** (solid line for ≤/≥, dashed line for < or >).
2. **Shade the correct region** (above or below the line).
3. **Find where shaded regions overlap**—this is the solution set.

Example 4: Solving a System of Inequalities

Graph the solution for the system:

$$y \leq 2x + 4$$

$$y > -x + 1$$

✓ **Graph the boundary lines:**

- $y \leq 2x + 4$ (solid line, shade **below**)
- $y > -x + 1$ (dashed line, shade **above**)

✓ **Final Answer:** The solution set is where the shaded regions overlap.

SAT Strategy:
✓ Use the **Desmos calculator** to shade inequality regions and find overlaps.

4. Real-World Applications of Systems of Equations and Inequalities

Many SAT word problems involve **real-world applications** of systems.

Example 5: Word Problem - Ticket Sales

A concert venue sells **adult tickets for** $12 ** and ** studentticketsfor$**8**. If **150 tickets were sold for a total of $1,500**, how many student tickets were sold?

✓ **Step 1: Define variables**

- Let a = number of adult tickets
- Let s = number of student tickets

✓ **Step 2: Set up equations**

$$a + s = 150$$

$$12a + 8s = 1500$$

✓ **Step 3: Solve by Substitution or Elimination**

$$a = 150 - s$$

$$12(150 - s) + 8s = 1500$$

$$1800 - 12s + 8s = 1500$$

$$-4s = -300$$

$$s = 75$$

✓ **Final Answer:** 75 student tickets were sold.

SAT Strategy:
✓ Assign variables **clearly** and **use elimination for word problems**.

5. Summary of Key Strategies

Concept	Strategy
Solving Systems of Equations	Use **substitution** when one equation is solved for a variable; use **elimination** for standard form equations.

Graphing Systems	The solution is where two lines **intersect**.
Solving Inequalities	Shade regions and find **overlaps**.
Word Problems	Assign variables clearly and **translate into equations**.

6. Final Key Takeaways

✓ **Substitution is best when one equation is solved for a variable.**
✓ **Elimination is best when equations are in standard form.**
✓ **Graphing is useful for visualizing solutions.**
✓ **For inequalities, shade regions and find overlapping areas.**

By **mastering systems of equations and inequalities**, students can **improve their SAT Math accuracy, solve problems efficiently, and tackle real-world applications with confidence.**

11.3 Functions, Graphs, and Their Real-World Applications

The **Digital SAT Math section** frequently tests **functions and their graphs**, assessing students' ability to interpret, manipulate, and apply function concepts in real-world scenarios. Mastering these skills ensures students can solve **algebraic function equations, analyze graphs, and model real-life situations mathematically**.

This section will cover:
✓ **Understanding Functions and Function Notation**
✓ **Graphing Functions and Identifying Key Features**
✓ **Function Transformations**
✓ **Real-World Applications of Functions**

1. Understanding Functions and Function Notation

A **function** is a relation between inputs (x) and outputs (y) where each input has **only one output**.

Function Notation

Instead of using y, functions are often written as:

$$f(x) = mx + b$$

where:

- $f(x)$ is the function output (same as y)
- x is the input (independent variable)
- m is the slope (rate of change)
- b is the y-intercept (starting value)

Example 1: Evaluating a Function

If $f(x) = 3x - 4$, what is $f(5)$?

✓ **Solution:**

1. Substitute $x = 5$ into the function:

$$f(5) = 3(5) - 4$$

2. Simplify:

$$15 - 4 = 11$$

✓ **Final Answer:** $f(5) = 11$

SAT Strategy:
✓ **Plug in given values carefully**, ensuring the correct order of operations.

2. Graphing Functions and Identifying Key Features

A. Key Features of a Function Graph

Feature	Definition	Example
Intercepts	Points where the graph crosses the axes	y-intercept at $(0,3)$, x-intercept at $(-2,0)$
Slope	Rate of change $(\frac{\text{rise}}{\text{run}})$	$m = 2$ (line rises 2 units for every 1 unit right)
Domain	Set of all possible x-values	$-3 \leq x \leq 5$
Range	Set of all possible y-values	$-4 \leq y \leq 8$

Example 2: Identifying the y-Intercept

If a function is given by $f(x) = -2x + 7$, what is the y-intercept?

✓ **Solution:**

- The y-intercept occurs at $x = 0$, so plug in $x = 0$:

$$f(0) = -2(0) + 7 = 7$$

✓ **Final Answer: y-intercept is** $(0,7)$

SAT Strategy:
✓ **Identify the y-intercept directly from the equation** in slope-intercept form $y = mx + b$.

B. Graphing a Linear Function

For the equation $y = 3x - 5$:

1. **Plot the y-intercept** at $(0, -5)$.
2. **Use the slope** $m = 3 \rightarrow$ Rise **3** units, Run **1** unit right.
3. **Draw the line through the points.**

SAT Strategy:
✓ **If given an equation, plot key points (intercepts, slope) before graphing.**

3. Function Transformations

A. Types of Function Transformations

Transformation	Equation Change	Effect on Graph
Vertical Shift	$f(x) + k$	Moves up if $k > 0$, down if $k < 0$
Horizontal Shift	$f(x - h)$	Moves right if $h > 0$, left if $h < 0$
Reflection	$-f(x)$	Flips across x-axis
Stretch or Compression	$af(x)$	Stretches if $

Example 3: Identifying a Transformation

How does the function $g(x) = f(x) - 3$ transform the graph of $f(x)$?

✓ **Solution:**

- The "-3" subtracts from the function, indicating a **downward shift by 3 units**.

✓ **Final Answer: Shift downward by 3 units.**

SAT Strategy:
✓ **Compare transformations to the base function $f(x)$ to determine movement.**

4. Real-World Applications of Functions

Functions are used in **real-world contexts** on the SAT, requiring students to interpret function models.

Example 4: Linear Function in a Real-World Scenario

A taxi company charges a base fare of $4plus2$ per mile. Write a function $C(x)$ representing the total cost of a ride for x miles.

✓ **Solution:**

1. The **base fare is 4**, so this is the **y-intercept** ($b = 4$).
2. The **cost increases by **$2 per mile**, so the **slope is 2(** m = 2).
3. Function equation:

$$C(x) = 2x + 4$$

✓ **Final Answer:** $C(x) = 2x + 4$

SAT Strategy:
✓ **Identify the constant (starting value) and rate of change when creating function models.**

Example 5: Finding the Input from the Output

Using the function $C(x) = 2x + 4$, how many miles were traveled if the total fare was $18?

✓ **Solution:**

1. Set $C(x) = 18$:

$$18 = 2x + 4$$

2. Solve for x:

$$14 = 2x$$

$$x = 7$$

✓ **Final Answer: 7 miles**

SAT Strategy:
✓ **Set up the function equation and solve for x when given an output value.**

5. Summary of Key Strategies

Concept	**Strategy**
Function Notation	Substitute values carefully to evaluate functions.
Graphing Functions	Identify slope, intercepts, and transformations.
Transformations	Recognize shifts, reflections, and stretches.
Word Problems	Define variables clearly and set up function models.

6. Final Key Takeaways

✓ **Understand function notation and how to evaluate functions.**
✓ **Identify and interpret key graph features (intercepts, slope, transformations).**
✓ **Use function transformations to recognize shifts, reflections, and scaling.**

✓ **Apply functions to real-world scenarios by creating and solving equations.**
✓ **Practice with the Desmos calculator for graphing and function visualization.**

By **mastering functions, graphs, and real-world applications**, students can **increase accuracy, improve problem-solving speed, and maximize their SAT Math score.**

CHAPTER 12

ADVANCED MATH

12.1 Quadratic and Polynomial Expressions

The **Digital SAT Math section** includes questions on **quadratic and polynomial expressions**, requiring students to manipulate, factor, solve, and analyze equations. These problems test a student's ability to **work with second-degree and higher-degree polynomials using algebraic techniques and graphing strategies**.

This section will cover:
✓ **Understanding Quadratic and Polynomial Expressions**
✓ **Factoring Quadratic Expressions**
✓ **Solving Quadratic Equations**
✓ **Working with Higher-Degree Polynomials**
✓ **Graphing Quadratics and Polynomials**

1. Understanding Quadratic and Polynomial Expressions

A **quadratic equation** is a second-degree polynomial, written as:

$$ax^2 + bx + c = 0$$

where:

- a, b, and c are constants
- x is the variable
- $a \neq 0$

Example Quadratic Equations:

✓ $x^2 - 5x + 6 = 0$
✓ $2x^2 + 7x - 3 = 0$

A **polynomial expression** is a sum of terms consisting of variables raised to whole-number exponents, written as:

$$a_n x^n + a_{n-1} x^{n-1} + \cdots + a_1 x + a_0$$

where:

- n is the highest exponent (degree)
- $a_n \neq 0$

Example Polynomial Expressions:

✓ **Cubic Polynomial:** $x^3 - 4x^2 + 3x - 5$
✓ **Quartic Polynomial:** $2x^4 + x^3 - 6x^2 + 8$

SAT Strategy:
✓ **Recognizing the degree of a polynomial helps determine its graph shape and number of solutions.**

2. Factoring Quadratic Expressions

Factoring is a key algebraic skill used to **simplify equations and solve for variables**.

A. Factoring Quadratics in Standard Form

$$ax^2 + bx + c$$

✓ **Step 1:** Find two numbers that **multiply to** c and **add to** b.
✓ **Step 2:** Rewrite as two binomials.

Example 1: Factoring a Simple Quadratic

Factor: $x^2 - 5x + 6$

✓ Find two numbers that multiply to **6** and add to **-5** → **(-3 and -2)**.

✓ **Factored Form:**

$$(x - 3)(x - 2)$$

SAT Strategy:
✓ **Check your answer by expanding the binomials** to verify it matches the original equation.

B. Factoring When $a \neq 1$

Example 2: Factoring a Quadratic with a Leading Coefficient

Factor: $2x^2 + 7x + 3$

✓ Multiply $2 \times 3 = 6$, then find two numbers that **multiply to 6 and add to 7** → **(6 and 1)**.

✓ Rewrite the middle term:

$$2x^2 + 6x + x + 3$$

✓ Factor by grouping:

$$2x(x + 3) + 1(x + 3)$$

✓ **Factored Form:**

$$(2x + 1)(x + 3)$$

SAT Strategy:
✓ **Use the "factor by grouping" method when the leading coefficient isn't 1.**

3. Solving Quadratic Equations

A. Solving by Factoring

Example 3: Solving a Quadratic by Factoring

Solve: $x^2 - 7x + 12 = 0$

✓ Factor:

$$(x - 3)(x - 4) = 0$$

✓ Solve for x:

$$x - 3 = 0 \quad \Rightarrow \quad x = 3$$

$$x - 4 = 0 \quad \Rightarrow \quad x = 4$$

✓ **Final Answer:** $x = 3, x = 4$

SAT Strategy:
✓ **If a quadratic is factorable, factoring is the fastest solving method.**

B. Solving Using the Quadratic Formula

If a quadratic **cannot be factored easily**, use the **quadratic formula**:

$$x = \frac{-b \pm \sqrt{b^2 - 4ac}}{2a}$$

Example 4: Using the Quadratic Formula

Solve: $2x^2 - 3x - 5 = 0$

✓ Identify $a = 2, b = -3, c = -5$.
✓ Apply the quadratic formula:

$$x = \frac{-(-3) \pm \sqrt{(-3)^2 - 4(2)(-5)}}{2(2)}$$

$$x = \frac{3 \pm \sqrt{9 + 40}}{4}$$

$$x = \frac{3 \pm \sqrt{49}}{4}$$

$$x = \frac{3 \pm 7}{4}$$

✓ **Final Answers:**

$$x = \frac{3 + 7}{4} = \frac{10}{4} = 2.5$$

$$x = \frac{3 - 7}{4} = \frac{-4}{4} = -1$$

SAT Strategy:
✓ Use the **quadratic formula** when factoring is difficult.
✓ **Check the discriminant** $(b^2 - 4ac)$ to determine the number of solutions:

- If **positive**, two solutions.
- If **zero**, one solution.
- If **negative**, no real solutions.

4. Working with Higher-Degree Polynomials

A. Factoring Higher-Degree Polynomials

✓ **Example 5: Factoring a Cubic Polynomial**

Factor: $x^3 - 3x^2 - 4x + 12$

✓ **Step 1:** Group terms:

$$(x^3 - 3x^2) + (-4x + 12)$$

✓ **Step 2:** Factor out common terms:

$$x^2(x - 3) - 4(x - 3)$$

✓ **Step 3:** Factor completely:

$$(x - 3)(x^2 - 4)$$

✓ **Step 4:** Recognize $x^2 - 4$ as a **difference of squares**:

$$(x - 3)(x - 2)(x + 2)$$

✓ **Final Answer:** $(x - 3)(x - 2)(x + 2)$

SAT Strategy:
✓ **Look for common factors and apply difference of squares when possible.**

5. Graphing Quadratics and Polynomials

A. Identifying Key Features of a Quadratic Graph

✓ **Standard Form:** $y = ax^2 + bx + c$

✓ **Vertex:** $x = -\frac{b}{2a}$ (Axis of symmetry)

✓ **Intercepts:** Solve for $y = 0$ (x-intercepts)

Example 6: Finding the Vertex of a Quadratic

Find the vertex of: $y = x^2 - 4x + 3$

✓ Use the vertex formula:

$$x = -\frac{-4}{2(1)} = 2$$

✓ Plug into the equation:

$$y = (2)^2 - 4(2) + 3 = 4 - 8 + 3 = -1$$

✓ **Final Answer: Vertex is** $(2, -1)$

SAT Strategy:
✓ **Use Desmos to quickly find key graphing features.**

6. Final Key Takeaways

✓ **Factor quadratics when possible; use the quadratic formula if necessary.**
✓ **Recognize polynomial patterns (difference of squares, grouping).**
✓ **Use the vertex formula for graphing quadratics.**
✓ **For higher-degree polynomials, look for common factors.**
✓ **Apply functions to real-world scenarios and model relationships algebraically.**

By mastering **quadratic and polynomial expressions**, students can **solve complex algebra problems and maximize their SAT Math score.**

12.2 Functions (Quadratic, Exponential, etc.) and Their Properties

The **Digital SAT Math section** frequently tests students' understanding of different types of functions, their properties, and how they are represented graphically. Functions describe relationships between variables, and mastering them is essential for success in algebra and real-world applications.

This section will cover:

- Understanding different types of functions
- Key properties of quadratic, exponential, and absolute value functions
- Identifying transformations and key points
- Applying functions to problem-solving

1. Understanding Different Types of Functions

A function is a relationship where each input (x) has exactly one output (y). The SAT tests several common function types, each with unique properties and applications.

Function Type	General Equation	Key Features
Linear	$f(x) = mx + b$	Constant rate of change, straight line
Quadratic	$f(x) = ax^2 + bx + c$	Parabolic shape, vertex, symmetry
Exponential	$f(x) = a \cdot b^x$	Rapid growth or decay, horizontal asymptote

Absolute Value	$ f(x) =	x

Understanding these function types helps students recognize their graphs, transformations, and applications in real-world contexts.

2. Quadratic Functions and Their Properties

Standard Form of a Quadratic Function

$$f(x) = ax^2 + bx + c$$

- a determines **concavity** (opens up if $a > 0$, down if $a < 0$).
- b influences the **axis of symmetry** and shifts the graph horizontally.
- c represents the **y-intercept**.

Vertex Form of a Quadratic Function

$$f(x) = a(x - h)^2 + k$$

- (h, k) is the **vertex** of the parabola.
- The function shifts **right or left** based on h, and **up or down** based on k.

Finding the Vertex from Standard Form

$$x = -\frac{b}{2a}$$

Once x is found, substitute it into the equation to find y.

Example 1: Finding the Vertex of a Quadratic Function

Find the vertex of $f(x) = x^2 - 6x + 5$.

1. Use the formula $x = -\frac{b}{2a}$:

$$x = -\frac{-6}{2(1)} = 3$$

2. Substitute $x = 3$ into $f(x)$:

$$f(3) = (3)^2 - 6(3) + 5 = 9 - 18 + 5 = -4$$

3. The vertex is **(3, -4)**.

3. Exponential Functions and Their Properties

General Form of an Exponential Function

$$f(x) = a \cdot b^x$$

- If $b > 1$, the function shows **exponential growth**.
- If $0 < b < 1$, the function shows **exponential decay**.
- The horizontal asymptote is usually at $y = 0$.

Example 2: Identifying Growth or Decay

Identify whether $f(x) = 5(1.2)^x$ represents growth or decay.

- The base $b = 1.2$, which is **greater than 1**, so this function represents **exponential growth**.

4. Absolute Value Functions and Their Properties

General Form of an Absolute Value Function

$$f(x) = a \mid x - h \mid +k$$

- The vertex is at (h, k).
- The graph is **V-shaped**, opening **up if** $a > 0$ and **down if** $a < 0$.

Example 3: Graphing an Absolute Value Function

What is the vertex of $f(x) = 3 \mid x + 2 \mid -5$?

- The function follows $f(x) = a \mid x - h \mid +k$.
- Here, $h = -2$ and $k = -5$.
- The vertex is **(-2, -5)**.

5. Identifying Transformations of Functions

Functions can be transformed through shifts, reflections, and stretches/compressions.

Transformation	Equation Change	Effect on Graph
Vertical Shift	$f(x) + k$	Moves up if $k > 0$, down if $k < 0$
Horizontal Shift	$f(x - h)$	Moves right if $h > 0$, left if $h < 0$
Reflection over x-axis	$-f(x)$	Flips graph upside down
Vertical Stretch	$af(x)$, $	a
Vertical Compression	$af(x)$, $ 0 <	a

Example 4: Identifying a Transformation

How does $g(x) = -2(x - 3)^2 + 4$ compare to $f(x) = x^2$?

- The **-2** reflects the graph over the x-axis and stretches it.
- The **(x - 3)** moves it **3 units right**.
- The **+4** shifts it **4 units up**.

6. Real-World Applications of Functions

Functions are used in real-world scenarios such as **business, science, and finance**.

Example 5: Exponential Growth Application

A bacteria colony doubles in size every hour. If it starts with 100 bacteria, how many will there be in 4 hours?

1. Use the exponential formula:

$$P = P_0 b^t$$

where $P_0 = 100$, $b = 2$, and $t = 4$.

2. Solve:

$$P = 100(2^4) = 100(16) = 1600$$

The bacteria population will be **1,600** after 4 hours.

7. Summary of Key Strategies

Concept	Strategy
Quadratic Functions	Identify **vertex, axis of symmetry, intercepts**

Exponential Functions	Recognize **growth vs. decay** from the base b
Absolute Value Functions	Identify **vertex and transformations**
Transformations	Compare to **parent function to determine shifts**
Real-World Problems	Set up **function equations to model scenarios**

8. Final Key Takeaways

- Quadratic functions create **parabolas**, and their vertex can be found using $x = -\frac{b}{2a}$.
- Exponential functions describe **growth and decay**, depending on the base b.
- Absolute value functions form **V-shaped graphs**, with transformations shifting their position.
- Function transformations involve **shifts, reflections, stretches, and compressions**.
- Real-world problems often require **setting up function equations and interpreting their solutions**.

By mastering **quadratic, exponential, and absolute value functions**, students can **improve their understanding of algebraic relationships, solve complex equations, and excel in the SAT Math section.**

12.3 Rational Expressions and Complex Numbers (Introduction)

The **Digital SAT Math section** includes questions on **rational expressions** and **complex numbers**, which test students' ability to manipulate fractions involving polynomials, simplify expressions, and understand imaginary numbers. These concepts appear in both multiple-choice and grid-in questions, often requiring algebraic manipulation and strategic problem-solving.

This section will cover:

- **Understanding Rational Expressions**
- **Simplifying and Operations with Rational Expressions**
- **Solving Equations Involving Rational Expressions**
- **Introduction to Complex Numbers**

1. Understanding Rational Expressions

A **rational expression** is a fraction where the numerator and denominator are both polynomials.

$$\frac{P(x)}{Q(x)}$$

where:

- $P(x)$ and $Q(x)$ are polynomials
- $Q(x) \neq 0$

Examples of Rational Expressions

- $\frac{x+2}{x-3}$
- $\frac{4x^2-9}{2x+1}$
- $\frac{x^2+5x+6}{x+2}$

These expressions follow the same algebraic rules as regular fractions but require additional steps for factoring and simplification.

2. Simplifying and Operations with Rational Expressions

A. Simplifying Rational Expressions

To simplify a rational expression:

1. **Factor both the numerator and denominator** if possible.
2. **Cancel out common factors** in the numerator and denominator.

Example 1: Simplifying a Rational Expression

Simplify:

$$\frac{x^2 - 9}{x^2 - 3x}$$

1. Factor the numerator and denominator:

$$\frac{(x - 3)(x + 3)}{x(x - 3)}$$

2. Cancel the common factor $(x - 3)$:

$$\frac{x + 3}{x}$$

Final Answer: $\frac{x+3}{x}$

B. Multiplying and Dividing Rational Expressions

Example 2: Multiplying Rational Expressions

Multiply:

$$\frac{x + 2}{x - 4} \times \frac{x - 4}{x + 5}$$

1. Cancel out common terms:

$$\frac{\cancel{x - 4}(x + 2)}{\cancel{x - 4}(x + 5)}$$

2. The final simplified expression is:

$$\frac{x + 2}{x + 5}$$

C. Adding and Subtracting Rational Expressions

To add or subtract rational expressions:

1. Find the **least common denominator (LCD)**.
2. Rewrite fractions with the LCD.
3. Add or subtract numerators while keeping the denominator.

Example 3: Adding Rational Expressions

Solve:

$$\frac{2}{x} + \frac{3}{x + 2}$$

1. The **LCD is** $x(x + 2)$.
2. Rewrite each fraction with the LCD:

$$\frac{2(x+2)}{x(x+2)}+\frac{3x}{x(x+2)}$$

3. Combine numerators:

$$\frac{2x+4+3x}{x(x+2)}$$

4. Final Answer:

$$\frac{5x+4}{x(x+2)}$$

3. Solving Equations Involving Rational Expressions

To solve an equation with rational expressions:

1. **Find the LCD** of all terms.
2. **Multiply every term by the LCD** to eliminate denominators.
3. **Solve the resulting equation**.
4. **Check for restrictions** (values that make any denominator zero).

Example 4: Solving a Rational Equation

Solve:

$$\frac{2}{x}+1=\frac{5}{x}$$

1. The **LCD is** x. Multiply everything by x:

$$2+x=5$$

2. Solve for x:

$$x=3$$

Final Answer: $x=3$

4. Introduction to Complex Numbers

A **complex number** is any number of the form:

$$a+bi$$

where:

- a is the **real part**
- bi is the **imaginary part**
- i is the **imaginary unit**, where $i^2=-1$

Basic Operations with Complex Numbers

A. Adding and Subtracting Complex Numbers

Treat i like a variable and combine like terms.

Example 5: Adding Complex Numbers

Simplify:

$$(3+2i)+(5-4i)$$

1. Add real parts:

$$3+5=8$$

2. Add imaginary parts:

$$2i - 4i = -2i$$

Final Answer: $8 - 2i$

B. Multiplying Complex Numbers

Use the distributive property and remember that $i^2 = -1$.

Example 6: Multiplying Complex Numbers

Multiply:

$$(2 + i)(3 - 2i)$$

1. Distribute:

$$2(3) + 2(-2i) + i(3) + i(-2i)$$

2. Simplify:

$$6 - 4i + 3i - 2i^2$$

3. Substitute $i^2 = -1$:

$$6 - 4i + 3i + 2$$

4. Final Answer:

$$8 - i$$

C. Finding the Conjugate of a Complex Number

The **conjugate** of $a + bi$ is $a - bi$. It is used to **rationalize denominators**.

Example 7: Rationalizing a Complex Denominator

Simplify:

$$\frac{5}{3 + 2i}$$

1. Multiply numerator and denominator by the conjugate $3 - 2i$:

$$\frac{5(3 - 2i)}{(3 + 2i)(3 - 2i)}$$

2. Expand:

$$\frac{15 - 10i}{9 - 4i^2}$$

3. Substitute $i^2 = -1$:

$$\frac{15 - 10i}{9 + 4} = \frac{15 - 10i}{13}$$

Final Answer: $\frac{15}{13} - \frac{10}{13}i$

5. Summary of Key Strategies

Concept	Strategy
Simplifying Rational Expressions	Factor numerators and denominators, then cancel common terms.
Solving Rational Equations	Multiply by the LCD to eliminate fractions before solving.

Operations with Complex Numbers	Treat i as a variable and simplify using $i^2 = -1$.
Multiplying Complex Numbers	Use the distributive property and combine like terms.
Rationalizing Complex Denominators	Multiply by the conjugate to remove imaginary numbers from the denominator.

6. Final Key Takeaways

- Rational expressions follow the **same rules as fractions** but involve polynomials.
- Complex numbers include an **imaginary component** represented by i.
- Multiplication of complex numbers requires recognizing that $i^2 = -1$.
- The **conjugate** is useful for rationalizing denominators in complex number fractions.

By mastering **rational expressions and complex numbers**, students can tackle **advanced algebra problems on the SAT with confidence.**

12.4 Problem-Solving Strategies for Advanced Topics

The **Digital SAT Math section** includes advanced algebra concepts such as **quadratic equations, polynomials, functions, rational expressions, and complex numbers**. Many of these questions require **multi-step reasoning and problem-solving strategies** rather than just straightforward calculations.

This section will cover:

- **Recognizing Key SAT Problem Types**
- **Breaking Down Multi-Step Problems**
- **Strategic Use of the Desmos Calculator**
- **Common Traps and How to Avoid Them**

1. Recognizing Key SAT Problem Types

Understanding the most common SAT problem structures allows students to approach them strategically rather than solving from scratch every time.

Problem Type	Recognizing the Question	Best Strategy
Word Problems with Equations	"A company sells tickets for $5 each…"	Define variables, set up an equation
Systems of Equations	"One equation describes price, another describes quantity…"	Solve using **substitution or elimination**
Quadratic Problems	"Find the value of x given $ax^2 + bx + c = 0$"	Factor when possible; use **quadratic formula** if needed
Function Transformations	"How does $g(x)$ compare to $f(x)$?"	Identify **shifts, reflections, and stretches**
Inequalities	"Which values satisfy $ax + b > c$?"	Solve normally but **flip sign when dividing by negatives**
Complex Numbers	"What is $(3 + 2i)(4 - i)$?"	Use **FOIL and simplify using** $i^2 = -1$

2. Breaking Down Multi-Step Problems

Some SAT math problems involve **multiple steps**, requiring students to keep track of different operations.

A. Solving Multi-Step Word Problems

Example 1: Multi-Step System of Equations

A bookstore sells fiction books for $12eachandnonfictionbooksfor15$ each. If a customer buys **10 books** and spends **$132**, how many of each type did they buy?

Step 1: Define Variables

- Let f be the number of fiction books.
- Let n be the number of nonfiction books.

Step 2: Set Up Equations

1. Total books equation:

$$f + n = 10$$

2. Total price equation:

$$12f + 15n = 132$$

Step 3: Solve Using Substitution or Elimination

1. Express n in terms of f:

$$n = 10 - f$$

2. Substitute into the second equation:

$$12f + 15(10 - f) = 132$$

3. Expand and solve:

$$12f + 150 - 15f = 132$$

$$-3f + 150 = 132$$

$$-3f = -18$$

$$f = 6$$

4. Find n:

$$n = 10 - 6 = 4$$

Final Answer: The customer bought **6 fiction** and **4 nonfiction** books.

B. Solving Multi-Step Quadratic Problems

Example 2: Quadratic Word Problem

A projectile is launched from the ground, and its height h, in meters, after t seconds is given by:

$$h(t) = -5t^2 + 20t$$

Find the time when the projectile reaches its maximum height.

Step 1: Identify the Key Feature

- The maximum height occurs at the **vertex** of the quadratic.
- Use the vertex formula:

$$t = -\frac{b}{2a}$$

where $a = -5, b = 20$.

Step 2: Calculate the Vertex

$$t = -\frac{20}{2(-5)}$$

$$t = \frac{20}{10} = 2$$

Final Answer: The projectile reaches its maximum height at **2 seconds**.

3. Strategic Use of the Desmos Calculator

Many problems on the Digital SAT can be **solved more efficiently using the Desmos graphing calculator**.

A. When to Use Desmos

Problem Type	**How Desmos Helps**
Graphing Quadratic Functions	Find the vertex, x-intercepts, or y-intercepts quickly
Solving Equations	Check solutions by graphing both sides of the equation
Finding Intersections	Solve systems of equations graphically
Inequalities	Shade and visualize solution sets

Example 3: Using Desmos for Solving a Quadratic

Solve for x in the equation:

$$2x^2 - 3x - 5 = 0$$

1. **Enter into Desmos:** $y = 2x^2 - 3x - 5$.
2. Find **x-intercepts**, which are the solutions.
3. The graph shows intersections at $x = -1$ and $x = 2.5$.

Final Answer: $x = -1, 2.5$

4. Common Traps and How to Avoid Them

A. Misinterpreting Word Problems

- **Trap:** Misreading "at least" or "no more than" can lead to using the wrong inequality sign.
- **Solution:** Carefully translate words into equations before solving.

B. Forgetting to Flip the Inequality Sign

- **Trap:** When dividing by a negative number in an inequality, students forget to flip the sign.
- **Solution:** Always check if multiplication/division involves a negative.

Example 4: Inequality Sign Flip

Solve for x:

$$-2x > 8$$

1. Divide by **-2**:

$$x < -4$$

2. **Sign flips** since dividing by a negative.

3. Final Answer: $x < -4$.

C. Missing the Second Solution in Quadratic Equations

- **Trap:** Solving $x^2 = 9$ and only writing $x = 3$, forgetting $x = -3$.
- **Solution:** Always consider **both positive and negative square roots**.

5. Summary of Key Strategies

Strategy	Why It Works
Recognizing Common Problem Types	Helps approach questions efficiently
Breaking Down Multi-Step Problems	Reduces errors and improves accuracy
Using the Desmos Calculator	Saves time on graphing and equation solving
Avoiding Common Traps	Prevents careless mistakes and loss of points

6. Final Key Takeaways

- **Understand common SAT math question types** to recognize the best approach.
- **Break down word problems step by step** by defining variables and setting up equations.
- **Use the Desmos calculator strategically** to check work and find solutions graphically.
- **Be mindful of common mistakes** like flipping inequality signs and missing second solutions in quadratic equations.
- **Practice multi-step problems regularly** to build confidence and improve problem-solving speed.

By mastering **advanced problem-solving strategies**, students can confidently tackle **complex algebraic and function-based questions on the SAT**, maximizing their accuracy and efficiency.

CHAPTER 13

PROBLEM SOLVING & DATA ANALYSIS

13.1 Ratios, Proportions, Percentages, and Units

The **Digital SAT Math section** includes numerous questions requiring students to work with **ratios, proportions, percentages, and unit conversions**. These topics are essential for solving real-world problems involving scaling, rates, and comparisons.

This section will cover:

- Understanding **ratios and proportions**
- Solving **percentage problems**
- Applying **unit conversions and dimensional analysis**
- Recognizing **common SAT problem structures**

1. Understanding Ratios and Proportions

A **ratio** is a relationship between two quantities. It is written in different forms:

$$\frac{a}{b}, \quad a:b, \quad \text{or} \quad a \text{ to } b$$

A **proportion** is an equation that sets two ratios equal to each other:

$$\frac{a}{b} = \frac{c}{d}$$

Example 1: Solving a Proportion

If a recipe requires **3 cups of flour** for every **5 cups of sugar**, how much sugar is needed for **9 cups of flour**?

1. Set up the proportion:

$$\frac{3}{5} = \frac{9}{x}$$

2. Cross-multiply:

$$3x = 45$$

3. Solve for x:

$$x = 15$$

Final Answer: 15 cups of sugar

Key SAT Strategy:

- **Cross-multiply to solve proportions quickly**.
- **Check if simplifying the ratio first can save time**.

2. Solving Percentage Problems

A. Percentage Formula

To calculate a percentage, use the formula:

$$\frac{\text{Part}}{\text{Whole}} \times 100\%$$

B. Finding a Percentage of a Number

Example 2: What is 30% of 250?

$$0.30 \times 250 = 75$$

Final Answer: 75

C. Percentage Increase and Decrease

$$\frac{\text{New Value} - \text{Old Value}}{\text{Old Value}} \times 100\%$$

Example 3: A jacket originally costs $80 but is now 64$***. What is the percentage decrease?***

$$\frac{80-64}{80} \times 100 = \frac{16}{80} \times 100 = 20\%$$

Final Answer: 20% decrease

Key SAT Strategy:

- Convert percentages to **decimals for easier multiplication**.
- Be careful with **increase vs. decrease calculations**.

3. Unit Conversions and Dimensional Analysis

A. Common Unit Conversions

Conversion	Equivalent Value
1 inch	2.54 cm
1 mile	1.609 km
1 kg	2.2 lbs
1 liter	1000 mL

B. Using Conversion Factors

To convert units, multiply by conversion factors:

Example 4: Convert 5 miles to kilometers.

$$5 \text{ miles} \times \frac{1.609 \text{ km}}{1 \text{ mile}} = 8.045 \text{ km}$$

Final Answer: 8.05 km (rounded to two decimal places)

C. Rate and Dimensional Analysis

Example 5: If a car travels at 60 mph, how many miles does it travel in 2.5 hours?

$$60 \text{ miles/hour} \times 2.5 \text{ hours} = 150 \text{ miles}$$

Final Answer: 150 miles

Key SAT Strategy:

- Use **conversion factors** to **cancel out units and solve step by step**.
- Always **double-check units in word problems**.

4. Common SAT Problem Structures and Shortcuts

A. Using Ratio Scaling Instead of Proportions

Example 6: A class has boys and girls in a ratio of 3:5. If there are 24 students total, how many are boys?

1. Add ratio parts: $3 + 5 = 8$

2. Find one part: $24 \div 8 = 3$
3. Multiply by boys' ratio: $3 \times 3 = 9$

Final Answer: 9 boys

B. Reverse Percentage Problems

Example 7: After a 20% increase, the price of an item is $72. What was the original price?

1. Let original price be x.
2. $x + 0.20x = 72$
3. $1.20x = 72$
4. $x = 72 \div 1.2 = 60$

Final Answer: $60

C. Unit Rate Problems

Example 8: A printer prints 90 pages in 6 minutes. How many pages per minute?

$$\frac{90 \text{ pages}}{6 \text{ minutes}} = 15 \text{ pages per minute}$$

Final Answer: 15 pages per minute

Key SAT Strategy:

- For ratio problems, **find one unit first**, then scale up or down.
- Work **backwards for percentage and rate problems**.

5. Summary of Key Strategies

Concept	Best Strategy
Ratios and Proportions	Use **cross-multiplication** or scale up/down when possible.
Percentage Problems	Convert percentages to **decimals for easier calculations**.
Unit Conversions	Use **conversion factors** and set up equations carefully.
Rate Problems	Solve using **unit rates** to find per unit values.
Reverse Percentage Problems	Work **backwards by dividing by the multiplier**.

6. Final Key Takeaways

- Ratios compare **two or more quantities**, and **proportions solve for missing values** in equivalent ratios.
- Percentages require understanding **increase, decrease, and reverse calculations**.
- Unit conversions use **conversion factors and dimensional analysis**.
- Rates and ratios appear in **real-world SAT problems** and can often be solved with **unit rate methods**.
- **Practice solving percentage and ratio problems efficiently** to save time on the SAT.

By **mastering ratios, proportions, percentages, and unit conversions**, students can approach **SAT word problems confidently and maximize accuracy on the math section.**

13.2 Data Interpretation (Charts, Tables, Graphs)

The **Digital SAT Math section** includes **data interpretation questions** that require students to analyze information presented in **charts, tables, graphs, and scatterplots**. These questions test a student's ability to **extract key details, identify trends, and apply mathematical reasoning to real-world scenarios**.

This section will cover:

- **Understanding Different Data Representations**
- **Extracting and Interpreting Information from Tables and Graphs**
- **Identifying Trends, Correlations, and Outliers**
- **Applying Data to Real-World Contexts**

1. Understanding Different Data Representations

A. Types of Graphs and When to Use Them

Graph Type	Best Used For	Example
Bar Graph	Comparing discrete categories	Population sizes of different countries
Line Graph	Showing trends over time	Temperature changes across months
Scatterplot	Identifying relationships between variables	Hours studied vs. test scores
Pie Chart	Displaying proportions of a whole	Budget allocation in a company
Table	Organizing numerical data	Sales figures for different products

B. Example SAT Question Setup

Many SAT questions will provide a **graph, chart, or table** and ask for an analysis, such as identifying **trends, relationships, and calculations**.

2. Extracting and Interpreting Information from Tables and Graphs

Let's analyze a **sample table** that could appear on the SAT.

Example 1: Reading a Table

Year	Company A Revenue ($M)	Company B Revenue ($M)	Company C Revenue ($M)
2020	45	55	60
2021	50	53	65
2022	55	58	70
2023	60	61	75

Question:

Which company had the greatest percentage increase in revenue from 2020 to 2023?

✓ Step 1: Use the Percentage Change Formula

$$\% \text{ Change} = \frac{\text{New Value} - \text{Old Value}}{\text{Old Value}} \times 100$$

✓ Step 2: Calculate for Each Company

- **Company A:**

$$\frac{60-45}{45} \times 100 = \frac{15}{45} \times 100 = 33.3\%$$

- **Company B:**

$$\frac{61-55}{55} \times 100 = \frac{6}{55} \times 100 = 10.9\%$$

- **Company C:**

$$\frac{75-60}{60} \times 100 = \frac{15}{60} \times 100 = 25\%$$

✓ **Final Answer: Company A had the greatest percentage increase at 33.3%.**

3. Identifying Trends, Correlations, and Outliers

Many SAT questions ask students to **interpret trends in line graphs or scatterplots**.

Example 2: Identifying Trends in a Line Graph

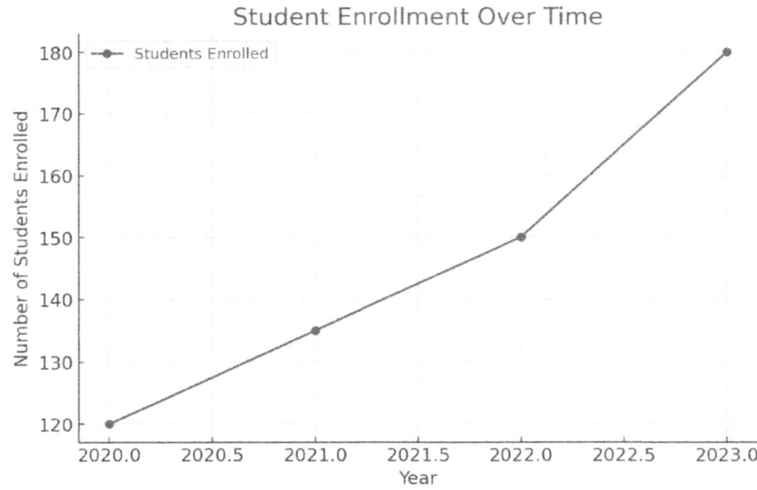

Question:

Based on the line graph, what was the approximate percentage increase in student enrollment from 2020 to 2023?

1. Use the percentage change formula:

$$\% \text{ Change} = \frac{\text{New Value} - \text{Old Value}}{\text{Old Value}} \times 100$$

2. Plug in values:

$$\frac{180-120}{120} \times 100 = \frac{60}{120} \times 100 = 50\%$$

Final Answer: 50% increase in student enrollment

4. Applying Data to Real-World Contexts

A. Scatterplots and Correlation

Scatterplots help determine whether **two variables are related**.

- **Positive correlation:** As one variable increases, the other increases.
- **Negative correlation:** As one variable increases, the other decreases.
- **No correlation:** No clear pattern exists.

Example 3: Identifying Correlation in a Scatterplot

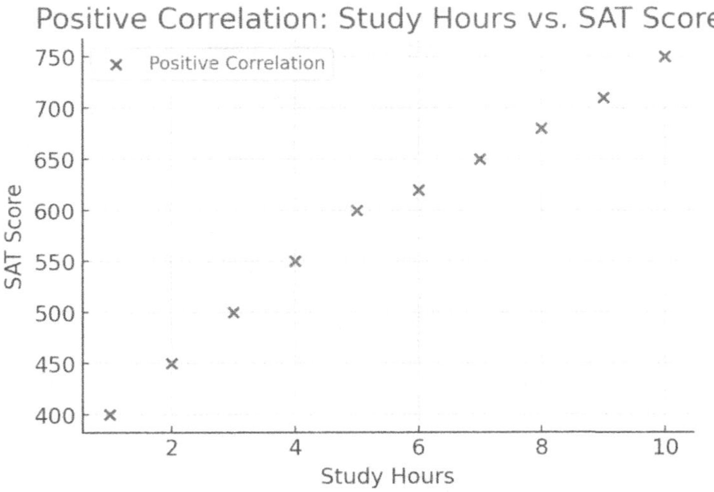

A study examines the **relationship between the number of study hours and SAT scores**. The scatterplot shows a general upward trend.

Question:
What type of correlation does this scatterplot represent?

Answer:
Since **higher study hours are associated with higher SAT scores**, this is a **positive correlation**.

5. Summary of Key Strategies

Concept	Strategy
Reading Tables	Identify trends, use correct formulas for percentages and comparisons.
Interpreting Line Graphs	Focus on trends (increase, decrease, or plateau).
Using Scatterplots	Identify correlation type (positive, negative, or none).
Solving Multi-Step Word Problems	Convert word problems into mathematical equations.

6. Final Key Takeaways

- **Tables, charts, and graphs** contain valuable data that must be interpreted correctly.
- **Line graphs show trends**, while **bar graphs compare categories**.
- **Scatterplots reveal correlations**, helping identify relationships between variables.
- **Real-world applications involve understanding how data represents business, science, or economics.**
- **Practice identifying trends and calculating changes efficiently** to improve SAT performance.

By mastering **data interpretation techniques**, students can approach SAT **problem-solving with confidence and accuracy**.

13.3 Basic Probability and Statistics (Mean, Median, Mode, etc.)

The **Digital SAT Math section** includes questions that assess a student's understanding of **probability and statistics**, including measures of central tendency (mean, median, mode), variability (range, standard deviation), and probability calculations. These concepts are essential for **interpreting data and making informed predictions**.

This section will cover:

- **Measures of Central Tendency (Mean, Median, Mode)**
- **Measures of Variability (Range, Standard Deviation)**

- **Fundamentals of Probability**
- **Applying Probability and Statistics to SAT Word Problems**

1. Measures of Central Tendency: Mean, Median, and Mode

A. Mean (Average)

The **mean** is the sum of all values divided by the number of values.

$$\text{Mean} = \frac{\sum \text{values}}{\text{number of values}}$$

Example 1: Finding the Mean

Find the mean of the numbers: **5, 7, 8, 12, 18**

1. Sum of values:

$$5 + 7 + 8 + 12 + 18 = 50$$

2. Divide by the number of values:

$$\frac{50}{5} = 10$$

Final Answer: 10

B. Median (Middle Value of Ordered Data)

The **median** is the middle number when values are arranged in **ascending order**.

- If there are **odd** numbers, the median is the middle value.
- If there are **even** numbers, the median is the average of the two middle values.

Example 2: Finding the Median

Find the median of **3, 6, 10, 14, 22, 25, 31**

Since there are **7 numbers (odd count)**, the middle value is the **4th number**:
Median = 14

Find the median of **4, 8, 12, 20, 26, 30**

Since there are **6 numbers (even count)**, find the average of the two middle numbers **(12 and 20)**:

$$\frac{12 + 20}{2} = \frac{32}{2} = 16$$

Final Answer: 16

C. Mode (Most Frequently Occurring Value)

The **mode** is the number that appears most frequently.

- A dataset can have **one mode, multiple modes, or no mode**.

Example 3: Finding the Mode

Find the mode of **2, 4, 6, 6, 8, 9, 6, 10**

Since **6 appears most frequently**, the **mode = 6**.

If no number repeats, the dataset has **no mode**.

2. Measures of Variability: Range and Standard Deviation

A. Range (Difference Between Max and Min Values)

The **range** measures how spread out the data is.

$$\text{Range} = \text{Maximum} - \text{Minimum}$$

Example 4: Finding the Range

Find the range of **5, 12, 18, 22, 35**

1. Maximum: **35**, Minimum: **5**
2. Range = **35 - 5 = 30**

Final Answer: 30

B. Standard Deviation (Spread of Data from Mean)

The **standard deviation** measures how much values deviate from the mean.

- A **low standard deviation** means values are **closer to the mean**.
- A **high standard deviation** means values are **more spread out**.

The SAT does **not** require students to calculate standard deviation but may ask **which dataset has a higher/lower deviation** based on the spread of numbers.

Example 5: Comparing Standard Deviation

Dataset A: **5, 6, 7, 8, 9**
Dataset B: **1, 10, 20, 30, 40**

Question: Which dataset has a higher standard deviation?

Since Dataset B has **numbers spread further apart**, it has a **higher standard deviation**.

3. Fundamentals of Probability

A. Probability Formula

Probability measures the likelihood of an event occurring.

$$P(\text{event}) = \frac{\text{favorable outcomes}}{\text{total outcomes}}$$

Example 6: Rolling a Die

What is the probability of rolling an even number on a standard six-sided die?

1. Favorable outcomes: **2, 4, 6** (3 outcomes)
2. Total outcomes: **6**
3. Probability:

$$P = \frac{3}{6} = \frac{1}{2}$$

Final Answer: $\frac{1}{2}$ **or 50%**

B. Independent vs. Dependent Probability

Probability Type	**Definition**	**Example**
Independent Events	The outcome of one event does **not** affect another	Rolling a die twice
Dependent Events	The outcome of one event **affects** another	Drawing cards without replacement

Example 7: Probability of Two Independent Events

A coin is flipped twice. What is the probability of getting **two heads**?

Since **each flip is independent**, multiply the probabilities:

$$P(\text{heads}) = \frac{1}{2} \times \frac{1}{2} = \frac{1}{4}$$

Final Answer: $\frac{1}{4}$ or 25%

C. Expected Value in Probability Questions

Some SAT problems require finding the expected value of repeated probabilities.

Example 8: Probability in Word Problems

A bag contains 3 red balls, 2 blue balls, and 5 green balls. If one ball is randomly selected, what is the probability it is **not red**?

1. Total balls = **3 + 2 + 5 = 10**
2. Non-red balls = **2 blue + 5 green = 7**
3. Probability:

$$P(\text{not red}) = \frac{7}{10}$$

Final Answer: $\frac{7}{10}$ or 70%

4. Applying Probability and Statistics to SAT Word Problems

A. Real-World Application of Mean

Example 9: Finding the Missing Value in an Average

The average score of 4 students on a test is **85**. Three students scored **90, 85, and 80**. What was the fourth student's score?

1. Use the mean formula:

$$\frac{90 + 85 + 80 + x}{4} = 85$$

2. Multiply both sides by 4:

$$255 + x = 340$$

3. Solve for x:

$$x = 85$$

Final Answer: 85

B. Probability in Real-World Contexts

Example 10: Conditional Probability

In a school, **60% of students play a sport**. Of those, **40% play soccer**. What percentage of students **play soccer**?

Multiply probabilities:

$$P(\text{soccer}) = 0.6 \times 0.4 = 0.24$$

Final Answer: 24%

5. Summary of Key Strategies

Concept	Best Strategy
Mean, Median, Mode	Organize data first, identify middle values correctly.
Probability Problems	Identify total outcomes, then count favorable outcomes.
Real-World Statistics	Use the **average formula** for missing values.
Comparing Data Spread	Look for **range and standard deviation differences**.

6. Final Key Takeaways

- **Mean, median, and mode** are key tools for understanding data sets.
- **Probability problems require counting outcomes carefully.**
- **Recognizing independent vs. dependent events is crucial.**
- **Real-world SAT problems involve applying these concepts to word problems.**

By **mastering probability and statistics**, students can improve their **problem-solving speed and accuracy** on the SAT.

13.4 Understanding Margins of Error and Data Trends

The **Digital SAT Math section** includes questions on **margins of error, confidence intervals, and identifying trends in data**. These concepts are critical for understanding **statistical accuracy and making predictions based on sample data**.

This section will cover:

- **What is the Margin of Error?**
- **Confidence Intervals and Their Interpretation**
- **Identifying Trends and Outliers in Data**
- **SAT Strategies for Data Trend Analysis**

1. What is the Margin of Error?

A. Definition

The **margin of error (MOE)** represents the possible variation in a survey or statistical result due to **sampling limitations**. It tells us how much the sample data might differ from the actual population value.

B. Formula for Margin of Error

$$\text{Margin of Error} = Z \times \frac{\sigma}{\sqrt{n}}$$

Where:

- Z = **Z-score** (based on confidence level)
- σ = **Standard deviation of the population**
- n = **Sample size**

C. Common Z-Scores for Confidence Levels

Confidence Level	Z-Score
90%	1.645
95%	1.96

99%	2.576

A **higher confidence level** results in a **larger margin of error**, indicating **greater certainty but a wider range**.

Example 1: Calculating Margin of Error

A survey of **400 students** shows an average SAT score of **1200** with a standard deviation of **100**. What is the margin of error for a **95% confidence level**?

1. Identify values:
    - $Z = 1.96$ (for 95% confidence)
    - $\sigma = 100$
    - $n = 400$
2. Apply the formula:

$$\text{MOE} = 1.96 \times \frac{100}{\sqrt{400}}$$

3. Simplify:

$$\text{MOE} = 1.96 \times \frac{100}{20} = 1.96 \times 5 = 9.8$$

Final Answer: ± 9.8

This means the **true SAT average** is likely between **1190.2 and 1209.8**.

2. Confidence Intervals and Their Interpretation

A **confidence interval** provides a range where the true population value is expected to lie.

$$\text{Confidence Interval} = \text{Sample Mean} \pm \text{Margin of Error}$$

Example 2: Finding the Confidence Interval

From the previous example:

- Sample Mean = **1200**
- MOE = ± 9.8

$$1200 \pm 9.8$$

$$(1190.2, 1209.8)$$

Interpretation:
We are **95% confident** that the **true average SAT score** of all students falls within this range.

3. Identifying Trends and Outliers in Data

A. Recognizing Trends in Graphs and Tables

Trend Type	How It Looks in a Graph	Meaning
Positive Trend	Line slopes **upward**	One variable **increases** as the other increases
Negative Trend	Line slopes **downward**	One variable **decreases** as the other increases
No Trend	Points are **scattered randomly**	No clear relationship

Example 3: Identifying a Trend in a Scatterplot

A study tracks **weekly study hours vs. SAT scores** for 50 students.

Question:
What trend does the scatterplot likely show?

Answer:
Since **more study hours** should correlate with **higher SAT scores**, the scatterplot likely shows a **positive correlation**.

B. Outliers in Data

An **outlier** is a data point that **differs significantly** from the rest.

Example 4: Identifying an Outlier in a Data Set

Data Set: **72, 75, 78, 80, 82, 150**

Question:
Which value is an outlier?

Answer:
The number **150** is an outlier because it is **far outside the range of other values**.

4. SAT Strategies for Data Trend Analysis

A. Estimating Based on Trends

If a **data trend shows steady growth, predict values using the pattern**.

Example 5: Predicting a Value Based on a Trend

Year	Population (millions)
2010	100
2015	120
2020	140
2025	?

Question:
What is the estimated population in 2025?

1. The population **increases by 20 million** every **5 years**.
2. If the pattern continues, in **2025**, the population will be **160 million**.

Final Answer: 160 million

B. Using Line of Best Fit in a Scatterplot

A **line of best fit** is used to **approximate relationships** between variables.

Example 6: Predicting from a Line of Best Fit

A scatterplot of **years of work experience vs. salary** shows a **positive correlation**.

Question:
If a person has **6 years of experience**, what can we predict about their salary?

Answer:
If the trend shows an increase of **$5,000 per year**, and a person with **5 years of experience** earns **$55,000**, then:

- A person with **6 years** would earn **$60,000**.

5. Summary of Key Strategies

Concept	Strategy
Margin of Error	Use $Z \times \frac{\sigma}{\sqrt{n}}$ to estimate accuracy
Confidence Intervals	Find the range by adding/subtracting MOE from the mean
Recognizing Trends	Look for **upward, downward, or no trend** in graphs
Identifying Outliers	Check for **values that differ greatly** from the rest
Using Line of Best Fit	Estimate values by extending the trendline

6. Final Key Takeaways

- **The margin of error** quantifies uncertainty in sample data.
- **Confidence intervals** give a range where the true population value is expected to lie.
- **Trends in data** help predict future values and make statistical decisions.
- **Outliers can distort averages and trends**, making them crucial to identify.
- **Understanding data trends and applying estimation techniques** is essential for the SAT.

By mastering **margins of error, confidence intervals, and data trends**, students can **improve their data interpretation skills** and confidently answer SAT questions involving **statistics and probability**.

CHAPTER 14

ADDITIONAL TOPICS: GEOMETRY & TRIGONOMETRY

14.1 Congruence, Similarity, and Basic Theorems

The **Digital SAT Math section** includes geometry questions that require students to understand **congruence, similarity, and fundamental geometric theorems**. Mastering these concepts is essential for solving problems involving **triangles, quadrilaterals, transformations, and proportional reasoning**.

This section will cover:

- **Congruence and Similarity Definitions**
- **Triangle Congruence and Similarity Theorems**
- **Key Angle and Parallel Line Theorems**
- **Real-World Applications of Geometry on the SAT**

1. Understanding Congruence and Similarity

A. What is Congruence?

Two figures are **congruent** if they have **the same shape and size**. This means:

- Corresponding **sides** are **equal in length**.
- Corresponding **angles** are **equal in measure**.
- The figures can be **transformed** through **rotation, reflection, or translation** but not resized.

Notation:

$$\triangle ABC \cong \triangle DEF$$

indicates that **triangle ABC is congruent to triangle DEF**.

B. What is Similarity?

Two figures are **similar** if they have **the same shape but not necessarily the same size**. This means:

- Corresponding **angles** are **equal**.
- Corresponding **sides are proportional** (same ratio).

Notation:

$$\triangle ABC \sim \triangle DEF$$

indicates that **triangle ABC is similar to triangle DEF**.

Example 1: Identifying Similar Triangles

Given that $\triangle ABC \sim \triangle DEF$, and that $AB = 6$, $BC = 8$, and $AC = 10$, while $DE = 9$, find EF.

1. Since the triangles are **similar**, their sides are **proportional**.
2. Set up a proportion using corresponding sides:

$$\frac{AB}{DE} = \frac{BC}{EF}$$

$$\frac{6}{9} = \frac{8}{x}$$

3. Cross multiply:

$$6x = 72$$

4. Solve for x:

$$x = 12$$

Final Answer: $EF = 12$

2. Triangle Congruence and Similarity Theorems

A. Triangle Congruence Theorems

To prove that two triangles are **congruent**, we use these postulates:

Postulate	Definition
SSS (Side-Side-Side)	If three sides of one triangle are equal to three sides of another triangle, they are congruent.
SAS (Side-Angle-Side)	If two sides and the included angle of one triangle are equal to those of another, they are congruent.
ASA (Angle-Side-Angle)	If two angles and the included side are equal, the triangles are congruent.
AAS (Angle-Angle-Side)	If two angles and a non-included side are equal, the triangles are congruent.
HL (Hypotenuse-Leg, Right Triangles Only)	If the hypotenuse and a leg of two right triangles are equal, the triangles are congruent.

Example 2: Using SAS to Prove Congruence

Given that $AB = DE$, $BC = EF$, **and** $\angle B = \angle E$, prove $\triangle ABC \cong \triangle DEF$.

Since **two sides and the included angle** are equal, we can conclude:

$$\triangle ABC \cong \triangle DEF \quad \text{(SAS Postulate)}$$

B. Triangle Similarity Theorems

To prove that two triangles are **similar**, we use these theorems:

Theorem	Definition
AA (Angle-Angle)	If two corresponding angles are equal, the triangles are similar.
SSS (Side-Side-Side) Similarity	If all three pairs of sides are proportional, the triangles are similar.
SAS (Side-Angle-Side) Similarity	If two sides are proportional and the included angle is the same, the triangles are similar.

Example 3: Using AA to Prove Similarity

If $\triangle XYZ$ and $\triangle ABC$ have $\angle X = \angle A$ and $\angle Y = \angle B$, prove similarity.

Since **two corresponding angles** are equal, the triangles are similar by:

$$\triangle XYZ \sim \triangle ABC \quad \text{(AA Similarity)}$$

3. Key Angle and Parallel Line Theorems

A. Parallel Lines and Transversals

When a **transversal** cuts two **parallel lines**, it creates **several important angle relationships**.

Angle Type	Definition
Corresponding Angles	Equal when lines are parallel
Alternate Interior Angles	Equal when lines are parallel
Alternate Exterior Angles	Equal when lines are parallel
Same-Side Interior Angles	Add up to 180°

Example 4: Solving for x in a Parallel Line Diagram

Given two parallel lines cut by a transversal, if one angle is 65°, find the alternate interior angle.

Since alternate interior angles are equal:

$$x = 65^\circ$$

4. Real-World Applications of Geometry on the SAT

A. Similar Triangles in Real Life

Example 5: Finding the Height of a Tree Using Shadows

A **6-foot person** casts a **4-foot shadow**. A **tree** nearby casts a **20-foot shadow**. How tall is the tree?

Since the person and tree form **similar triangles**, set up a proportion:

$$\frac{\text{Person's Height}}{\text{Person's Shadow}} = \frac{\text{Tree's Height}}{\text{Tree's Shadow}}$$

$$\frac{6}{4} = \frac{x}{20}$$

Cross-multiply:

$$6 \times 20 = 4x$$

$$120 = 4x$$

$$x = 30$$

Final Answer: The tree is 30 feet tall.

B. Scale Factor in Map Problems

Example 6: Using Scale Factor in a Map

A map uses a scale of **1 inch = 5 miles**. If two cities are **3 inches apart** on the map, how far apart are they in real life?

Multiply the distance by the scale factor:

$$3 \times 5 = 15$$

Final Answer: 15 miles.

5. Summary of Key Strategies

Concept	Best Strategy
Congruence	Use **SSS, SAS, ASA, AAS, or HL** to prove triangles are congruent.
Similarity	Use **AA, SSS, or SAS** for proving similarity.
Parallel Lines	Identify **corresponding, alternate interior, and same-side interior angles**.

Proportions in Similar Figures	Use **ratios and cross-multiplication** to solve problems.
Real-World Problems	Apply **similar triangles, scale factors, and shadow problems** to solve geometry questions.

6. Final Key Takeaways

- **Congruent figures** have **equal sides and angles**.
- **Similar figures** have **proportional sides and equal angles**.
- **Parallel lines with transversals** create **equal angle pairs**.
- **Proportions solve real-world problems like heights, distances, and maps**.
- **Practice applying triangle similarity and congruence rules to SAT geometry questions**.

By mastering **congruence, similarity, and key theorems**, students can confidently solve **SAT geometry problems and improve their overall test performance**.

14.2 Circles, Triangles, and Polygon Properties

The **Digital SAT Math section** includes geometry questions on **circles, triangles, and polygons**, requiring students to apply **key properties, theorems, and formulas** to solve problems. Mastering these topics is essential for **identifying angles, calculating perimeters and areas, and understanding geometric relationships**.

This section will cover:

- **Properties of Circles**
- **Triangle Classification and Theorems**
- **Properties of Polygons (Quadrilaterals, Pentagons, etc.)**
- **SAT Geometry Problem-Solving Strategies**

1. Properties of Circles

A **circle** is a set of points equidistant from a fixed point called the **center**.

A. Key Terms in a Circle

Term	Definition
Radius (r)	Distance from the center to any point on the circle
Diameter (d)	Longest chord, $d = 2r$
Circumference	The perimeter of a circle, $C = 2\pi r$
Area	The space inside a circle, $A = \pi r^2$
Chord	A segment joining two points on the circle
Tangent	A line that touches the circle at exactly one point
Arc	A portion of the circle's circumference
Sector	A "slice" of a circle, defined by two radii

B. Important Circle Formulas

1. **Circumference of a Circle:**

$$C = 2\pi r$$

2. **Area of a Circle:**

$$A = \pi r^2$$

3. **Arc Length Formula:**

$$\text{Arc Length} = \frac{\theta}{360} \times 2\pi r$$

4. **Sector Area Formula:**

$$\text{Sector Area} = \frac{\theta}{360} \times \pi r^2$$

Example 1: Finding the Arc Length

A circle has a radius of **6 cm**. What is the arc length of a **90° sector**?

1. Use the arc length formula:

$$\frac{90}{360} \times 2\pi(6)$$

2. Simplify:

$$\frac{1}{4} \times 12\pi = 3\pi$$

Final Answer: 3π **cm** or **9.42 cm** (approximate).

2. Triangle Classification and Theorems

A. Types of Triangles

Triangle Type	Properties
Equilateral	All sides equal, all angles = **60°**
Isosceles	Two equal sides, two equal angles
Scalene	No sides or angles are equal
Right Triangle	One angle is **90°**

B. Triangle Angle Sum Theorem

The sum of the interior angles of a triangle is always **180°**.

Example 2: Finding a Missing Triangle Angle

In a triangle, two angles measure **50°** and **60°**. Find the third angle.

$$x + 50 + 60 = 180$$

$$x = 70^\circ$$

Final Answer: 70°

C. Pythagorean Theorem (Right Triangles Only)

$$a^2 + b^2 = c^2$$

where:

- a and b are the legs
- c is the **hypotenuse**

Example 3: Solving for the Hypotenuse

A right triangle has legs **6 cm** and **8 cm**. Find the hypotenuse.

1. Apply the Pythagorean theorem:

$$6^2 + 8^2 = c^2$$

2. Compute:

$$36 + 64 = c^2$$

$$c^2 = 100$$

$$c = 10$$

Final Answer: 10 cm

3. Properties of Polygons (Quadrilaterals, Pentagons, etc.)

A **polygon** is a closed figure with three or more sides.

A. Sum of Interior Angles

For an n**-sided polygon**, the sum of interior angles is:

$$\text{Sum} = (n - 2) \times 180$$

Polygon	Sides (n)	Sum of Interior Angles
Triangle	3	180°
Quadrilateral	4	360°
Pentagon	5	540°
Hexagon	6	720°

Example 4: Finding a Missing Interior Angle in a Pentagon

A pentagon has **four angles measuring 110°, 95°, 120°, and 100°**. Find the missing angle.

1. Compute total sum:

$$(5 - 2) \times 180 = 540^\circ$$

2. Find the missing angle x:

$$x + 110 + 95 + 120 + 100 = 540$$

3. Solve for x:

$$x = 115^\circ$$

Final Answer: 115°

B. Properties of Special Quadrilaterals

Shape	Key Properties
Parallelogram	Opposite sides equal, opposite angles equal
Rectangle	All angles **90°**, opposite sides equal
Rhombus	All sides equal, opposite angles equal
Square	All sides and angles equal (special case of rhombus and rectangle)
Trapezoid	One pair of parallel sides

Example 5: Solving for the Missing Side in a Rectangle

A rectangle has **one side of 7 cm** and a **perimeter of 28 cm**. Find the other side.

1. Use the perimeter formula:

$$P = 2(l + w)$$

2. Plug in known values:

$$28 = 2(7 + w)$$

3. Solve for w:

$$14 = 7 + w$$

$$w = 7$$

Final Answer: 7 cm

4. SAT Geometry Problem-Solving Strategies

Concept	Strategy
Circle Problems	Use formulas for circumference and area. Identify key terms like radius, diameter, and tangent.
Triangle Theorems	Apply the **Pythagorean theorem** for right triangles and **angle sum theorem** for missing angles.
Polygon Angle Sum	Use $(n - 2) \times 180$ to find missing angles in polygons.
Parallel Lines	Identify **corresponding, alternate interior, and same-side interior angles**.
Quadrilateral Properties	Recognize special quadrilaterals (rectangles, squares, rhombuses) and apply their properties.

5. Final Key Takeaways

- **Circles:** Use formulas for circumference, area, arc length, and sector area.
- **Triangles:** Apply the **Pythagorean theorem, triangle congruence, and similarity rules**.
- **Polygons:** Use **angle sum formulas and special quadrilateral properties**.
- **SAT Geometry Strategy:** Recognize **common question structures and use process of elimination**.

By mastering **circles, triangles, and polygon properties**, students can efficiently solve SAT geometry problems and maximize their performance.

14.3 Right Triangle Trigonometry and the Unit Circle

The **Digital SAT Math section** includes **right triangle trigonometry** and **unit circle concepts**, testing students on their ability to work with **sine, cosine, tangent, and radian measures**. These concepts are essential for solving problems involving **angles, distances, and periodic functions**.

This section will cover:

- **Right Triangle Trigonometry (Sine, Cosine, Tangent)**
- **Special Right Triangles (30-60-90 and 45-45-90)**
- **The Unit Circle and Radian Measure**
- **SAT Strategies for Trigonometry Questions**

1. Right Triangle Trigonometry (Sine, Cosine, Tangent)

A **right triangle** has one **90° angle** and two acute angles. The relationships between the **side lengths and angles** of right triangles are described by **trigonometric ratios**:

$$\sin\theta = \frac{\text{opposite}}{\text{hypotenuse}}$$

$$\cos\theta = \frac{\text{adjacent}}{\text{hypotenuse}}$$

$$\tan\theta = \frac{\text{opposite}}{\text{adjacent}}$$

Where:

- **Opposite** = Side opposite the given angle
- **Adjacent** = Side next to the given angle
- **Hypotenuse** = Longest side of the right triangle

Example 1: Finding a Side Length Using Trigonometry

In a right triangle, $\theta = 30°$ and the hypotenuse is **10**. Find the length of the opposite side.

1. Use the **sine function**:

$$\sin 30° = \frac{\text{opposite}}{\text{hypotenuse}}$$

2. Plug in values:

$$\frac{x}{10} = \frac{1}{2}$$

3. Solve for x:

$$x = 10 \times \frac{1}{2} = 5$$

Final Answer: 5 units

2. Special Right Triangles (30-60-90 and 45-45-90)

A. 30-60-90 Triangle Properties

A **30-60-90 triangle** follows a specific ratio:

$$1 : \sqrt{3} : 2$$

- **Shortest side** = x (opposite 30°)
- **Longer leg** = $x\sqrt{3}$ (opposite 60°)
- **Hypotenuse** = $2x$

Example 2: Finding a Missing Side in a 30-60-90 Triangle

A **30-60-90 triangle** has a hypotenuse of **12**. Find the shorter leg.

1. The hypotenuse is **2x**, so set up the equation:

$$2x = 12$$

2. Solve for x:

$$x = 6$$

Final Answer: 6 units

B. 45-45-90 Triangle Properties

A **45-45-90 triangle** follows a specific ratio:

$$1 : 1 : \sqrt{2}$$

- **Legs are equal**
- **Hypotenuse** = $x\sqrt{2}$, where x is the leg length

Example 3: Finding the Hypotenuse in a 45-45-90 Triangle

A **45-45-90 triangle** has legs of **8**. Find the hypotenuse.

1. Use the formula:

$$\text{Hypotenuse} = x\sqrt{2}$$

2. Plug in $x = 8$:

$$8\sqrt{2}$$

Final Answer: $8\sqrt{2}$ or **approximately 11.3**

3. The Unit Circle and Radian Measure

A. Understanding the Unit Circle

The **unit circle** is a circle centered at the origin with **radius = 1**. It helps define **trigonometric values for standard angles**.

Angle (Degrees)	**Angle (Radians)**	**Coordinates** $(\cos\theta, \sin\theta)$
0°	0	$(1,0)$
30°	$\frac{\pi}{6}$	$\left(\frac{\sqrt{3}}{2}, \frac{1}{2}\right)$
45°	$\frac{\pi}{4}$	$\left(\frac{\sqrt{2}}{2}, \frac{\sqrt{2}}{2}\right)$
60°	$\frac{\pi}{3}$	$\left(\frac{1}{2}, \frac{\sqrt{3}}{2}\right)$
90°	$\frac{\pi}{2}$	$(0,1)$

B. Converting Between Degrees and Radians

To convert degrees to radians:

$$\text{Radians} = \text{Degrees} \times \frac{\pi}{180}$$

Example 4: Convert 120° to Radians

$$120^\circ \times \frac{\pi}{180} = \frac{2\pi}{3}$$

Final Answer: $\frac{2\pi}{3}$ **radians**

To convert radians to degrees:

$$\text{Degrees} = \text{Radians} \times \frac{180}{\pi}$$

Example 5: Convert $\frac{\pi}{3}$ ***to Degrees***

$$\frac{\pi}{3} \times \frac{180}{\pi} = 60^\circ$$

Final Answer: 60°

4. SAT Strategies for Trigonometry Questions

A. Using Reference Angles in the Unit Circle

If an angle is **greater than 90°**, use **symmetry** in the unit circle to determine values.

Example 6: Finding the Sine of 150°

1. **Reference Angle:** $180° - 150° = 30°$.
2. **Since 150° is in Quadrant II,** sine remains **positive**.
3. $\sin 150° = \sin 30° = \frac{1}{2}$.

Final Answer: $\frac{1}{2}$

B. Identifying the Quadrant of an Angle

- **Quadrant I**: $\sin, \cos, \tan$ **positive**
- **Quadrant II**: $\sin$ **positive**, $\cos, \tan$ **negative**
- **Quadrant III**: $\tan$ **positive**, $\sin, \cos$ **negative**
- **Quadrant IV**: $\cos$ **positive**, $\sin, \tan$ **negative**

5. Summary of Key Strategies

Concept	Best Strategy
Trigonometric Ratios	Use **SOH-CAH-TOA** to solve right triangles.
Special Right Triangles	Memorize **30-60-90** and **45-45-90** ratios.
Unit Circle	Understand **quadrants, reference angles, and coordinate pairs**.
Radians to Degrees	Multiply by $\frac{180}{\pi}$ and vice versa.
SAT Problem-Solving	Identify **quadrants and reference angles** for trigonometry questions.

6. Final Key Takeaways

- **Right triangle trigonometry uses sine, cosine, and tangent ratios** to solve for unknown sides and angles.
- **Special right triangles (30-60-90 and 45-45-90) have fixed side ratios** that simplify calculations.
- **The unit circle provides sine and cosine values for common angles** and allows for conversion between degrees and radians.
- **On the SAT, trigonometry problems often involve recognizing angle properties and applying ratios efficiently.**

By mastering **right triangle trigonometry and the unit circle**, students can tackle **complex SAT trigonometry questions with confidence** and **boost their overall score**.

14.4 Visualizing Geometry in Desmos

The **Digital SAT Math section** allows students to use the **Desmos graphing calculator**, which can be an invaluable tool for **visualizing geometric concepts**. Many geometry problems on the SAT involve **circles, lines, triangles, transformations, and coordinate geometry**, and Desmos provides a quick way to confirm solutions.

This section will cover:

- **Graphing Lines, Circles, and Polygons in Desmos**
- **Using Desmos for Distance, Midpoint, and Slope Calculations**
- **Visualizing Transformations (Reflections, Rotations, Translations)**
- **SAT Problem-Solving with Desmos**

1. Graphing Lines, Circles, and Polygons in Desmos

A. Graphing a Line in Slope-Intercept Form

The **slope-intercept form** of a line is:

$$y = mx + b$$

where:

- m is the **slope** (rise/run)
- b is the **y-intercept**

Example 1: Graphing a Line

Graph the equation $y = 2x - 3$ in Desmos.

1. Open Desmos and enter:

   y = 2x - 3

2. Identify the **y-intercept (0, -3)**.
3. Use the slope **rise 2, run 1** to plot more points.

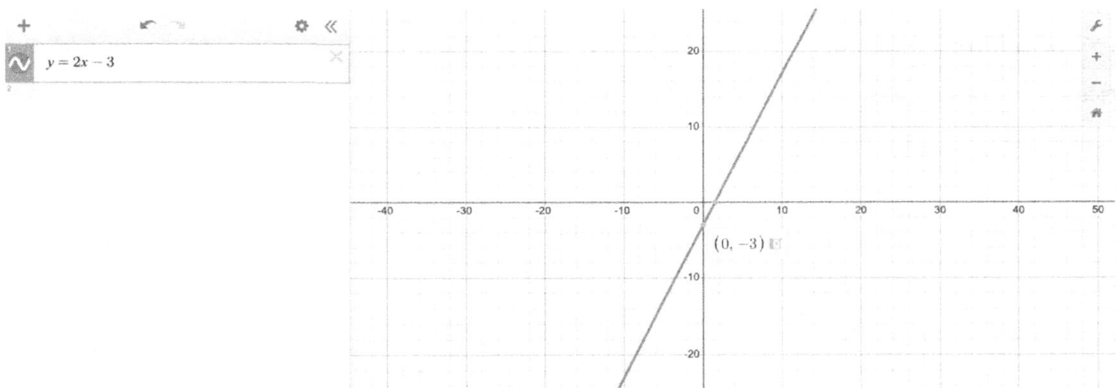

Key SAT Application: Use Desmos to **confirm linear equations** and **find intersections between two lines.**

B. Graphing a Circle in Desmos

The **standard equation of a circle** is:

$$(x - h)^2 + (y - k)^2 = r^2$$

where:

- (h, k) is the **center**
- r is the **radius**

Example 2: Graphing a Circle

Graph the circle centered at **(2, -1)** with a radius of **5**.

1. Open Desmos and enter:

$$(x-2)^2+(y+1)^2=25$$

2. The circle is centered at **(2, -1)** and has a radius of **5**.

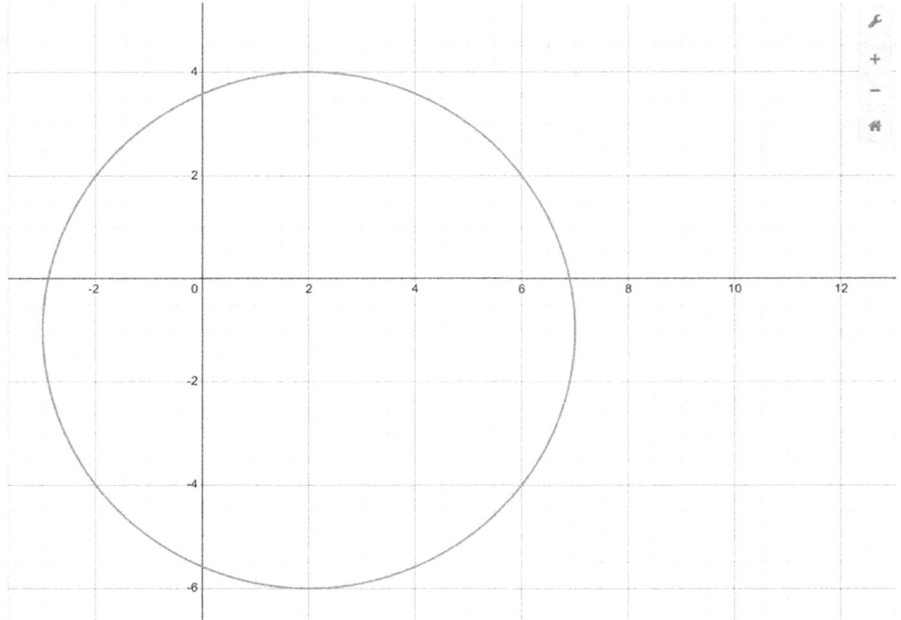

Key SAT Application: Quickly check circle equations and **find points of intersection with lines**.

C. Plotting Polygons in Desmos

Example 3: Graphing a Triangle

Graph a triangle with **vertices (0,0), (4,0), and (2,3)**.

1. Open Desmos and enter:

$$polygon\ ((0,0),(4,0),(2,3))$$

2. Desmos will create a **closed triangle**.

polygon((0,0),(4,0),(2,3))

Key SAT Application:

- Find **triangle side lengths using Desmos distance formula**.
- Confirm **similarity and congruence transformations**.

2. Using Desmos for Distance, Midpoint, and Slope Calculations

A. Distance Formula

The distance between two points (x_1, y_1) and (x_2, y_2) is:

$$d = \sqrt{(x_2 - x_1)^2 + (y_2 - y_1)^2}$$

Example 4: Finding Distance Between Two Points

Find the distance between **(1,2) and (4,6)**.

1. Open Desmos and enter:

$$\sqrt{(4-1)^2 + (6-2)^2}$$

2. The answer is 5.

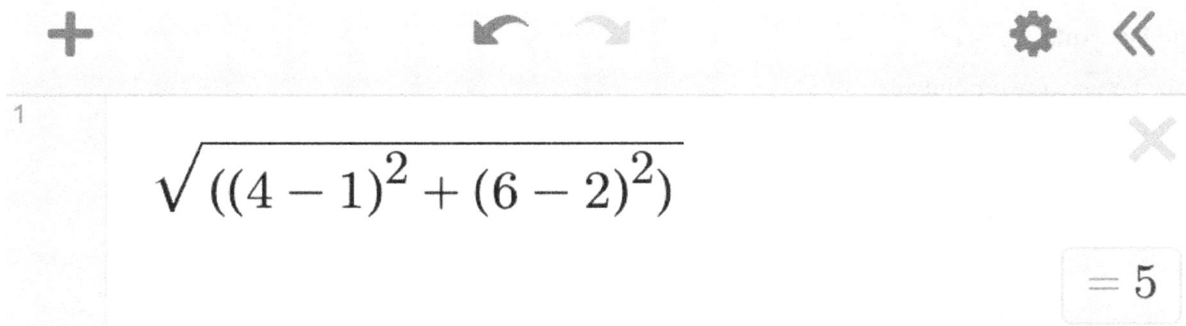

B. Midpoint Formula

The midpoint of two points is:

$$M = \left(\frac{x_1 + x_2}{2}, \frac{y_1 + y_2}{2}\right)$$

Example 5: Finding the Midpoint

Find the midpoint between **(-2, 4) and (6, 8)**.

1. Open Desmos and enter:

$$\left(\frac{(-2+6)}{2}, \frac{(4+8)}{2}\right)$$

2. The midpoint it returns is **(2,6)**.

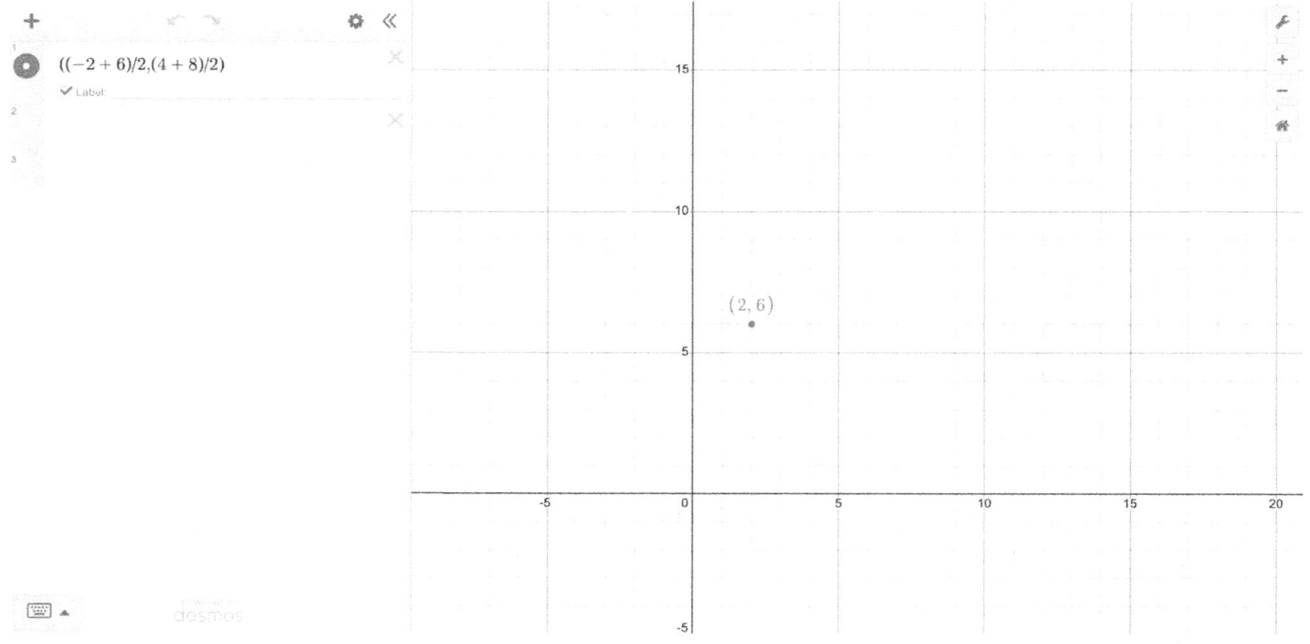

C. Slope Formula

The slope between two points is:

$$m = \frac{y_2 - y_1}{x_2 - x_1}$$

Example 6: Finding the Slope

Find the slope of a line through **(3, 7) and (6, 2)**.

1. Open Desmos and enter:

   (2 - 7) / (6 - 3)

2. The answer is $-\frac{5}{3}$.

Key SAT Application: Use Desmos for **quick calculations of distance, midpoint, and slope**, reducing algebraic errors.

3. Visualizing Transformations (Reflections, Rotations, Translations)

A. Reflections in Desmos

To reflect a function **across the x-axis**, use:

$$y = -f(x)$$

To reflect across the **y-axis**, use:

$$y = f(-x)$$

Example 7: Reflecting a Function

Reflect $y = x^2 - 4$ across the **x-axis**.

1. Open Desmos and enter:

$$y = -(x_2 - 4)$$

2. The new graph **flips over the x-axis**.

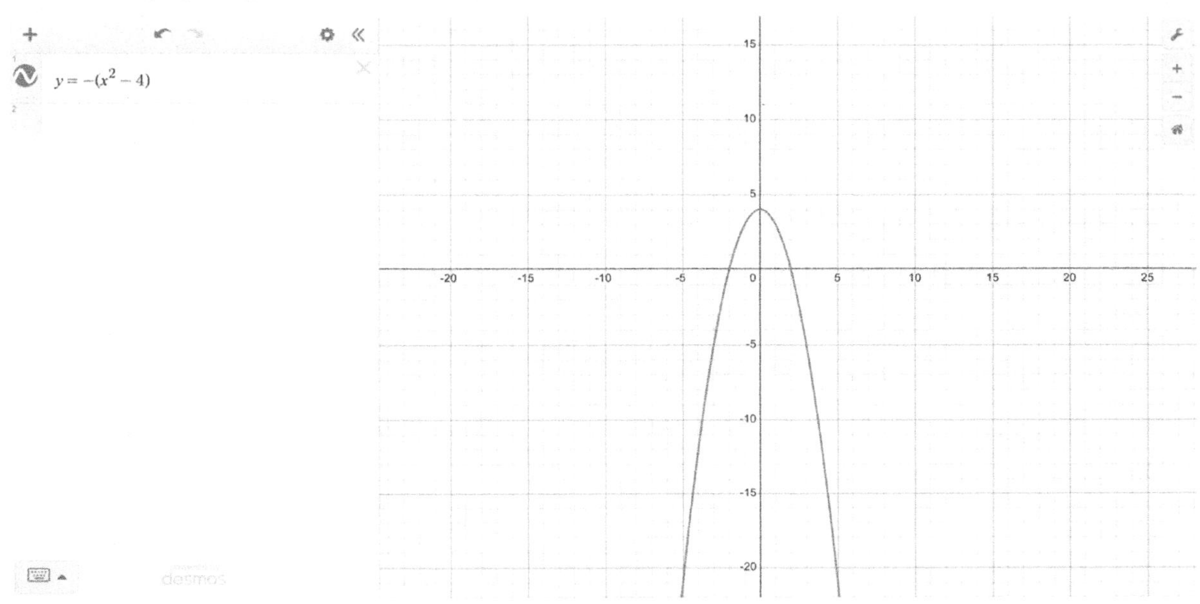

B. Translations in Desmos

To shift a function **up/down by k**:

$$y = f(x) + k$$

To shift **left/right by h**:

$$y = f(x - h)$$

Example 8: Translating a Function

Shift $y = x^2$ **2 units right and 3 units up**.

1. Open Desmos and enter:

$$\mathrm{y} = (\mathrm{x} - 2)^2 + 3$$

2. The parabola moves **right and up**.

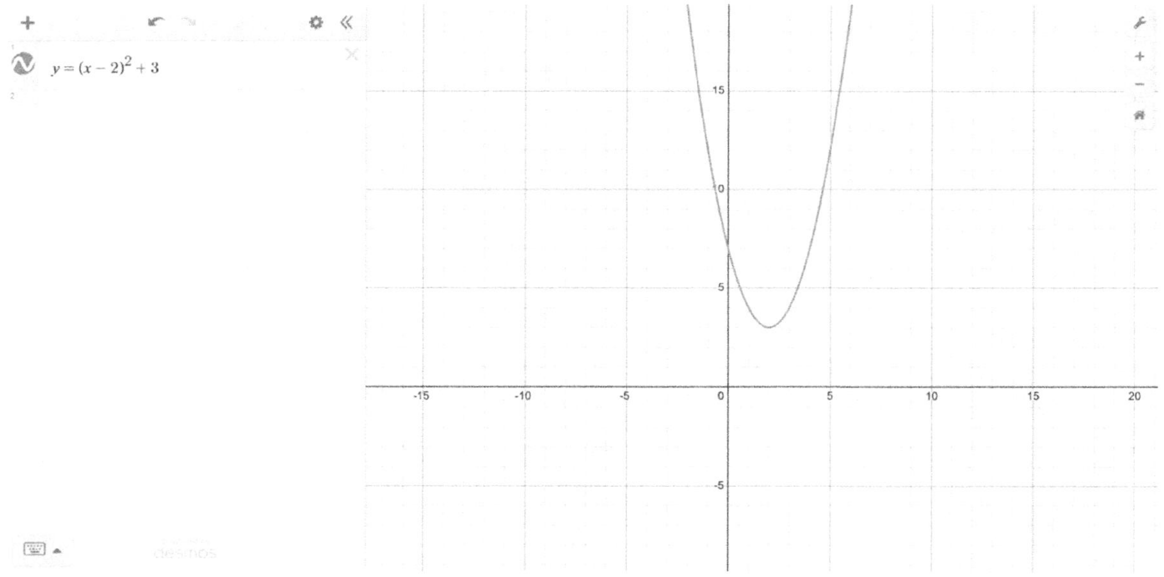

4. SAT Problem-Solving with Desmos

A. Finding Intersections Between Functions

If two functions are given, find their intersection points.

Example 9: Finding Intersection of Two Equations

Find where $y = x^2 - 3x + 2$ **and** $y = 2x - 5$ **intersect.**

1. Open Desmos and enter:

$$y = x^2 - 3x + 2$$

$$y = 2x - 4$$

2. Identify where the graphs **cross**.

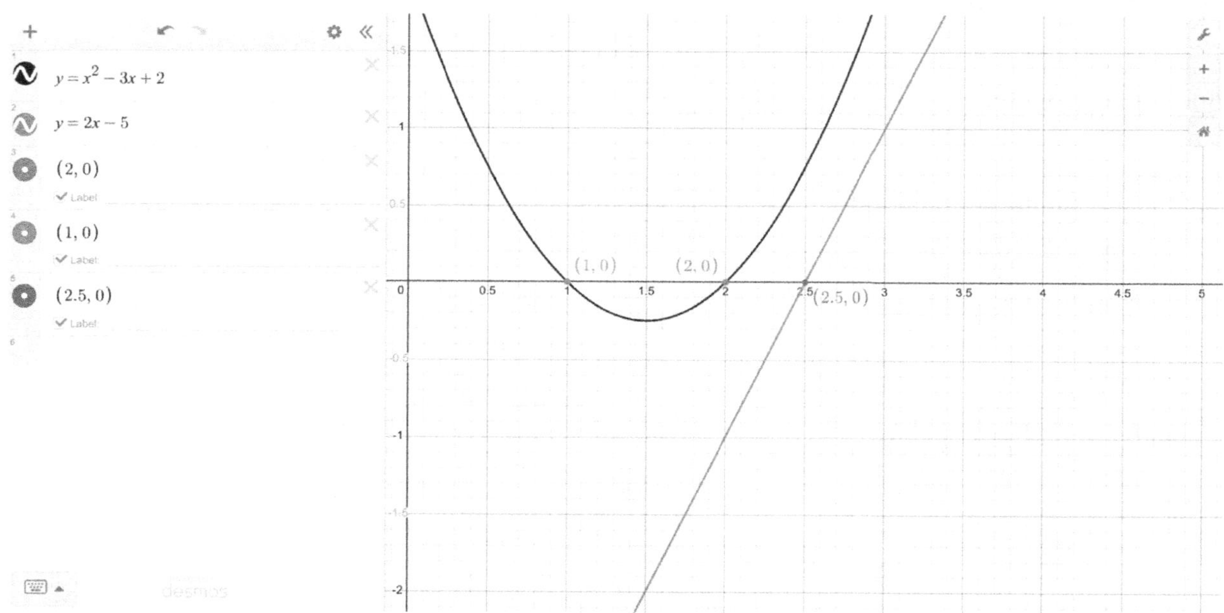

B. Solving Quadratics with Desmos

Instead of using the **quadratic formula**, graph the function and find **x-intercepts**.

Example 10: Solving $x^2 - 5x + 6 = 0$

1. Open Desmos and enter: $$y = x^2 - 5x + 6$$
2. Identify **x-values where the graph crosses the x-axis.**
3. The solutions are $x = 2$ **and** $x = 3$.

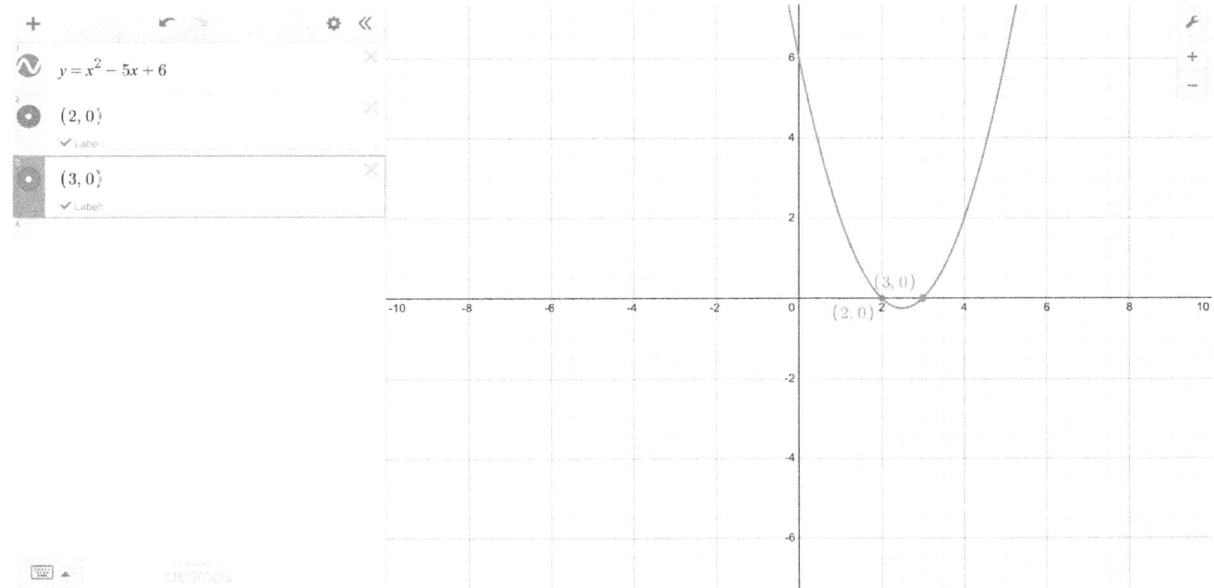

5. Summary of Key Strategies

Concept	Desmos Strategy
Graphing Lines	Enter the equation in slope-intercept form
Graphing Circles	Use the equation $(x - h)^2 + (y - k)^2 = r^2$
Distance & Midpoint	Use Desmos functions to compute quickly
Reflections & Translations	Modify equations using $f(x)$ transformations
Finding Intersections	Graph both equations and identify crossing points

6. Final Key Takeaways

- **Desmos is a powerful tool for visualizing geometry concepts**, from **lines and circles to transformations and distance calculations**.
- **Use Desmos to check solutions** for equations, intersections, and graph-based problems.
- **For SAT problems involving functions, graphing in Desmos can save time** and reduce algebraic errors.
- **Practice using Desmos before test day** to maximize efficiency during the SAT Math section.

By **mastering Desmos for geometry**, students can **increase accuracy, improve problem-solving speed, and confidently tackle SAT geometry questions**.

CHAPTER 15

STRATEGIES FOR MATH SUCCESS

15.1 Pacing and Organization in Adaptive Modules

The **Digital SAT Math section** is **adaptive**, meaning **Module 2 changes in difficulty based on performance in Module 1**. Efficient **pacing and organization** are crucial to ensuring that students **answer all questions accurately within the time limit** while maximizing their potential score.

This section will cover:

- **Understanding Time Constraints and Adaptive Scoring**
- **Pacing Strategies for Module 1 and Module 2**
- **Managing Difficult Questions and Time Allocation**
- **Best Practices for Staying Organized**

1. Understanding Time Constraints and Adaptive Scoring

The **Digital SAT Math section** consists of two **adaptive modules**, each with **22 questions and 35 minutes**, for a total of **44 questions in 70 minutes**.

Module	Number of Questions	Time Per Module	Average Time Per Question
Module 1	22	35 minutes	~1 minute 35 seconds
Module 2	22	35 minutes	~1 minute 35 seconds

Since the **difficulty of Module 2 depends on Module 1 performance**, pacing **in Module 1 is crucial**. Strong performance unlocks a **harder Module 2**, leading to a **higher score range**.

Key Time Management Challenges

- **Overthinking on early questions** can **consume too much time**, leaving less time for harder problems later.
- **Skipping too many questions in Module 1** may prevent access to a **higher-scoring Module 2**.
- **Not pacing properly in Module 2** can result in **missed or rushed answers** at the end.

2. Pacing Strategies for Module 1 and Module 2

A. Module 1 Pacing Strategy: Build Momentum

- **Goal:** Answer questions **efficiently and accurately** to maximize performance.
- **Strategy:**
  - **First 10 questions (Easy/Medium):** ~12–14 minutes (**focus on speed and accuracy**).
  - **Middle 7 questions (Medium):** ~12 minutes (**slightly more complex, don't rush**).
  - **Final 5 questions (Harder):** ~8–10 minutes (**skip time-consuming ones if necessary**).

Example: How to Pace the First 5 Questions

- These are typically **basic algebra, percentages, or geometry problems**.
- Solve them **in under 1 minute each** to **bank extra time for later questions**.

B. Module 2 Pacing Strategy: Handle Increased Difficulty

- **Goal:** Adapt to either **a harder or easier module** based on Module 1 performance.
- **Strategy:**
  - **First 5 questions:** ~6–7 minutes (**build confidence, avoid careless mistakes**).
  - **Middle 10 questions:** ~14 minutes (**expect multi-step problems**).
  - **Final 7 questions:** ~12 minutes (**expect abstract or function-based problems**).

3. Managing Difficult Questions and Time Allocation

Since **some problems require multiple steps**, knowing when to **skip, flag, or return** is essential.

A. When to Skip and Return Later

- **If a problem takes longer than 90 seconds**, **flag it** and move on.
- **If a question requires complex algebraic manipulation**, check if **Desmos can be used**.
- **Skip if unsure and return only if time allows**.

Example: Skipping a Multi-Step Word Problem

If a problem requires multiple equations and calculations:

1. **Estimate a possible answer range**.
2. **Flag it if too time-consuming**, then **return if time allows**.

B. Prioritizing Easier Questions for Maximum Points

- The **SAT Math section does not penalize wrong answers**, so **answer every question**.
- Spending **too much time on one hard question** might cost you **multiple correct answers elsewhere**.

4. Best Practices for Staying Organized

A. Tracking Answer Progress

- **Flag questions** that need review but attempt them first.
- If unsure, **eliminate wrong choices first** and guess strategically.

B. Staying Focused Under Time Pressure

- **Use scratch paper for multi-step problems** to avoid confusion.
- **Write down key values and equations** before using Desmos to avoid miscalculations.

C. Mental Strategies to Maintain Confidence

- **Breathe and reset if stuck** on a difficult problem.
- **Use checkpoints every 10 questions** to ensure pacing is on track.

5. Summary of Key Strategies

Strategy	Why It Works
Build momentum in Module 1	Maximizes chances of unlocking a higher-difficulty Module 2.
Use a time breakdown for each module	Prevents running out of time.
Skip hard questions and return later	Saves time for more solvable problems.
Track time every 10 questions	Ensures even pacing throughout the section.
Use scratch paper for complex problems	Reduces careless mistakes and confusion.

6. Final Key Takeaways

- **Answer easier questions quickly** in Module 1 to maximize **accuracy and pacing**.
- **If stuck on a question, flag it and move on**, then return if time allows.
- **Module 2 difficulty depends on Module 1 performance**, so **early accuracy is crucial**.
- **Use Desmos for complex equations but avoid unnecessary calculator use**.
- **Check your pacing every 10 questions** to stay on track.

By **mastering pacing and organization in adaptive modules**, students can efficiently **navigate the SAT Math section, optimize their time, and maximize their overall score**.

15.2 When to Use the Calculator and When Not To

The **Digital SAT Math section** allows calculator use throughout the test, with the built-in **Desmos graphing calculator** available on-screen. However, **using the calculator effectively** is crucial—while it can speed up complex calculations, over-reliance can waste time on simple problems that could be solved mentally or with algebraic techniques.

This section will cover:

- **Understanding When the Calculator Saves Time**
- **When NOT to Use the Calculator**
- **SAT Calculator Efficiency Tips**
- **Example Questions: Calculator vs. Mental Math**

1. Understanding When the Calculator Saves Time

The calculator is most useful for:

- **Complex arithmetic** (fractions, exponents, large numbers)
- **Graphing functions and finding intersections**
- **Solving equations quickly**
- **Statistical calculations (mean, standard deviation, etc.)**
- **Multi-step problems involving square roots, logs, or trigonometry**

A. Solving Equations Efficiently with Desmos

For **quadratic equations** or equations with multiple variables, using Desmos to **graph both sides and find intersections** can be **faster than factoring or using the quadratic formula**.

Example 1: Solving a Quadratic Equation Using Desmos

Solve $x^2 - 5x + 6 = 0$.

1. Enter in Desmos:

$$y = x^2 - 5x + 6$$

2. Find where the graph crosses the **x-axis**.
3. The solutions are $x = 2, x = 3$.

Final Answer: $x = 2,3$

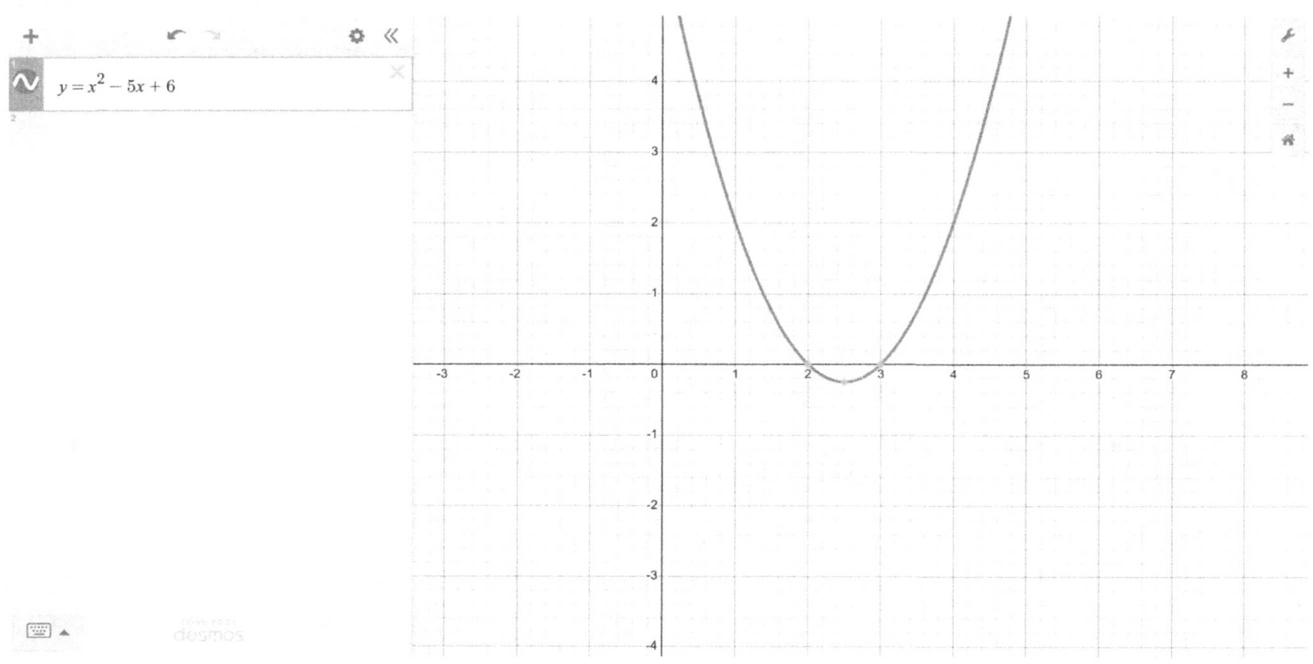

Key Takeaway:

- If an equation can be **factored quickly**, do it manually.
- If factoring is **not obvious**, graph in Desmos to find the **x-intercepts**.

B. Graphing Systems of Equations

Graphing is **faster than substitution or elimination** when solving systems of equations.

Example 2: Solving a System of Equations

Solve for x and y:

$$y = 2x + 3$$
$$y = -x + 5$$

1. Enter both equations into Desmos:

$$y = 2x + 3$$
$$y = -x + 5$$

2. Find where the graphs **intersect**.
3. The intersection is at $(1,5)$.

Final Answer: $x = 1, y = 5$

Key Takeaway:

- **Use the calculator when solving systems algebraically takes too long**.
- If both equations are in **y = mx + b form**, **graph them** to find their intersection.

2. When NOT to Use the Calculator

The calculator is **not needed** when:

- A problem involves **simple arithmetic** (e.g., 7×8, $45 \div 5$)
- The equation can be **solved quickly with algebra**
- A problem requires **recognizing a pattern** rather than computation
- A question is about **concepts rather than calculations**

A. Mental Math for Simple Arithmetic

Example 3: Evaluating an Expression

Compute $24 \div 8 + 5 \times 3$.

1. Division first:

$$24 \div 8 = 3$$

2. Multiplication next:

$$5 \times 3 = 15$$

3. Add:

$$3 + 15 = 18$$

Final Answer: 18

Key Takeaway:

- **Basic operations should be done mentally** to save time.

- **Using a calculator for simple math slows you down.**

B. Avoiding Calculator Overuse for Fractions

Example 4: Simplifying a Fraction Without a Calculator

Simplify $\frac{36}{48}$.

1. Find the **greatest common factor (GCF)**:
    - GCF of 36 and 48 is **12**.
2. Divide both numerator and denominator by 12:

$$\frac{36 \div 12}{48 \div 12} = \frac{3}{4}$$

Final Answer: $\frac{3}{4}$

Key Takeaway:

- **Use mental math for simple fraction reductions** instead of the calculator.
- **If the numbers are large, then use the calculator for division.**

3. SAT Calculator Efficiency Tips

Task	Best Approach
Basic arithmetic (addition, subtraction, multiplication, division)	Mental math (no calculator needed)
Complex fractions, square roots, exponents	Use Desmos or a scientific calculator
Solving equations (linear, quadratic, systems of equations)	Graph functions in Desmos for quick solutions
Finding intersections of functions	Graph both equations and find points of intersection
Percentage problems	Use the percentage formula manually unless large numbers are involved
Statistics (mean, standard deviation, etc.)	Calculator is useful for long calculations

4. Example Questions: Calculator vs. Mental Math

A. When the Calculator Helps

A researcher collects data on **cell phone battery life**. A phone lasts **4.5 hours** on a **full charge**, and the power decreases by **3% per hour**. How much battery remains after **5 hours**?

Using **exponential decay formula**:

$$P = P_0(1 - r)^t$$

where:

- $P_0 = 100\%$
- $r = 0.03$
- $t = 5$

Using Desmos:

100 * (1 - 0.03)^5

Final result: **85.87% battery remaining**.

B. When Mental Math is Faster

What is **15% of 80**?

1. Convert **15% to a decimal**:

$$0.15$$

2. Multiply:

$$0.15 \times 80 = 12$$

Final Answer: 12

Using a calculator would take **longer than mental math**.

5. Summary of Key Strategies

Concept	Best Strategy
Simple math operations	Solve mentally to save time
Equations with complex numbers	Use Desmos or a calculator
Finding intersections of functions	Graph in Desmos instead of solving manually
Percentage and fraction simplifications	Use mental math or quick shortcuts when possible
Word problems involving exponential functions	Use Desmos for quick calculations

6. Final Key Takeaways

- **The SAT allows calculators, but using them wisely is key**—overuse can slow you down.
- **Use Desmos for solving equations, graphing, and finding intersections** efficiently.
- **Mental math should be used for basic calculations, fractions, and percentages**.
- **Knowing when to use vs. not use the calculator** improves pacing and ensures more time for complex questions.
- **Practice using Desmos before test day** to become **familiar with graphing and solving equations quickly**.

By **mastering calculator efficiency**, students can **increase their SAT Math speed, reduce errors, and maximize their overall score**.

15.3 Avoiding Common Math Pitfalls: Misreading Graphs & Data

The **Digital SAT Math section** often includes questions that require students to **interpret graphs, tables, and charts**. A significant number of errors occur **not because of difficult calculations, but due to misreading the given data**. Mastering **data interpretation strategies** can help prevent these common mistakes and improve accuracy.

This section will cover:

- **Common Mistakes When Interpreting Graphs and Tables**
- **Understanding Scales, Units, and Labels**
- **Recognizing Trends and Avoiding False Assumptions**
- **SAT Strategies to Improve Accuracy on Graph and Data Questions**

1. Common Mistakes When Interpreting Graphs and Tables

Many students make **avoidable mistakes** when answering questions based on **bar graphs, line charts, scatterplots, and tables**. Below are the most frequent errors:

A. Confusing Different Data Sets

- **Mistake:** Selecting data from the wrong column, row, or category.
- **Solution:** Always **double-check labels** before making calculations.

Example 1: Misreading a Table

Year	Total Sales (Million $)	Online Sales (Million $)	In-Store Sales (Million $)
2020	150	50	100
2021	180	70	110
2022	210	90	120

Question: What was the increase in online sales from 2020 to 2022?

- **Common Mistake:** Some students mistakenly look at **Total Sales** instead of **Online Sales**.
- **Correct Calculation:**

$$90 - 50 = 40 \text{ million dollars}$$

Final Answer: 40 million dollars

B. Ignoring Axis Scales on Graphs

- **Mistake:** Assuming each tick mark represents **one unit** when the graph actually represents **larger intervals**.
- **Solution:** Always **check the scale on both axes** before making conclusions.

Example 2: Misreading a Line Graph Scale

A line graph tracks **population growth over time**, and the **y-axis scale increases by 10,000 per unit**. A student mistakenly assumes it increases by 1,000, leading to **miscalculations in the growth rate**.

Key SAT Strategy:

- Always **identify what each unit on the graph represents** before making estimates or calculations.

2. Understanding Scales, Units, and Labels

A. Checking the Units of Measurement

- **Mistake:** Mixing different units (e.g., **miles vs. kilometers**, **minutes vs. hours**).
- **Solution:** Convert all measurements to a **common unit** before solving.

Example 3: Incorrect Unit Conversion

A car travels **60 miles per hour**. A graph shows the **distance in kilometers**. If 1 mile = 1.609 km, how far does the car travel in **2 hours**?

1. Convert miles to kilometers:

$$60 \times 1.609 = 96.54 \text{ km per hour}$$

2. Multiply by 2 hours:

$$96.54 \times 2 = 193.08 \text{ km}$$

Final Answer: 193.08 km

B. Recognizing Percentage vs. Actual Value

- **Mistake:** Confusing percentage change with actual value change.
- **Solution:** Convert percentages into **actual numbers before making conclusions**.

Example 4: Understanding Percentage Change

A store increases sales from **500 units to 600 units**. A student mistakenly thinks this is a **600% increase** instead of a **20% increase**.

$$\text{Percentage Increase} = \frac{\text{New Value} - \text{Old Value}}{\text{Old Value}} \times 100$$

$$= \frac{600 - 500}{500} \times 100 = \frac{100}{500} \times 100 = 20\%$$

Final Answer: 20% increase, not 600%

3. Recognizing Trends and Avoiding False Assumptions

A. Correlation vs. Causation

- **Mistake:** Assuming **correlation implies causation** (i.e., one event directly causes another).
- **Solution:** Look for **additional context** before making conclusions.

Example 5: Misinterpreting Correlation in a Scatterplot

A scatterplot shows that **students who sleep more tend to score higher on the SAT**.

- **Incorrect Conclusion:** "Sleeping longer **causes** higher SAT scores."
- **Correct Conclusion:** "There is a **correlation** between sleep and SAT scores, but other factors (like study habits) might also play a role."

Key SAT Strategy:

- If a question asks **whether one factor causes another**, check if there is **enough evidence** beyond just a correlation.

B. Identifying Trends in Data

- **Mistake:** Misreading whether a trend is **increasing, decreasing, or fluctuating**.
- **Solution:** Carefully analyze the **entire dataset** before making judgments.

Example 6: Identifying a Trend in a Table

Year	Temperature (°F)
2019	60
2020	62
2021	61
2022	65

- **Incorrect Answer:** "Temperatures increase every year."
- **Correct Answer:** "Temperatures fluctuate but show an **overall increasing trend**."

4. SAT Strategies to Improve Accuracy on Graph and Data Questions

Common Mistake	Strategy to Avoid It
Misreading the **table column or row**	Double-check labels before selecting an answer.
Ignoring the **graph scale**	Always check **units and intervals** before interpreting data.
Assuming **percentage and actual values are the same**	Convert percentages into real numbers first.

Confusing **correlation with causation**	Correlation does **not always imply causation**.
Misidentifying trends	Look at **all the data points** before making a conclusion.

5. Summary of Key Strategies

Concept	**Best Strategy**
Interpreting Tables & Graphs	Double-check labels and read all values carefully.
Understanding Graph Scales	Identify axis intervals before making calculations.
Avoiding Correlation Mistakes	Check if the question is asking for **correlation vs. causation**.
Recognizing Trends	Look at **multiple data points, not just one change**.
Percentage Problems	Convert percentages into actual numbers before solving.

6. Final Key Takeaways

- **Carefully read tables and graphs** to avoid simple misinterpretations.
- **Check axis labels, scales, and units** before making calculations.
- **Convert percentages into real numbers** to prevent common percentage errors.
- **Correlation does not imply causation**—look for **additional supporting evidence**.
- **Analyze the full dataset** before drawing conclusions about trends.

By **avoiding common pitfalls when interpreting graphs and data**, students can **improve their SAT accuracy and ensure they are answering questions based on correct assumptions and interpretations**.

15.4 Smart Guessing: Elimination Tactics and Checking Work

The **Digital SAT Math section** does not penalize for incorrect answers, meaning **students should always answer every question**. When unsure of an answer, using **strategic guessing and elimination tactics** can significantly improve accuracy.

This section will cover:

- **Why Smart Guessing is Essential on the SAT**
- **Elimination Strategies for Multiple-Choice Questions**
- **Checking Work for Common Errors**
- **How to Make an Educated Guess in Grid-In Questions**

1. Why Smart Guessing is Essential on the SAT

A. No Penalty for Guessing

Unlike older versions of the SAT, the **Digital SAT has no penalty for incorrect answers**.

- **Leaving a question blank = 0% chance of getting it right**.
- **Guessing randomly = 25% chance on multiple-choice** (1 in 4).
- **Guessing with elimination = 50–75% chance of success**.

2. Elimination Strategies for Multiple-Choice Questions

A. Step-by-Step Process for Eliminating Wrong Answers

4. **Scan answer choices before solving**—sometimes you can eliminate choices immediately.
5. **Check for extreme or illogical values**—the SAT rarely uses **absolute extremes**.
6. **Substitute answer choices into the equation (if applicable)** to test correctness.
7. **Use estimation to eliminate obviously wrong choices**.

B. Recognizing Common Wrong Answer Traps

Trap Type	Description	Example
Too Large/Too Small	An answer is **unrealistically high or low**	The population of a town is increasing by 5% annually. If the current population is 10,000, which is closest to the population in 5 years? (Answer choices: **10,500, 12,763, 100,000, 1,000,000 → Eliminate 100,000 and 1,000,000**)
Sign Error	The correct answer is positive, but a negative option is given	Solve for x: $-3x = 9$. (Answer choices: **-3, 3, 6, -6 → Eliminate -3 and -6**)
Irrelevant Calculation	Some choices are based on performing **the wrong operation**	A rectangle has an area of 24 and a width of 4. What is its length? (Answer choices: **6, 20, 28, 12 → Eliminate choices that use addition instead of division**)

C. Example: Using Elimination to Narrow Choices

Question:
Solve for x:

$$5x + 3 = 23$$

Answer choices:
(A) 3, (B) 4, (C) 5, (D) 6

1. **Estimate**: Since **5x must be close to 20**, x should be **around 4**.
2. **Test** $x = 3$ **(A)**:

$$5(3) + 3 = 15 + 3 = 18$$

   Wrong—eliminate A.
3. **Test** $x = 4$ **(B)**:

$$5(4) + 3 = 20 + 3 = 23$$

   Correct answer is **(B) 4**.

By **eliminating options before solving completely**, students can **save time and increase accuracy**.

3. Checking Work for Common Errors

Many SAT mistakes come from **misreading the problem, sign errors, or miscalculations**.

A. Common Calculation Errors to Watch For

Error Type	Example	How to Check Work
Sign Mistakes	$-x = 5$ mistakenly solved as $x = 5$ instead of $x = -5$	Check negatives carefully
Distributive Property Mistakes	$3(x + 2) = 3x + 2$ (should be $3x + 6$)	Expand parentheses step-by-step
Order of Operations Mistakes	$4 + 3 \times 2 = 14$ (should be 10)	Use PEMDAS (Parentheses, Exponents, Multiplication/Division, Addition/Subtraction)

Misreading a Word Problem	"Twice the sum of x and 3" written as $2x + 3$ instead of $2(x + 3)$	Carefully translate words into math

Example: Checking for a Sign Error

Solve for x:

$$-2x + 6 = 12$$

1. Subtract 6 from both sides:

$$-2x = 6$$

2. **Divide by -2**:

$$x = -3$$

If a student mistakenly wrote $x = 3$, **double-checking signs** would catch the error.

4. How to Make an Educated Guess in Grid-In Questions

Grid-in questions do not have answer choices, but **educated guessing can still be used**.

A. Key Strategies for Grid-In Guessing

1. **Eliminate impossible values**—if a question asks for **a positive number**, **negative values can be ignored**.
2. **Estimate answers when exact calculations are too slow**.
3. **Use answer choices from previous multiple-choice questions as hints**—sometimes the SAT reuses answer structures.

B. Example: Guessing a Grid-In Answer with Estimation

A rectangle has an **area of 84 square inches** and a **length of 12 inches**. Estimate its width.

1. Use the formula:

$$A = \text{length} \times \text{width}$$

$$84 = 12 \times w$$

2. **Estimate** w:
    - $12 \times 7 = 84$, so $w = 7$.

Final Answer: 7

5. Summary of Key Strategies

Strategy	Why It Works
Use elimination for multiple-choice	Increases probability of selecting the correct answer
Look for extreme or unrealistic values	SAT rarely has very large or small answers
Estimate answers before solving fully	Saves time and prevents miscalculations
Check signs and calculations	Eliminates common algebra errors
Use logical reasoning for grid-in questions	Helps avoid impossible or unreasonable guesses

6. Final Key Takeaways

- **Eliminate wrong answers first** to improve guessing accuracy.
- **Estimate before solving completely**—this prevents miscalculations.

- **Check work for sign errors, order of operations mistakes, and misread word problems**.
- **Use the process of elimination for grid-in questions** by ruling out unreasonable values.
- **Never leave a question blank**—even a random guess gives you a **25% chance on multiple-choice and some chance on grid-ins**.

By **applying elimination tactics and checking work systematically**, students can **reduce careless mistakes and improve accuracy on the SAT Math section**.

PART IV

PRACTICE EXERCISES AND FULL-LENGTH TESTS

CHAPTER 16

FOUNDATIONAL PRACTICE EXERCISES

16.1 Warm-Up Drills for Reading Comprehension

The **Digital SAT Reading & Writing section** requires strong reading comprehension skills to quickly extract key information from short passages and answer questions efficiently. To build these skills, warm-up drills should focus on:

- **Identifying main ideas and key details**
- **Recognizing tone, style, and purpose**
- **Making logical inferences**
- **Understanding vocabulary in context**

This section provides **targeted practice drills** to help students **increase reading speed, comprehension, and accuracy**.

1. Drill: Identifying the Main Idea

The **main idea** is the central point or argument the author is making. To find it, focus on:

- **The first and last sentences** of the passage
- **Repeated themes or key phrases**
- **The author's purpose (inform, persuade, entertain, or explain)**

Warm-Up Practice Exercises: Finding the Main Idea

Q.1 -

Passage:

Renewable energy sources, such as solar and wind power, are increasingly seen as the future of electricity generation. With growing concerns about climate change and depleting fossil fuels, many governments are investing heavily in sustainable technologies. The shift towards renewables is expected to reduce greenhouse gas emissions and promote environmental sustainability.

Question: What is the main idea of the passage?

(A) Renewable energy sources are unreliable compared to fossil fuels.

(B) Governments are hesitant to invest in renewable energy.

(C) Renewable energy is a promising solution to environmental challenges.

(D) Fossil fuels are completely outdated.

Q.2 -

Passage:

Regular physical activity not only benefits physical health by reducing the risk of chronic diseases but also plays a crucial role in improving mental well-being. Studies indicate that exercise can alleviate symptoms of depression and anxiety by releasing endorphins and enhancing mood. Consequently, incorporating regular physical activity into daily routines is increasingly recommended by health professionals.

Question: What is the main idea of the passage?

(A) Exercise is only important for physical health.

(B) Regular exercise has positive effects on both physical and mental health.

(C) Endorphins are the only benefit of exercise.

(D) Health professionals are unsure about the benefits of exercise.

Q.3 -

Passage:

Social media has revolutionized the way people communicate by enabling instant sharing of information across the globe. While it has enhanced connectivity and provided platforms for diverse voices, critics argue that it has also contributed to superficial interactions and the spread of misinformation. Nevertheless, social media continues to be an integral part of modern communication.

Question: What is the main idea of the passage?

(A) Social media is the sole source of misinformation.

(B) Social media has both positive and negative effects on communication.

(C) People should avoid social media to have meaningful interactions.

(D) The global impact of social media is minimal.

Q.4 -

Passage:

TechNova, a leading technology firm, recently unveiled its latest innovation: a wearable device that monitors vital health metrics in real-time. This breakthrough product combines advanced sensors with artificial intelligence to provide personalized health insights, revolutionizing how individuals manage their well-being.

Question: What is the main idea of the passage?

(A) TechNova's previous products were ineffective.

(B) The new wearable device is a significant innovation in personal health management.

(C) Artificial intelligence is difficult to integrate with health monitoring.

(D) Wearable devices are becoming obsolete.

Q.5 -

Passage:

The invention of the printing press in the 15th century marked a pivotal moment in history. By enabling the mass production of books, it democratized access to information, facilitated the spread of knowledge, and played a crucial role in the Reformation and scientific revolution.

Question: What is the main idea of the passage?

(A) The printing press was invented in the 15th century.

(B) The printing press is the sole cause of modern democracy.

(C) The printing press revolutionized the dissemination of knowledge and influenced major historical movements.

(D) The invention of the printing press had little effect on society.

Q.6 -

Passage:

Many environmentalists argue that preserving natural habitats is essential for maintaining biodiversity. Protecting these ecosystems not only safeguards countless species from extinction but also ensures that natural processes, such as pollination and water purification, continue uninterrupted. Conservation efforts are therefore vital for sustaining life on Earth.

Question: What is the main idea of the passage?

(A) Biodiversity is irrelevant to ecosystem function.

(B) Natural habitats are only important for rare species.

(C) Protecting natural habitats is crucial for preserving biodiversity and essential ecological processes.

(D) Environmental conservation hinders human progress.

Q.7 -

Passage:

Recent debates over education reform have centered on the need for a more holistic approach to learning. Advocates argue that traditional methods, which emphasize rote memorization, should be replaced with strategies that foster critical thinking, creativity, and problem-solving skills. This shift aims to better prepare students for the complexities of the modern world.

Question: What is the main idea of the passage?

(A) Rote memorization is the best method for education.

(B) Education reform should focus on a holistic approach that develops critical thinking and creativity.

(C) The modern world does not require problem-solving skills.

(D) Traditional education methods are sufficient for today's challenges.

Q.8 -

Passage:

With the growing global population, sustainable agriculture has become a pressing issue. By employing eco-friendly practices such as crop rotation, organic farming, and reduced pesticide use, farmers can produce food in a way that minimizes environmental impact while ensuring long-term productivity. This approach not only preserves soil health but also promotes food security.

Question: What is the main idea of the passage?

(A) Conventional farming methods are more efficient than sustainable agriculture.

(B) Sustainable agriculture is a critical practice for reducing environmental impact and promoting food security.

(C) Organic farming is the only method to achieve sustainable agriculture.

(D) Crop rotation is an outdated practice.

Q.9 -

Passage:

Throughout history, art has served as a powerful medium for expressing cultural identity and emotions. From painting and sculpture to literature and music, artistic expression allows individuals to communicate ideas that transcend language barriers. This universal form of expression enriches society by fostering empathy and understanding among diverse groups.

Question: What is the main idea of the passage?

(A) Art is exclusively about personal expression.

(B) Artistic expression only benefits the cultural elite.

(C) Art is a universal medium that communicates ideas and fosters understanding across cultures.

(D) Visual art is superior to other forms of artistic expression.

Q.10 -

Passage:

The trend towards remote work has accelerated in recent years, driven by advances in technology and shifting attitudes towards work-life balance. Companies are increasingly adopting flexible work arrangements that allow employees to work from anywhere, leading to a reevaluation of traditional office spaces. This shift is reshaping the future of employment and workplace culture.

Question: What is the main idea of the passage?

(A) Remote work is a temporary trend that will soon fade.

(B) Advances in technology have made traditional offices obsolete.

(C) The rise of remote work is transforming employment practices and workplace culture.

(D) Work-life balance is no longer a priority in modern workplaces.

Q.11 -

Passage:

Global policies aimed at mitigating climate change have become a central focus of international relations. Governments are collaborating on initiatives to reduce carbon emissions, invest in renewable energy, and protect vulnerable ecosystems. These efforts reflect a growing recognition of the need to address environmental challenges on a global scale.

Question: What is the main idea of the passage?

(A) Climate change is solely the responsibility of individual nations.

(B) International collaboration is crucial for addressing the challenges of climate change.
(C) Renewable energy is the only solution to climate change.
(D) Carbon emissions cannot be reduced effectively.

Q.12 -

Passage:

Recent advances in medical technology have significantly improved patient outcomes. Innovations such as robotic surgery, telemedicine, and personalized treatment plans have enhanced the precision and effectiveness of healthcare. These developments are paving the way for a future where medical care is more efficient and tailored to individual needs.

Question: What is the main idea of the passage?
(A) Medical technology has become overly complex and expensive.
(B) Traditional methods of medical treatment remain superior.
(C) Advances in medical technology are transforming healthcare by improving patient outcomes.
(D) Telemedicine is replacing all traditional healthcare practices.

Q.13 -

Passage:

Reading offers numerous benefits that extend beyond simple entertainment. It enhances vocabulary, stimulates mental processes, and improves concentration. Moreover, reading allows individuals to explore diverse perspectives, fostering empathy and critical thinking skills. These benefits make reading an essential activity for personal development.

Question: What is the main idea of the passage?
(A) Reading is only a leisure activity with minimal benefits.
(B) The primary benefit of reading is improving vocabulary.
(C) Reading is a valuable activity that contributes to personal and intellectual growth.
(D) Concentration is the only skill improved by reading.

Q.14 -

Passage:

Incorporating technology into the classroom has transformed traditional educational methods. Interactive tools, digital textbooks, and online resources have made learning more engaging and accessible for students. This integration not only enhances the learning experience but also equips students with essential digital skills for the future.

Question: What is the main idea of the passage?
(A) Technology in classrooms has complicated the learning process.
(B) Digital textbooks have replaced traditional teaching methods.
(C) The integration of technology in education improves both engagement and skill development.
(D) Online resources are less effective than traditional textbooks.

Q.15 -

Passage:

Community gardens have emerged as a popular solution to urban food deserts and environmental challenges. These gardens provide residents with access to fresh produce, promote community engagement, and contribute to greener urban spaces. As a result, they play a vital role in enhancing both social and environmental well-being in cities.

Question: What is the main idea of the passage?
(A) Urban areas have no need for community gardens.
(B) Community gardens are primarily recreational spaces.
(C) Community gardens address urban food scarcity and enhance social and environmental well-being.
(D) Fresh produce is the only benefit provided by community gardens.

Q.16 -

Passage:
Recent studies have highlighted a growing gap between the wealthy and the poor. Economic inequality has far-reaching implications, affecting access to education, healthcare, and opportunities for social mobility. Addressing this disparity is essential for fostering a more equitable and prosperous society.

Question: What is the main idea of the passage?

(A) Economic inequality has no real impact on society.

(B) The gap between the wealthy and the poor is narrowing.

(C) Economic inequality poses significant challenges that must be addressed to promote social fairness.

(D) Access to education is unaffected by economic disparity.

Q.17 -

Passage:
Space exploration continues to captivate the imagination of scientists and the public alike. Recent missions have yielded valuable data about distant planets and the origins of our solar system. These discoveries not only advance our scientific knowledge but also inspire future generations to pursue careers in science and technology.

Question: What is the main idea of the passage?

(A) Space exploration is a waste of resources.

(B) Only scientists are interested in space exploration.

(C) Space exploration provides valuable scientific insights and inspires future innovation.

(D) The primary purpose of space exploration is to colonize other planets.

Q.18 -

Passage:
Over the past century, the evolution of music has reflected changes in technology, culture, and society. From the advent of radio broadcasting to the rise of digital streaming platforms, each innovation has reshaped how music is created, distributed, and enjoyed by audiences around the world. These shifts have democratized access to music and diversified artistic expression.

Question: What is the main idea of the passage?

(A) Traditional music will eventually disappear.

(B) The evolution of music is solely driven by technology.

(C) Technological and cultural shifts have transformed the music industry and broadened access to music.

(D) Digital streaming platforms are harmful to music quality.

Q.19 -

Passage:
Modern urban planning emphasizes the creation of sustainable, livable cities that balance economic growth with environmental stewardship. By integrating green spaces, efficient public transportation, and mixed-use developments, urban planners aim to enhance the quality of life for city residents while reducing environmental impact.

Question: What is the main idea of the passage?

(A) Urban planning solely focuses on economic growth.

(B) Sustainable urban planning is critical for creating livable cities that balance growth and environmental concerns.

(C) Public transportation is the only aspect of urban planning.

(D) Green spaces are more important than economic growth.

Q.20 -

Passage:
Nutrition experts emphasize that a balanced diet plays a crucial role in maintaining overall health. Consuming a variety of fruits, vegetables, whole grains, and lean proteins provides the body with essential nutrients and helps prevent chronic diseases. Adopting healthy eating habits is therefore a fundamental component of a healthy lifestyle.

Question: What is the main idea of the passage?
(A) A balanced diet is only important for weight management.
(B) Healthy eating is a minor factor in overall well-being.
(C) A balanced diet is essential for maintaining health and preventing chronic diseases.
(D) Nutrients can be obtained solely through supplements.

Answers and Explanations for Identifying the Main Idea Exercises

Q.1:

- **Correct Answer:** (C) Renewable energy is a promising solution to environmental challenges.
- **Explanation:** The passage emphasizes the growing investment in renewable energy to combat climate change and reduce emissions, positioning it as a promising solution.

Q.2:

- **Correct Answer:** (B) Regular exercise has positive effects on both physical and mental health.
- **Explanation:** The passage discusses how exercise benefits not only the body by reducing disease risk but also the mind by alleviating symptoms of depression and anxiety.

Q.3:

- **Correct Answer:** (B) Social media has both positive and negative effects on communication.
- **Explanation:** The passage outlines the dual impact of social media by highlighting both its ability to enhance connectivity and its role in spreading misinformation.

Q.4:

- **Correct Answer:** (B) The new wearable device is a significant innovation in personal health management.
- **Explanation:** The passage focuses on TechNova's latest product, emphasizing its advanced features and potential to revolutionize personal health management.

Q.5:

- **Correct Answer:** (C) The printing press revolutionized the dissemination of knowledge and influenced major historical movements.
- **Explanation:** The passage underlines how the printing press democratized information, thereby significantly impacting historical events such as the Reformation and scientific revolution.

Q.6:

- **Correct Answer:** (C) Protecting natural habitats is crucial for preserving biodiversity and essential ecological processes.
- **Explanation:** The passage stresses the importance of conservation in maintaining biodiversity and supporting processes like pollination and water purification.

Q.7:

- **Correct Answer:** (B) Education reform should focus on a holistic approach that develops critical thinking and creativity.
- **Explanation:** The passage argues that moving away from rote memorization towards methods that foster critical thinking and creativity is necessary for modern education.

Q.8:

- **Correct Answer:** (B) Sustainable agriculture is a critical practice for reducing environmental impact and promoting food security.
- **Explanation:** The passage explains how eco-friendly agricultural practices help maintain soil health and secure long-term food production while minimizing environmental damage.

Q.9:

- **Correct Answer:** (C) Art is a universal medium that communicates ideas and fosters understanding across cultures.

- **Explanation:** The passage highlights art's role in transcending language barriers and promoting empathy, thereby uniting diverse cultures.

Q.10:

- **Correct Answer:** (C) The rise of remote work is transforming employment practices and workplace culture.
- **Explanation:** The passage discusses how advances in technology and new work-life balance attitudes are reshaping traditional office setups and employment practices.

Q.11:

- **Correct Answer:** (B) International collaboration is crucial for addressing the challenges of climate change.
- **Explanation:** The passage describes how global cooperation through various initiatives is necessary to effectively tackle climate change.

Q.12:

- **Correct Answer:** (C) Advances in medical technology are transforming healthcare by improving patient outcomes.
- **Explanation:** The passage focuses on how modern innovations such as robotic surgery and telemedicine are making healthcare more efficient and personalized.

Q.13:

- **Correct Answer:** (C) Reading is a valuable activity that contributes to personal and intellectual growth.
- **Explanation:** The passage outlines the diverse benefits of reading—including enhanced vocabulary, concentration, and empathy—emphasizing its role in personal development.

Q.14:

- **Correct Answer:** (C) The integration of technology in education improves both engagement and skill development.
- **Explanation:** The passage shows how digital tools and online resources make learning more engaging and equip students with necessary digital skills.

Q.15:

- **Correct Answer:** (C) Community gardens address urban food scarcity and enhance social and environmental well-being.
- **Explanation:** The passage explains that community gardens not only provide fresh produce but also strengthen community ties and promote environmental health.

Q.16:

- **Correct Answer:** (C) Economic inequality poses significant challenges that must be addressed to promote social fairness.
- **Explanation:** The passage highlights the broad impact of economic disparities on access to education, healthcare, and social mobility, underscoring the need for change.

Q.17:

- **Correct Answer:** (C) Space exploration provides valuable scientific insights and inspires future innovation.
- **Explanation:** The passage details how discoveries from space missions expand our scientific understanding and motivate future generations to pursue science and technology.

Q.18:

- **Correct Answer:** (C) Technological and cultural shifts have transformed the music industry and broadened access to music.
- **Explanation:** The passage discusses how innovations—from radio to digital streaming—have reshaped the music industry and made it more accessible and diverse.

Q.19:

- **Correct Answer:** (B) Sustainable urban planning is critical for creating livable cities that balance growth and environmental concerns.
- **Explanation:** The passage emphasizes the importance of integrating green spaces and efficient transportation to create urban areas that balance economic and environmental priorities.

Q.20:

- **Correct Answer:** (C) A balanced diet is essential for maintaining health and preventing chronic diseases.
- **Explanation:** The passage underscores that a variety of nutritious foods is key to overall health and effective prevention of chronic conditions.

2. Drill: Recognizing Tone, Style, and Author's Purpose

The **tone** reflects the author's attitude (neutral, positive, negative), while the **purpose** explains why the passage was written.

Author's Purpose	Key Clues
To Inform	Facts, neutral tone, balanced discussion
To Persuade	Opinion, strong arguments, emotional language
To Entertain	Storytelling, humor, engaging descriptions

Warm-Up Practice Exercises: Identifying Author's Purpose

Q.1 -

Passage:

The new environmental policy, as outlined in the recent government report, meticulously details the steps necessary to reduce urban pollution. With a focus on sustainable development and stringent regulations on industrial emissions, the report reflects a clear commitment to environmental stewardship and public health.

Question: What is the primary purpose of the passage?

(A) To entertain the reader with a humorous take on government policies.

(B) To inform readers about a new environmental policy and its objectives.

(C) To criticize government efforts to control urban pollution.

(D) To describe the historical background of environmental regulations.

Q.2 -

Passage:

In a world that increasingly values individual success, the power of community volunteering stands out as a beacon of hope. Through selfless acts of service, volunteers not only help those in need but also strengthen the bonds that tie society together. The call to volunteer is a call to rebuild a more compassionate, interconnected community.

Question: What is the primary purpose of the passage?

(A) To inform readers about the historical origins of volunteerism.

(B) To entertain readers with anecdotes about volunteering mishaps.

(C) To persuade readers to engage in community volunteering by highlighting its benefits.

(D) To criticize modern society for neglecting traditional values.

Q.3 -

Passage:

While some marvel at the latest smartphone's capabilities, others wonder if the device can do more than just take selfies and order pizza. The tone of this piece is light-hearted and slightly sarcastic, as it pokes fun at our overreliance on technology for even the simplest tasks.

Question: Which best describes the tone and purpose of the passage?

(A) Humorous and critical of modern technology's trivial applications.

(B) Solemn and analytical about technological advancements.

(C) Informative and objective about smartphone features.
(D) Persuasive, urging readers to abandon technology.

Q.4 -

Passage:

In her latest essay, the author reminisces about her childhood summers spent in the countryside, emphasizing the simplicity and beauty of a life close to nature. The narrative is filled with warm nostalgia and gentle longing, inviting readers to appreciate the quiet moments often lost in the hustle of modern urban life.

Question: What is the primary purpose of the passage?
(A) To provide a factual account of rural living.
(B) To evoke nostalgia and encourage reflection on the simplicity of nature.
(C) To criticize modern urban lifestyles harshly.
(D) To persuade readers to move to the countryside.

Q.5 -

Passage:

Recent scientific studies have confirmed that human activity is accelerating climate change at an unprecedented rate. The report presents compelling evidence from multiple research teams, emphasizing the urgent need for policy reforms and global cooperation to mitigate environmental damage. The tone is serious and authoritative.

Question: What is the primary purpose of the passage?
(A) To entertain readers with personal anecdotes about climate.
(B) To inform and warn readers about the seriousness of climate change and the need for action.
(C) To dismiss concerns about environmental issues.
(D) To criticize research methodologies in climate science.

Q.6 -

Passage:

The city's new public transportation initiative, while touted as a revolutionary step forward, has left many residents frustrated. The program is marred by delays, overcrowding, and a lack of clear communication from officials. The writer's tone is critical and disapproving.

Question: What is the primary purpose of the passage?
(A) To celebrate the successes of the public transportation initiative.
(B) To inform readers about the technical specifications of the transit system.
(C) To criticize the public transportation initiative for its shortcomings.
(D) To entertain readers with humorous stories about commuting.

Q.7 -

Passage:

A recent study conducted by educational researchers reveals that integrating technology into the classroom can significantly improve student engagement. The report presents data from controlled experiments and concludes with recommendations for schools to adopt digital learning tools. The style is formal, precise, and objective.

Question: What is the primary purpose of the passage?
(A) To persuade schools to abandon traditional teaching methods entirely.
(B) To provide an objective overview of research findings on the impact of technology in education.
(C) To entertain readers with quirky classroom anecdotes.
(D) To criticize technology for distracting students.

Q.8 -

Passage:

In today's consumer-driven society, the relentless pursuit of material possessions often overshadows the true sources of happiness. The author reflects on the emptiness that can accompany excessive consumption, urging readers to seek fulfillment beyond the accumulation of goods. The tone is reflective and subtly critical of modern consumerism.

Question: What is the primary purpose of the passage?
(A) To inform readers about the latest consumer trends.
(B) To entertain with humorous anecdotes about shopping.
(C) To critique consumerism and encourage a more meaningful approach to happiness.
(D) To provide statistical data on consumer spending.

Q.9 -

Passage:

The transition to renewable energy is not merely a technological challenge but a moral imperative. The author passionately argues that embracing solar and wind power will lead to a more sustainable future, urging policymakers and citizens alike to invest in green technologies. The style is persuasive and impassioned.

Question: What is the primary purpose of the passage?
(A) To entertain readers with futuristic predictions about energy.
(B) To inform about the basic principles of renewable energy without bias.
(C) To persuade readers to support the adoption of renewable energy sources.
(D) To compare renewable energy with fossil fuels in a neutral tone.

Q.10 -

Passage:

Political campaigns often promise a revolution in governance, yet the reality is far more predictable. With witty observations and biting satire, the writer exposes the performative nature of modern politics, suggesting that campaign promises are little more than elaborate marketing ploys. The tone is sarcastic and mocking.

Question: What is the primary purpose of the passage?
(A) To praise political campaigns for their transparency.
(B) To entertain readers with a humorous and satirical critique of political campaigns.
(C) To provide a factual account of campaign strategies.
(D) To offer policy recommendations for future elections.

Q.11 -

Passage:

Despite facing numerous setbacks, individuals who persevere often emerge stronger and more resilient. The narrative is filled with inspiring examples of people overcoming adversity, and it emphasizes the importance of determination and self-belief. The tone is sincere and motivational.

Question: What is the primary purpose of the passage?
(A) To entertain readers with dramatic personal stories.
(B) To inform about the psychological effects of adversity.
(C) To motivate and inspire readers by highlighting the power of perseverance.
(D) To criticize society for not supporting those in need.

Q.12 -

Passage:

Social media platforms are awash with trends that are as fleeting as they are bizarre. From dance challenges to viral memes, the digital landscape is a constant parade of absurdity. The author's tone is humorous and ironic, offering a wry commentary on the ever-changing world of online trends.

Question: What is the primary purpose of the passage?
(A) To provide a comprehensive history of social media.
(B) To inform readers about the technical aspects of social media platforms.
(C) To entertain readers with humorous observations about social media trends.
(D) To advocate for stricter regulations on social media content.

Q.13 -

Passage:

In the quiet moments following a personal loss, one is often confronted with the profound silence that remains.

The reflective narrative explores the depths of grief and the slow journey towards healing, capturing a somber and contemplative mood. The tone is thoughtful and mournful.

Question: What is the primary purpose of the passage?

(A) To inform readers about the biological processes of grief.

(B) To provide a step-by-step guide to overcoming loss.

(C) To evoke empathy and encourage reflection on the nature of grief.

(D) To criticize cultural practices surrounding mourning.

Q.14 -

Passage:

The rapid pace of technological innovation in the 21st century has transformed everyday life in ways once thought impossible. From smart devices to artificial intelligence, these advancements are celebrated as milestones of human ingenuity. The tone is upbeat and enthusiastic.

Question: What is the primary purpose of the passage?

(A) To lament the loss of traditional skills in the digital age.

(B) To inform readers about recent technological advancements in a neutral manner.

(C) To celebrate the achievements of modern technology and inspire optimism about the future.

(D) To criticize the societal impact of rapid technological change.

Q.15 -

Passage:

Preserving historical sites is not merely about conserving old structures; it is about maintaining a tangible connection to our past. The essay argues that these landmarks serve as educational tools and reminders of cultural heritage, stressing the moral duty to protect them. The tone is instructive and earnest.

Question: What is the primary purpose of the passage?

(A) To entertain readers with anecdotes about historical sites.

(B) To provide detailed architectural analyses of historic buildings.

(C) To educate readers on the importance of preserving historical landmarks and cultural heritage.

(D) To argue for the demolition of outdated structures.

Q.16 -

Passage:

Literature has long been a mirror reflecting the complexities of society. Through its narratives, readers gain insight into diverse human experiences, fostering empathy and critical thinking. The writer adopts a reflective and analytical tone to explore how literature shapes our understanding of the world.

Question: What is the primary purpose of the passage?

(A) To entertain with fictional stories.

(B) To analyze the influence of literature on societal values and individual perspectives.

(C) To provide a chronological history of literary movements.

(D) To criticize modern literature for lacking depth.

Q.17 -

Passage:

The degradation of natural habitats has reached a critical point, and immediate action is necessary to preserve the planet's biodiversity. The author passionately argues for increased conservation efforts, advocating for policies that balance development with environmental protection. The tone is urgent and persuasive.

Question: What is the primary purpose of the passage?

(A) To provide an unbiased review of environmental policies.

(B) To entertain with anecdotes about wildlife encounters.

(C) To persuade readers to support conservation initiatives by emphasizing the urgent need for action.

(D) To criticize economic development projects.

Q.18 -

Passage:
Art has the unique ability to capture the fleeting emotions of a moment, offering viewers a glimpse into the artist's inner world. The narrative is reflective and appreciative, highlighting how art serves as a bridge between personal expression and universal experiences.
Question: What is the primary purpose of the passage?
(A) To provide a technical analysis of art techniques.
(B) To persuade readers to become art critics.
(C) To celebrate the power of art in conveying emotions and connecting people.
(D) To critique the commercialization of the art world.
Q.19 -
Passage:
Education is the cornerstone of progress, offering individuals the tools to transform their lives and their communities. The author writes with a motivational tone, urging students to embrace learning as a lifelong journey that unlocks opportunities and fosters innovation.
Question: What is the primary purpose of the passage?
(A) To provide statistical data on educational attainment.
(B) To argue that education is overrated in modern society.
(C) To inspire readers to value education and view it as a key to personal and societal transformation.
(D) To entertain with humorous school stories.
Q.20 -
Passage:
In today's media landscape, the subtle influence of bias can often distort the presentation of facts. The writer examines how selective reporting and sensationalism shape public opinion, adopting a critical and analytical tone. The passage scrutinizes the media's role in perpetuating certain narratives.
Question: What is the primary purpose of the passage?
(A) To entertain readers with amusing media bloopers.
(B) To inform readers about the history of journalism in a neutral manner.
(C) To critically analyze the impact of media bias on public perception and encourage skepticism.
(D) To promote a specific news outlet as unbiased.

Answers and Explanations for Recognizing Tone, Style, and Author's Purpose Exercises

Q.1:

- **Correct Answer:** (B) To inform readers about a new environmental policy and its objectives.
- **Explanation:** The passage provides detailed information about the policy's focus and intended outcomes in a formal, informative tone.

Q.2:

- **Correct Answer:** (C) To persuade readers to engage in community volunteering by highlighting its benefits.
- **Explanation:** The passage uses inspirational language and emphasizes the positive impact of volunteering, aiming to motivate action.

Q.3:

- **Correct Answer:** (A) Humorous and critical of modern technology's trivial applications.
- **Explanation:** The light-hearted and sarcastic tone critiques the overuse of technology for trivial matters rather than offering a neutral analysis.

Q.4:

- **Correct Answer:** (B) To evoke nostalgia and encourage reflection on the simplicity of nature.
- **Explanation:** The passage's warm, nostalgic tone is designed to make readers reflect on past experiences and appreciate nature's simplicity.

Q.5:

- **Correct Answer:** (B) To inform and warn readers about the seriousness of climate change and the need for action.
- **Explanation:** The authoritative tone and presentation of scientific evidence aim to educate and alert readers about climate change.

Q.6:

- **Correct Answer:** (C) To criticize the public transportation initiative for its shortcomings.
- **Explanation:** The passage's critical tone and focus on issues like delays and overcrowding indicate its purpose to highlight and critique the program's failures.

Q.7:

- **Correct Answer:** (B) To provide an objective overview of research findings on the impact of technology in education.
- **Explanation:** The formal and precise style of the passage is intended to inform readers about research data without persuading them toward a particular opinion.

Q.8:

- **Correct Answer:** (C) To critique consumerism and encourage a more meaningful approach to happiness.
- **Explanation:** The reflective and subtly critical tone directs readers to reconsider the value of material possessions compared to genuine sources of fulfillment.

Q.9:

- **Correct Answer:** (C) To persuade readers to support the adoption of renewable energy sources.
- **Explanation:** The impassioned and persuasive language underscores the moral and practical imperatives of renewable energy, urging support for green technologies.

Q.10:

- **Correct Answer:** (B) To entertain readers with a humorous and satirical critique of political campaigns.
- **Explanation:** The witty, sarcastic tone is used to mock the superficiality of campaign promises, making the passage primarily entertaining.

Q.11:

- **Correct Answer:** (C) To motivate and inspire readers by highlighting the power of perseverance.
- **Explanation:** The sincere and motivational tone, along with inspiring examples, is intended to encourage readers to overcome adversity.

Q.12:

- **Correct Answer:** (C) To entertain readers with humorous observations about social media trends.
- **Explanation:** The humorous and ironic tone is aimed at entertaining the reader while commenting on the fleeting nature of online trends.

Q.13:

- **Correct Answer:** (C) To evoke empathy and encourage reflection on the nature of grief.
- **Explanation:** The contemplative and somber tone invites readers to reflect deeply on personal loss and the emotions tied to grief.

Q.14:

- **Correct Answer:** (C) To celebrate the achievements of modern technology and inspire optimism about the future.
- **Explanation:** The upbeat and enthusiastic tone serves to highlight technological advancements and promote a positive outlook on future innovations.

Q.15:

- **Correct Answer:** (C) To educate readers on the importance of preserving historical landmarks and cultural heritage.
- **Explanation:** The instructive and earnest tone is used to stress the value of historical preservation as a means of maintaining cultural identity.

Q.16:

- **Correct Answer:** (B) To analyze the influence of literature on societal values and individual perspectives.
- **Explanation:** The reflective and analytical tone supports a discussion on literature's role in shaping empathy and critical thought.

Q.17:

- **Correct Answer:** (C) To persuade readers to support conservation initiatives by emphasizing the urgent need for action.
- **Explanation:** The urgent, persuasive tone and impassioned language call for immediate support for environmental conservation.

Q.18:

- **Correct Answer:** (C) To celebrate the power of art in conveying emotions and connecting people.
- **Explanation:** The reflective and appreciative tone highlights art's ability to bridge personal expression with universal experiences.

Q.19:

- **Correct Answer:** (C) To inspire readers to value education and view it as a key to personal and societal transformation.
- **Explanation:** The motivational tone is designed to uplift and encourage readers to see education as fundamental to progress.

Q.20:

- **Correct Answer:** (C) To critically analyze the impact of media bias on public perception and encourage skepticism.
- **Explanation:** The analytical tone is employed to scrutinize the influence of biased reporting, urging readers to question the presented narratives.

3. Drill: Making Logical Inferences

Inference questions require students to **read between the lines** and determine **implied** ideas.

Warm-Up Practice 3: Making an Inference

Q.1 -

Passage:

Lila sat quietly at the back of the school library, her eyes scanning a thick textbook. Although she appeared deeply engrossed, her occasional glances at the clock suggested that she was anxious about an upcoming deadline.

Question: What can be inferred from the passage?

(A) Lila prefers studying alone rather than in groups.
(B) Lila is worried about the time she has left to finish her work.
(C) Lila is not very interested in the subject of her textbook.
(D) Lila is planning to leave the library soon.

Q.2 -

Passage:

After returning from the grocery store, Tom immediately began unpacking boxes and preparing a meal. His actions, including checking his pantry and organizing ingredients by type, indicated that he followed a well-planned routine when cooking.

Question: What inference can be made from the passage?

(A) Tom rarely cooks at home.
(B) Tom's meal preparation is spontaneous.
(C) Tom follows a structured routine when cooking.
(D) Tom is dissatisfied with the grocery store's selection.

Q.3 -

Passage:
During the morning meeting, the manager frowned as she reviewed the quarterly reports. Though she did not express her concerns verbally, her quiet sighs and the tapping of her pen on the desk hinted at her dissatisfaction with the results.
Question: What can be inferred from the passage?
(A) The manager is highly satisfied with the quarterly reports.
(B) The manager's team performed exceptionally well.
(C) The manager is quietly disappointed with the quarterly results.
(D) The manager will announce new policies during the meeting.
Q.4 -
Passage:
When asked about her weekend plans, Sarah simply smiled and mentioned she had "big ideas" in mind. As she spoke, her eyes lit up when referring to a new art project, leaving her friends curious for more details.
Question: What can be inferred from the passage?
(A) Sarah is planning to attend a concert.
(B) Sarah is excited about starting a creative project.
(C) Sarah is avoiding discussing her weekend plans.
(D) Sarah's friends are not interested in art projects.
Q.5 -
Passage:
Every morning, the dog wagged its tail vigorously when it saw its owner at the door. Even on rainy days, it waited patiently by the window, its ears perking up at the sound of approaching footsteps.
Question: What can be inferred from the passage?
(A) The dog dislikes going outside on rainy days.
(B) The dog is indifferent to its owner's presence.
(C) The dog is extremely loyal and affectionate toward its owner.
(D) The dog prefers to sleep all day.
Q.6 -
Passage:
The classroom was unusually silent as the teacher began distributing graded assignments. A few students exchanged nervous glances and whispered among themselves, suggesting that many were anxious about their academic performance.
Question: What can be inferred from the passage?
(A) All students are confident about their performance.
(B) The teacher did not return any assignments.
(C) Many students are anxious about their academic performance.
(D) The classroom is unresponsive to feedback.
Q.7 -
Passage:
Dark clouds gathered ominously overhead, and a strong wind began to pick up. Neighbors hurriedly closed their windows and moved outdoor furniture inside, clearly preparing for an approaching storm.
Question: What can be inferred from the passage?
(A) The weather was clear and sunny.
(B) The neighbors are accustomed to frequent storms.
(C) A severe storm was imminent.
(D) The outdoor furniture was newly purchased.
Q.8 -

Passage:
During dinner, Maria's plate remained largely untouched. Although she said nothing, the slow pace at which she used her fork and the pained expression on her face suggested that she was not feeling well.
Question: What can be inferred from the passage?
(A) Maria is enjoying her meal.
(B) Maria is likely feeling unwell or upset.
(C) Maria's food is cold.
(D) Maria has already finished eating.
Q.9 -
Passage:
After a lengthy discussion in the meeting, Mark quickly gathered his notes and left without saying goodbye. His sudden, hurried exit left his colleagues wondering if he was preoccupied with another urgent matter.
Question: What can be inferred from the passage?
(A) Mark was deeply engaged in the meeting.
(B) Mark is known for his punctuality.
(C) Mark was likely in a rush or preoccupied with another commitment.
(D) Mark enjoys surprising his colleagues with abrupt departures.
Q.10 -
Passage:
During the press conference, the spokesperson maintained a calm and measured tone while addressing a controversial issue. Despite sharp questions from reporters, the consistent answers and unruffled demeanor suggested confidence in the organization's strategy.
Question: What can be inferred from the passage?
(A) The spokesperson was nervous and unsure of the answers.
(B) The organization is likely unprepared for the controversy.
(C) The spokesperson is confident about the organization's strategy.
(D) The spokesperson avoided answering any difficult questions.
Q.11 -
Passage:
Even though the project had faced numerous setbacks, Jenna worked late into the night, revising plans and seeking solutions. Her continued effort implied that she was deeply committed to the project's success despite the challenges.
Question: What can be inferred from the passage?
(A) Jenna has little interest in the project.
(B) Jenna is determined to overcome obstacles and succeed.
(C) Jenna is planning to quit the project soon.
(D) Jenna finds the project uninteresting.
Q.12 -
Passage:
As the clock ticked past midnight, the usually bustling office had grown nearly silent. The few remaining employees worked quietly at their desks, suggesting that a major deadline was either already met or was in full progress.
Question: What can be inferred from the passage?
(A) The office is always empty at midnight.
(B) The employees are likely working under a tight deadline.
(C) The company has no important deadlines.
(D) The employees prefer working alone.
Q.13 -

Passage:

When the manager praised the team's efforts during the meeting, there was a noticeable lift in morale. Colleagues exchanged smiles and relaxed their postures, indicating that positive feedback was both unexpected and greatly appreciated.

Question: What can be inferred from the passage?

(A) The team often receives criticism from their manager.

(B) The manager rarely provides any feedback.

(C) Positive feedback from leadership has a favorable impact on team morale.

(D) The team is indifferent to praise.

Q.14 -

Passage:

At the start of the new academic year, the campus was abuzz with activity. While freshmen eagerly participated in orientation events, senior students appeared more reserved—possibly due to the anticipation of challenging final projects.

Question: What can be inferred from the passage?

(A) Freshmen are less interested in academic activities than seniors.

(B) Senior students are likely more focused on upcoming academic responsibilities.

(C) Both freshmen and seniors dislike campus events.

(D) The campus is unusually quiet at the beginning of the academic year.

Q.15 -

Passage:

The local bakery opened its doors early in the morning, and by mid-morning, a steady line of customers had formed. The cheerful chatter and satisfied expressions on the patrons' faces indicated that the bakery was very popular within the community.

Question: What can be inferred from the passage?

(A) The bakery is struggling to attract customers.

(B) The bakery's products are likely well-loved by the community.

(C) The bakery opens late every day.

(D) Customers prefer shopping at other bakeries.

Q.16 -

Passage:

In the weeks following the release of the new novel, literary critics and readers alike praised its innovative narrative style. The book's unconventional structure and unexpected plot twists left many impressed, suggesting that it offered a fresh take on modern literature.

Question: What can be inferred from the passage?

(A) The novel follows a traditional narrative structure.

(B) The novel is likely to be considered boring by readers.

(C) The novel is celebrated for its originality and creativity.

(D) The critics uniformly disliked the book.

Q.17 -

Passage:

At the annual marathon, spectators cheered enthusiastically as runners crossed the finish line. Despite the fatigue evident on their faces, the tired smiles and upbeat greetings from the runners revealed a strong sense of accomplishment and pride.

Question: What can be inferred from the passage?

(A) The runners were disappointed with their performance.

(B) The marathon was canceled due to extreme conditions.

(C) The runners felt a strong sense of achievement after completing the race.
(D) The spectators were uninterested in the event.

Q.18 -

Passage:

During the family reunion, cousins gathered around the dining table, sharing stories and laughing heartily. Although the overall atmosphere was joyful, occasional reflective pauses indicated that the event also evoked bittersweet memories of relatives no longer present.

Question: What can be inferred from the passage?
(A) The family reunion was solely a joyful celebration.
(B) The gathering evoked both happy and sad emotions among the family members.
(C) The cousins were uninterested in family history.
(D) The reunion was a somber event with no laughter.

Q.19 -

Passage:

After a long day at work, Sam settled into his favorite armchair with a cup of tea and a well-worn book. The relaxed expression on his face and the leisurely pace of his reading suggested that he was keen on unwinding and escaping the stresses of the day.

Question: What can be inferred from the passage?
(A) Sam is planning to work late into the night.
(B) Sam finds reading to be a stressful activity.
(C) Sam uses reading as a way to relax and de-stress.
(D) Sam prefers watching television over reading.

Q.20 -

Passage:

While preparing dinner, Jenna paused as the kitchen light flickered briefly before stabilizing. A slight frown crossed her face, and she walked over to check the circuit breaker—actions that indicated she was concerned about a potential electrical issue.

Question: What can be inferred from the passage?
(A) Jenna is uninterested in cooking dinner.
(B) Jenna is unaware of electrical safety.
(C) Jenna is cautious and concerned about household safety.
(D) Jenna enjoys troubleshooting electrical problems.

Answers and Explanations for Making Logical Inferences Exercises

Q.1:

- **Correct Answer:** (B) Lila is worried about the time she has left to finish her work.
- **Explanation:** Lila's repeated glances at the clock imply anxiety about an impending deadline.

Q.2:

- **Correct Answer:** (C) Tom follows a structured routine when cooking.
- **Explanation:** Tom's actions—checking his pantry and organizing ingredients—indicate a deliberate, planned approach to cooking.

Q.3:

- **Correct Answer:** (C) The manager is quietly disappointed with the quarterly results.
- **Explanation:** Her frowning, sighing, and pen tapping suggest discontent with the report outcomes.

Q.4:

- **Correct Answer:** (B) Sarah is excited about starting a creative project.
- **Explanation:** Her smile, reference to "big ideas," and the sparkle in her eyes when mentioning an art project imply excitement about a new creative endeavor.

Q.5:

- **Correct Answer:** (C) The dog is extremely loyal and affectionate toward its owner.
- **Explanation:** The dog's eager greeting and patient behavior even in poor weather suggest strong loyalty and affection.

Q.6:

- **Correct Answer:** (C) Many students are anxious about their academic performance.
- **Explanation:** The nervous glances and whispers among students indicate widespread anxiety regarding their grades.

Q.7:

- **Correct Answer:** (C) A severe storm was imminent.
- **Explanation:** The dark clouds, rising winds, and hurried actions of the neighbors strongly imply that a severe storm was approaching.

Q.8:

- **Correct Answer:** (B) Maria is likely feeling unwell or upset.
- **Explanation:** Her untouched plate, slow eating, and pained expression imply that she is not feeling well.

Q.9:

- **Correct Answer:** (C) Mark was likely in a rush or preoccupied with another commitment.
- **Explanation:** His quick, silent exit suggests he had another urgent matter or was in a hurry.

Q.10:

- **Correct Answer:** (C) The spokesperson is confident about the organization's strategy.
- **Explanation:** A calm, consistent response in the face of tough questions indicates confidence.

Q.11:

- **Correct Answer:** (B) Jenna is determined to overcome obstacles and succeed.
- **Explanation:** Her late-night work and continued efforts despite setbacks demonstrate her determination.

Q.12:

- **Correct Answer:** (B) The employees are likely working under a tight deadline.
- **Explanation:** The deserted office late at night and focused work suggest that a significant deadline is in progress.

Q.13:

- **Correct Answer:** (C) Positive feedback from leadership has a favorable impact on team morale.
- **Explanation:** The team's uplift in mood following praise indicates that encouragement boosts morale.

Q.14:

- **Correct Answer:** (B) Senior students are likely more focused on upcoming academic responsibilities.
- **Explanation:** Their reserved behavior, contrasted with freshmen enthusiasm, suggests seniors are preoccupied with future academic tasks.

Q.15:

- **Correct Answer:** (B) The bakery's products are likely well-loved by the community.
- **Explanation:** The long line of customers and their cheerful expressions imply that the bakery is very popular.

Q.16:

- **Correct Answer:** (C) The novel is celebrated for its originality and creativity.
- **Explanation:** Praise from both critics and readers for its innovative style indicates that the novel is valued for its originality.

Q.17:

- **Correct Answer:** (C) The runners felt a strong sense of achievement after completing the race.
- **Explanation:** The tired smiles and positive interactions after the marathon indicate a feeling of accomplishment.

Q.18:

- **Correct Answer:** (B) The gathering evoked both happy and sad emotions among the family members.
- **Explanation:** The mix of laughter with reflective pauses suggests that the reunion stirred bittersweet memories.

Q.19:

- **Correct Answer:** (C) Sam uses reading as a way to relax and de-stress.
- **Explanation:** The relaxed setting and Sam's leisurely reading indicate that he is using the activity to unwind.

Q.20:

- **Correct Answer:** (C) Jenna is cautious and concerned about household safety.
- **Explanation:** Her pause during dinner and the action of checking the circuit breaker indicate a concern for electrical safety.

4. Drill: Understanding Vocabulary in Context

Vocabulary questions test how **words are used in a passage**, often requiring **choosing a synonym that fits the meaning in context**.

Warm-Up Practice 4: Vocabulary in Context

Q.1 -
Sentence in Passage:
The professor's explanation was so **lucid** that even students who struggled with the subject found it easy to understand.
Question: What does the word **"lucid"** most nearly mean in the sentence?
(A) Confusing
(B) Clear
(C) Elaborate
(D) Brief

Q.2 -
Sentence in Passage:
During the debate, the candidate presented a **cogent** argument that convinced even her harshest critics.
Question: What does the word **"cogent"** most nearly mean in the sentence?
(A) Weak
(B) Unconvincing
(C) Persuasive
(D) Disorganized

Q.3 -
Sentence in Passage:
The old mansion had an **austere** appearance, with plain furnishings and little decoration.
Question: What does the word **"austere"** most nearly mean in the sentence?
(A) Lavish
(B) Plain
(C) Cheerful
(D) Chaotic

Q.4 -
Sentence in Passage:
Despite his groundbreaking achievements, the scientist remained **modest** about his contributions.
Question: What does the word **"modest"** most nearly mean in the sentence?
(A) Boastful
(B) Humble

(C) Arrogant
(D) Extravagant

Q.5 -

Sentence in Passage:
The critic's **trenchant** review left the director both impressed and a little disconcerted by its sharp observations.
Question: What does the word **"trenchant"** most nearly mean in the sentence?
(A) Mild
(B) Vague
(C) Incisive
(D) Cheerful

Q.6 -

Sentence in Passage:
The novel's **somber** tone perfectly matched the tragic events that unfolded throughout the story.
Question: What does the word **"somber"** most nearly mean in the sentence?
(A) Joyful
(B) Gloomy
(C) Humorous
(D) Enthusiastic

Q.7 -

Sentence in Passage:
Her **meticulous** research ensured that every detail of the project was accurate and complete.
Question: What does the word **"meticulous"** most nearly mean in the sentence?
(A) Careless
(B) Thorough
(C) Hasty
(D) Superficial

Q.8 -

Sentence in Passage:
His **facetious** remark during the meeting lightened the mood, even though the topic was quite serious.
Question: What does the word **"facetious"** most nearly mean in the sentence?
(A) Sincere
(B) Humorous
(C) Offensive
(D) Somber

Q.9 -

Sentence in Passage:
The artist's work was considered **avant-garde**, pushing the boundaries of traditional art with radical techniques.
Question: What does the word **"avant-garde"** most nearly mean in the sentence?
(A) Conventional
(B) Radical
(C) Outdated
(D) Derivative

Q.10 -

Sentence in Passage:
Although initially met with skepticism, the scientist's theory proved to be **sound** after rigorous testing.
Question: What does the word **"sound"** most nearly mean in the sentence?
(A) Faulty
(B) Reliable

(C) Simplistic
(D) Controversial

Q.11 -

Sentence in Passage:

Known for his **laconic** style, the speaker conveyed complex ideas in very few words.

Question: What does the word **"laconic"** most nearly mean in the sentence?

(A) Verbose
(B) Brief
(C) Ambiguous
(D) Persuasive

Q.12 -

Sentence in Passage:

The poet's **eloquent** verses captivated the audience with their expressive and graceful language.

Question: What does the word **"eloquent"** most nearly mean in the sentence?

(A) Awkward
(B) Inarticulate
(C) Articulate
(D) Disorganized

Q.13 -

Sentence in Passage:

The detective's **astute** observations quickly uncovered details that others had overlooked.

Question: What does the word **"astute"** most nearly mean in the sentence?

(A) Oblivious
(B) Sharp
(C) Careless
(D) Unobservant

Q.14 -

Sentence in Passage:

Critics often complained that the writer's **verbose** style made his books unnecessarily long.

Question: What does the word **"verbose"** most nearly mean in the sentence?

(A) Concise
(B) Wordy
(C) Clear
(D) Straightforward

Q.15 -

Sentence in Passage:

The CEO's decision was **pragmatic**, focusing on realistic solutions rather than idealistic theories.

Question: What does the word **"pragmatic"** most nearly mean in the sentence?

(A) Impractical
(B) Theoretical
(C) Realistic
(D) Speculative

Q.16 -

Sentence in Passage:

The film received **scathing** reviews from critics who lambasted its weak plot and poor character development.

Question: What does the word **"scathing"** most nearly mean in the sentence?

(A) Complimentary
(B) Glowing

(C) Harsh
(D) Indifferent
Q.17 -
Sentence in Passage:
The researcher's **revolutionary** discovery challenged long-held theories and paved the way for new advancements.
Question: What does the word **"revolutionary"** most nearly mean in the sentence?
(A) Trivial
(B) Outdated
(C) Innovative
(D) Conventional
Q.18 -
Sentence in Passage:
The dessert was absolutely **delectable**, leaving everyone at the table eager for a second serving.
Question: What does the word **"delectable"** most nearly mean in the sentence?
(A) Unappetizing
(B) Bland
(C) Delicious
(D) Ordinary
Q.19 -
Sentence in Passage:
The politician's **equivocal** response left the audience unsure of his true stance on the issue.
Question: What does the word **"equivocal"** most nearly mean in the sentence?
(A) Clear
(B) Ambiguous
(C) Decisive
(D) Forthright
Q.20 -
Sentence in Passage:
Her **resilient** spirit allowed her to bounce back quickly after the many setbacks she experienced.
Question: What does the word **"resilient"** most nearly mean in the sentence?
(A) Fragile
(B) Easily discouraged
(C) Able to recover quickly
(D) Slow to adapt

Answers and Explanations for Vocabulary in Context Exercises

Q.1:

- **Correct Answer:** (B) Clear
- **Explanation:** "Lucid" means expressed clearly; easy to understand.

Q.2:

- **Correct Answer:** (C) Persuasive
- **Explanation:** "Cogent" refers to an argument that is convincing and logically compelling.

Q.3:

- **Correct Answer:** (B) Plain
- **Explanation:** "Austere" describes something that is simple, without ornamentation.

Q.4:

- **Correct Answer:** (B) Humble

- **Explanation:** "Modest" means not boastful or arrogant; showing humility.

Q.5:
- **Correct Answer:** (C) Incisive
- **Explanation:** "Trenchant" means sharply effective, cutting to the heart of the matter.

Q.6:
- **Correct Answer:** (B) Gloomy
- **Explanation:** "Somber" means dark, gloomy, or solemn in mood.

Q.7:
- **Correct Answer:** (B) Thorough
- **Explanation:** "Meticulous" means showing great attention to detail; very careful and precise.

Q.8:
- **Correct Answer:** (B) Humorous
- **Explanation:** "Facetious" means treating serious issues with deliberately inappropriate humor.

Q.9:
- **Correct Answer:** (B) Radical
- **Explanation:** "Avant-garde" describes innovative, experimental, or unconventional ideas.

Q.10:
- **Correct Answer:** (B) Reliable
- **Explanation:** "Sound" in this context means solid, well-founded, or reliable.

Q.11:
- **Correct Answer:** (B) Brief
- **Explanation:** "Laconic" means using few words; concise.

Q.12:
- **Correct Answer:** (C) Articulate
- **Explanation:** "Eloquent" means expressing oneself clearly and effectively.

Q.13:
- **Correct Answer:** (B) Sharp
- **Explanation:** "Astute" refers to being perceptive and able to accurately assess situations.

Q.14:
- **Correct Answer:** (B) Wordy
- **Explanation:** "Verbose" means using more words than necessary; overly long-winded.

Q.15:
- **Correct Answer:** (C) Realistic
- **Explanation:** "Pragmatic" means dealing with things sensibly and realistically, based on practical considerations.

Q.16:
- **Correct Answer:** (C) Harsh
- **Explanation:** "Scathing" means severely critical; expressing strong disapproval.

Q.17:
- **Correct Answer:** (C) Innovative
- **Explanation:** "Revolutionary" means radically new or innovative, challenging the old ways.

Q.18:
- **Correct Answer:** (C) Delicious
- **Explanation:** "Delectable" means highly pleasing to the senses, especially taste.

Q.19:
- **Correct Answer:** (B) Ambiguous
- **Explanation:** "Equivocal" means having more than one possible meaning; unclear or ambiguous.

Q.20:

- **Correct Answer:** (C) Able to recover quickly
- **Explanation:** "Resilient" describes someone or something that can recover quickly from difficulties.

5. Summary of Key Strategies

Skill	Best Strategy
Main Idea	Focus on the **first and last sentences** for clues.
Tone & Purpose	Identify **neutral vs. persuasive vs. entertaining language**.
Inference Questions	Read between the lines but **don't assume too much**.
Vocabulary in Context	Use **context clues** to determine word meaning.

6. Final Key Takeaways

- **Skim first, then read carefully** to save time and focus on key information.
- **For main idea questions, check the first and last sentences.**
- **For inference questions, find implied meanings rather than direct statements.**
- **For vocabulary in context, check how the word is used, not just its dictionary definition.**
- **Eliminate extreme or unrelated answer choices first.**

By **practicing these warm-up drills**, students can **increase reading comprehension speed and accuracy**, leading to **higher scores on the SAT Reading & Writing section**.

16.2 Grammar Drills: Editing and Revising Short Passages

The **Digital SAT Writing & Language section** tests a student's ability to **identify and correct grammar errors, improve sentence clarity, and enhance organization in short passages**. This section provides targeted **grammar drills** focusing on common SAT-tested concepts.

This section will cover:

- **Subject-Verb Agreement and Verb Tense Consistency**
- **Pronoun Clarity and Agreement**
- **Parallel Structure and Wordiness**
- **Sentence Structure and Logical Flow**

1. Drill: Subject-Verb Agreement and Verb Tense Consistency

A **verb must agree with its subject** in number and remain consistent in **tense** throughout a passage.

Warm-Up Practice 1: Correcting Subject-Verb Agreement

Q.1 -
Sentence:
The team of engineers have completed their project ahead of schedule.
Question: Which revision best corrects the error?
(A) The team of engineers has completed its project ahead of schedule.
(B) The team of engineers has completed their project ahead of schedule.
(C) The team of engineers have completed its project ahead of schedule.
(D) The team of engineers are completing its project ahead of schedule.

Q.2 -
Sentence:
The list of items on the desk are arranged alphabetically.
Question: Which revision best corrects the error?
(A) The list of items on the desk is arranged alphabetically.

(B) The list of items on the desk are arranged in alphabetical order.
(C) The list of items on the desk is arranged in alphabetic order.
(D) The list of items on the desk have been arranged alphabetically.

Q.3 -

Sentence:

Each of the participants were given a certificate at the end of the event.

Question: Which revision best corrects the error?

(A) Each of the participants was given a certificate at the end of the event.
(B) Each of the participants were given certificates at the end of the event.
(C) Each of the participants is given a certificate at the end of the event.
(D) Each of the participants have been given a certificate at the end of the event.

Q.4 -

Sentence:

The pair of scissors are on the desk.

Question: Which revision best corrects the error?

(A) The pair of scissors is on the desk.
(B) The pair of scissors are on the desk.
(C) The pair of scissors have been on the desk.
(D) A pair of scissors is on the desk.

Q.5 -

Sentence:

Neither the teacher nor the students has completed their work on time.

Question: Which revision best corrects the error?

(A) Neither the teacher nor the students has completed their work on time.
(B) Neither the teacher nor the students have completed their work on time.
(C) Neither the teacher nor the students has completed its work on time.
(D) Neither the teacher nor the students have completed its work on time.

Q.6 -

Sentence:

Yesterday, John and his sister goes to the market.

Question: Which revision best corrects the error?

(A) Yesterday, John and his sister went to the market.
(B) Yesterday, John and his sister go to the market.
(C) Yesterday, John and his sister are going to the market.
(D) Yesterday, John and his sister has gone to the market.

Q.7 -

Sentence:

After the meeting, the manager explained that the reports is due on Monday.

Question: Which revision best corrects the error?

(A) After the meeting, the manager explained that the reports are due on Monday.
(B) After the meeting, the manager explained that the reports is due on Monday.
(C) After the meeting, the manager explained that the report is due on Monday.
(D) After the meeting, the manager explains that the reports are due on Monday.

Q.8 -

Sentence:

She always enjoyed reading novels, but last week she enjoy reading biographies instead.

Question: Which revision best corrects the error?

(A) She always enjoyed reading novels, but last week she enjoyed reading biographies instead.

(B) She always enjoys reading novels, but last week she enjoy reading biographies instead.
(C) She always enjoyed reading novels, but last week she enjoys reading biographies instead.
(D) She always enjoys reading novels, but last week she enjoyed reading biography instead.

Q.9 -

Sentence:
The athletes trains every morning to prepare for the championship.
Question: Which revision best corrects the error?
(A) The athletes train every morning to prepare for the championship.
(B) The athletes trains every morning to prepare for the championship.
(C) The athletes training every morning to prepare for the championship.
(D) The athletes have trained every morning to prepare for the championship.

Q.10 -

Sentence:
Either the committee members or the chairperson are attending the conference.
Question: Which revision best corrects the error?
(A) Either the committee members or the chairperson is attending the conference.
(B) Either the committee members or the chairperson are attending the conference.
(C) Either the committee members or the chairperson were attending the conference.
(D) Either the committee members or the chairperson have attended the conference.

Q.11 -

Sentence:
The number of students in the class have increased since last year.
Question: Which revision best corrects the error?
(A) The number of students in the class has increased since last year.
(B) The number of students in the class have increased since last year.
(C) The numbers of students in the class has increased since last year.
(D) The number of students in the class increased since last year.

Q.12 -

Sentence:
There was many mistakes in the report that needed to be corrected.
Question: Which revision best corrects the error?
(A) There were many mistakes in the report that needed to be corrected.
(B) There was many mistakes in the report that needed to be corrected.
(C) There are many mistakes in the report that needed to be corrected.
(D) There were many mistakes in the report which needed to be corrected.

Q.13 -

Sentence:
If he is finished his work, he goes home early.
Question: Which revision best corrects the error?
(A) If he has finished his work, he goes home early.
(B) If he is finished with his work, he goes home early.
(C) If he finished his work, he goes home early.
(D) If he finishes his work, he goes home early.

Q.14 -

Sentence:
The teacher explains the lesson and then gave the students a quiz.
Question: Which revision best corrects the error?
(A) The teacher explains the lesson and then gives the students a quiz.

(B) The teacher explained the lesson and then gave the students a quiz.
(C) The teacher explains the lesson and then gave the students a quiz.
(D) The teacher explained the lesson and then gives the students a quiz.

Q.15 -

Sentence:
At the conference last week, the speaker discusses the importance of renewable energy.
Question: Which revision best corrects the error?
(A) At the conference last week, the speaker discussed the importance of renewable energy.
(B) At the conference last week, the speaker discusses the importance of renewable energy.
(C) At the conference last week, the speaker has discussed the importance of renewable energy.
(D) At the conference last week, the speaker is discussing the importance of renewable energy.

Q.16 -

Sentence:
The data collected during the experiment is analyzed carefully.
Question: Which revision best corrects the error?
(A) The data collected during the experiment are analyzed carefully.
(B) The data collected during the experiment is analyzed carefully.
(C) The data collected during the experiment was analyzed carefully.
(D) The data collected during the experiment have been analyzed carefully.

Q.17 -

Sentence:
Neither the manager nor the assistants was aware of the changes in the schedule.
Question: Which revision best corrects the error?
(A) Neither the manager nor the assistants were aware of the changes in the schedule.
(B) Neither the manager nor the assistants was aware of the changes in the schedule.
(C) Neither the manager nor the assistants are aware of the changes in the schedule.
(D) Neither the manager nor the assistants were aware of the change in the schedule.

Q.18 -

Sentence:
After finishing her homework, Jessica goes to the library and studied for her exams.
Question: Which revision best corrects the error?
(A) After finishing her homework, Jessica goes to the library and studies for her exams.
(B) After finishing her homework, Jessica went to the library and studied for her exams.
(C) After finishing her homework, Jessica goes to the library and study for her exams.
(D) After finishing her homework, Jessica went to the library and studies for her exams.

Q.19 -

Sentence:
During the summer, the volunteers organized a fundraiser and raise money for the local charity.
Question: Which revision best corrects the error?
(A) During the summer, the volunteers organized a fundraiser and raised money for the local charity.
(B) During the summer, the volunteers organized a fundraiser and raise money for the local charity.
(C) During the summer, the volunteers organize a fundraiser and raised money for the local charity.
(D) During the summer, the volunteers organized a fundraiser and are raising money for the local charity.

Q.20 -

Sentence:
Every morning, the gardener waters the plants and trimmed the hedges.
Question: Which revision best corrects the error?
(A) Every morning, the gardener waters the plants and trims the hedges.

(B) Every morning, the gardener waters the plants and trimmed the hedges.
(C) Every morning, the gardener water the plants and trims the hedges.
(D) Every morning, the gardener waters the plants and is trimming the hedges.

Answers and Explanations for Subject-Verb Agreement and Verb Tense Consistency Exercises

Q.1:

- **Correct Answer:** (A)
- **Explanation:** The collective noun "team" is singular; therefore, the singular verb "has" and the matching possessive pronoun "its" are required.

Q.2:

- **Correct Answer:** (A)
- **Explanation:** "List" is singular; thus, the verb should be "is arranged" rather than "are arranged."

Q.3:

- **Correct Answer:** (A)
- **Explanation:** "Each" is a distributive pronoun that requires a singular verb ("was given") rather than a plural verb.

Q.4:

- **Correct Answer:** (A)
- **Explanation:** Although "scissors" is plural in form, the phrase "a pair of scissors" is treated as a single unit, so a singular verb ("is") is correct.

Q.5:

- **Correct Answer:** (B)
- **Explanation:** With "neither/nor," the verb should agree with the nearer subject ("students" is plural), so "have completed" is correct.

Q.6:

- **Correct Answer:** (A)
- **Explanation:** The correct past tense for a compound subject is "went," ensuring proper verb tense consistency.

Q.7:

- **Correct Answer:** (A)
- **Explanation:** "Reports" is plural and requires the plural verb "are due" rather than "is due."

Q.8:

- **Correct Answer:** (A)
- **Explanation:** To maintain past tense consistency, "enjoy" should be corrected to "enjoyed."

Q.9:

- **Correct Answer:** (A)
- **Explanation:** The plural subject "athletes" requires the plural form "train" instead of "trains."

Q.10:

- **Correct Answer:** (A)
- **Explanation:** In an either/or construction, the verb should agree with the subject closest to it; "chairperson" is singular, so "is attending" is correct.

Q.11:

- **Correct Answer:** (A)
- **Explanation:** "The number" is singular; therefore, the verb should be "has increased."

Q.12:

- **Correct Answer:** (A)

- **Explanation:** "Mistakes" is plural, so the correct form is "There were many mistakes" instead of "There was."

Q.13:

- **Correct Answer:** (A)
- **Explanation:** The sentence requires the present perfect "has finished" to indicate a completed action relevant to the present.

Q.14:

- **Correct Answer:** (A)
- **Explanation:** Consistent present tense requires both verbs to be in the present: "explains" and "gives."

Q.15:

- **Correct Answer:** (A)
- **Explanation:** Since the event occurred last week, the past tense "discussed" correctly aligns with the time reference.

Q.16:

- **Correct Answer:** (A)
- **Explanation:** "Data" (when treated as a plural noun) requires the plural verb "are analyzed."

Q.17:

- **Correct Answer:** (A)
- **Explanation:** With "neither/nor," the verb agrees with the subject closest to it ("assistants" is plural), so "were aware" is correct.

Q.18:

- **Correct Answer:** (A)
- **Explanation:** To maintain consistent present tense ("goes"), the following verb should also be in the present tense ("studies").

Q.19:

- **Correct Answer:** (A)
- **Explanation:** The past tense "organized" requires the parallel past tense "raised" to maintain verb tense consistency.

Q.20:

- **Correct Answer:** (A)
- **Explanation:** Both actions occur routinely in the present; therefore, "waters" and "trims" are required for consistency.

2. Drill: Pronoun Clarity and Agreement

A **pronoun must clearly refer to a noun (antecedent) and agree in number and gender**.

Warm-Up Practice Exercises: Fixing Ambiguous Pronouns

Q.1 -

Sentence:

After the meeting, Jordan told Alex that his idea was brilliant.

Question: Which revision best improves pronoun clarity?

(A) After the meeting, Jordan told Alex that the idea was brilliant.

(B) After the meeting, Jordan told Alex that Alex's idea was brilliant.

(C) After the meeting, Jordan told Alex that Jordan's idea was brilliant.

(D) After the meeting, Jordan told Alex that their idea was brilliant.

Q.2 -

Sentence:

When the teacher spoke with the principal, she explained that the report needed revisions.

Question: Which revision best clarifies the pronoun reference?
(A) When the teacher spoke with the principal, the teacher explained that the report needed revisions.
(B) When the teacher spoke with the principal, the principal explained that the report needed revisions.
(C) When the teacher spoke with the principal, she explained that the report needed revisions.
(D) When the teacher spoke with the principal, the report was explained to be in need of revisions.

Q.3 -

Sentence:
If a candidate fails to include a resume, they will not be considered for the job.
Question: Which revision best corrects the pronoun agreement error?
(A) If a candidate fails to include a resume, he will not be considered for the job.
(B) If a candidate fails to include a resume, he or she will not be considered for the job.
(C) If candidates fail to include a resume, they will not be considered for the job.
(D) If a candidate fails to include a resume, one will not be considered for the job.

Q.4 -

Sentence:
When the dog chased the cat, it was very fast.
Question: Which revision best clarifies the ambiguous pronoun?
(A) When the dog chased the cat, the dog was very fast.
(B) When the dog chased the cat, it ran very fast.
(C) When the dog chased the cat, the cat was very fast.
(D) When chasing the cat, the dog was very fast.

Q.5 -

Sentence:
Emily told Jessica that her project had been selected for the award.
Question: Which revision best improves clarity by specifying the intended antecedent?
(A) Emily told Jessica that her project had been selected for the award.
(B) Emily told Jessica that the project had been selected for the award.
(C) Emily told Jessica that Jessica's project had been selected for the award.
(D) Emily told Jessica that Emily's project had been selected for the award.

Q.6 -

Sentence:
Maria and Laura went to the mall because she needed a new dress.
Question: Which revision best clarifies the pronoun reference?
(A) Maria and Laura went to the mall because they needed a new dress.
(B) Maria and Laura went to the mall because both needed a new dress.
(C) Maria and Laura went to the mall because Laura needed a new dress.
(D) Maria and Laura went to the mall because Maria needed a new dress.

Q.7 -

Sentence:
When the critics reviewed the film, it impressed them.
Question: Which revision best improves pronoun clarity?
(A) When the critics reviewed the film, the film impressed them.
(B) When the critics reviewed the film, it impressed the critics.
(C) When the critics reviewed the film, they were impressed.
(D) When the critics reviewed the film, the film was impressive.

Q.8 -

Sentence:
The committee told the manager that their decision was final.

Question: Which revision best corrects the pronoun agreement error?
(A) The committee told the manager that their decision was final.
(B) The committee told the manager that its decision was final.
(C) The committee told the manager that the decision was final.
(D) The committee told the manager that the manager's decision was final.

Q.9 -

Sentence:
When the students met the professor, they explained that the syllabus had been updated.
Question: Which revision best clarifies the pronoun reference?
(A) When the students met the professor, the students explained that the syllabus had been updated.
(B) When the students met the professor, the syllabus was explained to have been updated.
(C) When the students met the professor, the professor explained that the syllabus had been updated.
(D) When the students met the professor, he explained that the syllabus had been updated.

Q.10 -

Sentence:
Alex told Jordan that their presentation needed more work.
Question: Which revision best clarifies whose presentation is being discussed?
(A) Alex told Jordan that his presentation needed more work.
(B) Alex told Jordan that her presentation needed more work.
(C) Alex told Jordan that Jordan's presentation needed more work.
(D) Alex told Jordan that the presentation needed more work.

Q.11 -

Sentence:
Each of the team members received their feedback after practice.
Question: Which revision best corrects the pronoun agreement error?
(A) Each of the team members received its feedback after practice.
(B) Each of the team members received his or her feedback after practice.
(C) Each team member received their feedback after practice.
(D) The team members received feedback after practice.

Q.12 -

Sentence:
After reviewing the manuscript, the editor told the author that it needed extensive revisions.
Question: Which revision best clarifies the pronoun reference?
(A) After reviewing the manuscript, the editor told the author that the manuscript needed extensive revisions.
(B) After reviewing the manuscript, the editor told the author that he needed extensive revisions.
(C) After reviewing the manuscript, the editor told the author that revisions were needed.
(D) After reviewing the manuscript, the editor told the author that they needed extensive revisions.

Q.13 -

Sentence:
The doctor advised the patient to take their medication regularly.
Question: Which revision best corrects the pronoun agreement error?
(A) The doctor advised the patient to take his or her medication regularly.
(B) The doctor advised the patient to take his medication regularly.
(C) The doctor advised the patient to take the medication regularly.
(D) The doctor advised the patient to take their medication regularly.

Q.14 -

Sentence:
When an applicant submits their portfolio, the review committee evaluates it thoroughly.

Question: Which revision best corrects the pronoun agreement error?
(A) When an applicant submits his or her portfolio, the review committee evaluates it thoroughly.
(B) When an applicant submits its portfolio, the review committee evaluates it thoroughly.
(C) When applicants submit their portfolios, the review committee evaluates them thoroughly.
(D) When an applicant submits the portfolio, the review committee evaluates it thoroughly.

Q.15 -

Sentence:
When a student consults the counselor, she listens carefully.
Question: Which revision best improves pronoun clarity?
(A) When a student consults the counselor, the counselor listens carefully.
(B) When a student consults the counselor, the student listens carefully.
(C) When a student consults the counselor, he listens carefully.
(D) When a student consults the counselor, they listen carefully.

Q.16 -

Sentence:
Each employee should update their contact information by the end of the day.
Question: Which revision best corrects the pronoun agreement error?
(A) Each employee should update his or her contact information by the end of the day.
(B) All employees should update their contact information by the end of the day.
(C) Each employee should update their contact information by the end of the day.
(D) Each employee should update its contact information by the end of the day.

Q.17 -

Sentence:
The writer explained that the critic did not appreciate his work.
Question: Which revision best clarifies the pronoun reference?
(A) The writer explained that the critic did not appreciate his work.
(B) The writer explained that the critic did not appreciate the writer's work.
(C) The writer explained that the critic did not appreciate her work.
(D) The writer explained that the critic did not appreciate the work.

Q.18 -

Sentence:
During the rehearsal, the director told the actor that she needed to improve her performance.
Question: Which revision best improves pronoun clarity?
(A) During the rehearsal, the director told the actor that she needed to improve her performance.
(B) During the rehearsal, the director told the actor that the actor needed to improve her performance.
(C) During the rehearsal, the director told the actor that the director needed to improve her performance.
(D) During the rehearsal, the director told the actor that the actor needed to improve his performance.

Q.19 -

Sentence:
Lisa and Megan discussed their ideas, but she believed they were impractical.
Question: Which revision best clarifies the pronoun reference?
(A) Lisa and Megan discussed their ideas, but Lisa believed they were impractical.
(B) Lisa and Megan discussed their ideas, but Megan believed they were impractical.
(C) Lisa and Megan discussed their ideas, but one of them believed they were impractical.
(D) Lisa and Megan discussed their ideas, but both believed they were impractical.

Q.20 -

Sentence:
When a candidate receives feedback, they are encouraged to improve their skills.

Question: Which revision best corrects the pronoun agreement error?
(A) When a candidate receives feedback, he or she is encouraged to improve his or her skills.
(B) When a candidate receives feedback, he is encouraged to improve his skills.
(C) When candidates receive feedback, they are encouraged to improve their skills.
(D) When a candidate receives feedback, one is encouraged to improve skills.

Answers and Explanations for Pronoun Clarity and Agreement Exercises

Q.1:

- **Correct Answer:** (C)
- **Explanation:** Replacing the ambiguous pronoun with "Jordan's idea" clarifies that it is Jordan's idea that is being referred to.

Q.2:

- **Correct Answer:** (A)
- **Explanation:** Specifying "the teacher explained" removes ambiguity about who provided the explanation.

Q.3:

- **Correct Answer:** (B)
- **Explanation:** Using "he or she" ensures that the singular antecedent "a candidate" agrees with the pronoun.

Q.4:

- **Correct Answer:** (C)
- **Explanation:** Changing "it" to "the cat" clearly indicates that the cat was fast.

Q.5:

- **Correct Answer:** (C)
- **Explanation:** Replacing "her project" with "Jessica's project" removes the ambiguity regarding whose project was selected.

Q.6:

- **Correct Answer:** (C)
- **Explanation:** Specifying "Laura needed a new dress" clearly indicates which person is being referred to.

Q.7:

- **Correct Answer:** (C)
- **Explanation:** Rewriting the sentence as "they were impressed" clearly attributes the reaction to the critics.

Q.8:

- **Correct Answer:** (B)
- **Explanation:** Changing "their decision" to "its decision" correctly applies a singular possessive pronoun to the collective noun "committee."

Q.9:

- **Correct Answer:** (D)
- **Explanation:** Replacing the ambiguous "they" with "he" clearly identifies the professor as the one who explained the update.

Q.10:

- **Correct Answer:** (C)
- **Explanation:** Specifying "Jordan's presentation" clarifies that the presentation in question belongs to Jordan.

Q.11:

- **Correct Answer:** (B)
- **Explanation:** Using "his or her" ensures that the singular antecedent "each" is matched correctly with a singular pronoun.

Q.12:

- **Correct Answer:** (A)
- **Explanation:** Replacing "it" with "the manuscript" eliminates ambiguity regarding what needed revisions.

Q.13:

- **Correct Answer:** (A)
- **Explanation:** Changing "their medication" to "his or her medication" correctly aligns with the singular antecedent "the patient."

Q.14:

- **Correct Answer:** (A)
- **Explanation:** Replacing "their portfolio" with "his or her portfolio" properly matches the singular antecedent "an applicant."

Q.15:

- **Correct Answer:** (A)
- **Explanation:** Specifying "the counselor listens carefully" makes it clear that the counselor is the one taking the action.

Q.16:

- **Correct Answer:** (A)
- **Explanation:** Using "his or her" corrects the singular-pronoun error associated with "each employee."

Q.17:

- **Correct Answer:** (B)
- **Explanation:** Changing "his work" to "the writer's work" clarifies that the work being discussed belongs to the writer, not the critic.

Q.18:

- **Correct Answer:** (B)
- **Explanation:** Replacing "she" with "the actor" clarifies that it is the actor who needs to improve her performance.

Q.19:

- **Correct Answer:** (B)
- **Explanation:** Specifying "Megan believed" removes the ambiguity regarding which individual held the opinion.

Q.20:

- **Correct Answer:** (A)
- **Explanation:** Rewriting the sentence with "he or she" ensures the singular antecedent "a candidate" is paired with a matching pronoun.

3. Drill: Parallel Structure and Wordiness

Parallel structure ensures that **items in a list or comparison follow the same grammatical format**.

Warm-Up Practice Exercises: Fixing Parallelism Errors

Q.1 -

Sentence:
The manager expects employees to be punctual, working hard, and that they complete their assignments on time.
Question: Which revision best corrects the error?
(A) The manager expects employees to be punctual, work hard, and complete their assignments on time.
(B) The manager expects employees to be punctual, working hard, and completing their assignments on time.
(C) The manager expects employees to be punctual, work hard, and that they complete their assignments on time.

(D) The manager expects employees to be punctual, to work hard, and that they complete their assignments on time.

Q.2 -

Sentence:

She likes reading, to jog in the park, and watching movies on weekends.

Question: Which revision best corrects the error?

(A) She likes reading, to jog in the park, and watching movies on weekends.

(B) She likes reading, jogging in the park, and watching movies on weekends.

(C) She likes to read, jog in the park, and watch movies on weekends.

(D) She likes reading, jogging in the park, and to watch movies on weekends.

Q.3 -

Sentence:

The new software is designed to be user-friendly, efficient, and it provides accurate results.

Question: Which revision best corrects the error?

(A) The new software is designed to be user-friendly, efficient, and to provide accurate results.

(B) The new software is designed to be user-friendly, efficient, and provides accurate results.

(C) The new software is designed to be user-friendly, efficient, and accurately providing results.

(D) The new software is designed to be user-friendly, efficient, and accurate.

Q.4 -

Sentence:

To prepare for the exam, the students studied hard, reviewed their notes, and practiced problems.

Question: Which revision best corrects the error?

(A) To prepare for the exam, the students studied hard, reviewed their notes, and practiced problems.

(B) To prepare for the exam, the students studied hard, reviewing their notes, and practiced problems.

(C) To prepare for the exam, the students studied hard, reviewed their notes, and were practicing problems.

(D) To prepare for the exam, the students studied hard, were reviewing their notes, and practiced problems.

Q.5 -

Sentence:

The proposal is not only too complex but also it is too expensive and takes too long to implement.

Question: Which revision best corrects the error?

(A) The proposal is not only too complex but also too expensive and time-consuming to implement.

(B) The proposal is not only too complex but also too expensive and takes too long to implement.

(C) The proposal is too complex, too expensive, and takes too long to implement.

(D) The proposal is not only too complex, but also too expensive and takes too long to implement.

Q.6 -

Sentence:

The candidate promised to improve customer service, reduce response times, and lower costs.

Question: Which revision best corrects the error?

(A) The candidate promised to improve customer service, reduce response times, and lower costs.

(B) The candidate promised to improve customer service, reducing response times, and lower costs.

(C) The candidate promised to improve customer service, reduce response times, and to lower costs.

(D) The candidate promised to improve customer service, reducing response times, and to lower costs.

Q.7 -

Sentence:

The report was lengthy, filled with unnecessary details, and it was confusing.

Question: Which revision best corrects the error?

(A) The report was lengthy, with unnecessary details and confusing.

(B) The report was lengthy, included unnecessary details, and was confusing.

(C) The report was lengthy, included unnecessary details, and left readers confused.
(D) The report was lengthy, contained unnecessary details, and was confusing.

Q.8 -

Sentence:
To succeed in the competition, participants must be quick-thinking, have strong stamina, and be well-prepared.
Question: Which revision best corrects the error?
(A) To succeed in the competition, participants must be quick-thinking, have strong stamina, and be well-prepared.
(B) To succeed in the competition, participants must be quick-thinking, have strong stamina, and to be well-prepared.
(C) To succeed in the competition, participants must think quickly, have strong stamina, and be well-prepared.
(D) To succeed in the competition, participants must be quick-thinking, have strong stamina, and being well-prepared.

Q.9 -

Sentence:
The athlete's performance was not only impressive but also demonstrated a high level of determination, discipline, and that she had trained rigorously.
Question: Which revision best corrects the error?
(A) The athlete's performance was not only impressive but also demonstrated determination, discipline, and rigorous training.
(B) The athlete's performance was not only impressive but also showed a high level of determination, discipline, and rigorous training.
(C) The athlete's performance was not only impressive but also demonstrated a high level of determination, discipline, and rigorous training.
(D) The athlete's performance was impressive, demonstrated determination, discipline, and that she had trained rigorously.

Q.10 -

Sentence:
The committee decided to allocate funds for the project, hire new staff, and purchase updated equipment.
Question: Which revision best corrects the error?
(A) The committee decided to allocate funds for the project, hire new staff, and purchase updated equipment.
(B) The committee decided to allocate funds for the project, to hire new staff, and to purchase updated equipment.
(C) The committee decided to allocate funds for the project, hiring new staff, and purchasing updated equipment.
(D) The committee decided to allocate funds for the project, hire new staff, and they planned to purchase updated equipment.

Q.11 -

Sentence:
The report is long, contains unnecessary data, and is written in a way that is overly complicated.
Question: Which revision best corrects the error?
(A) The report is long, includes unnecessary data, and is written in an overly complicated manner.
(B) The report is long, has unnecessary data, and is overly complicated.
(C) The report is long, contains unnecessary data, and is overly complicated.
(D) The report is long, contains unnecessary data, and is written overly complicated.

Q.12 -

Sentence:
The marketing plan is designed to increase brand awareness, boost sales, and improve customer engagement.
Question: Which revision best corrects the error?
(A) The marketing plan is designed to increase brand awareness, boost sales, and improve customer engagement.

(B) The marketing plan is designed to increase brand awareness, to boost sales, and to improve customer engagement.
(C) The marketing plan is designed to increase brand awareness, boost sales, and with the aim of improving customer engagement.
(D) The marketing plan is designed to increase brand awareness, boost sales, and with the goal of improving customer engagement.

Q.13 -

Sentence:

To succeed in the job interview, candidates should dress professionally, be confident, and demonstrate their skills effectively.

Question: Which revision best corrects the error?

(A) To succeed in the job interview, candidates should dress professionally, be confident, and demonstrate their skills effectively.
(B) To succeed in the job interview, candidates should dress professionally, be confident, and demonstrating their skills effectively.
(C) To succeed in the job interview, candidates should dress professionally, be confident, and should demonstrate their skills effectively.
(D) To succeed in the job interview, candidates should dress professionally, be confident, and demonstrate their skills effectively.

Q.14 -

Sentence:

The new employee was instructed to update the database, checking the records, and to respond to client inquiries.

Question: Which revision best corrects the error?

(A) The new employee was instructed to update the database, check the records, and respond to client inquiries.
(B) The new employee was instructed to update the database, checking the records, and responding to client inquiries.
(C) The new employee was instructed to update the database, check the records, and responding to client inquiries.
(D) The new employee was instructed to update the database, update the records, and respond to client inquiries.

Q.15 -

Sentence:

Our marketing strategy involves creating innovative content, engaging with audiences on social media, and analyzing consumer behavior regularly.

Question: Which revision best corrects the error?

(A) Our marketing strategy involves creating innovative content, engaging with audiences on social media, and analyzing consumer behavior regularly.
(B) Our marketing strategy involves creating innovative content, engaging with audiences on social media, and to analyze consumer behavior regularly.
(C) Our marketing strategy involves the creation of innovative content, the engagement with audiences on social media, and the analysis of consumer behavior.
(D) Our marketing strategy involves creating innovative content, engaging with audiences on social media, and analyzing consumer behavior.

Q.16 -

Sentence:

The report not only covers the annual revenue figures but also explains how the trends have affected the company's market share, and provides recommendations for future growth.

Question: Which revision best corrects the error?

(A) The report covers the annual revenue figures, explains how the trends have affected the company's market share, and provides recommendations for future growth.

(B) The report not only covers the annual revenue figures but also explains how the trends have affected the company's market share and provides recommendations for future growth.
(C) The report not only covers the annual revenue figures, but also explains how the trends have affected the company's market share, and it provides recommendations for future growth.
(D) The report covers the annual revenue figures, it explains how the trends have affected the company's market share, and it provides recommendations for future growth.

Q.17 -

Sentence:
The curriculum is designed to develop critical thinking skills, foster creativity, and encourage problem-solving abilities.
Question: Which revision best corrects the error?
(A) The curriculum is designed to develop critical thinking skills, foster creativity, and encourage problem-solving abilities.
(B) The curriculum is designed to develop critical thinking skills, to foster creativity, and encourage problem-solving abilities.
(C) The curriculum is designed to develop critical thinking skills, to foster creativity, and to encourage problem-solving abilities.
(D) The curriculum is designed to develop critical thinking skills, foster creativity, and it encourages problem-solving abilities.

Q.18 -

Sentence:
The advertisement was effective because it was eye-catching, had a clear message, and had a modern, appealing design.
Question: Which revision best corrects the error?
(A) The advertisement was effective because it was eye-catching, had a clear message, and had a modern, appealing design.
(B) The advertisement was effective because it was eye-catching, had a clear message, and its design was modern and appealing.
(C) The advertisement was effective because it was eye-catching, clear in its message, and modern in design.
(D) The advertisement was effective because it was eye-catching, had a clear message, and modern and appealing in design.

Q.19 -

Sentence:
To be successful, the entrepreneur must be innovative, take risks, and he must work hard.
Question: Which revision best corrects the error?
(A) To be successful, the entrepreneur must be innovative, take risks, and work hard.
(B) To be successful, the entrepreneur must be innovative, take risks, and he must work hard.
(C) To be successful, the entrepreneur must be innovative, risk-taking, and hard-working.
(D) To be successful, the entrepreneur must be innovative, taking risks, and working hard.

Q.20 -

Sentence:
The writer's style is characterized by clarity, an ability to engage the reader, and that vivid imagery is effective.
Question: Which revision best corrects the error?
(A) The writer's style is characterized by clarity, engagement, and the use of vivid imagery.
(B) The writer's style is characterized by clarity, an ability to engage the reader, and the use of vivid imagery.
(C) The writer's style is characterized by clarity, the ability to engage the reader, and the effective use of vivid imagery.
(D) The writer's style is characterized by clarity, an ability to engage, and vivid imagery.

Answers and Explanations for Parallel Structure and Wordiness Exercises

Q.1:

- **Correct Answer:** (A)
- **Explanation:** The revision "to be punctual, work hard, and complete their assignments on time" uses parallel (bare infinitive) verb forms throughout.

Q.2:

- **Correct Answer:** (B)
- **Explanation:** This option uses consistent gerund forms ("reading, jogging, and watching") for all activities.

Q.3:

- **Correct Answer:** (A)
- **Explanation:** By replacing "and it provides" with "and to provide," the sentence aligns all elements as infinitives.

Q.4:

- **Correct Answer:** (A)
- **Explanation:** The verbs "studied," "reviewed," and "practiced" are all in the simple past, creating a parallel structure.

Q.5:

- **Correct Answer:** (A)
- **Explanation:** This revision preserves the "not only… but also" construction and uses parallel adjectives/adjective phrases ("too complex," "too expensive," and "time-consuming to implement").

Q.6:

- **Correct Answer:** (A)
- **Explanation:** The sentence now lists three parallel infinitives: "to improve, reduce, and lower."

Q.7:

- **Correct Answer:** (D)
- **Explanation:** Replacing "filled with unnecessary details" with "contained unnecessary details" aligns all descriptive phrases ("was lengthy," "contained unnecessary details," and "was confusing") in a parallel manner.

Q.8:

- **Correct Answer:** (A)
- **Explanation:** All items are expressed in a parallel form: "quick-thinking," "have strong stamina," and "be well-prepared."

Q.9:

- **Correct Answer:** (C)
- **Explanation:** The revised sentence consistently lists qualities and actions in a parallel series.

Q.10:

- **Correct Answer:** (A)
- **Explanation:** The revision uses a series of bare infinitives—"allocate, hire, and purchase"—which is both concise and parallel.

Q.11:

- **Correct Answer:** (B)
- **Explanation:** "Has unnecessary data" and "is overly complicated" form a parallel, concise description.

Q.12:

- **Correct Answer:** (B)
- **Explanation:** Using the full infinitive form ("to increase, to boost, and to improve") ensures that all parts of the series are parallel.

Q.13:

- **Correct Answer:** (A)
- **Explanation:** The sentence now lists three coordinated actions ("dress professionally, be confident, and demonstrate their skills") in a parallel structure.

Q.14:

- **Correct Answer:** (A)
- **Explanation:** Changing "checking the records" to "check the records" creates a consistent series of infinitives.

Q.15:

- **Correct Answer:** (A)
- **Explanation:** The revision uses three gerund phrases ("creating innovative content, engaging with audiences, and analyzing consumer behavior") that are parallel.

Q.16:

- **Correct Answer:** (B)
- **Explanation:** This option correctly maintains the "not only… but also" structure with parallel verbs ("covers" and "explains" along with "provides").

Q.17:

- **Correct Answer:** (A)
- **Explanation:** The revised sentence uses three parallel infinitive phrases ("to develop, foster, and encourage") that clearly convey the curriculum's goals.

Q.18:

- **Correct Answer:** (A)
- **Explanation:** By stating "was eye-catching, had a clear message, and had a modern, appealing design," the sentence consistently describes the advertisement with parallel adjectives and phrases.

Q.19:

- **Correct Answer:** (A)
- **Explanation:** This revision presents three parallel requirements—"be innovative, take risks, and work hard"—without unnecessary repetition.

Q.20:

- **Correct Answer:** (C)
- **Explanation:** The sentence now features a parallel series of noun phrases: "clarity, the ability to engage the reader, and the effective use of vivid imagery."

4. Drill: Sentence Structure and Logical Flow

SAT grammar questions often test **sentence structure and clarity**, requiring students to **revise run-on sentences, comma splices, and misplaced modifiers**.

Warm-Up Practice 4: Fixing a Misplaced Modifier

Q.1 -

Sentence:

The meeting ended late, many employees left the office immediately.

Question: Which revision best corrects the error?

(A) The meeting ended late; many employees left the office immediately.

(B) The meeting ended late, so many employees left the office immediately.

(C) The meeting ended late, and many employees left the office immediately.

(D) The meeting ended late. Many employees left the office immediately.

Q.2 -

Sentence:

Running to catch the bus, the rain started pouring.
Question: Which revision best corrects the error?
(A) While running to catch the bus, I experienced a sudden downpour.
(B) While I was running to catch the bus, the rain started pouring.
(C) I was running to catch the bus, and the rain started pouring.
(D) Running to catch the bus, I got soaked when the rain started pouring.

Q.3 -

Sentence:
The chef prepared a delicious meal, it was served to the guests.
Question: Which revision best corrects the error?
(A) The chef prepared a delicious meal and served it to the guests.
(B) The chef prepared a delicious meal; it was served to the guests.
(C) The chef prepared a delicious meal, and it was served to the guests.
(D) The chef prepared a delicious meal: it was served to the guests.

Q.4 -

Sentence:
Having finished the report, the computer was shut down.
Question: Which revision best corrects the error?
(A) Having finished the report, the report was sent and the computer was shut down.
(B) Having finished the report, John shut down the computer.
(C) After finishing the report, the computer was shut down by John.
(D) The report was finished, and then the computer was shut down.

Q.5 -

Sentence:
The project was challenging, the team succeeded nonetheless.
Question: Which revision best corrects the error?
(A) Although the project was challenging, the team succeeded nonetheless.
(B) The project was challenging; however, the team succeeded nonetheless.
(C) The project was challenging, yet the team succeeded nonetheless.
(D) Despite the project being challenging, the team succeeded nonetheless.

Q.6 -

Sentence:
She enjoys painting, and drawing is her favorite hobby.
Question: Which revision best corrects the error?
(A) She enjoys painting, and she enjoys drawing as her favorite hobby.
(B) She enjoys painting and drawing, and they are both her favorite hobbies.
(C) She enjoys both painting and drawing.
(D) She enjoys painting; drawing is her favorite hobby.

Q.7 -

Sentence:
The report was long, it contained detailed statistics and lengthy explanations.
Question: Which revision best corrects the error?
(A) The report was long; it contained detailed statistics and lengthy explanations.
(B) The report was long, and it contained detailed statistics and lengthy explanations.
(C) The report was long. It contained detailed statistics and lengthy explanations.
(D) The report was long, containing detailed statistics and lengthy explanations.

Q.8 -

Sentence:

Before leaving the house, the keys were not found in the usual spot.
Question: Which revision best corrects the error?
(A) Before leaving the house, the keys were missing from the usual spot.
(B) Before leaving the house, I could not find the keys in the usual spot.
(C) Before leaving the house, the usual spot had no keys.
(D) Before leaving the house, I did not find the keys in the usual spot.
Q.9 -
Sentence:
The experiment was conducted carefully, results were recorded accurately.
Question: Which revision best corrects the error?
(A) The experiment was conducted carefully; results were recorded accurately.
(B) The experiment was conducted carefully, and the results were recorded accurately.
(C) The experiment was conducted carefully. The results were recorded accurately.
(D) Carefully conducted, the experiment yielded accurately recorded results.
Q.10 -
Sentence:
The student, who struggled with the assignment, and he eventually sought help from the teacher.
Question: Which revision best corrects the error?
(A) The student, who struggled with the assignment, eventually sought help from the teacher.
(B) The student who struggled with the assignment eventually sought help from the teacher.
(C) The student, having struggled with the assignment, eventually sought help from the teacher.
(D) The student struggled with the assignment and eventually sought help from the teacher.
Q.11 -
Sentence:
After the meeting was over, the documents were reviewed, and they were distributed to the department.
Question: Which revision best corrects the error?
(A) After the meeting was over, the documents were reviewed and distributed to the department.
(B) After the meeting, the documents were reviewed and distributed to the department.
(C) The documents were reviewed and distributed to the department after the meeting ended.
(D) Once the meeting was finished, the documents were reviewed and distributed to the department.
Q.12 -
Sentence:
She likes to travel, she enjoys exploring new cultures, and she is fascinated by historical landmarks.
Question: Which revision best corrects the error?
(A) She likes to travel, enjoys exploring new cultures, and is fascinated by historical landmarks.
(B) She likes to travel and enjoys exploring new cultures, and she is fascinated by historical landmarks.
(C) She likes to travel; she enjoys exploring new cultures; and she is fascinated by historical landmarks.
(D) She likes to travel, enjoys exploring new cultures, and historical landmarks fascinate her.
Q.13 -
Sentence:
The policy was approved quickly, it has been implemented in all departments since last month.
Question: Which revision best corrects the error?
(A) The policy was approved quickly, and it has been implemented in all departments since last month.
(B) The policy was approved quickly; it has been implemented in all departments since last month.
(C) The policy was approved quickly and has been implemented in all departments since last month.
(D) Approved quickly, the policy has been implemented in all departments since last month.
Q.14 -
Sentence:

To succeed in business, networking is essential; it helps build connections and fosters new opportunities.
Question: Which revision best improves sentence structure and logical flow?
(A) Networking is essential because it helps build connections and fosters new opportunities.
(B) To succeed in business, networking is essential as it builds connections and fosters new opportunities.
(C) Networking, essential for business success, builds connections and fosters new opportunities.
(D) To succeed in business, networking is essential; it builds connections and fosters new opportunities.

Q.15 -

Sentence:
Due to the fact that the weather was bad, the event was canceled.
Question: Which revision best corrects the wordiness?
(A) Because the weather was bad, the event was canceled.
(B) Since the weather was bad, the event was canceled.
(C) Owing to the bad weather, the event was canceled.
(D) The event was canceled because of bad weather.

Q.16 -

Sentence:
After working for hours, a break was taken by the employees.
Question: Which revision best corrects the error?
(A) After working for hours, the employees took a break.
(B) After working for hours, a break was taken by the employees.
(C) After hours of work, a break was taken by the employees.
(D) After working for hours, the break was taken.

Q.17 -

Sentence:
The proposal, which was lengthy and complicated, needed to be revised and it was sent back to the author.
Question: Which revision best corrects the error?
(A) The lengthy and complicated proposal needed to be revised and was sent back to the author.
(B) The proposal, which was lengthy and complicated, needed revision and was sent back to the author.
(C) The proposal, lengthy and complicated, needed to be revised and sent back to the author.
(D) The lengthy proposal, which was complicated, needed to be revised and was sent back to the author.

Q.18 -

Sentence:
After the announcement, the employees cheered, and they celebrated their achievements.
Question: Which revision best corrects the error?
(A) After the announcement was made, the employees cheered and celebrated their achievements.
(B) Following the announcement, the employees cheered and celebrated their achievements.
(C) After the announcement, the employees cheered and celebrated their achievements.
(D) The announcement was made, and the employees cheered and celebrated their achievements.

Q.19 -

Sentence:
Although the instructions were confusing at first, the students understood them after reading the manual, they began working on the assignment.
Question: Which revision best corrects the error?
(A) Although the instructions were confusing at first, the students understood them after reading the manual and began working on the assignment.
(B) Although the instructions were confusing at first, after reading the manual, the students understood them and began working on the assignment.
(C) The instructions were confusing at first; however, the students understood them after reading the manual and

began working on the assignment.
(D) Although the instructions were confusing at first, the students understood them after reading the manual; they began working on the assignment.

Q.20 -

Sentence:
The director announced that the new policy would take effect immediately, and employees must comply with it without delay.
Question: Which revision best corrects the error?
(A) The director announced that the new policy would take effect immediately, and employees must comply with it without delay.
(B) The director announced that the new policy would take effect immediately, and that employees must comply with it without delay.
(C) The director announced that the new policy would take effect immediately and employees must comply with it without delay.
(D) The director announced the new policy would take effect immediately and employees must comply with it without delay.

Answers and Explanations for Sentence Structure and Logical Flow Exercises

Q.1:

- **Correct Answer:** (A)
- **Explanation:** Replacing the comma with a semicolon correctly separates two independent clauses without creating a run-on sentence.

Q.2:

- **Correct Answer:** (A)
- **Explanation:** By specifying the subject "I," the revision eliminates the misplaced modifier that originally made it seem as if the rain was running.

Q.3:

- **Correct Answer:** (A)
- **Explanation:** Combining the clauses with "and served it to the guests" corrects the comma splice and creates a concise, logical flow.

Q.4:

- **Correct Answer:** (B)
- **Explanation:** Including the subject "John" clarifies who finished the report and who shut down the computer, eliminating the dangling modifier.

Q.5:

- **Correct Answer:** (A)
- **Explanation:** Starting the sentence with "Although" properly introduces the dependent clause, ensuring a smooth logical connection between the challenge and the team's success.

Q.6:

- **Correct Answer:** (C)
- **Explanation:** The revision "She enjoys both painting and drawing" provides a concise, parallel structure without unnecessary repetition.

Q.7:

- **Correct Answer:** (D)
- **Explanation:** Using a participial phrase ("containing detailed statistics and lengthy explanations") links the description to the subject while eliminating the comma splice.

Q.8:

- **Correct Answer:** (D)

- **Explanation:** Changing the sentence to "Before leaving the house, I did not find the keys in the usual spot" corrects the dangling modifier by clearly identifying the subject.

Q.9:

- **Correct Answer:** (B)
- **Explanation:** Adding "and" properly connects the two independent clauses, ensuring a smooth logical flow.

Q.10:

- **Correct Answer:** (B)
- **Explanation:** Removing the extra pronoun "and he" eliminates redundancy and clarifies that the student alone sought help.

Q.11:

- **Correct Answer:** (B)
- **Explanation:** Dropping unnecessary words for conciseness, the revision "After the meeting, the documents were reviewed and distributed to the department" flows logically.

Q.12:

- **Correct Answer:** (A)
- **Explanation:** Removing repeated subjects and combining the clauses creates a parallel structure and eliminates the comma splice.

Q.13:

- **Correct Answer:** (C)
- **Explanation:** Joining the independent clauses with "and" produces a clear, coherent sentence that logically flows from approval to implementation.

Q.14:

- **Correct Answer:** (A)
- **Explanation:** Rewriting the sentence as "Networking is essential because it helps build connections and fosters new opportunities" establishes a clear cause-and-effect relationship.

Q.15:

- **Correct Answer:** (A)
- **Explanation:** Replacing "Due to the fact that" with "Because" removes unnecessary wordiness while preserving the intended meaning.

Q.16:

- **Correct Answer:** (A)
- **Explanation:** By stating "the employees took a break," the sentence clearly identifies the subject, correcting the dangling modifier.

Q.17:

- **Correct Answer:** (A)
- **Explanation:** The revision eliminates redundancy by removing the extra clause and presents a smooth, parallel structure.

Q.18:

- **Correct Answer:** (C)
- **Explanation:** This revision streamlines the sentence by removing extraneous words while maintaining a logical progression of ideas.

Q.19:

- **Correct Answer:** (A)
- **Explanation:** Combining the clauses with "and" eliminates the comma splice and ensures a coherent flow from confusion to understanding and action.

Q.20:

- **Correct Answer:** (B)

- **Explanation:** Inserting "that" before "employees" establishes parallel structure and clarifies that both the policy's immediate effect and the required compliance are part of the announcement.

5. Summary of Key Strategies

Concept	Best Strategy
Subject-Verb Agreement	Identify the subject and ensure the verb matches in number.
Pronoun Clarity	Ensure pronouns refer clearly to one noun and match in number.
Parallel Structure	Items in lists and comparisons must follow the same format.
Sentence Structure	Check for misplaced modifiers, run-ons, and comma splices.

6. Final Key Takeaways

- **Identify and correct subject-verb agreement errors**, especially with collective nouns.
- **Clarify ambiguous pronouns by repeating the noun when necessary.**
- **Use parallel structure in lists and comparisons to maintain consistency.**
- **Avoid misplaced modifiers by placing descriptive phrases near the nouns they modify.**
- **Practice revising short passages to build familiarity with common SAT grammar traps.**

By **mastering these grammar drills**, students can **improve their ability to edit and revise short passages effectively**, leading to **higher scores on the SAT Writing & Language section**.

16.3 Basic to Intermediate Math Problem Sets

The **Digital SAT Math section** includes a range of questions from **basic arithmetic and algebra** to **intermediate-level geometry and data analysis**. This section provides **practice problems** designed to reinforce **core math skills and problem-solving techniques**.

This section will cover:

- **Basic Arithmetic and Number Properties**
- **Algebraic Equations and Inequalities**
- **Geometry and Measurement**
- **Data Analysis and Probability**

1. Basic Arithmetic and Number Properties

These problems test **fractions, decimals, percentages, and integer properties**.

Practice Problem 1: Fractions and Operations

Q.1 -
Calculate:

$$\frac{2}{3}+\frac{3}{5}=?$$

Q.2 -
Calculate:

$$\frac{7}{8}-\frac{1}{4}=?$$

Q.3 -
Calculate:

$$\frac{5}{6}\times\frac{3}{4}=?$$

Q.4 -
Calculate:

$$\frac{9}{10} \div \frac{3}{5} = ?$$

Q.5 -

Calculate:

$$\frac{4}{7} + \frac{2}{3} = ?$$

Q.6 -

Calculate:

$$\frac{11}{12} - \frac{5}{8} = ?$$

Q.7 -

Calculate:

$$\frac{3}{5} \times \frac{10}{9} = ?$$

Q.8 -

Calculate:

$$\frac{8}{9} \div \frac{4}{7} = ?$$

Q.9 -

Calculate:

$$\frac{5}{6} + \frac{7}{12} = ?$$

Q.10 -

Calculate:

$$\frac{3}{4} - \frac{1}{8} = ?$$

Practice Problem 2: Percentage Increase

Q.11 -

A smartphone originally costs **$500**. If the price increases by **10%**, what is the new price?

Q.12 -

A pair of shoes originally costs **$80**. If the price increases by **25%**, what is the new price?

Q.13 -

A car is originally priced at **$20,000**. If the price increases by **5%**, what is the new price?

Q.14 -

A jacket originally costs **$120**. If its price increases by **15%**, what is the new price?

Q.15 -

A computer originally costs **$1,000**. If its price increases by **8%**, what is the new price?

Q.16 -

A bicycle originally costs **$300**. If its price increases by **20%**, what is the new price?

Q.17 -

A watch originally costs **$250**. If its price increases by **12%**, what is the new price?

Q.18 -

A book originally costs **$40**. If its price increases by **30%**, what is the new price?

Q.19 -

A piece of furniture originally costs **$700**. If its price increases by **10%**, what is the new price?

Q.20 -

A subscription service originally costs **$15** per month. If the monthly price increases by **18%**, what is the new monthly cost?

Answers and Explanations

Practice Problem 1: Fractions and Operations

Q.1:

- **Calculation:**

$$\frac{2}{3}+\frac{3}{5}=\frac{10}{15}+\frac{9}{15}=\frac{19}{15}=1\frac{4}{15}$$

- **Final Answer:** $1\frac{4}{15}$

Q.2:

- **Calculation:**

  Convert $\frac{1}{4}$ to $\frac{2}{8}$ since 7/8 is already with denominator 8:

$$\frac{7}{8}-\frac{1}{4}=\frac{7}{8}-\frac{2}{8}=\frac{5}{8}$$

- **Final Answer:** $\frac{5}{8}$

Q.3:

- **Calculation:**

$$\frac{5}{6}\times\frac{3}{4}=\frac{15}{24}=\frac{5}{8}\quad\text{(divide numerator and denominator by 3)}$$

- **Final Answer:** $\frac{5}{8}$

Q.4:

- **Calculation:**

$$\frac{9}{10}\div\frac{3}{5}=\frac{9}{10}\times\frac{5}{3}=\frac{45}{30}=\frac{3}{2}\quad\text{(or 1.5)}$$

- **Final Answer:** $\frac{3}{2}$ or 1.5

Q.5:

- **Calculation:**

  Common denominator for $\frac{4}{7}$ and $\frac{2}{3}$ is 21:

$$\frac{4}{7}=\frac{12}{21},\quad\frac{2}{3}=\frac{14}{21}$$
$$\frac{12}{21}+\frac{14}{21}=\frac{26}{21}$$

- **Final Answer:** $\frac{26}{21}$ (or $1\frac{5}{21}$)

Q.6:

- **Calculation:**

  Common denominator for $\frac{11}{12}$ and $\frac{5}{8}$ is 24:

$$\frac{11}{12}=\frac{22}{24},\quad\frac{5}{8}=\frac{15}{24}$$
$$\frac{22}{24}-\frac{15}{24}=\frac{7}{24}$$

- **Final Answer:** $\frac{7}{24}$

Q.7:

- **Calculation:**

$$\frac{3}{5}\times\frac{10}{9}=\frac{30}{45}=\frac{2}{3}\quad\text{(divide numerator and denominator by 15)}$$

- **Final Answer:** $\frac{2}{3}$

Q.8:

- **Calculation:**
  $$\frac{8}{9} \div \frac{4}{7} = \frac{8}{9} \times \frac{7}{4} = \frac{56}{36} = \frac{14}{9}$$ (simplify by dividing numerator and denominator by 4)
- **Final Answer:** $\frac{14}{9}$

Q.9:

- **Calculation:**
  Convert $\frac{5}{6}$ to twelfths:
  $$\frac{5}{6} = \frac{10}{12}; \quad \frac{10}{12} + \frac{7}{12} = \frac{17}{12} = 1\frac{5}{12}$$
- **Final Answer:** $\frac{17}{12}$ (or $1\frac{5}{12}$)

Q.10:

- **Calculation:**
  Convert $\frac{3}{4}$ to eighths:
  $$\frac{3}{4} = \frac{6}{8}; \quad \frac{6}{8} - \frac{1}{8} = \frac{5}{8}$$
- **Final Answer:** $\frac{5}{8}$

Practice Problem 2: Percentage Increase

Q.11:

- **Calculation:**
  Increase = 10% of \$500:
  $$0.10 \times 500 = 50$$
  New price = $500 + 50 = 550$
- **Final Answer:** \$550

Q.12:

- **Calculation:**
  Increase = 25% of \$80:
  $$0.25 \times 80 = 20$$
  New price = $80 + 20 = 100$
- **Final Answer:** \$100

Q.13:

- **Calculation:**
  Increase = 5% of \$20,000:
  $$0.05 \times 20000 = 1000$$
  New price = $20000 + 1000 = 21000$
- **Final Answer:** \$21,000

Q.14:

- **Calculation:**
  Increase = 15% of \$120:
  $$0.15 \times 120 = 18$$
  New price = $120 + 18 = 138$
- **Final Answer:** \$138

Q.15:

- **Calculation:**
  Increase = 8% of \$1,000:

$$0.08 \times 1000 = 80$$

New price = $1000 + 80 = 1080$

- **Final Answer:** $1,080

Q.16:

- **Calculation:**
  Increase = 20% of $300:

$$0.20 \times 300 = 60$$

New price = $300 + 60 = 360$

- **Final Answer:** $360

Q.17:

- **Calculation:**
  Increase = 12% of $250:

$$0.12 \times 250 = 30$$

New price = $250 + 30 = 280$

- **Final Answer:** $280

Q.18:

- **Calculation:**
  Increase = 30% of $40:

$$0.30 \times 40 = 12$$

New price = $40 + 12 = 52$

- **Final Answer:** $52

Q.19:

- **Calculation:**
  Increase = 10% of $700:

$$0.10 \times 700 = 70$$

New price = $700 + 70 = 770$

- **Final Answer:** $770

Q.20:

- **Calculation:**
  Increase = 18% of $15:

$$0.18 \times 15 = 2.70$$

New monthly cost = $15 + 2.70 = 17.70$

- **Final Answer:** $17.70 per month

2. Algebraic Equations and Inequalities

These problems test **solving equations, inequalities, and simplifying expressions**.

Practice Problem 3: Solving a Linear Equation

Q.1 -
Solve for x:

$$2x + 5 = 17$$

Q.2 -
Solve for x:

$$3x - 4 = 2x + 6$$

Q.3 -
Solve for x:

$$4(x - 3) = 2x + 8$$

Q.4 -
Solve for x:

$$5 - 3x = 2x + 10$$

Q.5 -
Solve for x:

$$\frac{1}{2}x + 3 = 7$$

Q.6 -
Solve for x:

$$2(3x + 1) = 4x + 10$$

Q.7 -
Solve for x:

$$7 - 2x = 3x + 2$$

Q.8 -
Solve for x:

$$\frac{4x}{3} + 2 = 10$$

Q.9 -
Solve for x:

$$6x - 5 = 3x + 16$$

Q.10 -
Solve for x:

$$8 - 2(x + 1) = 4x - 6$$

Practice Problem 4: Solving a Quadratic Equation

Q.11 -
Solve for x:

$$x^2 - 5x + 6 = 0$$

Q.12 -
Solve for x:

$$x^2 + 3x - 10 = 0$$

Q.13 -
Solve for x:

$$2x^2 - 8x + 6 = 0$$

Q.14 -
Solve for x:

$$x^2 - 4 = 0$$

Q.15 -
Solve for x:

$$x^2 + 2x - 8 = 0$$

Q.16 -
Solve for x:

$$3x^2 - 12 = 0$$

Q.17 -
Solve for x:

$$x^2 - x - 12 = 0$$

Q.18 -
Solve for x:

$$2x^2 + x - 6 = 0$$

Q.19 -
Solve for x:

$$x^2 - 9x + 14 = 0$$

Q.20 -
Solve for x:

$$x^2 + 6x + 9 = 0$$

Answers and Explanations

Practice Problem 3: Solving a Linear Equation

Q.1:

- **Solution:**
  Subtract 5 from both sides:
  $$2x = 12 \quad \Rightarrow \quad x = 6$$
- **Final Answer:** $x = 6$

Q.2:

- **Solution:**
  Subtract $2x$ from both sides:
  $$x - 4 = 6 \quad \Rightarrow \quad x = 10$$
- **Final Answer:** $x = 10$

Q.3:

- **Solution:**
  Expand the left side:
  $$4x - 12 = 2x + 8$$
  Subtract $2x$ from both sides:
  $$2x - 12 = 8 \quad \Rightarrow \quad 2x = 20 \quad \Rightarrow \quad x = 10$$
- **Final Answer:** $x = 10$

Q.4:

- **Solution:**
  Add $3x$ to both sides:
  $$5 = 5x + 10$$
  Subtract 10:
  $$-5 = 5x \quad \Rightarrow \quad x = -1$$
- **Final Answer:** $x = -1$

Q.5:

- **Solution:**
  Subtract 3:
  $$\frac{1}{2}x = 4 \quad \Rightarrow \quad x = 8$$
- **Final Answer:** $x = 8$

Q.6:

- **Solution:**
  Expand the left side:
  $$6x + 2 = 4x + 10$$
  Subtract $4x$:
  $$2x + 2 = 10 \quad \Rightarrow \quad 2x = 8 \quad \Rightarrow \quad x = 4$$
- **Final Answer:** $x = 4$

Q.7:

- **Solution:**
  Add $2x$ to both sides:

$$7 = 5x + 2 \quad \Rightarrow \quad 5x = 5 \quad \Rightarrow \quad x = 1$$

- **Final Answer:** $x = 1$

Q.8:

- **Solution:**
  Subtract 2:

$$\frac{4x}{3} = 8 \quad \Rightarrow \quad 4x = 24 \quad \Rightarrow \quad x = 6$$

- **Final Answer:** $x = 6$

Q.9:

- **Solution:**
  Subtract $3x$ from both sides:

$$3x - 5 = 16 \quad \Rightarrow \quad 3x = 21 \quad \Rightarrow \quad x = 7$$

- **Final Answer:** $x = 7$

Q.10:

- **Solution:**
  Expand the left side:

$$8 - 2x - 2 = 4x - 6 \quad \Rightarrow \quad 6 - 2x = 4x - 6$$

  Add $2x$ to both sides:

$$6 = 6x - 6 \quad \Rightarrow \quad 6x = 12 \quad \Rightarrow \quad x = 2$$

- **Final Answer:** $x = 2$

Practice Problem 4: Solving a Quadratic Equation

Q.11:

- **Solution:**
  Factor:

$$x^2 - 5x + 6 = (x - 2)(x - 3) = 0$$

  Set each factor equal to zero:

$$x = 2 \quad \text{or} \quad x = 3$$

- **Final Answer:** $x = 2$ or $x = 3$

Q.12:

- **Solution:**
  Factor:

$$x^2 + 3x - 10 = (x + 5)(x - 2) = 0$$

  Thus,

$$x = -5 \quad \text{or} \quad x = 2$$

- **Final Answer:** $x = -5$ or $x = 2$

Q.13:

- **Solution:**
  Factor out 2:

$$2(x^2 - 4x + 3) = 0$$

  Factor the quadratic:

$$(x - 1)(x - 3) = 0$$

  So,

$$x = 1 \quad \text{or} \quad x = 3$$

- **Final Answer:** $x = 1$ or $x = 3$

Q.14:

- **Solution:**
Recognize the difference of squares:
$$x^2 - 4 = (x - 2)(x + 2) = 0$$
Therefore,
$$x = 2 \quad \text{or} \quad x = -2$$
- **Final Answer:** $x = 2$ or $x = -2$

Q.15:

- **Solution:**
Factor:
$$x^2 + 2x - 8 = (x + 4)(x - 2) = 0$$
Hence,
$$x = -4 \quad \text{or} \quad x = 2$$
- **Final Answer:** $x = -4$ or $x = 2$

Q.16:

- **Solution:**
Factor out 3:
$$3x^2 - 12 = 3(x^2 - 4) = 0$$
Then, use the difference of squares:
$$x^2 - 4 = (x - 2)(x + 2) = 0$$
So,
$$x = 2 \quad \text{or} \quad x = -2$$
- **Final Answer:** $x = 2$ or $x = -2$

Q.17:

- **Solution:**
Factor:
$$x^2 - x - 12 = (x - 4)(x + 3) = 0$$
Thus,
$$x = 4 \quad \text{or} \quad x = -3$$
- **Final Answer:** $x = 4$ or $x = -3$

Q.18:

- **Solution:**
Multiply $2 \times (-6) = -12$. Find two numbers that multiply to -12 and add to 1: 4 and -3. Rewrite:
$$2x^2 + 4x - 3x - 6 = 0$$
Factor by grouping:
$$2x(x + 2) - 3(x + 2) = 0$$
Factor out $(x + 2)$:
$$(x + 2)(2x - 3) = 0$$
So,
$$x = -2 \quad \text{or} \quad x = \frac{3}{2}$$
- **Final Answer:** $x = -2$ or $x = \frac{3}{2}$

Q.19:

- **Solution:**
Factor:
$$x^2 - 9x + 14 = (x - 7)(x - 2) = 0$$

Hence,

$$x = 7 \quad \text{or} \quad x = 2$$

- **Final Answer:** $x = 7$ or $x = 2$

Q.20:

- **Solution:**
  Recognize a perfect square trinomial:
  $$x^2 + 6x + 9 = (x + 3)^2 = 0$$
  Therefore,
  $$x = -3$$
- **Final Answer:** $x = -3$

3. Geometry and Measurement

These problems test **shapes, angles, perimeter, area, and volume**.

Practice Problem 5: Pythagorean Theorem and Triangle Applications

Q.1 -
Find the length of the hypotenuse of a right triangle with legs of 9 cm and 12 cm.

Q.2 -
In a right triangle, one leg measures 8 m and the hypotenuse is 10 m. Find the length of the other leg.

Q.3 -
A ladder leans against a wall so that its base is 6 feet from the wall and its top touches the wall at a height of 8 feet. What is the length of the ladder?

Q.4 -
A square has a diagonal of $10\sqrt{2}$ cm. Find the side length of the square.

Q.5 -
In a right triangle, the lengths of the legs are in the ratio $3:4$ and the hypotenuse measures 10. Find the lengths of the legs.

Q.6 -
A right triangle has a hypotenuse of 17 and one leg of 8. Determine the length of the other leg.

Q.7 -
On a coordinate plane, the distance between two points is 13 units. If the horizontal distance is 5 units, what is the vertical distance between the points?

Q.8 -
A rectangular garden has a length of 14 m and a width of 48 m. Find the length of the diagonal of the garden.

Q.9 -
A right triangle has legs that differ by 2 units, and its hypotenuse is 10. Find the lengths of the two legs.

Q.10 -
In a right triangle, one leg measures 7 and the hypotenuse measures 25. Find the length of the other leg.

Practice Problem 6: Area, Perimeter, and Volume

Q.11 -
Find the area of a circle with a radius of 7 cm.

Q.12 -
Find the circumference of a circle with a diameter of 10 m.

Q.13 -
Calculate the area of a triangle with a base of 12 cm and a height of 5 cm.

Q.14 -
Determine the perimeter of a rectangle with a length of 15 m and a width of 8 m.

Q.15 -

Find the area of a trapezoid with bases of 10 m and 14 m, and a height of 6 m.

Q.16 -

Calculate the volume of a rectangular prism with a length of 4, a width of 3, and a height of 5.

Q.17 -

Find the surface area of a cube with a side length of 3.

Q.18 -

Calculate the volume of a cylinder with a radius of 4 and a height of 10.

Q.19 -

A circle has an area of 36π. Determine its radius.

Q.20 -

Find the surface area of a sphere with a radius of 6.

Answers and Explanations for Geometry and Measurement Exercises

Practice Problem 5: Pythagorean Theorem and Triangle Applications

Q.1:

- **Solution:**
  Using the Pythagorean Theorem:
  $$c = \sqrt{9^2 + 12^2} = \sqrt{81 + 144} = \sqrt{225} = 15$$
- **Final Answer: 15 cm**

Q.2:

- **Solution:**
  Let the unknown leg be x. Then:
  $$x = \sqrt{10^2 - 8^2} = \sqrt{100 - 64} = \sqrt{36} = 6$$
- **Final Answer: 6 m**

Q.3:

- **Solution:**
  The ladder's length is the hypotenuse of a right triangle with legs 6 and 8:
  $$\text{Ladder length} = \sqrt{6^2 + 8^2} = \sqrt{36 + 64} = \sqrt{100} = 10$$
- **Final Answer: 10 ft**

Q.4:

- **Solution:**
  In a square, the diagonal d and side s are related by:
  $$d = s\sqrt{2} \quad \Rightarrow \quad s = \frac{d}{\sqrt{2}} = \frac{10\sqrt{2}}{\sqrt{2}} = 10$$
- **Final Answer: 10 cm**

Q.5:

- **Solution:**
  Let the legs be $3k$ and $4k$; then the hypotenuse is $5k$. Since $5k = 10$, $k = 2$. Thus, the legs are:
  $$3k = 6 \quad \text{and} \quad 4k = 8$$
- **Final Answer: 6 and 8**

Q.6:

- **Solution:**
  Using the Pythagorean Theorem:
  $$x = \sqrt{17^2 - 8^2} = \sqrt{289 - 64} = \sqrt{225} = 15$$
- **Final Answer: 15**

Q.7:

- **Solution:**
  With total distance 13 and horizontal distance 5, the vertical distance is:
  $$\sqrt{13^2 - 5^2} = \sqrt{169 - 25} = \sqrt{144} = 12$$
- **Final Answer: 12**

Q.8:

- **Solution:**
  The diagonal of a rectangle:
  $$d = \sqrt{14^2 + 48^2} = \sqrt{196 + 2304} = \sqrt{2500} = 50$$
- **Final Answer: 50 m**

Q.9:

- **Solution:**
  Let the legs be x and $x + 2$. Then:
  $$x^2 + (x + 2)^2 = 10^2 \quad \Rightarrow \quad x^2 + x^2 + 4x + 4 = 100$$
  $$2x^2 + 4x - 96 = 0 \quad \Rightarrow \quad x^2 + 2x - 48 = 0$$
  Solve using the quadratic formula:
  $$x = \frac{-2 \pm \sqrt{2^2 - 4(1)(-48)}}{2} = \frac{-2 \pm \sqrt{4 + 192}}{2} = \frac{-2 \pm \sqrt{196}}{2}$$
  $$x = \frac{-2 + 14}{2} = 6 \quad \text{(reject the negative solution)}$$
  The legs are 6 and 8.
- **Final Answer: 6 and 8**

Q.10:

- **Solution:**
  Let the unknown leg be x. Then:
  $$x = \sqrt{25^2 - 7^2} = \sqrt{625 - 49} = \sqrt{576} = 24$$
- **Final Answer: 24**

Practice Problem 6: Area, Perimeter, and Volume

Q.11:

- **Solution:**
  Area of a circle:
  $$A = \pi r^2 = \pi(7^2) = 49\pi$$
- **Final Answer: 49π cm²**

Q.12:

- **Solution:**
  Circumference of a circle with diameter 10:
  $$C = \pi d = \pi \times 10 = 10\pi$$
- **Final Answer: 10π m**

Q.13:

- **Solution:**
  Area of a triangle:
  $$A = \frac{1}{2} \times \text{base} \times \text{height} = \frac{1}{2} \times 12 \times 5 = 30$$
- **Final Answer: 30 cm²**

Q.14:

- **Solution:**
Perimeter of a rectangle:
$$P = 2(\text{length} + \text{width}) = 2(15 + 8) = 2(23) = 46$$
- **Final Answer: 46 m**

Q.15:

- **Solution:**
Area of a trapezoid:
$$A = \frac{1}{2}(b_1 + b_2) \times h = \frac{1}{2}(10 + 14) \times 6 = \frac{1}{2}(24) \times 6 = 72$$
- **Final Answer: 72 m²**

Q.16:

- **Solution:**
Volume of a rectangular prism:
$$V = \text{length} \times \text{width} \times \text{height} = 4 \times 3 \times 5 = 60$$
- **Final Answer: 60**

Q.17:

- **Solution:**
Surface area of a cube:
$$SA = 6s^2 = 6(3^2) = 6 \times 9 = 54$$
- **Final Answer: 54**

Q.18:

- **Solution:**
Volume of a cylinder:
$$V = \pi r^2 h = \pi(4^2)(10) = \pi(16)(10) = 160\pi$$
- **Final Answer:** 160π

Q.19:

- **Solution:**
Given area $A = 36\pi$ for a circle:
$$A = \pi r^2 \quad \Rightarrow \quad r^2 = 36 \quad \Rightarrow \quad r = 6$$
- **Final Answer: 6**

Q.20:

- **Solution:**
Surface area of a sphere:
$$SA = 4\pi r^2 = 4\pi(6^2) = 4\pi \times 36 = 144\pi$$
- **Final Answer:** 144π

4. Data Analysis and Probability

These problems test **interpreting graphs, mean/median/mode, and probability**.

Practice Problem 7: Data Analysis (Mean, Median, Mode, Range, and Interpreting Data)

Q.1 -
Find the mean of the following numbers:
4,8,12,16,20

Q.2 -
Find the median of the following set of numbers:
3,5,7,9,11

Q.3 -
Find the mode of the following data set:
2,3,3,5,7,8
Q.4 -
Find the range of the following set of numbers:
10,4,15,9,6
Q.5 -
In a class, 5 students scored 80 and 3 students scored 90 on a test. Find the overall mean score.
Q.6 -
A survey of study hours yielded the following data (in hours):
2,4,5,3,4,6,5,5
Find the mean number of hours studied.
Q.7 -
For the following data set, find both the median and the mode:
12,15,12,18,20,15,15
Q.8 -
Find the mean of the following scores:
100,95,80,70,85
Q.9 -
Calculate the range of the following numbers:
22,35,27,30,40,28
Q.10 -
If the sum of 9 numbers is 81, what is their mean?

Practice Problem 8: Probability of an Event and Other Probability Problems
Q.11 -
A bag contains 4 red, 5 blue, and 3 green marbles. What is the probability of drawing a blue marble?
Q.12 -
If a fair six-sided die is rolled, what is the probability of rolling a number greater than 4?
Q.13 -
A card is drawn from a standard deck of 52 cards. What is the probability of drawing a heart?
Q.14 -
Two coins are tossed simultaneously. What is the probability of obtaining exactly one head?
Q.15 -
A jar contains 10 balls numbered 1 through 10. What is the probability of drawing an even number?
Q.16 -
A spinner is divided into 8 equal sections numbered 1 through 8. What is the probability that the spinner lands on a prime number?
Q.17 -
A box contains 6 defective bulbs and 24 non-defective bulbs. If one bulb is selected at random, what is the probability that it is defective?
Q.18 -
In a classroom of 30 students, 12 students wear glasses. What is the probability that a randomly selected student wears glasses?
Q.19 -
A jar contains 7 red, 5 blue, and 8 yellow candies. What is the probability of selecting either a red or a blue candy?

Q.20 -

A standard deck of 52 cards contains 12 face cards (Jacks, Queens, Kings). What is the probability of drawing a face card?

Answers and Explanations

Practice Problem 7: Data Analysis

Q.1:

- **Calculation:**

$$\text{Mean} = \frac{4 + 8 + 12 + 16 + 20}{5} = \frac{60}{5} = 12$$

- **Final Answer: 12**

Q.2:

- **Explanation:**
  The numbers in order are: 3, 5, 7, 9, 11. The middle (third) number is 7.
- **Final Answer: 7**

Q.3:

- **Explanation:**
  In the set 2,3,3,5,7,8, the number 3 appears twice (more often than any other value).
- **Final Answer: 3**

Q.4:

- **Calculation:**

$$\text{Range} = \text{Maximum} - \text{Minimum} = 15 - 4 = 11$$

- **Final Answer: 11**

Q.5:

- **Calculation:**
  Total score = $5 \times 80 + 3 \times 90 = 400 + 270 = 670$
  Total students = 8
  Mean score = $\frac{670}{8} = 83.75$
- **Final Answer: 83.75**

Q.6:

- **Calculation:**
  Sum = $2 + 4 + 5 + 3 + 4 + 6 + 5 + 5 = 34$
  Count = 8
  Mean = $\frac{34}{8} = 4.25$
- **Final Answer: 4.25 hours**

Q.7:

- **Explanation:**
  Sorted data: 12, 12, 15, 15, 15, 18, 20
  Median (middle value) = 15
  Mode (most frequent) = 15 (appears three times)
- **Final Answer: Median = 15; Mode = 15**

Q.8:

- **Calculation:**
  Sum = $100 + 95 + 80 + 70 + 85 = 430$
  Count = 5
  Mean = $\frac{430}{5} = 86$

- **Final Answer: 86**

Q.9:

- **Calculation:**
  Minimum = 22, Maximum = 40
  Range = $40 - 22 = 18$
- **Final Answer: 18**

Q.10:

- **Calculation:**
  Mean = $\frac{81}{9} = 9$
- **Final Answer: 9**

Practice Problem 8: Probability

Q.11:

- **Calculation:**
  Total marbles = $4 + 5 + 3 = 12$
  Favorable (blue) = 5
  Probability = $\frac{5}{12}$
- **Final Answer:** $\frac{5}{12}$

Q.12:

- **Explanation:**
  Numbers greater than 4 on a die: 5 and 6 (2 outcomes)
  Total outcomes = 6
  Probability = $\frac{2}{6} = \frac{1}{3}$
- **Final Answer:** $\frac{1}{3}$

Q.13:

- **Calculation:**
  There are 13 hearts in a deck of 52.
  Probability = $\frac{13}{52} = \frac{1}{4}$
- **Final Answer:** $\frac{1}{4}$

Q.14:

- **Explanation:**
  Two coins have 4 outcomes: HH, HT, TH, TT.
  Exactly one head occurs in HT and TH (2 outcomes).
  Probability = $\frac{2}{4} = \frac{1}{2}$
- **Final Answer:** $\frac{1}{2}$

Q.15:

- **Calculation:**
  Even numbers between 1 and 10: 2, 4, 6, 8, 10 (5 outcomes)
  Total = 10
  Probability = $\frac{5}{10} = \frac{1}{2}$
- **Final Answer:** $\frac{1}{2}$

Q.16:

- **Explanation:**
  Prime numbers between 1 and 8: 2, 3, 5, 7 (4 outcomes)

Total sections = 8

Probability = $\frac{4}{8} = \frac{1}{2}$

- **Final Answer:** $\frac{1}{2}$

Q.17:

- **Calculation:**

  Total bulbs = $6 + 24 = 30$

  Defective bulbs = 6

  Probability = $\frac{6}{30} = \frac{1}{5}$

- **Final Answer:** $\frac{1}{5}$

Q.18:

- **Calculation:**

  Total students = 30

  Students wearing glasses = 12

  Probability = $\frac{12}{30} = \frac{2}{5}$

- **Final Answer:** $\frac{2}{5}$

Q.19:

- **Calculation:**

  Total candies = $7 + 5 + 8 = 20$

  Red or blue candies = $7 + 5 = 12$

  Probability = $\frac{12}{20} = \frac{3}{5}$

- **Final Answer:** $\frac{3}{5}$

Q.20:

- **Explanation:**

  Total face cards = 12 in a 52-card deck

  Probability = $\frac{12}{52} = \frac{3}{13}$

- **Final Answer:** $\frac{3}{13}$

5. Summary of Key Strategies

Concept	Best Strategy
Fractions & Percentages	Find a **common denominator** or convert to decimals.
Equations & Inequalities	Isolate the variable step-by-step.
Geometry	Memorize key formulas for **area, perimeter, and volume**.
Data Interpretation	Organize values before solving for mean, median, or probability.

6. Final Key Takeaways

- **Review basic arithmetic operations** (fractions, decimals, percentages).
- **Practice solving algebraic equations efficiently** using factoring or formulas.
- **Memorize key geometry formulas** for area, volume, and Pythagorean theorem applications.
- **Develop strong data interpretation skills** to quickly analyze graphs and probability problems.

By **completing these practice problems**, students can **strengthen their foundation in SAT Math and improve their speed and accuracy**.

Below is a complete mixed drill chapter with 50 questions covering a variety of problem types from the Digital SAT Math section. The questions are organized into five sections—each addressing different content areas. After the list of questions, you will find all the answers with detailed explanations.

16.4 Mixed Question Drills to Build Stamina (Digital SAT Math)

The Digital SAT Math section tests your skills in algebra, geometry, data analysis, probability, and more. Use these 50 mixed questions to build both speed and accuracy under timed conditions.

Section 1: Algebra and Functions Drill (Questions Q.1–Q.10)

Q.1 –
Solve for x:

$$3x + 7 = 22$$

Q.2 –
Solve for x:

$$2x - 5 = x + 4$$

Q.3 –
Solve for x:

$$4(x - 2) = 2x + 8$$

Q.4 –
Solve for x:

$$\frac{1}{3}x + 6 = 10$$

Q.5 –
Evaluate the function $f(x) = 2x^2 - 3x + 1$ at $x = -2$.

Q.6 –
If $g(x) = \frac{x+5}{2}$, what is $g(3)$?

Q.7 –
Solve for x in the quadratic equation:

$$x^2 - 4x - 5 = 0$$

Q.8 –
Solve the system of equations:

$$\begin{cases} 2x + y = 7 \\ x - y = 1 \end{cases}$$

Q.9 –
Simplify the expression:

$$3(x - 4) + 2(2x + 1)$$

Q.10 –
Solve for x:

$$5(x + 2) = 3(2x + 4)$$

Section 2: Geometry and Trigonometry Drill (Questions Q.11–Q.20)

Q.11 –
Find the hypotenuse of a right triangle with legs of lengths 5 and 12.

Q.12 –
A circle has a radius of 6. Find its area.

Q.13 –
Find the circumference of a circle with a diameter of 14.

Q.14 –
Find the area of a triangle with a base of 8 and a height of 5.
Q.15 –
A rectangle has a length of 10 and a width of 4. Find its perimeter.
Q.16 –
Find the volume of a rectangular prism with dimensions: length = 3, width = 4, and height = 5.
Q.17 –
In a right triangle, if $\sin\theta = \frac{3}{5}$, find $\cos\theta$ (assume θ is acute).
Q.18 –
A square has an area of 49. What is its side length?
Q.19 –
A rectangle has a diagonal of 13 and one side of length 5. Find the length of the other side.
Q.20 –
Find the surface area of a cube with a side length of 4.

Section 3: Word Problems and Data Analysis Drill (Questions Q.21–Q.30)

Q.21 –
A map has a scale of 1 inch = 20 miles. If two cities are 3.5 inches apart on the map, how far apart are they in reality?
Q.22 –
Find the mode of the following test scores:
72,85,90,85,78,92,85
Q.23 –
Find the median of the following numbers:
45,67,55,72,60
Q.24 –
Calculate the mean of these numbers:
10,15,20,25,30
Q.25 –
A recipe requires a flour-to-sugar ratio of 4:1. If you have 12 cups of flour, how many cups of sugar are needed?
Q.26 –
If 5 pencils cost $3, what is the cost of 12 pencils?
Q.27 –
A car travels 150 miles in 3 hours. What is its average speed in miles per hour?
Q.28 –
A survey collected the following scores from 20 students:
7,8,9,7,6,8,8,9,7,7,8,6,9,8,7,8,9,7,8,7
Find the mean score (round to one decimal place).
Q.29 –
The total cost of 8 notebooks is $24. What is the cost per notebook?
Q.30 –
A store sells 3 shirts for $45. How much would 7 shirts cost at the same rate?

Section 4: Probability and Statistics Drill (Questions Q.31–Q.40)

Q.31 –
A bag contains 5 red, 7 blue, and 8 green marbles. What is the probability of drawing a green marble?
Q.32 –
When a standard six-sided die is rolled, what is the probability of rolling a number less than 4?

Q.33 –
Two coins are tossed. What is the probability of obtaining two heads?
Q.34 –
From a standard deck of 52 cards, what is the probability of drawing a spade?
Q.35 –
A jar contains 3 white, 4 black, and 5 red balls. What is the probability that a ball drawn at random is either black or red?
Q.36 –
A spinner divided into 10 equal sections (numbered 1–10) is spun. What is the probability that it lands on a multiple of 3?
Q.37 –
In a group of 40 students, 10 are left-handed. What is the probability that a randomly selected student is left-handed?
Q.38 –
A box contains 6 defective and 24 non-defective items. What is the probability of picking a defective item?
Q.39 –
A box contains 4 red, 4 blue, and 4 green pens. If one pen is selected at random, what is the probability that it is not blue?
Q.40 –
In a class, 18 students passed a test and 12 failed. What is the probability that a randomly chosen student passed?

Section 5: Mixed Review Drill (Questions Q.41–Q.50)

Q.41 –
Solve for x:

$$3(x + 4) = 2x + 15$$

Q.42 –
Solve for x:

$$4x - 7 = 5x + 2$$

Q.43 –
Simplify the expression:

$$2(3x - 5) - 4(x - 2)$$

Q.44 –
Solve for x:

$$\frac{2x - 3}{4} = \frac{x + 5}{2}$$

Q.45 –
If $f(x) = x^2 + 2x - 3$, find $f(-1)$.
Q.46 –
Solve for x:

$$x^2 + 2x = 15$$

Q.47 –
A rectangle has a length of $x + 3$ and a width of x. If its area is 40, find x.
Q.48 –
Solve the system of equations:

$$\begin{cases} 2x + 3y = 12 \\ x - y = 2 \end{cases}$$

Q.49 –
Find the slope of the line that passes through the points $(2,3)$ and $(8,15)$.

Q.50 –

If $g(x) = 3x - 4$ and $h(x) = x^2$, find $(g \circ h)(2)$ (i.e., evaluate $g(h(2))$).

Answers and Explanations

Section 1: Algebra and Functions Drill

Q.1:

- **Solution:**

$$3x + 7 = 22 \quad \Rightarrow \quad 3x = 15 \quad \Rightarrow \quad x = 5$$

- **Final Answer:** $x = 5$

Q.2:

- **Solution:**

$$2x - 5 = x + 4 \quad \Rightarrow \quad x - 5 = 4 \quad \Rightarrow \quad x = 9$$

- **Final Answer:** $x = 9$

Q.3:

- **Solution:**

$$4(x - 2) = 2x + 8 \quad \Rightarrow \quad 4x - 8 = 2x + 8 \quad \Rightarrow \quad 2x = 16 \quad \Rightarrow \quad x = 8$$

- **Final Answer:** $x = 8$

Q.4:

- **Solution:**

$$\frac{1}{3}x + 6 = 10 \quad \Rightarrow \quad \frac{1}{3}x = 4 \quad \Rightarrow \quad x = 12$$

- **Final Answer:** $x = 12$

Q.5:

- **Solution:**

$$f(-2) = 2(-2)^2 - 3(-2) + 1 = 2(4) + 6 + 1 = 8 + 6 + 1 = 15$$

- **Final Answer: 15**

Q.6:

- **Solution:**

$$g(3) = \frac{3 + 5}{2} = \frac{8}{2} = 4$$

- **Final Answer: 4**

Q.7:

- **Solution:**
  Factor the quadratic:

$$x^2 - 4x - 5 = (x - 5)(x + 1) = 0 \quad \Rightarrow \quad x = 5 \text{ or } x = -1$$

- **Final Answer:** $x = 5$ **or** $x = -1$

Q.8:

- **Solution:**
  From the system:

$$x - y = 1 \quad \Rightarrow \quad x = y + 1$$

  Substitute into $2x + y = 7$:

$$2(y + 1) + y = 7 \quad \Rightarrow \quad 2y + 2 + y = 7 \quad \Rightarrow \quad 3y = 5 \quad \Rightarrow \quad y = \frac{5}{3}$$

  Then, $x = \frac{5}{3} + 1 = \frac{8}{3}$.

- **Final Answer: $x = \frac{8}{3},\text{\:\,}y = \frac{5}{3}$**

Q.9:

- **Solution:**

$$3(x-4)+2(2x+1)=3x-12+4x+2=7x-10$$

- **Final Answer:** $7x-10$

Q.10:

- **Solution:**

$$5(x+2)=3(2x+4) \quad \Rightarrow \quad 5x+10=6x+12 \quad \Rightarrow \quad x=-2$$

- **Final Answer:** $x=-2$

Section 2: Geometry and Trigonometry Drill

Q.11:

- **Solution:**

  Hypotenuse $=\sqrt{5^2+12^2}=\sqrt{25+144}=\sqrt{169}=13$
- **Final Answer: 13**

Q.12:

- **Solution:**

  Area $=\pi r^2=\pi(6^2)=36\pi$
- **Final Answer:** 36π

Q.13:

- **Solution:**

  Radius $=\frac{14}{2}=7$; Circumference $=2\pi r=14\pi$
- **Final Answer:** 14π

Q.14:

- **Solution:**

  Area $=\frac{1}{2}\times$ base $\times$ height $=\frac{1}{2}\times 8\times 5=20$
- **Final Answer: 20 square units**

Q.15:

- **Solution:**

  Perimeter $=2(\text{length}+\text{width})=2(10+4)=28$
- **Final Answer: 28**

Q.16:

- **Solution:**

  Volume $=3\times 4\times 5=60$
- **Final Answer: 60**

Q.17:

- **Solution:**

  Since $\sin\theta=\frac{3}{5}$, then

$$\cos\theta=\sqrt{1-\left(\frac{3}{5}\right)^2}=\sqrt{1-\frac{9}{25}}=\sqrt{\frac{16}{25}}=\frac{4}{5}$$

- **Final Answer:** $\frac{4}{5}$

Q.18:

- **Solution:**

  Side length $=\sqrt{49}=7$
- **Final Answer: 7**

Q.19:

- **Solution:**
  Let the unknown side be w. Then,
  $$13^2 = 5^2 + w^2 \quad \Rightarrow \quad 169 = 25 + w^2 \quad \Rightarrow \quad w^2 = 144 \quad \Rightarrow \quad w = 12$$
- **Final Answer: 12**

Q.20:

- **Solution:**
  Surface area of a cube $= 6s^2 = 6(4^2) = 6 \times 16 = 96$
- **Final Answer: 96**

Section 3: Word Problems and Data Analysis Drill

Q.21:

- **Solution:**
  Distance $= 3.5 \times 20 = 70$ miles
- **Final Answer: 70 miles**

Q.22:

- **Solution:**
  The number 85 appears most frequently.
- **Final Answer: 85**

Q.23:

- **Solution:**
  Ordered set: $45,55,60,67,72$. The median is the middle value, 60.
- **Final Answer: 60**

Q.24:

- **Solution:**
  Mean $= \frac{10+15+20+25+30}{5} = \frac{100}{5} = 20$
- **Final Answer: 20**

Q.25:

- **Solution:**
  Ratio 4:1 means for every 4 cups flour, 1 cup sugar is needed. With 12 cups flour:
  $$\frac{12}{4} = 3 \text{ cups sugar}$$
- **Final Answer: 3 cups**

Q.26:

- **Solution:**
  Cost per pencil $= \frac{3}{5} = 0.60$ dollars; 12 pencils cost $12 \times 0.60 = 7.20$ dollars.
- **Final Answer: $7.20**

Q.27:

- **Solution:**
  Average speed $= \frac{150}{3} = 50$ mph.
- **Final Answer: 50 mph**

Q.28:

- **Solution:**
  Sum of scores $= 7+8+9+7+6+8+8+9+7+7+8+6+9+8+7+8+9+7+8+7 = 153$
  Mean $= \frac{153}{20} = 7.65$, which rounds to **7.7**.
- **Final Answer: 7.7**

Q.29:

- **Solution:**
  Cost per notebook $= \frac{24}{8} = 3$ dollars.
- **Final Answer: $3**

Q.30:

- **Solution:**
  Cost per shirt $= \frac{45}{3} = 15$ dollars; 7 shirts cost $7 \times 15 = 105$ dollars.
- **Final Answer: $105**

Section 4: Probability and Statistics Drill

Q.31:

- **Solution:**
  Total marbles $= 5 + 7 + 8 = 20$; Probability (green) $= \frac{8}{20} = \frac{2}{5}$.
- **Final Answer:** $\frac{2}{5}$

Q.32:

- **Solution:**
  Numbers less than 4 on a die: 1, 2, 3 (3 outcomes); Probability $= \frac{3}{6} = \frac{1}{2}$.
- **Final Answer:** $\frac{1}{2}$

Q.33:

- **Solution:**
  Two coins yield 4 outcomes: HH, HT, TH, TT; Only HH gives two heads; Probability $= \frac{1}{4}$.
- **Final Answer:** $\frac{1}{4}$

Q.34:

- **Solution:**
  Spades in a deck $= 13$; Probability $= \frac{13}{52} = \frac{1}{4}$.
- **Final Answer:** $\frac{1}{4}$

Q.35:

- **Solution:**
  Total balls $= 3 + 4 + 5 = 12$; Favorable (black or red) $= 4 + 5 = 9$; Probability $= \frac{9}{12} = \frac{3}{4}$.
- **Final Answer:** $\frac{3}{4}$

Q.36:

- **Solution:**
  Multiples of 3 among 1–10: 3, 6, 9 (3 outcomes); Probability $= \frac{3}{10}$.
- **Final Answer:** $\frac{3}{10}$

Q.37:

- **Solution:**
  Probability $= \frac{10}{40} = \frac{1}{4}$.
- **Final Answer:** $\frac{1}{4}$

Q.38:

- **Solution:**
  Total items $= 6 + 24 = 30$; Probability (defective) $= \frac{6}{30} = \frac{1}{5}$.

- **Final Answer:** $\frac{1}{5}$

Q.39:

- **Solution:**

  Total pens $= 4 + 4 + 4 = 12$; Not blue means red or green: $12 - 4 = 8$; Probability $= \frac{8}{12} = \frac{2}{3}$.
- **Final Answer:** $\frac{2}{3}$

Q.40:

- **Solution:**

  Total students $= 18 + 12 = 30$; Probability (passed) $= \frac{18}{30} = \frac{3}{5}$.
- **Final Answer:** $\frac{3}{5}$

Section 5: Mixed Review Drill

Q.41:

- **Solution:**

$$3(x + 4) = 2x + 15$$

  Expand: $3x + 12 = 2x + 15$
  Subtract $2x$: $x + 12 = 15$
  Subtract 12: $x = 3$
- **Final Answer:** $x = 3$

Q.42:

- **Solution:**

$$4x - 7 = 5x + 2$$

  Rearranging: $-7 - 2 = 5x - 4x$

$$-9 = x$$

- **Final Answer:** $x = -9$

Q.43:

- **Solution:**
  Expand: $2(3x - 5) - 4(x - 2) = 6x - 10 - 4x + 8 = 2x - 2$
- **Final Answer:** $2x - 2$

Q.44:

- **Solution:**

$$\frac{2x - 3}{4} = \frac{x + 5}{2}$$

  Cross-multiply: $2(2x - 3) = 4(x + 5)$

$$4x - 6 = 4x + 20$$

  Subtract $4x$: $-6 = 20$ (a contradiction)
- **Final Answer: No solution**

Q.45:

- **Solution:**

$$f(-1) = (-1)^2 + 2(-1) - 3 = 1 - 2 - 3 = -4$$

- **Final Answer:** -4

Q.46:

- **Solution:**

$$x^2 + 2x - 15 = 0$$

  Factor: $(x + 5)(x - 3) = 0$
  $x = -5$ or $x = 3$

- **Final Answer:** $x = -5$ **or** $x = 3$

Q.47:

- **Solution:**
  Area $= x(x+3) = 40$
  $$x^2 + 3x - 40 = 0$$
  Factor: $(x+8)(x-5) = 0$
  $x = 5$ (reject $x = -8$ as a length)
- **Final Answer:** $x = 5$

Q.48:

- **Solution:**
  From $x - y = 2$, $x = y + 2$. Substitute in $2x + 3y = 12$:
  $$2(y+2) + 3y = 12$$
  $$2y + 4 + 3y = 12$$
  $5y = 8$ so $y = \frac{8}{5}$, then $x = \frac{8}{5} + 2 = \frac{18}{5}$
- **Final Answer:** $x = \frac{18}{5}$, $y = \frac{8}{5}$

Q.49:

- **Solution:**
  Slope $= \frac{15-3}{8-2} = \frac{12}{6} = 2$
- **Final Answer: 2**

Q.50:

- **Solution:**
  $(g \circ h)(x) = g\big(h(x)\big) = g(x^2) = 3x^2 - 4;$
  $$(g \circ h)(2) = 3(2^2) - 4 = 3(4) - 4 = 12 - 4 = 8$$
- **Final Answer: 8**

Final Key Takeaways

- **Algebra and Functions:** Practice isolating variables, evaluating functions, and solving systems for efficient problem-solving.
- **Geometry and Trigonometry:** Know key formulas (area, perimeter, volume) and apply the Pythagorean Theorem and trigonometric ratios accurately.
- **Word Problems and Data Analysis:** Convert real-world scenarios into equations and compute statistical measures (mean, median, mode, range) carefully.
- **Probability and Statistics:** Determine probabilities by correctly counting favorable and total outcomes.
- **Mixed Review:** Build endurance by practicing a wide variety of problems in a single session.

By working through these 50 mixed questions and reviewing the detailed explanations, you will build stamina and enhance your accuracy for the Digital SAT Math section. Good luck with your practice!

CHAPTER 17

ADVANCED PRACTICE EXERCISES

17.1 Challenging Reading & Writing Passages with Complex Vocabulary

The **Digital SAT Reading & Writing section** often includes passages with **advanced vocabulary, complex sentence structures, and nuanced rhetorical devices**. To excel, students must develop strong **context-based word recognition, analytical reading skills, and precise comprehension**.

This section will cover:

- **Reading Passages with Advanced Vocabulary**
- **Context Clues for Understanding Unfamiliar Words**
- **Recognizing Subtle Tone and Authorial Intent**
- **Practice Drills for Advanced Reading Comprehension**

1. Reading Passages with Advanced Vocabulary

Passages on the SAT often include **formal, historical, or academic language** that requires understanding **nuance and implied meaning**.

Example Passage with Complex Vocabulary
Passage:
The philosopher's discourse on human nature was profoundly **erudite**, drawing upon a compendium of historical references to substantiate his argument. Though his reasoning was sound, some critics found his **prolixity** unnecessary, arguing that brevity would have rendered his assertions more persuasive.
Question: What does the word "erudite" most nearly mean in the passage?
(A) Careless
(B) Scholarly
(C) Insulting
(D) Informal
Correct Answer: (B) Scholarly

Strategy for Complex Vocabulary Questions

- **Look for context clues**—the passage states that the discourse was "drawing upon a compendium of historical references," implying **deep knowledge**.
- **Avoid extreme choices**—words like "careless" and "insulting" don't fit the passage's academic tone.

2. Context Clues for Understanding Unfamiliar Words

When faced with an unfamiliar word, use **context clues** to infer meaning.

Context Clue Type	Definition	Example
Definition Clue	The word is explicitly defined	"The scientist's hypothesis was **untenable**, meaning it could not be supported by evidence."
Contrast Clue	The sentence shows an opposite meaning	"Unlike her **parsimonious** brother, she was extremely generous with her money."
Inference Clue	The passage suggests meaning through description	"His **vociferous** objections drowned out the speaker, disrupting the entire debate."

Example Passage Using Context Clues

The senator's **obsequious** behavior toward influential donors was noted by critics, who claimed he prioritized corporate interests over public welfare.

Question: What does "obsequious" most nearly mean in the passage?

(A) Loyal

(B) Submissive

(C) Indifferent

(D) Deceptive

Correct Answer: (B) Submissive

Why?

- The passage suggests that the senator was **overly accommodating to donors**, which implies **excessive submissiveness**.

3. Recognizing Subtle Tone and Authorial Intent

SAT passages often require students to analyze **tone** and **authorial intent**.

Tone Type	Example Passage	Common SAT Words
Analytical	The study meticulously outlines the discrepancies between the two theories.	Meticulous, Objective, Pragmatic
Critical	The journalist's **acerbic** commentary exposed the flaws in the new policy.	Acerbic, Scathing, Derisive
Neutral/Informative	The report delineates the economic impact of tax reforms.	Delineate, Expound, Convey

Example Question on Tone

Passage:

While some herald the new technological advancements as groundbreaking, others caution against potential ethical concerns, arguing that the rush for progress often outpaces moral deliberation.

Question: What is the tone of the passage?

(A) Optimistic

(B) Cautious

(C) Indifferent

(D) Sarcastic

Correct Answer: (B) Cautious

Why?

- The phrase **"caution against potential ethical concerns"** suggests a **concerned, careful** tone rather than enthusiastic optimism.

4. Practice Drills for Advanced Reading Comprehension

Drill 1: Identifying the Main Idea in a Dense Passage

Passage:

The Industrial Revolution heralded an era of unprecedented economic expansion. However, while urban centers flourished, rural populations experienced a dramatic shift in labor demands, forcing many into unfavorable working conditions. The prosperity of industry came at a social cost, creating a rift between wealth and labor that shaped economic policies for decades.

Question: What is the main idea of the passage?

(A) The Industrial Revolution only benefited the wealthy.

(B) Urbanization improved living conditions for all workers.

(C) Economic progress during the Industrial Revolution had both benefits and drawbacks.
(D) The Industrial Revolution slowed economic expansion.
Correct Answer: (C) Economic progress during the Industrial Revolution had both benefits and drawbacks.

Why?

- The passage discusses **both economic expansion and social challenges**, making (C) the best choice.

Drill 2: Understanding Logical Transitions

Passage:
The discovery of penicillin transformed medical treatment. _____, it significantly reduced mortality rates from bacterial infections.
Question: Which transition word best completes the sentence?
(A) However
(B) Consequently
(C) Nevertheless
(D) Meanwhile
Correct Answer: (B) Consequently

Why?

- The second sentence **explains the effect** of penicillin's discovery, so **"consequently"** is the best fit.

Drill 3: Matching Word Meaning to Context

Sentence:
The CEO's **magnanimous** gesture of donating his entire annual bonus to charity was praised by employees.
Question: What does "magnanimous" most nearly mean?
(A) Generous
(B) Foolish
(C) Secretive
(D) Wealthy
Correct Answer: (A) Generous

Why?
- The phrase **"donating his entire annual bonus to charity"** suggests **kindness and generosity**.

5. Summary of Key Strategies

Skill	Best Strategy
Understanding Complex Vocabulary	Use **context clues** (definition, contrast, inference).
Identifying the Main Idea	Look at **first and last sentences** for central themes.
Recognizing Authorial Tone	Pay attention to **word choice and key phrases**.
Logical Transitions	Identify **cause-effect, contrast, or continuation** words.
Analyzing Sentence Structure	Break complex sentences into **simpler components**.

6. Final Key Takeaways
- **Advanced SAT passages require close reading**—use **context clues to determine vocabulary meaning**.
- **The author's tone and purpose are key indicators of meaning**—watch for **subtle language cues**.
- **Main idea questions require identifying the core argument**, not minor details.
- **Logical transitions help connect ideas effectively**, reinforcing comprehension.

- **Consistent practice with high-level vocabulary and dense passages improves fluency and reading speed.**

By **mastering challenging reading comprehension and vocabulary**, students can confidently tackle **complex passages on the SAT**, improving both **accuracy and efficiency**.

17.2 High-Level Grammar and Rhetorical Exercises

The **Digital SAT Writing & Language section** requires students to recognize **complex grammatical structures** and apply **advanced rhetorical skills** to improve sentence clarity, organization, and effectiveness. This section provides **high-level practice exercises** focusing on:

- **Advanced Grammar and Sentence Structure**
- **Conciseness and Wordiness**
- **Logical Flow and Transitions**
- **Effective Argumentation and Rhetorical Strategies**

1. Advanced Grammar and Sentence Structure

A. Subject-Verb Agreement with Complex Subjects

When the subject is separated from the verb by **intervening phrases**, students must ensure agreement remains correct.

Example 1: Correcting Subject-Verb Agreement in Complex Sentences
Sentence:
The collection of rare books **were** displayed in the museum.
Question: Which revision best corrects the sentence?
(A) The collection of rare books **were** displayed in the museum.
(B) The collection of rare books **was** displayed in the museum.
(C) The collection of rare books **is** displayed in the museum.
(D) The collection of rare books **are** displayed in the museum.
Correct Answer: (B) The collection of rare books was displayed in the museum.

Why?

- The **subject is "collection" (singular)**, not "books" (plural).
- **Intervening phrases do not change subject-verb agreement.**

B. Correcting Dangling and Misplaced Modifiers

A **modifier** must be **placed next to the noun it modifies**.

Example 2: Fixing a Misplaced Modifier
Sentence:
Running down the hill, the backpack slipped off Jake's shoulders.
Question: Which revision best improves the sentence?
(A) Running down the hill, Jake's backpack slipped off his shoulders.
(B) The backpack slipped off Jake's shoulders running down the hill.
(C) Running down the hill, Jake felt his backpack slip off his shoulders.
(D) Jake's backpack slipped off his shoulders as he was running down the hill.
Correct Answer: (C) Running down the hill, Jake felt his backpack slip off his shoulders.

Why?

- In the original sentence, the **backpack appears to be running** instead of Jake.
- The correction ensures **Jake is the subject being modified**.

2. Conciseness and Wordiness

A. Eliminating Redundant Phrases

Redundancy occurs when **a sentence repeats the same idea unnecessarily**.

Example 3: Removing Wordiness
Sentence:
In the year 2020, a time that was recent, technology advanced at a rapid speed.
Question: Which revision best improves conciseness?
(A) In the year 2020, technology advanced rapidly.
(B) In 2020, technology advanced at a very rapid speed.
(C) In the recent past of the year 2020, technology was advancing.
(D) Technology, during 2020, advanced very fast.
Correct Answer: (A) In the year 2020, technology advanced rapidly.

Why?

- The phrase **"a time that was recent"** is unnecessary because "2020" already specifies the timeframe.
- "At a rapid speed" is **redundant**—"rapidly" conveys the same meaning.

3. Logical Flow and Transitions

A. Identifying Effective Transitions

Transitions should **logically connect ideas between sentences**.

Example 4: Choosing the Best Transition
Sentence:
Many students believe that test preparation improves scores. ____, research suggests that repeated practice tests are the most effective study method.
Question: Which transition word best fits the blank?
(A) However
(B) Similarly
(C) Consequently
(D) Meanwhile
Correct Answer: (A) However

Why?

- The second sentence **contrasts** the first by presenting a **more specific claim**, making "However" the best choice.

B. Sentence Placement for Logical Flow

Sometimes, a sentence must be **rearranged to maintain logical progression**.

Example 5: Sentence Placement in a Paragraph
Paragraph:
(1) Solar energy is becoming an increasingly popular renewable energy source. (2) Unlike fossil fuels, solar power does not release carbon dioxide into the atmosphere. (3) ____. (4) As a result, many governments have invested in solar panel technology.
Question: Which sentence best completes the paragraph?
(A) Wind energy is another alternative energy source.
(B) Solar panels require minimal maintenance and have long lifespans.
(C) Some critics argue that solar energy is unreliable on cloudy days.
(D) The sun produces enough energy to power the world for an entire year.

Correct Answer: (B) Solar panels require minimal maintenance and have long lifespans.

Why?

- The sentence logically follows the **benefits of solar energy** discussed in (2), leading into (4) about government investments.

4. Effective Argumentation and Rhetorical Strategies

A. Strengthening an Argument with Evidence

A strong argument requires **specific, relevant, and well-supported evidence**.

Example 6: Choosing the Strongest Supporting Detail
Sentence:
Studies indicate that eating a balanced diet improves overall health.
Question: Which sentence best supports this claim?
(A) Many people like eating vegetables.
(B) Fast food is unhealthy and lacks proper nutrition.
(C) A study from the American Journal of Nutrition found that individuals who consumed more fruits and vegetables had a 30% lower risk of heart disease.
(D) Some people avoid certain foods due to allergies.
Correct Answer: (C) A study from the American Journal of Nutrition found that individuals who consumed more fruits and vegetables had a 30% lower risk of heart disease.

Why?

- This choice provides **specific data and a credible source**, making it the strongest supporting detail.

High-Level Grammar and Rhetorical Exercises – Mixed Drill (40 Questions)

The Digital SAT Writing & Language section requires advanced skills in grammar, conciseness, logical flow, and effective argumentation. Use these 40 challenging exercises to sharpen your editing and rhetorical abilities under exam-like conditions.

Section 1: Advanced Grammar and Sentence Structure (Questions Q.1–Q.10)

Q.1 – Subject-Verb Agreement:
Select the best revision for the sentence:
"The array of completed projects **were** displayed in the conference hall."
(A) The array of completed projects were displayed in the conference hall.
(B) The array of completed projects was displayed in the conference hall.
(C) The array of completed projects is displayed in the conference hall.
(D) The array of completed projects are displayed in the conference hall.
Q.2 – Subject-Verb Agreement:
Select the best revision for the sentence:
"A bouquet of roses and lilies **add** beauty to the room."
(A) A bouquet of roses and lilies add beauty to the room.
(B) A bouquet of roses and lilies adds beauty to the room.
(C) A bouquet of roses and lilies is adding beauty to the room.
(D) A bouquet of roses and lilies have added beauty to the room.
Q.3 – Subject-Verb Agreement in Complex Sentences:
Select the best revision for the sentence:
"The team of experts, along with several advisors, **have** reached a consensus."
(A) The team of experts, along with several advisors, have reached a consensus.
(B) The team of experts, along with several advisors, has reached a consensus.

(C) The team of experts, as well as several advisors, have reached a consensus.
(D) The team of experts, accompanied by several advisors, are reaching a consensus.

Q.4 – Subject-Verb Agreement with Intervening Phrases:

Select the best revision for the sentence:
"The collection of ancient manuscripts, along with several modern texts, **were** examined by the scholar."
(A) The collection of ancient manuscripts, along with several modern texts, were examined by the scholar.
(B) The collection of ancient manuscripts, along with several modern texts, was examined by the scholar.
(C) The collection of ancient manuscripts and several modern texts were examined by the scholar.
(D) The collection of ancient manuscripts, along with several modern texts, are examined by the scholar.

Q.5 – Neither/Nor Agreement:

Select the best revision for the sentence:
"Neither the CEO nor the board members **agrees** with the new policy."
(A) Neither the CEO nor the board members agrees with the new policy.
(B) Neither the CEO nor the board members agree with the new policy.
(C) Neither the CEO nor the board members is agreeing with the new policy.
(D) Neither the CEO nor the board members are in agreement with the new policy.

Q.6 – Dangling Modifier:

Select the best revision for the sentence:
"After reading the book, the movie was disappointing."
(A) After reading the book, the movie was disappointing.
(B) After reading the book, the viewer found the movie disappointing.
(C) After reading the book, I found the movie disappointing.
(D) After reading the book, disappointment arose when watching the movie.

Q.7 – Misplaced Modifier:

Select the best revision for the sentence:
"Walking through the park, the flowers caught my attention."
(A) Walking through the park, I noticed that the flowers caught my attention.
(B) While walking through the park, the flowers caught my attention.
(C) Walking through the park, I noticed the flowers.
(D) While I was walking through the park, I noticed the flowers that caught my attention.

Q.8 – Dangling Modifier:

Select the best revision for the sentence:
"Having completed the assignment, the deadline was met."
(A) Having completed the assignment, the deadline was met.
(B) Having completed the assignment, the teacher noted the deadline was met.
(C) Having completed the assignment, I met the deadline.
(D) After completing the assignment, the deadline was met by the student.

Q.9 – Misplaced Modifier:

Select the best revision for the sentence:
"After finishing the exam, the answers were submitted."
(A) After finishing the exam, the answers were submitted.
(B) After finishing the exam, the proctor collected the answers.
(C) After finishing the exam, I submitted the answers.
(D) After finishing the exam, the answers quickly were submitted.

Q.10 – Misplaced Modifier:

Select the best revision for the sentence:
"Shouting loudly, the classroom was filled with noise."

(A) Shouting loudly, the classroom was filled with noise.
(B) Shouting loudly, the students filled the classroom with noise.
(C) The classroom was filled with noise, shouting loudly.
(D) Shouting loudly, the noise filled the classroom.

Section 2: Conciseness and Wordiness (Questions Q.11–Q.20)

Q.11 – Redundancy Elimination:
Select the best revision for the sentence:
"Due to the fact that the meeting was cancelled, no one attended the event."
(A) Because the meeting was cancelled, no one attended the event.
(B) The meeting was cancelled, so no one attended the event.
(C) Since the meeting was cancelled, attendance was nil.
(D) Owing to the cancellation of the meeting, no one attended the event.

Q.12 – Redundant Phrases:
Select the best revision for the sentence:
"In my personal opinion, I believe that the new policy is beneficial."
(A) In my opinion, the new policy is beneficial.
(B) I believe that the new policy is beneficial.
(C) Personally, I believe that the new policy is beneficial.
(D) In my personal opinion, the new policy is beneficial.

Q.13 – Wordiness Reduction:
Select the best revision for the sentence:
"At this point in time, we are currently reviewing the data."
(A) At this point in time, we are reviewing the data.
(B) Currently, we are reviewing the data.
(C) We are reviewing the data.
(D) Right now, we are reviewing the data.

Q.14 – Redundant Explanation:
Select the best revision for the sentence:
"The reason is because he did not study for the exam."
(A) He did not study for the exam.
(B) The reason he did not do well on the exam is that he did not study.
(C) Because he did not study for the exam, he failed.
(D) The reason is that he did not study for the exam.

Q.15 – Unnecessary Introductory Phrases:
Select the best revision for the sentence:
"In order to achieve success, it is necessary to work hard."
(A) To achieve success, you must work hard.
(B) Achieving success requires working hard.
(C) Success is achieved by working hard.
(D) In order to be successful, hard work is necessary.

Q.16 – Verbosity in Descriptions:
Select the best revision for the sentence:
"There are a number of different ways in which one can solve the problem."
(A) There are several ways to solve the problem.
(B) There are a number of ways to solve the problem.
(C) One can solve the problem in different ways.
(D) Multiple methods exist for solving the problem.

Q.17 – Eliminating Unnecessary Adverbs:
Select the best revision for the sentence:
"It is absolutely essential that we take immediate action."
(A) We must take immediate action.
(B) It is essential that we take immediate action.
(C) Immediate action is absolutely necessary.
(D) We absolutely must take immediate action.

Q.18 – Wordiness in Time Expressions:
Select the best revision for the sentence:
"At this point in time, we are in the process of reviewing the documents."
(A) We are reviewing the documents.
(B) Currently, we are reviewing the documents.
(C) We are in the process of reviewing the documents.
(D) Right now, we are reviewing the documents.

Q.19 – Redundant Time Indicators:
Select the best revision for the sentence:
"The meeting is scheduled to take place at 9:00 in the morning."
(A) The meeting is scheduled for 9:00 a.m.
(B) The meeting is scheduled at 9:00 a.m.
(C) The meeting is scheduled for 9:00 in the morning.
(D) The meeting is at 9:00 a.m.

Q.20 – Streamlining Contrast:
Select the best revision for the sentence:
"Despite the fact that the project was challenging, the team managed to complete it on time."
(A) Although the project was challenging, the team completed it on time.
(B) Even though the project was challenging, the team completed it on time.
(C) The project was challenging, but the team completed it on time.
(D) Despite its challenges, the team completed the project on time.

Section 3: Logical Flow and Transitions (Questions Q.21–Q.30)

Q.21 – Choosing a Transition Word:
Select the best word to fill in the blank:
"The study indicates that regular exercise improves cardiovascular health. _____, further research shows that it also enhances mental well-being."
(A) However
(B) Moreover
(C) Consequently
(D) Meanwhile

Q.22 – Establishing Cause and Effect:
Select the best word to fill in the blank:
"The experiment was a failure. _____, the team decided to revise their hypothesis."
(A) Therefore
(B) Nevertheless
(C) As a result
(D) However

Q.23 – Adding a Similar Point:
Select the best word to fill in the blank:
"The product received excellent reviews for its durability. _____, many customers praised its reliability."

(A) In contrast
(B) Similarly
(C) Conversely
(D) On the contrary

Q.24 – Adding Additional Information:

Select the best word to fill in the blank:

"She planned to study abroad in Europe. _____, her scholarship application was accepted by a prestigious university."

(A) Consequently
(B) Furthermore
(C) However
(D) As a result

Q.25 – Introducing a Contrasting Idea:

Select the best phrase to fill in the blank:

"Many employees prefer remote work because it offers flexibility. _____, some argue that working from home reduces productivity."

(A) On the other hand
(B) In addition
(C) Similarly
(D) Consequently

Q.26 – Reinforcing with an Additional Benefit:

Select the best word to fill in the blank:

"The new software update improved security measures. _____, it enhanced system performance significantly."

(A) Moreover
(B) Nevertheless
(C) However
(D) Although

Q.27 – Acknowledging a Limitation:

Select the best phrase to fill in the blank:

"The team was underprepared for the project. _____, they still managed to deliver a satisfactory presentation."

(A) Despite this
(B) Consequently
(C) In contrast
(D) Furthermore

Q.28 – Highlighting a Contrast:

Select the best word to fill in the blank:

"The report was comprehensive. _____, it failed to address the key issues raised by stakeholders."

(A) In addition
(B) However
(C) Moreover
(D) Similarly

Q.29 – Expressing a Result:

Select the best phrase to fill in the blank:

"Traffic was heavy during the morning rush hour. _____, commuters arrived late for work."

(A) As a result
(B) Nevertheless
(C) Moreover
(D) Similarly

Q.30 – Enhancing an Argument:

Select the best word to fill in the blank:

"The author presented strong arguments in support of renewable energy. ____, she provided detailed evidence and expert opinions to back up her claims."

(A) Consequently

(B) Furthermore

(C) However

(D) Alternatively

Section 4: Effective Argumentation and Rhetorical Strategies (Questions Q.31–Q.40)

Q.31 – Strengthening an Argument:

Select the best revision that adds strong evidence to support the claim:

"The proposal asserts that increasing green spaces improves urban life."

(A) Many people enjoy parks.

(B) A study by the Urban Planning Institute showed that cities with more green spaces have a 20% lower rate of respiratory illnesses.

(C) Green spaces are popular.

(D) Urban areas often lack parks.

Q.32 – Strengthening an Argument:

Select the best sentence to support the claim that education is vital:

"Education is essential for personal and societal growth."

(A) Education is important.

(B) Studies have shown that individuals with higher education levels earn significantly more over their lifetime.

(C) Many countries invest in education.

(D) Some people attend college.

Q.33 – Supporting a Claim with Data:

Select the best sentence to reinforce the claim that remote work boosts employee satisfaction:

(A) Employees enjoy flexible schedules.

(B) Surveys indicate that remote workers report a 30% increase in job satisfaction compared to those in traditional offices.

(C) Remote work is common.

(D) Many companies now allow remote work.

Q.34 – Providing Specific Evidence:

Select the best addition to an argument in favor of renewable energy:

(A) The paragraph should include a statistic that 40% of energy consumption in the U.S. comes from renewable sources.

(B) Renewable energy is popular.

(C) The paragraph should list various types of renewable energy.

(D) Fossil fuels are harmful.

Q.35 – Using Data for Persuasion:

Select the best sentence to support the benefits of a balanced diet:

(A) A balanced diet is good for health.

(B) A study published in the Journal of Nutrition found that individuals who maintained a balanced diet had a 25% lower risk of developing chronic diseases.

(C) Many people eat a balanced diet.

(D) A balanced diet includes fruits and vegetables.

Q.36 – Providing Evidence with Credibility:

Select the best sentence to support the claim that technological advances have improved quality of life:

(A) Technology is everywhere.
(B) Advances in medical technology have increased life expectancy by reducing mortality rates.
(C) Many people use smartphones.
(D) Technology is a modern convenience.

Q.37 – Engaging the Reader with a Rhetorical Question:

Select the sentence that most effectively uses a rhetorical question to engage readers on the topic of climate change:

(A) Climate change is a serious problem.
(B) Can we afford to ignore the overwhelming evidence of climate change, knowing that our future is at stake?
(C) The climate is changing.
(D) Scientists have proven that climate change is real.

Q.38 – Enhancing Transition Between Ideas:

Select the best revision that improves the transition between contrasting ideas:

(A) Although the policy has some benefits, it remains flawed.
(B) The policy has benefits; however, it is flawed in many ways.
(C) While the policy offers benefits, it also presents significant challenges that must be addressed.
(D) The policy is both beneficial and flawed.

Q.39 – Removing Ambiguity:

Select the best revision that removes ambiguity in an argument for increased funding for public education:

(A) Increasing funding for public education can help improve student outcomes.
(B) Increasing funding for public education, which is underfunded in many areas, can lead to better resources, more qualified teachers, and improved student performance.
(C) More funding is needed for public education.
(D) Education funding should be increased.

Q.40 – Employing Parallel Structure:

Select the best revision that uses parallel structure to strengthen an argument on the importance of civic engagement:

(A) Civic engagement is essential because it promotes community involvement, builds leadership skills, and helps to create positive change.
(B) Civic engagement is essential because it promotes community involvement, builds leadership skills, and the creation of positive change.
(C) Civic engagement is essential because it promotes community involvement, it builds leadership skills, and creates positive change.
(D) Civic engagement is essential because it promotes community involvement, it builds leadership skills, and it is a way to create positive change.

Answers and Explanations

Section 1: Advanced Grammar and Sentence Structure

Q.1:

Answer: (B)

Explanation: The subject is “collection” (singular), so the verb must be singular (“was” displayed).

Q.2:

Answer: (B)

Explanation: “Bouquet” is the singular subject, so “adds” is correct.

Q.3:

Answer: (B)

Explanation: The main subject “team” (singular) dictates that the verb be “has reached,” regardless of the intervening phrase.

Q.4:
Answer: (B)
Explanation: "Collection" is singular; therefore, "was examined" is the proper verb form.
Q.5:
Answer: (B)
Explanation: With a "neither/nor" construction, the verb should agree with the subject closer to it. Here, "board members" (plural) follow "CEO" (singular), so the correct verb is "agree." However, to remove ambiguity, a better revision is to use a construction that ensures agreement. In this case, option (B) "agree" is correct.
Note: Option (B) in Q.5 assumes that the intended correction is to have the plural verb form, so the best revision is:
"Neither the CEO nor the board members agree with the new policy."
Q.6:
Answer: (C)
Explanation: The revision "After reading the book, I found the movie disappointing" clearly assigns the modifier "after reading the book" to the proper subject (I).
Q.7:
Answer: (C)
Explanation: "Walking through the park, I noticed the flowers" clearly identifies the subject performing the action, eliminating ambiguity.
Q.8:
Answer: (C)
Explanation: "Having completed the assignment, I met the deadline" correctly connects the modifier with the subject performing the action.
Q.9:
Answer: (C)
Explanation: "After finishing the exam, I submitted the answers" correctly attributes the action to the subject, eliminating the dangling modifier.
Q.10:
Answer: (B)
Explanation: "Shouting loudly, the students filled the classroom with noise" properly assigns the modifier to "the students" instead of the inanimate "classroom."

Section 2: Conciseness and Wordiness

Q.11:
Answer: (A)
Explanation: "Because the meeting was cancelled, no one attended the event" removes unnecessary wordiness.
Q.12:
Answer: (B)
Explanation: "I believe that the new policy is beneficial" is concise and eliminates redundancy.
Q.13:
Answer: (C)
Explanation: "We are reviewing the data" is the most direct and concise revision.
Q.14:
Answer: (A)
Explanation: Simply stating "He did not study for the exam" eliminates the redundant phrase "the reason is because."
Q.15:
Answer: (A)
Explanation: "To achieve success, you must work hard" is clear, direct, and concise.

Q.16:
Answer: (A)
Explanation: "There are several ways to solve the problem" removes unnecessary verbosity while conveying the same meaning.
Q.17:
Answer: (A)
Explanation: "We must take immediate action" is concise and eliminates superfluous adverbs.
Q.18:
Answer: (A)
Explanation: "We are reviewing the documents" is direct and removes wordy expressions.
Q.19:
Answer: (A)
Explanation: "The meeting is scheduled for 9:00 a.m." is succinct and clear.
Q.20:
Answer: (A)
Explanation: "Although the project was challenging, the team completed it on time" is concise and effectively conveys the contrast without redundancy.

Section 3: Logical Flow and Transitions

Q.21:
Answer: (B)
Explanation: "Moreover" adds additional, related information, enhancing the flow between the two ideas.
Q.22:
Answer: (C)
Explanation: "As a result" properly indicates the consequence of the experiment's failure.
Q.23:
Answer: (B)
Explanation: "Similarly" appropriately adds another supporting point that is like the first statement.
Q.24:
Answer: (B)
Explanation: "Furthermore" adds additional positive information, linking the two sentences logically.
Q.25:
Answer: (A)
Explanation: "On the other hand" introduces a contrasting idea effectively.
Q.26:
Answer: (A)
Explanation: "Moreover" emphasizes an additional benefit of the software update.
Q.27:
Answer: (A)
Explanation: "Despite this" acknowledges the limitation while still presenting the positive outcome.
Q.28:
Answer: (B)
Explanation: "However" introduces a contrast between the comprehensive report and its shortcomings.
Q.29:
Answer: (A)
Explanation: "As a result" clearly shows the effect of heavy traffic on commuter punctuality.
Q.30:
Answer: (B)

Explanation: "Furthermore" effectively adds detailed evidence, strengthening the argument for renewable energy.

Section 4: Effective Argumentation and Rhetorical Strategies

Q.31:
Answer: (B)
Explanation: The sentence citing a study with specific statistics provides strong, credible evidence that supports the proposal.
Q.32:
Answer: (B)
Explanation: The statement about lifetime earnings backed by studies is a specific and persuasive piece of evidence.
Q.33:
Answer: (B)
Explanation: The sentence with survey data quantifying the increase in job satisfaction is the most persuasive and specific.
Q.34:
Answer: (A)
Explanation: Including a specific statistic about energy consumption directly supports the claim with concrete evidence.
Q.35:
Answer: (B)
Explanation: The sentence with a study from a reputable source, including a precise percentage, is the strongest support for the benefits of a balanced diet.
Q.36:
Answer: (B)
Explanation: Providing specific evidence regarding advances in medical technology offers strong support with credible details.
Q.37:
Answer: (B)
Explanation: The rhetorical question "Can we afford to ignore the overwhelming evidence of climate change, knowing that our future is at stake?" is engaging and thought-provoking.
Q.38:
Answer: (C)
Explanation: "While the policy offers benefits, it also presents significant challenges that must be addressed" clearly states the contrast in a balanced, logical manner.
Q.39:
Answer: (B)
Explanation: This revision adds specific details—mentioning underfunding, improved resources, and teacher quality—to remove ambiguity and strengthen the argument.
Q.40:
Answer: (A)
Explanation: The sentence "Civic engagement is essential because it promotes community involvement, builds leadership skills, and helps to create positive change" uses parallel structure effectively to list the benefits in a balanced and persuasive way.

5. Summary of Key Strategies

Concept	Best Strategy

Subject-Verb Agreement	Identify the subject and ensure agreement, even in complex sentences.
Modifiers	Place modifiers near the words they modify to avoid ambiguity.
Conciseness	Remove redundant words and phrases for clarity.
Transitions	Choose words that logically connect sentences.
Sentence Placement	Ensure sentence order follows a logical progression.
Supporting Evidence	Use specific, relevant facts to strengthen arguments.

6. Final Key Takeaways

- **Advanced grammar skills** help correct subject-verb agreement, misplaced modifiers, and parallel structure.
- **Conciseness and clarity** improve sentence effectiveness by removing redundancy.
- **Logical transitions and sentence placement** enhance reading comprehension and coherence.
- **Rhetorical strategies strengthen arguments** by ensuring **relevant, specific evidence** supports claims.

By **practicing high-level grammar and rhetorical exercises**, students can refine their **editing and writing skills**, leading to **higher accuracy in the SAT Writing & Language section**.

17.3 Advanced Math Sets (Quadratics, Exponential Functions, Trig)

The **Digital SAT Math section** includes **quadratic equations, exponential functions, and trigonometry**, testing students on their ability to solve equations, interpret functions, and apply key mathematical properties. This section provides **challenging practice exercises** covering:

- **Quadratic Equations and Functions**
- **Exponential Growth and Decay**
- **Trigonometric Ratios and Applications**

1. Quadratic Equations and Functions

Quadratic functions appear in the form:

$$f(x) = ax^2 + bx + c$$

where $a \neq 0$. They can be solved using:

- **Factoring**
- **The Quadratic Formula**
- **Graphing (Vertex, Axis of Symmetry, Roots)**

A. Solving Quadratic Equations by Factoring

Example 1: Factoring a Quadratic Equation

Solve:

$$x^2 - 7x + 12 = 0$$

Solution:

1. Factor the quadratic:

$$(x - 3)(x - 4) = 0$$

2. Solve for x:

$$x = 3, x = 4$$

Final Answer: $x = 3,4$

B. Solving Using the Quadratic Formula

The **quadratic formula** is used when factoring is difficult:

$$x = \frac{-b \pm \sqrt{b^2 - 4ac}}{2a}$$

Example 2: Using the Quadratic Formula

Solve:

$$2x^2 - 3x - 5 = 0$$

Solution:

1. Identify $a = 2, b = -3, c = -5$.
2. Compute discriminant:

$$(-3)^2 - 4(2)(-5) = 9 + 40 = 49$$

3. Solve using the formula:

$$x = \frac{3 \pm \sqrt{49}}{4}$$

$$x = \frac{3 \pm 7}{4}$$

Final Answer: $x = 2.5, x = -1$

C. Finding the Vertex of a Parabola

The **vertex** of a quadratic function is given by:

$$x = -\frac{b}{2a}$$

Example 3: Finding the Vertex of $f(x) = x^2 - 6x + 5$

1. Compute x-coordinate:

$$x = -\frac{-6}{2(1)} = 3$$

2. Substitute into the function:

$$f(3) = (3)^2 - 6(3) + 5 = -4$$

Final Answer: Vertex = $(3, -4)$

2. Exponential Growth and Decay

Exponential functions take the form:

$$f(x) = a \cdot b^x$$

where:

- a = **initial value**
- b = **growth/decay factor**
  - $b > 1$ = **growth**
  - $0 < b < 1$ = **decay**

A. Exponential Growth Example

Example 4: Population Growth

A city's population starts at **50,000** and grows **4% per year**. Find the population after **5 years**.

Solution:
Use the exponential growth formula:

$$P = P_0(1 + r)^t$$

where:

- $P_0 = 50{,}000$
- $r = 0.04$
- $t = 5$

$$P = 50{,}000(1.04)^5$$

$$P \approx 50{,}000(1.216)$$

$$P \approx 60{,}800$$

Final Answer: 60,800 people

B. Exponential Decay Example

Example 5: Radioactive Decay

A substance loses **12% of its mass per hour**. If it starts with **200 grams**, how much remains after **3 hours**?

Solution:
Use the exponential decay formula:

$$M = M_0(1 - r)^t$$

where:

- $M_0 = 200$
- $r = 0.12$
- $t = 3$

$$M = 200(0.88)^3$$

$$M \approx 200(0.681)$$

$$M \approx 136.2$$

Final Answer: 136.2 grams

3. Trigonometric Ratios and Applications

A. SOH-CAH-TOA for Right Triangles

Function	**Ratio**
Sine ($\sin\theta$)	$\frac{\text{opposite}}{\text{hypotenuse}}$
Cosine ($\cos\theta$)	$\frac{\text{adjacent}}{\text{hypotenuse}}$
Tangent ($\tan\theta$)	$\frac{\text{opposite}}{\text{adjacent}}$

Example 6: Finding a Missing Side

In a right triangle, $\sin 30^\circ = \frac{1}{2}$ and the hypotenuse is **10**. Find the opposite side.

1. Use $\sin\theta$ formula:

$$\sin 30^\circ = \frac{\text{opposite}}{\text{hypotenuse}}$$

2. Plug in values:

$$\frac{x}{10} = \frac{1}{2}$$

3. Solve for x:

$$x = 10 \times \frac{1}{2} = 5$$

Final Answer: 5 units

B. Using Trigonometry in the Unit Circle

The **unit circle** helps solve trigonometric equations involving radian measures.

Angle (Degrees)	**Sine**	**Cosine**	**Tangent**
0°	0	1	0
30° ($\frac{\pi}{6}$)	$\frac{1}{2}$	$\frac{\sqrt{3}}{2}$	$\frac{\sqrt{3}}{3}$
45° ($\frac{\pi}{4}$)	$\frac{\sqrt{2}}{2}$	$\frac{\sqrt{2}}{2}$	1

Example 7: Finding the Sine of 150°

What is $\sin 150^\circ$?

1. **Find the reference angle:**

$$180^\circ - 150^\circ = 30^\circ$$

2. Since **150° is in Quadrant II**, sine is **positive**.
3. From the unit circle, $\sin 30^\circ = \frac{1}{2}$.

Final Answer: $\frac{1}{2}$

Advanced Math Sets (Quadratics, Exponential Functions, Trigonometry)

Section 1: Quadratic Equations and Functions (Questions Q.1–Q.15)

Q.1 –
Solve for x:

$$x^2 - 9x + 20 = 0$$

Q.2 –
Solve for x using the quadratic formula:

$$2x^2 + 3x - 5 = 0$$

Q.3 –
Find the vertex of the function:

$$f(x) = 3x^2 - 12x + 7$$

Q.4 –
Determine the maximum value of the quadratic function:

$$f(x) = -x^2 + 4x + 1$$

Q.5 –
Solve and describe the roots of:

$$x^2 + 6x + 9 = 0$$

Q.6 –
Solve for x (express your answer in simplest radical form):

$$3x^2 - 2x - 8 = 0$$

Q.7 –
Find the axis of symmetry for:

$$f(x) = 4x^2 + 8x - 3$$

Q.8 –
For the quadratic function $f(x) = x^2 + bx + 16$ to have exactly one real root, determine the value(s) of b.

Q.9 –
Find all values of k for which the quadratic

$$x^2 - 2kx + k^2 - 9 = 0$$

has two distinct real solutions.

Q.10 –
Solve:

$$2(x - 3)^2 - 5 = 0$$

Q.11 –
A quadratic function $f(x) = ax^2 + bx + c$ has roots 2 and 7, and $f(0) = 14$. Write $f(x)$ in factored form.

Q.12 –
Solve for x given

$$x + \frac{1}{x} = 5.$$

Then, find the value of

$$x^2 + \frac{1}{x^2}.$$

Q.13 –
Solve the inequality:

$$x^2 - 5x + 6 < 0.$$

Q.14 –
Find the sum of the roots of:

$$4x^2 - 12x + 9 = 0.$$

Q.15 –
If the quadratic equation

$$x^2 - (k + 1)x + k = 0$$

has a repeated (double) root, determine k.

Section 2: Exponential Functions (Questions Q.16–Q.25)

Q.16 –
A bacteria population doubles every 3 hours. If the initial population is 500, what is the population after 12 hours?

Q.17 –
An investment of $2000 grows at an annual rate of 6% compounded annually. What is the amount after 10 years? (Express your answer to the nearest cent.)

Q.18 –
A car depreciates by 15% per year. If its initial value is $25,000, what is its approximate value after 4 years?

Q.19 –
Solve for x:
$$3 \cdot 2^x = 48.$$
Q.20 –
A radioactive substance loses 8% of its mass each day. If it starts with 150 grams, how many grams remain after 5 days? (Round your answer to one decimal place.)
Q.21 –
A population model is given by
$$P(t) = 1000(0.95)^t.$$
Find the time t (to two decimal places) at which the population falls to 500.
Q.22 –
The value of a computer decreases according to the function
$$V(t) = 1500e^{-0.2t},$$
where t is in years. What is its value after 3 years? (Round to the nearest dollar.)
Q.23 –
A population of insects increases by 25% each week. If there are initially 80 insects, what is the number of insects after 4 weeks? (Round to the nearest whole number.)
Q.24 –
Solve for x:
$$5^{x+1} = 125.$$
Q.25 –
A substance decays according to the formula
$$M(t) = 300(0.85)^t.$$
If t is measured in hours, find the mass remaining after 6 hours. (Round to one decimal place.)

Section 3: Trigonometric Ratios and Applications (Questions Q.26–Q.40)

Q.26 –
In a right triangle, if $\tan\theta = \frac{3}{4}$ and the adjacent side is 8, find the length of the opposite side.
Q.27 –
In a right triangle, if $\sin\theta = \frac{5}{13}$, find $\cos\theta$.
Q.28 –
Find the value of $\tan 45°$.
Q.29 –
Find the value of $\sin 120°$.
Q.30 –
Find the value of $\cos\frac{\pi}{3}$.
Q.31 –
In a right triangle with hypotenuse 17 and one leg of length 15, find the measure (in degrees) of the acute angle opposite the 15-unit side.
Q.32 –
A ladder leans against a wall forming a 60° angle with the ground. If the ladder is 10 feet long, find the height reached on the wall (in feet).
Q.33 –
Solve for θ (in degrees) in the interval $0 \leq \theta < 360°$ such that
$$\cos\theta = -\frac{1}{2}.$$

Q.34 –
Given that $\sin\theta = 0.8$ and θ is acute, find θ (in degrees, rounded to the nearest degree).
Q.35 –
Find the value of $\tan\frac{\pi}{4}$ using the unit circle.
Q.36 –
Express $\sin(2\theta)$ in terms of $\sin\theta$ and $\cos\theta$.
Q.37 –
In a $30°$-$60°$-$90°$ right triangle, if the side opposite $30°$ is 5, find the length of the side opposite $60°$.
Q.38 –
Using the cosine addition formula, find the exact value of $\cos 75°$.
Q.39 –
If $\sec\theta = \frac{5}{3}$ and $0 \leq \theta < 90°$, find $\cos\theta$.
Q.40 –
Solve for θ (in radians) in the interval $0 \leq \theta < 2\pi$ such that

$$\sin\theta = \frac{\sqrt{2}}{2}.$$

Answers and Explanations
Below are the detailed answers and explanations for each question.

Section 1: Quadratic Equations and Functions

Q.1 Answer: $x = 5$ or $x = 4$
Explanation: Factor the equation:

$$x^2 - 9x + 20 = (x-5)(x-4) = 0.$$

Thus, $x = 5$ or $x = 4$.

Q.2 Answer: $x = 1$ or $x = -2.5$
Explanation: Using the quadratic formula with $a = 2$, $b = 3$, $c = -5$:

$$x = \frac{-3 \pm \sqrt{3^2 - 4(2)(-5)}}{2 \cdot 2} = \frac{-3 \pm \sqrt{9+40}}{4} = \frac{-3 \pm \sqrt{49}}{4} = \frac{-3 \pm 7}{4}.$$

So, $x = \frac{4}{4} = 1$ or $x = \frac{-10}{4} = -2.5$.

Q.3 Answer: Vertex = $(2, -5)$
Explanation: The vertex's x-coordinate is given by

$$x = -\frac{b}{2a} = -\frac{-12}{2 \cdot 3} = 2.$$

Then, $f(2) = 3(2)^2 - 12(2) + 7 = 12 - 24 + 7 = -5$.

Q.4 Answer: Maximum value = 5
Explanation: For $f(x) = -x^2 + 4x + 1$, the vertex is at

$$x = -\frac{4}{2(-1)} = 2.$$

Then, $f(2) = -4 + 8 + 1 = 5$. Since the coefficient of x^2 is negative, the vertex represents a maximum.

Q.5 Answer: $x = -3$ (double root)
Explanation: The equation factors as

$$(x+3)^2 = 0,$$

so the only solution is $x = -3$ (a repeated root).

Q.6 Answer: $x = 2$ or $x = -\frac{4}{3}$
Explanation: Use the quadratic formula for $3x^2 - 2x - 8 = 0$:

$$\Delta = (-2)^2 - 4(3)(-8) = 4 + 96 = 100.$$

Thus,

$$x = \frac{2 \pm 10}{6} \Rightarrow x = \frac{12}{6} = 2 \quad \text{or} \quad x = \frac{-8}{6} = -\frac{4}{3}.$$

Q.7 Answer: $x = -1$
Explanation: The axis of symmetry is

$$x = -\frac{b}{2a} = -\frac{8}{2 \cdot 4} = -1.$$

Q.8 Answer: $b = 8$ or $b = -8$
Explanation: For a single (repeated) real root, the discriminant must be zero:

$$b^2 - 4(1)(16) = 0 \quad \Rightarrow \quad b^2 = 64 \quad \Rightarrow \quad b = \pm 8.$$

Q.9 Answer: All real numbers k
Explanation: The discriminant of

$$x^2 - 2kx + k^2 - 9 = 0$$

is

$$(2k)^2 - 4(k^2 - 9) = 4k^2 - 4k^2 + 36 = 36,$$

which is always positive. Thus, for any real k the equation has two distinct real solutions.

Q.10 Answer: $x = 3 \pm \sqrt{\frac{5}{2}}$

Explanation: Solve:

$$2(x-3)^2 = 5 \quad \Rightarrow \quad (x-3)^2 = \frac{5}{2} \quad \Rightarrow \quad x - 3 = \pm\sqrt{\frac{5}{2}},$$

so $x = 3 \pm \sqrt{\frac{5}{2}}$.

Q.11 Answer: $f(x) = (x-2)(x-7)$
Explanation: With roots 2 and 7, the function is $f(x) = A(x-2)(x-7)$. Since $f(0) = A(-2)(-7) = 14A = 14$, we have $A = 1$.

Q.12 Answer:
$x = \frac{5 \pm \sqrt{21}}{2}$ and $x^2 + \frac{1}{x^2} = 23.$
Explanation: Multiply $x + \frac{1}{x} = 5$ by x to get

$$x^2 + 1 = 5x \quad \Rightarrow \quad x^2 - 5x + 1 = 0.$$

Thus, by the quadratic formula,

$$x = \frac{5 \pm \sqrt{25 - 4}}{2} = \frac{5 \pm \sqrt{21}}{2}.$$

Also, $(x + 1/x)^2 = x^2 + 2 + 1/x^2 = 25$, so $x^2 + 1/x^2 = 25 - 2 = 23$.

Q.13 Answer: $2 < x < 3$
Explanation: Factor the quadratic:

$$x^2 - 5x + 6 = (x - 2)(x - 3) < 0.$$

The inequality holds for values between the roots.

Q.14 Answer: 3

Explanation: For any quadratic $ax^2 + bx + c = 0$, the sum of the roots is $-\frac{b}{a}$. Here, $-\frac{-12}{4} = 3$.

Q.15 Answer: $k = 1$
Explanation: For $x^2 - (k + 1)x + k = 0$ to have a repeated root, the discriminant must be zero:

$$(k + 1)^2 - 4k = 0 \quad \Rightarrow \quad k^2 + 2k + 1 - 4k = k^2 - 2k + 1 = 0,$$

which factors as $(k - 1)^2 = 0$.

Section 2: Exponential Functions

Q.16 Answer: 8000

Explanation: The population doubles every 3 hours. In 12 hours, there are $\frac{12}{3} = 4$ doublings, so

$$500 \times 2^4 = 500 \times 16 = 8000.$$

Q.17 Answer: Approximately $3,581.70
Explanation: Using the formula $A = 2000(1.06)^{10}$.
$(1.06)^{10} \approx 1.79085$ so $A \approx 2000 \times 1.79085 \approx 3581.70$.

Q.18 Answer: Approximately $13,050
Explanation: Value after 4 years:

$$25000 \times (0.85)^4 \approx 25000 \times 0.5220 \approx 13050.$$

Q.19 Answer: 4
Explanation: Divide both sides by 3:

$$2^x = 16 \quad \Rightarrow \quad 2^x = 2^4 \quad \Rightarrow \quad x = 4.$$

Q.20 Answer: Approximately 98.9 grams
Explanation:

$$150 \times (0.92)^5 \approx 150 \times 0.6591 \approx 98.9.$$

Q.21 Answer: Approximately 13.52
Explanation: Solve

$$1000(0.95)^t = 500 \quad \Rightarrow \quad (0.95)^t = 0.5.$$

Taking logarithms:

$$t = \frac{\ln 0.5}{\ln 0.95} \approx \frac{-0.69315}{-0.051293} \approx 13.52.$$

Q.22 Answer: Approximately $823
Explanation:

$$V(3) = 1500e^{-0.2\times 3} = 1500e^{-0.6} \approx 1500 \times 0.5488 \approx 823.$$

Q.23 Answer: Approximately 195 insects
Explanation:

$$80 \times (1.25)^4 \approx 80 \times 2.4414 \approx 195.$$

Q.24 Answer: 2
Explanation:

$$5^{x+1} = 125 \quad \Rightarrow \quad 125 = 5^3 \quad \Rightarrow \quad x + 1 = 3 \quad \Rightarrow \quad x = 2.$$

Q.25 Answer: Approximately 113.1 grams
Explanation:

$$300 \times (0.85)^6 \approx 300 \times 0.3771 \approx 113.1.$$

Section 3: Trigonometric Ratios and Applications

Q.26 Answer: 6
Explanation:

$$\tan\theta = \frac{\text{opposite}}{\text{adjacent}} = \frac{3}{4}; \quad \text{if adjacent} = 8, \quad \text{opposite} = 8 \times \frac{3}{4} = 6.$$

Q.27 Answer: $\frac{12}{13}$
Explanation: Use $\sin^2\theta + \cos^2\theta = 1$. With $\sin\theta = \frac{5}{13}$,

$$\cos\theta = \sqrt{1 - \left(\frac{5}{13}\right)^2} = \sqrt{\frac{169 - 25}{169}} = \frac{12}{13}.$$

Q.28 Answer: 1
Explanation: $\tan 45° = 1$.

Q.29 Answer: $\frac{\sqrt{3}}{2}$

Explanation: $\sin 120° = \sin(180° - 60°) = \sin 60° = \frac{\sqrt{3}}{2}$.

Q.30 Answer: $\frac{1}{2}$
Explanation: $\cos\frac{\pi}{3} = \cos 60° = \frac{1}{2}$.

Q.31 Answer: Approximately 62°
Explanation: In the triangle,

$$\sin\theta = \frac{15}{17} \quad \Rightarrow \quad \theta = \arcsin\left(\frac{15}{17}\right) \approx 62°.$$

Q.32 Answer: Approximately 8.66 feet

Explanation: $\sin 60° = \frac{\sqrt{3}}{2}$; height = $10 \times \frac{\sqrt{3}}{2} = 5\sqrt{3} \approx 8.66$.

Q.33 Answer: 120° and 240°

Explanation: $\cos\theta = -\frac{1}{2}$ when $\theta = 120°$ and $240°$ in the interval $[0, 360°)$.

Q.34 Answer: Approximately 53°
Explanation: $\theta = \arcsin(0.8) \approx 53.13°$, which rounds to 53°.

Q.35 Answer: 1
Explanation: $\tan\frac{\pi}{4} = 1$ from the unit circle.

Q.36 Answer: $2\sin\theta\cos\theta$
Explanation: The double-angle formula states $\sin(2\theta) = 2\sin\theta\cos\theta$.

Q.37 Answer: $5\sqrt{3}$

Explanation: In a $30°$-$60°$-$90°$ triangle, the side opposite $60°$ is $\sqrt{3}$ times the side opposite $30°$; thus, $5 \times \sqrt{3}$.

Q.38 Answer: $\frac{\sqrt{6}-\sqrt{2}}{4}$

Explanation: Use the cosine addition formula:

$$\cos75° = \cos(45° + 30°) = \cos45°\cos30° - \sin45°\sin30° = \frac{\sqrt{2}}{2} \cdot \frac{\sqrt{3}}{2} - \frac{\sqrt{2}}{2} \cdot \frac{1}{2} = \frac{\sqrt{6}-\sqrt{2}}{4}.$$

Q.39 Answer: $\frac{3}{5}$

Explanation: $\sec\theta = \frac{1}{\cos\theta}$, so $\cos\theta = \frac{1}{\sec\theta} = \frac{3}{5}$.

Q.40 Answer: $\theta = \frac{\pi}{4}$ and $\theta = \frac{3\pi}{4}$

Explanation: In $[0,2\pi)$, $\sin\theta = \frac{\sqrt{2}}{2}$ when $\theta = \frac{\pi}{4}$ and $\theta = \frac{3\pi}{4}$.

4. Summary of Key Strategies

Concept	Best Strategy
Quadratic Equations	Factor if possible; otherwise use the quadratic formula.
Exponential Growth/Decay	Use $P = P_0(1 \pm r)^t$ to calculate changes over time.
Trigonometric Ratios	Use **SOH-CAH-TOA** for right triangles.
Unit Circle	Memorize **key sine, cosine, and tangent values**.

5. Final Key Takeaways

- **Quadratic equations appear frequently**—factor when possible, use the quadratic formula when necessary.
- **Exponential functions model growth and decay**, requiring **multiplication by a percentage factor over time**.
- **Trigonometry problems require understanding SOH-CAH-TOA and the unit circle**.
- **Practice solving problems efficiently and using the Desmos calculator for verification**.

By **mastering quadratics, exponential functions, and trigonometry**, students can **tackle complex SAT Math problems with confidence and efficiency**.

17.4 Data Analysis and Real-World Problem Scenarios

The **Digital SAT Math section** includes **data interpretation and real-world application problems**, requiring students to analyze **graphs, charts, tables, and statistical measures** to make informed decisions. These questions test a student's ability to **interpret trends, apply formulas, and solve practical problems**.

This section will cover:

- **Analyzing Graphs, Tables, and Data Sets**
- **Statistical Measures (Mean, Median, Mode, Range, and Standard Deviation)**
- **Real-World Word Problems (Rates, Financial Growth, Probability)**
- **SAT Strategies for Complex Data Analysis Questions**

1. Analyzing Graphs, Tables, and Data Sets

A. Understanding Graph Types

Graph Type	Use Case

Bar Graph	Comparing quantities across categories
Line Graph	Showing trends over time
Scatterplot	Identifying relationships between variables
Pie Chart	Displaying proportions of a whole

Example 1: Reading a Bar Graph

Year	Company A Revenue ($M)	Company B Revenue ($M)
2020	50	60
2021	55	68
2022	62	75
2023	70	82

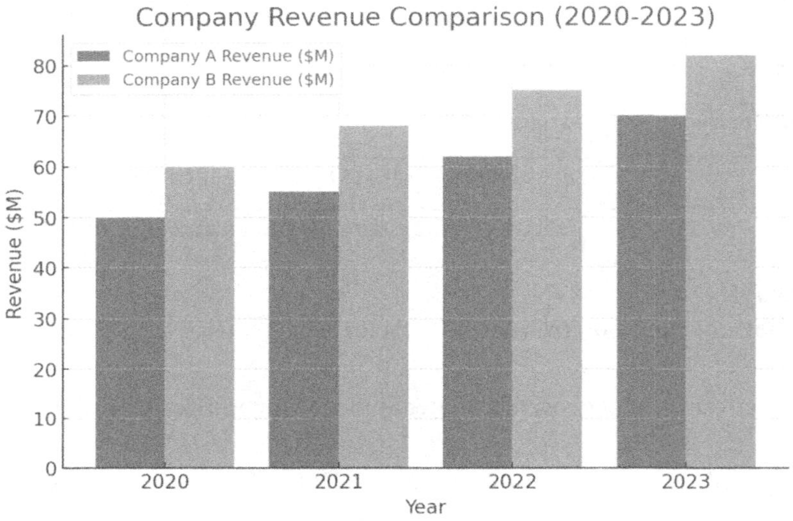

Question: What was the percentage increase in revenue for Company A from 2020 to 2023?

Solution:

1. Use the **percentage increase formula**:

$$\frac{\text{New Value} - \text{Old Value}}{\text{Old Value}} \times 100$$

2. Substitute values:

$$\frac{70-50}{50} \times 100 = \frac{20}{50} \times 100 = 40\%$$

Final Answer: 40% increase

2. Statistical Measures: Mean, Median, Mode, and Standard Deviation

A. Key Definitions

Measure	Definition
Mean (Average)	Sum of values divided by the number of values

Median	The middle value when numbers are ordered
Mode	The most frequently occurring value
Range	The difference between the highest and lowest values
Standard Deviation	A measure of data spread from the mean

Example 2: Finding the Median

Find the median of the set: **8, 12, 5, 20, 15**.

Solution:

1. Order the values: **5, 8, 12, 15, 20**.
2. Identify the middle value: **12**.

Final Answer: 12

3. Real-World Word Problems (Rates, Financial Growth, Probability)

A. Solving Rate Problems

Example 3: Speed and Distance Calculation

A train travels **300 miles** in **5 hours**. What is its average speed?

Solution:
Use the formula:

$$\text{Speed} = \frac{\text{Distance}}{\text{Time}}$$

$$\text{Speed} = \frac{300}{5} = 60 \text{ mph}$$

Final Answer: 60 mph

B. Compound Interest and Financial Growth

$$A = P(1 + r/n)^{nt}$$

where:

- P = Initial amount
- r = Annual interest rate
- n = Number of times compounded per year
- t = Number of years

Example 4: Compound Interest Calculation

A deposit of **$2,000** earns **5% annual interest**, compounded **annually**. What will the balance be after **3 years**?

Solution:

1. Use the formula:

$$A = 2000(1.05)^3$$

2. Compute:

$$A = 2000(1.1576) = 2315.20$$

Final Answer: $2,315.20

C. Probability in Real-Life Scenarios

Example 5: Drawing Cards from a Deck

A standard deck has **52 cards**, with **4 aces**. What is the probability of drawing an **ace**?

Solution:
Use the probability formula:

$$P = \frac{\text{Favorable Outcomes}}{\text{Total Outcomes}}$$

$$P = \frac{4}{52} = \frac{1}{13}$$

Final Answer: $\frac{1}{13}$ or **7.69%**

4. SAT Strategies for Complex Data Analysis Questions

A. Identifying Trends in Data

- Look for **increasing, decreasing, or fluctuating trends** in graphs and tables.

Example 6: Predicting a Trend

A company's revenue grows by $5Mperyear **. Ifrevenuewas **$**50M in 2020**, what will it be in **2025**?

$$50 + (5 \times 5) = 75M$$

Final Answer: $75M

B. Avoiding Common Pitfalls

Mistake	**Solution**
Misreading graph axes	Check **scale and labels** before answering
Confusing percentage increase with absolute increase	Convert percentages into **actual numbers**
Ignoring outliers in data analysis	Identify **values that differ significantly**

5. Summary of Key Strategies

Concept	**Best Strategy**
Graph and Table Interpretation	Read axes, scales, and labels carefully.
Statistical Measures	Memorize mean, median, mode, and standard deviation formulas.
Rate and Growth Problems	Use **speed = distance/time** and compound interest formulas.
Probability	Use **total outcomes vs. favorable outcomes** to find probability.

6. Final Key Takeaways

- **Data interpretation requires careful reading of graphs, tables, and charts** to avoid errors.
- **Mean, median, and mode help summarize data**, while standard deviation measures spread.
- **Real-world math includes rates, financial growth, and probability calculations.**
- **Recognizing trends and avoiding common data misinterpretations** can prevent mistakes on SAT questions.

By **practicing real-world problem-solving and data analysis**, students can confidently tackle **complex SAT math questions** and improve their overall performance.

CHAPTER 18

FULL-LENGTH PRACTICE TEST 1

MODULE 1 – READING & WRITING

Passage 1 – "The Attic Discovery"

Read the passage below and then answer Questions Q1–Q4.

Deep within the attic of her grandmother's old farmhouse, Lena discovered a dusty wooden chest that had long been forgotten. As sunlight filtered through a narrow window, it illuminated the intricate carvings on the chest—suggesting untold stories of generations past. With a mixture of curiosity and trepidation, Lena knelt down and gently opened the lid. Inside, among faded photographs and brittle letters, lay a small, ornate key. Though tarnished by time, the key exuded an aura of mystery and promise.

Embracing her newfound role as a detective of the past, Lena spent long evenings poring over handwritten journals and faded maps. Each discovery deepened her sense of wonder as she imagined lives lived in a different era. The once mundane attic transformed into a portal to history, igniting Lena's passion for uncovering hidden truths. Though moments of doubt arose, the key remained a constant symbol of hope—urging her ever forward into the labyrinth of her family's legacy.

Q1. What is the primary purpose of the passage?
(A). To describe the physical features of an old farmhouse.
(B). To recount Lena's discovery of a mysterious key and its significance.
(C). To explain the history of the wooden chest in detail.
(D). To compare different family heirlooms found in the attic.
Q2. Which detail most strongly suggests that the key holds sentimental value?
(A). The key is described as "ornate" and "tarnished by time."
(B). Lena finds faded photographs alongside the key.
(C). Sunlight illuminates the carvings on the chest.
(D). Lena spends evenings reading handwritten journals.
Q3. The word "trepidation" in the passage most nearly means:
(A). Excitement
(B). Fear or apprehension
(C). Disgust
(D). Confidence
Q4. Based on the passage, what can be inferred about Lena's character?
(A). She is indifferent to her family's past.
(B). She is curious and values history.
(C). She is primarily interested in material wealth.
(D). She dislikes spending time alone.

Passage 2 – "Unearthing the Past: The Mineral of Remembrance"

Read the passage below and answer Questions Q5–Q8.

In a remote region of the high Andes, a team of geologists recently uncovered a rare mineral that appears to defy conventional classification. The mineral's shimmering iridescence and peculiar crystalline structure have prompted experts to reexamine longstanding theories about geological formation. Field researchers describe the discovery as serendipitous—occurring during an expedition aimed at mapping tectonic fault lines. Preliminary analyses suggest that the mineral may have formed under unique environmental conditions that no longer exist on Earth. Although its precise composition remains under study, the mineral's unusual properties have already sparked interest among both academics and the mining industry. Some critics caution that rapid commercial exploitation could jeopardize further scientific investigation, urging a balanced approach that preserves the integrity of the natural site. As research continues, the discovery stands as a testament to the enduring mysteries hidden deep within our planet.

Q5. What is the central focus of the passage?
(A). The commercial potential of rare minerals.
(B). The unexpected discovery of a mineral that challenges existing theories.
(C). A detailed history of geological expeditions in the Andes.
(D). The dangers of exploiting natural resources.
Q6. The term "serendipitous" in the passage most nearly means:
(A). Deliberate
(B). Fortunate
(C). Unpredictable
(D). Cautious
Q7. Which statement best reflects the authors' attitude toward the discovery?
(A). Skeptical about its scientific value.
(B). Enthusiastic about the prospect of new research.
(C). Alarmed by the potential for commercial misuse.
(D). Indifferent to the mineral's formation process.
Q8. According to the passage, why do some experts oppose rapid commercial exploitation of the mineral?
(A). It might lead to environmental degradation.
(B). It could interfere with ongoing scientific research.
(C). It would diminish the mineral's market value.
(D). It conflicts with international mining regulations.

Independent Grammar & Writing Questions (Module 1)

Answer Questions Q9–Q27.

Q9. Select the best version of the underlined portion in the sentence:
"After several hours of searching, Lena **found out that** the attic held many secrets."
(A). found out that
(B). discovered that
(C). realized that
(D). observed that
Q10. Choose the option that best corrects the error in parallel structure:
"Lena spent her evenings reading journals, scanning old maps, and **to explore** the dusty corners of the farmhouse."
(A). No change
(B). exploring the dusty corners of the farmhouse
(C). to explore the dusty corners and reading journals
(D). explore the dusty corners of the farmhouse
Q11. Identify the sentence written in a grammatically correct manner.
(A). Neither the old chest nor the mysterious key have lost their charm over the years.
(B). Neither the old chest nor the mysterious key has lost their charm over the years.
(C). Neither the old chest nor the mysterious key has lost its charm over the years.
(D). Neither the old chest nor the mysterious key have lost its charm over the years.
Q12. In the following sentence, which choice best maintains verb tense consistency?
"While Lena **investigated** the attic, she **finds** clues that hint at her family's past."
(A). investigated / finds
(B). investigates / finds

(C). investigated / found
(D). investigates / found
Q13. Choose the best revision for clarity in the sentence:
"The key, which had been hidden away among old papers and fragile trinkets, **it seemed, carried** a history that was both mysterious and profound."
(A). The key, hidden among old papers and fragile trinkets, carried a mysterious and profound history.
(B). The key, which was hidden among old papers and fragile trinkets, carried a mysterious, profound history.
(C). Hidden among old papers and fragile trinkets, the key it carried a mysterious and profound history.
(D). The key carried a mysterious and profound history, hidden among old papers and fragile trinkets.
Q14. Which sentence uses commas correctly?
(A). Lena who had always been curious, found the key in the attic.
(B). Lena, who had always been curious found the key in the attic.
(C). Lena, who had always been curious, found the key in the attic.
(D). Lena who had always been curious found, the key in the attic.
Q15. Select the sentence that best corrects the misplaced modifier:
(A). While exploring the farmhouse, Lena discovered the mysterious key.
(B). Lena discovered the mysterious key while exploring the farmhouse.
(C). The mysterious key was discovered by Lena while exploring the farmhouse.
(D). While the mysterious key was discovered, Lena was exploring the farmhouse.
Q16. Choose the best version of the sentence to eliminate wordiness:
"**In view of the fact that** Lena was very curious, she took the time to search every nook and cranny of the attic."
(A). Because Lena was curious, she searched every nook of the attic.
(B). Since Lena was curious, she searched every nook and cranny of the attic.
(C). Lena, being very curious, took time to search every nook and cranny of the attic.
(D). Lena was curious; thus, she searched every nook and cranny of the attic.
Q17. Which option best corrects the pronoun–antecedent agreement error?
"Each of the letters and photographs **were** placed carefully in its own envelope."
(A). …were placed carefully in their own envelopes.
(B). …was placed carefully in its own envelope.
(C). …was placed carefully in their own envelope.
(D). …were placed carefully in its own envelope.
Q18. In the sentence below, which revision best corrects the error in word choice?
"Lena's adventure was not only exciting, but also **a unique** opportunity to learn about her ancestry."
(A). exciting, but also unique
(B). exciting, and also a unique
(C). exciting and also unique
(D). exciting, but also an unique
Q19. Which version of the sentence is punctuated correctly?
(A). Lena studied the old journals, the letters, and the photographs that were discovered in the attic.
(B). Lena studied the old journals, the letters and the photographs, that were discovered in the attic.
(C). Lena studied the old journals, the letters, and the photographs, that were discovered in the attic.
(D). Lena studied the old journals the letters, and the photographs that were discovered, in the attic.
Q20. Select the option that best corrects the sentence structure:
"Having completed her search, a sense of wonder overwhelmed Lena."
(A). Having completed her search, Lena was overwhelmed by a sense of wonder.
(B). Lena completed her search, and a sense of wonder overwhelmed her.
(C). After completing her search, a sense of wonder overwhelmed Lena.
(D). Completing her search, a sense of wonder was felt by Lena.

Q21. In the following sentence, choose the option that best clarifies the comparison:
"Unlike her cousins, who preferred quiet evenings, Lena enjoyed the adventure of uncovering secrets in the attic."
(A). No change
(B). Unlike her cousins who preferred quiet evenings, Lena enjoyed uncovering secrets.
(C). Unlike her cousins, Lena enjoyed the adventure of uncovering secrets.
(D). Unlike her cousins who preferred quiet evenings, Lena enjoyed the adventure of uncovering secrets.
Q22. Choose the version that best improves sentence coherence:
"Lena was curious; however, the key remained locked away, mysteriously, with no apparent connection to her family history."
(A). Lena was curious, yet the key remained mysteriously locked away with no apparent connection to her family history.
(B). Lena was curious; however, the key remained locked away with no apparent connection to her family history.
(C). Lena, curious as she was, found that the key remained mysteriously locked away with no apparent connection to her family history.
(D). Although Lena was curious, the key, locked away mysteriously, showed no connection to her family history.
Q23. Identify the sentence with correct subject–verb agreement:
(A). The collection of artifacts in the attic were impressive.
(B). The collection of artifacts in the attic was impressive.
(C). The collections of artifacts in the attic was impressive.
(D). The collections of artifacts in the attic were impressive.
Q24. Choose the best revision to avoid a dangling modifier:
"Walking through the hall, the ancient portraits caught Lena's attention."
(A). While walking through the hall, Lena noticed the ancient portraits.
(B). Walking through the hall, the ancient portraits caught Lena's attention.
(C). The ancient portraits caught Lena's attention as she was walking through the hall.
(D). As the ancient portraits caught Lena's attention, she walked through the hall.
Q25. Which sentence correctly uses a semicolon?
(A). Lena enjoyed her discovery; because it connected her to her past.
(B). Lena enjoyed her discovery; it connected her to her past.
(C). Lena enjoyed her discovery, it connected her to her past.
(D). Lena enjoyed her discovery: it connected her to her past.
Q26. Choose the best revision to correct the error in the sentence:
"The journals, which **was** filled with handwritten notes, offered a glimpse into the family's bygone days."
(A). which was filled with handwritten notes
(B). which were filled with handwritten notes
(C). that was filled with handwritten notes
(D). that were filled with handwritten notes
Q27. Select the version that improves clarity and conciseness:
"In the process of searching through the myriad items in the attic, Lena was able to uncover many clues regarding her family history."
(A). While searching through the many items in the attic, Lena uncovered numerous clues about her family history.
(B). In searching through the myriad of items in the attic, Lena uncovered many clues regarding her family history.
(C). While in the process of searching through the myriad items in the attic, Lena was able to uncover many

clues regarding her family history.
(D). By searching the attic, Lena uncovered many clues about her family history.

MODULE 2 – READING & WRITING

Passage 1 – "Reflections in the Mirror of Memory"

Read the passage below and answer Questions Q1–Q5 (Module 2).

In the fading light of autumn, Adrian found himself drawn to an old mirror that hung in an abandoned manor. The mirror—its surface etched with delicate patterns and whispers of a bygone era—seemed to capture more than mere reflections; it held echoes of lives once lived. As he stood before it, the interplay of light and shadow stirred memories that were both haunting and beautiful. Adrian recalled fragments of conversations, lost laughter, and quiet sorrows that had long since faded into obscurity. It was as if the mirror, imbued with a mysterious consciousness, compelled him to confront the transient nature of time and the inevitability of change. In that silent moment, past and present merged, leaving him with a profound awareness of his own impermanence. The experience was at once disquieting and liberating—a reminder that even fleeting moments can leave an indelible mark on one's soul. With each subtle distortion in the glass, he perceived a narrative of loss, renewal, and the delicate balance between memory and oblivion.

Q1. What is the primary theme of the passage?
(A). The beauty of old architecture.
(B). The interplay between memory, time, and impermanence.
(C). The restoration of abandoned manors.
(D). Vivid descriptions of autumn scenery.
Q2. The phrase "echoes of lives once lived" most nearly suggests:
(A). Actual sound recordings from the past.
(B). The lingering influence of past experiences.
(C). The physical presence of former residents.
(D). A collection of historical artifacts.
Q3. Which of the following best describes Adrian's reaction upon viewing the mirror?
(A). Indifference mixed with curiosity.
(B). Overwhelming nostalgia and introspection.
(C). Disgust and repulsion.
(D). Joy and unbridled excitement.
Q4. The passage implies that the mirror serves as a metaphor for:
(A). The physical decay of old buildings.
(B). A tool for divination.
(C). The way memories distort with time.
(D). A means to reconnect with lost loved ones.
Q5. Which detail most strongly supports the idea that time is transient?
(A). The mirror's delicate etched patterns.
(B). The interplay of light and shadow on the mirror.
(C). Adrian's recognition of his own impermanence.
(D). The abandoned state of the manor.

Passage 2 – "The Imperative of Environmental Accountability"

Read the passage below and answer Questions Q6–Q10 (Module 2).

In recent years, the discourse surrounding climate change has shifted from abstract scientific debates to urgent calls for environmental accountability. Critics argue that while technological advances have ushered in prosperity, they have also contributed to an unsustainable exploitation of natural resources. Industrial growth, unchecked consumption, and lax regulatory oversight have collectively accelerated the degradation of ecosystems. Proponents of stringent environmental policies contend that society must balance economic progress with ecological stewardship. They warn that failure to do so not only jeopardizes the natural world but also imperils the well-being of future generations. In response, some policymakers are advocating a paradigm shift—a transformation that prioritizes renewable energy, conservation efforts, and sustainable practices over short-term gains. This emerging perspective challenges traditional models of development and calls for a reexamination of the values underpinning modern society. As mounting evidence underscores the stakes, it becomes increasingly clear that the cost of inaction far exceeds the investments required for a resilient, equitable future.

Q6. What is the primary argument presented in the passage?
(A). Technological advances have solely benefited modern society.
(B). Economic progress should always be prioritized over environmental concerns.
(C). A balance between economic growth and environmental stewardship is essential.
(D). Traditional models of development are sufficient to address climate change.
Q7. The term "paradigm shift" in the passage most nearly means:
(A). A temporary change in policy.
(B). A fundamental change in approach or underlying assumptions.
(C). A minor adjustment in regulatory measures.
(D). An incremental improvement in industrial practices.
Q8. Which of the following best supports the argument that environmental degradation poses a threat to future generations?
(A). The mention of renewable energy initiatives.
(B). The critique of industrial growth and unchecked consumption.
(C). The call for a reexamination of modern societal values.
(D). The reference to technological advances and prosperity.
Q9. According to the passage, what is a key reason for the call for environmental accountability?
(A). The immediate economic benefits of strict regulation.
(B). The unsustainable exploitation of natural resources.
(C). The preservation of historical industrial practices.
(D). The desire to maintain traditional models of development.
Q10. What does the passage suggest is necessary to achieve a more sustainable future?
(A). Increased investment in fossil fuels.
(B). A transformation of societal values and practices toward sustainability.
(C). A reduction in technological innovation.
(D). A return to past economic models.

Independent Grammar & Writing Questions (Module 2)

Answer Questions Q11–Q27.
Q11. Select the best revision to correct the error in parallel structure:
"Adrian not only reflected on his memories but also **was considering** the future."
(A). Adrian not only reflected on his memories but also considered the future.
(B). Adrian not only reflected on his memories but also was considering the future.
(C). Adrian reflected on his memories and considered the future.
(D). Adrian not only was reflecting on his memories but also considered the future.
Q12. In the sentence below, choose the option that corrects the pronoun–antecedent agreement:
"Each of the environmental policies **were** designed to mitigate its impact on climate change."
(A). …were designed to mitigate their impact on climate change.
(B). …was designed to mitigate its impact on climate change.

(C). …was designed to mitigate their impact on climate change.
(D). …were designed to mitigate its impact on climate change.

Q13. Choose the best version of the sentence to correct the misplacement of a modifier:
"Advocating for renewable energy, the current policies were criticized by environmental activists."
(A). Environmental activists criticized the current policies, advocating for renewable energy.
(B). The current policies, which advocate for renewable energy, were criticized by environmental activists.
(C). Advocating for renewable energy, environmental activists criticized the current policies.
(D). Environmental activists, advocating for renewable energy, criticized the current policies.

Q14. Which sentence correctly uses a colon to introduce an explanation?
(A). The solution is simple: reducing carbon emissions.
(B). The solution is simple, reducing carbon emissions.
(C). The solution is: simple reducing carbon emissions.
(D). The solution: is simple, reducing carbon emissions.

Q15. Identify the sentence that is free of redundancy.
(A). The policy was implemented in its entirety, completely.
(B). The policy was fully implemented.
(C). The policy was implemented completely in every aspect.
(D). The policy was implemented in a complete and total manner.

Q16. Choose the best revision for clarity in the sentence:
"Critics argue that, **due to the fact that** technological advances have contributed to economic growth, they have also negatively affected the environment."
(A). Critics argue that technological advances have contributed to economic growth while also negatively affecting the environment.
(B). Critics argue that because technological advances have contributed to economic growth, they negatively affect the environment.
(C). Critics argue that technological advances, contributing to economic growth, have negatively affected the environment.
(D). Critics argue that, due to technological advances contributing to economic growth, there has been negative environmental impact.

Q17. In the sentence below, which choice best corrects the error in verb tense consistency?
"While policymakers **advocated** for change, new reports **emerge** about environmental degradation."
(A). …advocated / emerged
(B). …advocated / emerge
(C). …advocate / emerge
(D). …advocated / emerge

Q18. Choose the sentence that best eliminates a wordiness issue:
"**In light of the fact that** the evidence overwhelmingly supports the need for renewable energy, many experts are calling for immediate policy reform."
(A). Because the evidence overwhelmingly supports renewable energy, many experts are calling for immediate policy reform.
(B). Given that the evidence overwhelmingly supports the need for renewable energy, many experts are calling for immediate policy reform.
(C). Since the evidence overwhelmingly supports renewable energy, many experts are calling for immediate policy reform.
(D). Due to overwhelming evidence supporting renewable energy, many experts are calling for immediate policy reform.

Q19. Identify the sentence that best corrects the punctuation error:
"Industrial growth unchecked, consumption unbridled and regulatory oversight lax, have all contributed to

environmental degradation."

(A). Industrial growth, unchecked consumption, unbridled consumption, and lax regulatory oversight have all contributed to environmental degradation.

(B). Industrial growth, unchecked; consumption unbridled; and regulatory oversight lax have all contributed to environmental degradation.

(C). Industrial growth, unchecked consumption, and lax regulatory oversight have all contributed to environmental degradation.

(D). Industrial growth—unchecked, consumption unbridled, and regulatory oversight lax—have all contributed to environmental degradation.

Q20. In the following sentence, select the best revision to correct the faulty comparison:

"More than any previous policy, the new environmental law has been criticized for its lack of effectiveness."

(A). More than any previous policy, critics have criticized the new environmental law for its lack of effectiveness.

(B). The new environmental law has been criticized more than any previous policy for its lack of effectiveness.

(C). The new environmental law, more than any previous policy, has been criticized for its lack of effectiveness.

(D). No revision is necessary.

Q21. Choose the sentence that best corrects the misuse of the passive voice:

(A). The new regulations achieved significant improvements in air quality.

(B). The new regulations resulted in significant improvements in air quality.

(C). Significant improvements in air quality were achieved by the new regulations.

(D). The new regulations achieved air quality improvements significantly.

Q22. Which sentence best revises the dangling modifier?

"After reviewing the data, the conclusion was evident."

(A). After reviewing the data, the researchers found the conclusion to be evident.

(B). After the data was reviewed, the conclusion was evident.

(C). After reviewing the data, the conclusion became evident.

(D). The data, once reviewed, made the conclusion evident.

Q23. Select the best revision to improve sentence flow and coherence:

"Many experts argue that renewable energy is not only necessary for economic growth but **it is also** crucial for environmental sustainability."

(A). Many experts argue that renewable energy is necessary for economic growth and crucial for environmental sustainability.

(B). Many experts argue that renewable energy is not only necessary for economic growth, but also for environmental sustainability.

(C). Many experts argue that renewable energy is necessary not only for economic growth but also for environmental sustainability.

(D). Many experts argue that renewable energy is both necessary for economic growth and crucial for environmental sustainability.

Q24. In the sentence below, choose the answer that best corrects the pronoun usage:

"Those who believe that progress is inevitable must accept that **their opinions** are always correct."

(A). …must accept that its opinions are always correct.

(B). …must accept that their opinion is always correct.

(C). No change.

(D). …must accept that their viewpoints are always correct.

Q25. Identify the sentence that best eliminates an extraneous word.

(A). Many advocates strongly believe that immediate and urgent measures are needed to combat climate change.

(B). Many advocates strongly believe that immediate measures are needed to combat climate change.

(C). Many advocates believe that urgent measures are needed to combat climate change.
(D). Many advocates strongly believe that urgent measures are needed to combat climate change.

Q26. Choose the sentence that corrects the error in modifier placement:
"With an emphasis on sustainability, the conference discussed policies and innovations."
(A). With an emphasis on sustainability, the conference organizers discussed policies and innovations.
(B). The conference discussed policies and innovations with an emphasis on sustainability.
(C). The conference, with an emphasis on sustainability, discussed policies and innovations.
(D). The conference discussed sustainability, policies, and innovations.

Q27. Select the best revision to ensure consistency in point of view:
"If one wants to improve society, **you must** actively engage in civic duties."
(A). If one wants to improve society, one must actively engage in civic duties.
(B). If you want to improve society, you must actively engage in civic duties.
(C). If one wants to improve society, you must actively engage in civic duties.
(D). If you want to improve society, one must actively engage in civic duties.

MATH MODULE 1

Q1. Solve for x:

$2x - 7 = 9$

(A). 4
(B). 8
(C). 7
(D). 9

Q2. If $f(x) = 3x + 2$, what is $f(4)$?

(A). 10
(B). 12
(C). 14
(D). 16

Q3. Simplify the expression:

$(2x^2 \cdot 3x) \div (6x)$

(A). x^3
(B). x^2
(C). $6x^2$
(D). $1/x^2$

Q4. Solve for y:

$(5y)/2 = 15$

(A). 3
(B). 5
(C). 6
(D). 10

Q5. What is the slope of the line through the points (2, 3) and (8, 15)?

(A). 2
(B). 4
(C). 6
(D). 8

Q6. Solve the inequality:

$3x - 4 < 11$

(A). $x < 4$
(B). $x < 5$

(C). $x < 3$
(D). $x < 6$

Q7. If $5/x = 10$, what is the value of x?
(A). 0.5
(B). 2
(C). 5
(D). 10

Q8. A rectangle has a length of 8 and a width of 3. What is its area?
(A). 11
(B). 22
(C). 24
(D). 26

Q9. The ratio of apples to oranges in a basket is 3:5. If there are 15 apples, how many oranges are there?
(A). 20
(B). 23
(C). 25
(D). 30

Q10. Simplify the expression:
$4(3x - 2) - 2x$
(A). $10x - 8$
(B). $12x - 2$
(C). $12x - 8$
(D). $10x + 8$

Q11. Solve for x:
$x/4 + 3 = 7$
(A). 12
(B). 14
(C). 16
(D). 18

Q12. What is the value of $\sqrt{81}$?
(A). 7
(B). 8
(C). 9
(D). 10

Q13. A car travels 60 miles in 1.5 hours. What is its average speed (in mph)?
(A). 30
(B). 35
(C). 40
(D). 45

Q14. Find the value of x in the proportion:
$4/7 = x/21$
(A). 10
(B). 11
(C). 12
(D). 13

Q15. What is the solution set for the equation:
$2(x - 3) = 2x - 6$?
(A). $x = 3$

(B). $x = 0$
(C). All real numbers
(D). No solution

Q16. If $f(x) = x^2$, what is $f(3)$?
(A). 3
(B). 6
(C). 9
(D). 12

Q17. Solve the equation:
$|x - 4| = 3$
(A). $x = 7$ only
(B). $x = 1$ only
(C). $x = 1$ or 7
(D). $x = -1$ or 7

Q18. Find the solutions to the equation:
$3x^2 - 12 = 0$
(A). $x = 2$
(B). $x = -2$
(C). $x = 2$ or -2
(D). $x = 4$ or -4

Q19. A triangle has a base of 10 and a height of 6. What is its area?
(A). 30
(B). 20
(C). 60
(D). 15

Q20. Simplify the expression:
$(x^2 - 9)/(x - 3)$ (Assume $x \neq 3$)
(A). $x - 3$
(B). $x + 3$
(C). $x^2 - 3$
(D). $x^2 + 3$

Q21. Solve for x:
$(1/2)x + 3 = 7$
(A). 6
(B). 7
(C). 8
(D). 9

Q22. What is the distance between the points $(2, -1)$ and $(5, 3)$?
(A). 4
(B). 5
(C). 6
(D). 7

MATH MODULE 2

Q1. Solve for x:
$2x^2 - 5x - 3 = 0$
(A). $x = -1/2$ or $x = 3$
(B). $x = 1/2$ or $x = -3$

(C). $x = -1$ or $x = 3$

(D). $x = 1/2$ or $x = 3$

Q2. If $g(x) = \sqrt{(x + 4)}$, what is $g(5)$?

(A). 2

(B). 3

(C). 4

(D). 5

Q3. Solve the system of equations:

$2x + 3y = 12$

$x - y = 1$

(A). $x = 3, y = 2$

(B). $x = 2, y = 3$

(C). $x = 4, y = 2$

(D). $x = 3, y = 3$

Q4. Express the quadratic:

$x^2 - 4x + 4$

in factored form.

(A). $(x - 2)^2$

(B). $(x + 2)^2$

(C). $(x - 4)^2$

(D). $(x + 4)^2$

Q5. If $h(x) = 2x^2 - 3x + 5$, what is $h(-1)$?

(A). 6

(B). 8

(C). 10

(D). 12

Q6. Simplify the radical expression:

$\sqrt{50} - 2\sqrt{2}$

(A). $\sqrt{2}$

(B). $2\sqrt{2}$

(C). $3\sqrt{2}$

(D). $4\sqrt{2}$

Q7. For what value of x is the rational expression

$(x^2 - 9)/(x - 3)$

undefined?

(A). 3

(B). −3

(C). 0

(D). 9

Q8. Solve the inequality:

$x^2 - 4x - 5 < 0$

(A). $x < -1$ or $x > 5$

(B). $-1 < x < 5$

(C). $-1 \leq x \leq 5$

(D). $x > 5$

Q9. Find the vertex of the parabola given by:

$y = x^2 - 6x + 8$

(A). $(3, -1)$

(B). (−3, −1)
(C). (1, 3)
(D). (−1, 3)

Q10. If f(x) = (3x − 4)/(x + 2), what is f(0)?
(A). −2
(B). −4
(C). 2
(D). 4

Q11. A circle has an area of 25π. What is its radius?
(A). 4
(B). 5
(C). 6
(D). 7

Q12. Solve for x:
$\log_2(x) = 3$
(A). 4
(B). 8
(C). 16
(D). 3

Q13. If a function is defined as f(x) = 1/(x − 1), what is f(3)?
(A). 1/3
(B). 1/2
(C). 2
(D). 3

Q14. What is the sum of the first five terms of an arithmetic sequence with a first term of 2 and a common difference of 3?
(A). 35
(B). 40
(C). 45
(D). 50

Q15. Simplify the expression:
$(2x^2 - 8)/(4x)$
(A). (x − 2)(x + 2)/(2x)
(B). (x − 2)/(2x)
(C). (x + 2)/(2x)
(D). (x − 2)(x + 2)/(4x)

Q16. If the probability of event A is 0.3 and the probability of event B is 0.5, and the events are independent, what is the probability that both occur?
(A). 0.15
(B). 0.8
(C). 0.5
(D). 0.3

Q17. Solve for y in terms of x:
3y − 2x = 6
(A). y = (2/3)x + 2
(B). y = (3/2)x + 2
(C). y = (2/3)x − 2
(D). y = (3/2)x − 2

Q18. What is the sum of the infinite geometric series with a first term of 10 and a common ratio of 1/2?
(A). 10
(B). 15
(C). 20
(D). 25

Q19. If sin θ = 0.6 for an acute angle θ, what is cos θ?
(A). 0.6
(B). 0.8
(C). 1.0
(D). 0.4

Q20. For the function $f(x) = x^3 - 3x$, find f(2).
(A). 2
(B). 4
(C). 6
(D). 8

Q21. Solve the equation:
$4/(x + 2) = 2$
(A). −2
(B). 0
(C). 2
(D). 4

Q22. A rectangular prism has a length of 4, a width of 3, and a height of 5. What is its volume?
(A). 30
(B). 45
(C). 60
(D). 75

ANSWER KEY READING & WRITING

Module 1 Answer Key

Passage 1 (Reading): Q1. (B) Q2. (A) Q3. (B) Q4. (B)
Passage 2 (Reading): Q5. (B) Q6. (B) Q7. (C) Q8. (B)
Independent Grammar & Writing: Q9. (B) Q10. (B) Q11. (C) Q12. (C) Q13. (A) Q14. (C) Q15. (A)

Q16. (B) Q17. (B) Q18. (A) Q19. (A) Q20. (A) Q21. (A) Q22. (A) Q23. (B) Q24. (A) Q25. (B) Q26. (B) Q27. (A)

Module 2 Answer Key

Passage 1 (Reading): Q1. (B) Q2. (B) Q3. (B) Q4. (C) Q5. (C)
Passage 2 (Reading): Q6. (C) Q7. (B) Q8. (B) Q9. (B) Q10. (B)
Independent Grammar & Writing: Q11. (A) Q12. (B) Q13. (D) Q14. (A) Q15. (B) Q16. (A) Q17. (A) Q18. (D) Q19. (C) Q20. (C) Q21. (B) Q22. (A) Q23. (C) Q24. (C) Q25. (B) Q26. (A) Q27. (A)

ANSWER KEY MATH

Module 1 Answer Key

Q1. (B)
Q2. (C)
Q3. (B)
Q4. (C)
Q5. (A)
Q6. (B)
Q7. (A)
Q8. (C)
Q9. (C)
Q10. (A)
Q11. (C)
Q12. (C)
Q13. (C)
Q14. (C)
Q15. (C)
Q16. (C)
Q17. (C)
Q18. (C)
Q19. (A)
Q20. (B)
Q21. (C)
Q22. (B)

Module 2 Answer Key

Q1. (A)
Q2. (B)
Q3. (A)
Q4. (A)
Q5. (C)
Q6. (C)
Q7. (A)
Q8. (B)
Q9. (A)

Q10. (A)
Q11. (B)
Q12. (B)
Q13. (B)
Q14. (B)
Q15. (A)
Q16. (A)
Q17. (A)
Q18. (C)
Q19. (B)
Q20. (A)
Q21. (B)
Q22. (C)

CHAPTER 19

FULL-LENGTH PRACTICE TEST 2

MODULE 1 – READING & WRITING

Passage 1 – "The Garden of Echoes"

Read the passage below and then answer Questions Q1–Q4.

In the heart of a forgotten town lay a garden shrouded in the mists of time. Once the pride of an illustrious family, the garden was renowned for its rare flora and labyrinthine pathways. Over the years, the vibrant blossoms faded under nature's steady embrace, yet the space retained a quiet dignity. Visitors often remarked that beneath weathered stone benches and vine-wrapped arches, whispers of long-lost memories seemed to echo.

Marian, a young local historian, became captivated by the garden's enigmatic charm. With each measured step along its winding trails, she discovered subtle clues—a carved inscription on a bench, a peculiar bloom hidden behind overgrown shrubs—that hinted at a storied past. To her, the garden was not merely a relic; it was a living chronicle, inviting her to piece together the legacy of those who had once nurtured it.

Q1. What is the primary purpose of the passage?
(A). To detail the physical layout of an old garden.
(B). To convey the historical significance and mysterious atmosphere of a forgotten garden.
(C). To explain the botanical reasons behind the garden's fading colors.
(D). To describe modern restoration efforts at historical sites.
Q2. Which detail best supports the idea that the garden exudes mystery?
(A). "A garden shrouded in the mists of time."
(B). "Renowned for its rare flora and labyrinthine pathways."
(C). "Whispers of long-lost memories seemed to echo beneath weathered stone benches."
(D). "Marian discovered subtle clues along its winding trails."
Q3. The word "shrouded" in the first sentence most nearly means:
(A). Hidden
(B). Illuminated
(C). Adorned
(D). Revitalized
Q4. Based on the passage, what can be inferred about Marian's attitude toward the garden?
(A). She is indifferent to its past.
(B). She sees it as a burdensome relic of history.
(C). She regards it as a living chronicle worthy of exploration.
(D). She plans to modernize and change it completely.

Passage 2 – "City in Motion: The Rhythm of Urban Life"

Read the passage below and answer Questions Q5–Q8.

The city pulsed with energy at every corner. In the early light of dawn, commuters, street vendors, and early risers converged on sidewalks, their movements forming a choreographed dance of urgency and purpose. Towering skyscrapers and neon billboards testified to rapid urban evolution, while tucked-away alleys and timeworn cafés preserved hints of a bygone era. Amid this continuous flow, residents embraced a mosaic of cultures and ideas, each adding to the urban symphony.

For many, the metropolis was more than a mere backdrop—it was an ever-changing canvas of human endeavor. Poets found inspiration in its contrasts, and musicians captured its heartbeat in rhythms that resonated across neighborhoods. As twilight settled, the vigorous daytime energy softened into reflective moods, inviting both connection and introspection.

Q5. What is the main focus of the passage?
(A). To provide a detailed history of urban architecture.
(B). To describe the dynamic and multifaceted nature of city life.
(C). To critique the modern commercialization of urban centers.
(D). To explain the technical design of skyscrapers and billboards.
Q6. The term "mosaic" in the context of the passage most nearly means:
(A). A fragmented collection
(B). A harmonious blend
(C). A rigid structure
(D). A temporary arrangement
Q7. Which statement best captures the contrast presented in the passage?
(A). The city's modern elements coexist with remnants of its past.
(B). The city completely abandons its historical roots in favor of modernity.
(C). Urban life is chaotic and lacks any form of harmony.
(D). Modern urban design has replaced all traces of history.
Q8. What can be inferred about the impact of the city on its inhabitants?
(A). It isolates them from creative expression.
(B). It inspires both energetic activity and reflective thought.
(C). It forces them into monotonous routines.
(D). It discourages cultural diversity.

Independent Grammar & Writing Questions (Module 1)

Answer Questions Q9–Q27.

Q9. Select the best revision for clarity:
"After the lecture, the students, they went to the library."
(A). After the lecture, the students went to the library.
(B). After the lecture, the students, they proceeded to the library.
(C). After the lecture went to the library by the students.
(D). The students, after the lecture, they went to the library.
Q10. Choose the sentence with correct punctuation:
(A). The committee's decision however, was unexpected.
(B). The committee's decision, however was unexpected.
(C). The committee's decision, however, was unexpected.
(D). The committee's decision however was unexpected.
Q11. Identify the sentence with correct parallel structure:
"She likes reading, to jog, and baking."
(A). She likes reading, jogging, and baking.
(B). She likes to read, jogging, and baking.
(C). She likes reading, to jog, and to bake.
(D). She likes to read, jog, and baking.
Q12. Identify the sentence with correct subject–verb agreement:
"Each of the essays were revised."
(A). Each of the essays was revised.
(B). Each of the essays were revised.
(C). Every of the essays was revised.
(D). Every of the essays were revised.

Q13. Select the best revision for pronoun–antecedent agreement:
"Every student must bring their pencil to the test."
(A). Every student must bring his or her pencil to the test.
(B). Every student must bring their pencil to the test.
(C). Every student must bring a pencil to the test.
(D). Every student must bring his pencil to the test.
Q14. Choose the best revision for eliminating wordiness:
"Due to the fact that the experiment was not successful, the researchers decided to try a different method."
(A). Because the experiment was not successful, the researchers tried a different method.
(B). The experiment was not successful, so the researchers decided to try a different method.
(C). As the experiment failed, the researchers decided to try a different method.
(D). The experiment was not successful; therefore, the researchers tried a different method.
Q15. Select the best revision to correct the dangling modifier:
"While driving to work, a deer suddenly appeared in the road."
(A). While driving to work, I saw a deer suddenly appear in the road.
(B). While driving to work, the deer suddenly appeared in the road.
(C). A deer suddenly appeared in the road while I was driving to work.
(D). Driving to work, I noticed a deer suddenly appear in the road.
Q16. Which sentence is punctuated correctly with commas?
(A). My brother who is an avid reader loves historical novels.
(B). My brother, who is an avid reader, loves historical novels.
(C). My brother who is an avid reader, loves historical novels.
(D). My brother, who is an avid reader loves historical novels.
Q17. Identify the sentence with correct use of a semicolon:
(A). The lecture was lengthy; it covered many topics.
(B). The lecture was lengthy, it covered many topics.
(C). The lecture was lengthy: it covered many topics.
(D). The lecture was lengthy it covered many topics.
Q18. Select the best revision to correct verb tense consistency:
"She is planning to visit the museum and she visited the new exhibit yesterday."
(A). She is planning to visit the museum and she is visiting the new exhibit.
(B). She planned to visit the museum and visited the new exhibit yesterday.
(C). She is planning to visit the museum and will visit the new exhibit.
(D). She plans to visit the museum and visited the new exhibit yesterday.
Q19. Which sentence best improves clarity?
"In order to solve the problem, a solution was found by the team after extensive discussion."
(A). The team found a solution to the problem after extensive discussion.
(B). After extensive discussion, the team found a solution to the problem.
(C). The team, after extensive discussion, found a solution to the problem.
(D). A solution to the problem was found by the team after extensive discussion.
Q20. Select the sentence that best revises the sentence for parallelism:
"She likes dancing, singing, and to paint."
(A). She likes dancing, singing, and painting.
(B). She likes to dance, sing, and to paint.
(C). She likes dancing, to sing, and painting.
(D). She likes to dance, singing, and painting.
Q21. Identify the sentence with correct modifier placement:
"Covered in glitter, the star performance dazzled the audience."

(A). Covered in glitter, the star performance dazzled the audience.
(B). The star performance, covered in glitter, dazzled the audience.
(C). Dazzling the audience, the star performance was covered in glitter.
(D). Glitter covered the star performance, dazzling the audience.

Q22. Which sentence uses a colon correctly?
"He has one main goal ____ to travel the world."
(A). He has one main goal: to travel the world.
(B). He has one main goal; to travel the world.
(C). He has one main goal, to travel the world.
(D). He has one main goal - to travel the world.

Q23. Choose the best revision to correct the following sentence:
"The proposal, which was not well-received, and needed significant revisions, was approved."
(A). The proposal, which was not well-received and needed significant revisions, was approved.
(B). The proposal, which was not well-received, needed significant revisions, and was approved.
(C). The proposal which was not well-received and needed significant revisions was approved.
(D). The proposal was not well-received, needed significant revisions, and was approved.

Q24. Select the best revision to correct the error in word choice:
"He was extremely literally surprised by the news."
(A). He was extremely surprised by the news.
(B). He was literally surprised by the news.
(C). He was both extremely and literally surprised by the news.
(D). He was surprisingly shocked by the news.

Q25. Which sentence best corrects the following sentence for clarity:
"Before starting his project, his tools were organized by him carefully."
(A). Before starting his project, he carefully organized his tools.
(B). He organized his tools carefully before starting his project.
(C). His tools were carefully organized before he started his project.
(D). Before his project began, his tools were organized carefully by him.

Q26. Choose the sentence that best maintains consistency in point of view:
"When one starts a project, you must plan carefully."
(A). When one starts a project, one must plan carefully.
(B). When one starts a project, you must plan carefully.
(C). When you start a project, one must plan carefully.
(D). When you start a project, you must plan carefully.

Q27. Identify the sentence that best revises the sentence for conciseness:
"In the event that it rains, the game will be canceled."
(A). If it rains, the game will be canceled.
(B). Should it rain, the game will be canceled.
(C). If it rains, the game is canceled.
(D). Rain will cancel the game.

MODULE 2 – READING & WRITING

Passage 1 – "The Echoes of Innovation"

Read the passage below and answer Questions Q1–Q5.

In the crucible of modern creativity, innovation often emerges from unexpected intersections of art and science. At a newly unveiled research center, architects and engineers joined forces with painters and musicians to explore the boundaries of form and function. Their collaborative projects produced installations that defied conventional categorization, inviting viewers to engage with both aesthetic beauty and technical ingenuity.

Critics have hailed this interdisciplinary convergence as emblematic of a new era—one where the rigid lines between science and art blur to give rise to transformative ideas. Yet, some remain skeptical, contending that such collaborations risk diluting the rigor of scientific inquiry. Still, the experiments continue, fueling debates about the future of knowledge and the true nature of creativity.

Q1. What is the main purpose of the passage?
(A). To detail specific projects at a research center.
(B). To explore how the merging of art and science fosters innovation.
(C). To criticize interdisciplinary collaborations.
(D). To recount the history of a research center.
Q2. The phrase "crucible of modern creativity" most nearly means:
(A). A difficult environment where ideas are suppressed.
(B). A setting in which diverse ideas are forged.
(C). A marketplace of outdated methods.
(D). A traditional studio for artistic endeavors.
Q3. Which detail best supports the idea that the innovation described is unconventional?
(A). Architects and engineers collaborating with painters and musicians.
(B). The research center's modern design.
(C). A dialogue about solving societal issues.
(D). Skeptical critics warning against diluted scientific rigor.
Q4. The word "convergence" in the passage most nearly means:
(A). Separation
(B). Meeting
(C). Divergence
(D). Opposition
Q5. Based on the passage, what can be inferred about the critics' perspective?
(A). They fully support the interdisciplinary approach.
(B). They believe merging art and science may compromise scientific rigor.
(C). They are indifferent to the new innovations.
(D). They reject any form of artistic collaboration in science.

Passage 2 – "The Weight of Words in a Digital Age"

Read the passage below and answer Questions Q6–Q10.

In an era dominated by digital communication, the power of words has undergone a profound transformation. Social media platforms amplify voices across the globe, rendering language both a tool for connection and a potential weapon of division. Activists and writers harness this duality to mobilize movements, while advertisers exploit persuasive techniques to capture attention in an ever-crowded digital landscape. Amid this clamor, the written word retains its ability to influence, challenge, and inspire, even as its forms evolve with technology.

Yet, this digital milieu also raises questions about authenticity and depth. Critics argue that the rapid pace of online discourse often encourages superficial engagement, where sentiment replaces substance. Nonetheless, proponents maintain that digital platforms democratize expression—offering marginalized voices a rare opportunity to be heard. As debates persist, the evolution of language in the digital age remains a dynamic and contested terrain.

Q6. What is the central theme of the passage?
(A). The decline of traditional writing.
(B). The evolving impact of digital communication on language.

(C). The technical design of social media platforms.
(D). The history of online discourse.
Q7. The term "clamor" in the passage most nearly means:
(A). A harmonious chorus
(B). A loud, confused noise
(C). A subtle murmur
(D). An organized speech
Q8. Which statement best reflects the authors' perspective on digital communication?
(A). It has entirely undermined authentic expression.
(B). It fosters both superficiality and powerful inspiration.
(C). It is solely a tool for advertisers and marketers.
(D). It has eliminated the influence of the written word.
Q9. According to the passage, what is one criticism of online discourse?
(A). It promotes deep and reflective engagement.
(B). It encourages superficiality at the expense of substance.
(C). It completely excludes marginalized voices.
(D). It slows down communication processes.
Q10. Based on the passage, which best describes the debate about language in the digital age?
(A). It centers only on technological challenges.
(B). It involves conflicting views on democratization versus depth of engagement.
(C). It is solely about the decline of literacy.
(D). It has been conclusively resolved in favor of digital media.

Independent Grammar & Writing Questions (Module 2)

Answer Questions Q11–Q27.

Q11. Select the best revision for the sentence:
"The professor, along with her students, are planning to attend the conference."
(A). The professor, along with her students, is planning to attend the conference.
(B). The professor, along with her students, are planning to attend the conference.
(C). The professor and her students is planning to attend the conference.
(D). The professor and her students are planning to attend the conference.
Q12. Choose the option that best corrects the error in parallel structure:
"The committee was tasked with reviewing the report, to revise the proposal, and making recommendations."
(A). Reviewing the report, revising the proposal, and making recommendations.
(B). Review the report, revising the proposal, and making recommendations.
(C). Reviewing the report, to revise the proposal, and to make recommendations.
(D). Review the report, revise the proposal, and make recommendations.
Q13. Identify the sentence that best corrects the pronoun ambiguity:
"If a student forgets their notebook, they should report to the office."
(A). If a student forgets his or her notebook, he or she should report to the office.
(B). If a student forgets their notebook, they should report to the office.
(C). If students forget their notebooks, they should report to the office.
(D). If one forgets a notebook, that person should report to the office.
Q14. Select the best revision to eliminate redundancy:
"In my personal opinion, I believe that the plan is feasible."
(A). In my opinion, the plan is feasible.
(B). Personally, I believe the plan is feasible.

(C). I believe the plan is feasible.
(D). In my personal opinion, the plan is feasible.
Q15. Which sentence best corrects the error in subject–verb agreement:
"Neither the teacher nor the students was aware of the schedule change."
(A). Neither the teacher nor the students were aware of the schedule change.
(B). Neither the teacher nor the students was aware of the schedule change.
(C). Neither the teacher nor the students is aware of the schedule change.
(D). Neither the teacher nor the students are aware of the schedule change.
Q16. Choose the best revision for clarity:
"While reading the novel, the movie was adapted by the director."
(A). While reading the novel, the director adapted it into a movie.
(B). The director adapted the novel into a movie while reading it.
(C). While reading the novel, a movie adaptation was made by the director.
(D). The novel was adapted by the director while being read.
Q17. Select the sentence that best corrects the dangling modifier:
"After finishing the assignment, the TV was turned on."
(A). After finishing the assignment, I turned on the TV.
(B). After finishing the assignment, the TV was turned on by me.
(C). After the assignment was finished, the TV was turned on.
(D). After finishing the assignment, turning on the TV was my next step.
Q18. Which sentence uses commas correctly?
(A). My colleague who is an experienced editor loves revising manuscripts.
(B). My colleague, who is an experienced editor loves revising manuscripts.
(C). My colleague, who is an experienced editor, loves revising manuscripts.
(D). My colleague who is an experienced editor, loves revising manuscripts.
Q19. Identify the sentence with correct use of a semicolon:
(A). She wanted to join the meeting; but she was too busy.
(B). She wanted to join the meeting; however, she was too busy.
(C). She wanted to join the meeting, however; she was too busy.
(D). She wanted to join the meeting however, she was too busy.
Q20. Select the best revision to fix the sentence:
"Because of the heavy traffic, the meeting, which was scheduled for 9 a.m., was delayed."
(A). Due to heavy traffic, the 9 a.m. meeting was delayed.
(B). Heavy traffic delayed the meeting, which was scheduled for 9 a.m.
(C). Owing to heavy traffic, the 9 a.m. meeting was delayed.
(D). The heavy traffic caused the meeting at 9 a.m. to be delayed.
Q21. Choose the sentence that best corrects the error in parallel structure:
"The artist enjoyed painting, to sculpt, and drawing."
(A). The artist enjoyed painting, sculpting, and drawing.
(B). The artist enjoyed painting, to sculpt, and to draw.
(C). The artist enjoyed to paint, sculpt, and drawing.
(D). The artist enjoyed painting, sculpting, and to draw.
Q22. Select the sentence that best corrects the error in subject–verb agreement:
"The manager, along with his team, are organizing the event."
(A). The manager, along with his team, is organizing the event.
(B). The manager, along with his team, are organizing the event.
(C). The manager and his team is organizing the event.
(D). The manager and his team are organizing the event.

Q23. Which sentence correctly employs a colon?
"He has one dream _____ to travel the world."
(A). He has one dream: to travel the world.
(B). He has one dream; to travel the world.
(C). He has one dream, to travel the world.
(D). He has one dream - to travel the world.
Q24. Select the best revision for conciseness:
"In the process of making a decision, she took into consideration all the possible outcomes."
(A). She considered all possible outcomes before making a decision.
(B). She took into consideration all possible outcomes before deciding.
(C). In making a decision, she considered all outcomes.
(D). She considered all the possible outcomes in the decision-making process.
Q25. Choose the sentence that best maintains consistent verb tense:
"Yesterday, she writes in her journal and discussed her day with a friend."
(A). Yesterday, she wrote in her journal and discussed her day with a friend.
(B). Yesterday, she wrote in her journal and discusses her day with a friend.
(C). Yesterday, she writes in her journal and discusses her day with a friend.
(D). Yesterday, she writes in her journal and discussed her day with a friend.
Q26. Identify the sentence that best revises the error in wordiness:
"At this point in time, we are in agreement with the proposal."
(A). We are in agreement with the proposal.
(B). At this point, we agree with the proposal.
(C). Currently, we are in agreement with the proposal.
(D). We are currently in agreement with the proposal.
Q27. Select the best revision to ensure consistency in point of view:
"If one wishes to succeed, you must work diligently."
(A). If one wishes to succeed, one must work diligently.
(B). If one wishes to succeed, you must work diligently.
(C). If you wish to succeed, you must work diligently.
(D). If you wish to succeed, one must work diligently.

MATH MODULE 1

Q1. Solve for x:

$3x + 4 = 19$

(A). 3
(B). 4
(C). 5
(D). 6

Q2. If $f(x) = 2x^2 - 3$, what is f(2)?

(A). 3
(B). 5
(C). 7
(D). 9

Q3. Simplify the expression:

$(8x^2 - 2x) \div (2x)$

(A). $4x - 1$
(B). $4x + 1$

(C). $4x - 2$
(D). $4x$

Q4. Solve for x:
$(x/3) + 4 = 7$
(A). 6
(B). 9
(C). 12
(D). 15

Q5. Find the slope of the line through the points (1, 2) and (4, 8).
(A). 1
(B). 2
(C). 3
(D). 4

Q6. Solve the inequality:
$4x - 5 \geq 11$
(A). $x \geq 2$
(B). $x \geq 3$
(C). $x \geq 4$
(D). $x \geq 5$

Q7. Solve for x:
$12/x = 3$
(A). 3
(B). 4
(C). 5
(D). 6

Q8. What is the area of a triangle with a base of 10 and a height of 4?
(A). 20
(B). 24
(C). 30
(D). 40

Q9. The ratio of red to blue marbles is 2:3. If there are 14 red marbles, how many blue marbles are there?
(A). 18
(B). 19
(C). 20
(D). 21

Q10. Expand and simplify:
$5(2x - 1) - 3x$
(A). $7x - 5$
(B). $7x + 5$
(C). $8x - 5$
(D). $8x + 5$

Q11. Solve for x:
$3(x - 2) = 9$
(A). 3
(B). 4
(C). 5
(D). 6

Q12. What is the value of $\sqrt{144}$?

(A). 10
(B). 11
(C). 12
(D). 13

Q13. A car travels 150 miles in 3 hours. What is its average speed in mph?

(A). 40
(B). 45
(C). 50
(D). 55

Q14. Find the value of x in the proportion:

$5/8 = x/16$

(A). 8
(B). 9
(C). 10
(D). 11

Q15. What is the solution set for the equation:

$4(x - 1) = 4x - 4$?

(A). $x = 1$
(B). $x = 0$
(C). All real numbers
(D). No solution

Q16. If $g(x) = x^2 + 1$, what is $g(-3)$?

(A). 8
(B). 9
(C). 10
(D). 11

Q17. Solve the equation:

$|x + 2| = 5$

(A). $x = 3$ only
(B). $x = -7$ only
(C). $x = 3$ or -7
(D). $x = -3$ or 7

Q18. Find the solutions to the equation:

$x^2 - 16 = 0$

(A). $x = 4$ only
(B). $x = -4$ only
(C). $x = 4$ or -4
(D). $x = 2$ or -2

Q19. What is the area of a rectangle with a length of 12 and a width of 5?

(A). 55
(B). 60
(C). 65
(D). 70

Q20. Simplify the expression (assume $x \neq -2$):

$(x^2 - 4) \div (x + 2)$

(A). $x + 2$
(B). $x - 2$

(C). $x^2 - 2$
(D). $x - 4$

Q21. Solve for x:
$(3/4)x + 2 = 5$
(A). 3
(B). 4
(C). 5
(D). 6

Q22. What is the distance between the points (–1, 4) and (3, –2)?
(A). $2\sqrt{13}$
(B). $2\sqrt{14}$
(C). $2\sqrt{11}$
(D). $2\sqrt{12}$

MATH MODULE 2

Q1. Solve for x:
$2x^2 + 3x - 5 = 0$
(A). $x = 1$ or $x = -5/2$
(B). $x = -1$ or $x = 5/2$
(C). $x = 1/2$ or $x = -5$
(D). $x = 5/2$ or $x = -1$

Q2. If $f(x) = \sqrt{(3x + 9)}$, what is $f(0)$?
(A). 1
(B). 2
(C). 3
(D). 4

Q3. Solve the system of equations:
$x + y = 7$
$2x - y = 1$
(A). $x = 8/3$, $y = 13/3$
(B). $x = 13/3$, $y = 8/3$
(C). $x = 3$, $y = 4$
(D). $x = 4$, $y = 3$

Q4. Factor the quadratic:
$x^2 + 5x + 6$
(A). $(x + 1)(x + 6)$
(B). $(x + 2)(x + 3)$
(C). $(x - 2)(x - 3)$
(D). $(x + 3)^2$

Q5. If $h(x) = 4x^2 - x + 2$, what is $h(1)$?
(A). 4
(B). 5
(C). 6
(D). 7

Q6. Simplify the radical expression:
$\sqrt{72} - 2\sqrt{8}$
(A). $2\sqrt{2}$
(B). $4\sqrt{2}$

(C). $\sqrt{2}$
(D). 2

Q7. For what value of x is the rational expression
$(x^2 - 4)/(x - 2)$
undefined?
(A). 2
(B). –2
(C). 0
(D). 4

Q8. Solve the inequality:
$x^2 - 9 < 0$
(A). $x < -3$ or $x > 3$
(B). $-3 \leq x \leq 3$
(C). $-3 < x < 3$
(D). $x > -3$

Q9. Find the vertex of the parabola given by:
$y = 2x^2 - 8x + 3$
(A). (2, –5)
(B). (2, 5)
(C). (–2, –5)
(D). (4, –5)

Q10. If $f(x) = (5x - 7)/(2x + 1)$, what is f(0)?
(A). –7
(B). 7
(C). 0
(D). 1

Q11. A circle has a circumference of 10π. What is its area?
(A). 10π
(B). 25π
(C). 50π
(D). 100π

Q12. Solve for x:
$\log_3(x) = 2$
(A). 3
(B). 6
(C). 9
(D). 12

Q13. If $f(x) = 1/(2x - 1)$, what is f(1)?
(A). ½
(B). 1
(C). 2
(D). Undefined

Q14. What is the sum of the first 6 terms of an arithmetic sequence with first term 4 and common difference 3?
(A). 69
(B). 68
(C). 70
(D). 72

Q15. Simplify the expression:

$(6x^2 - 12) \div (3x)$

(A). $2(x^2 - 2)/x$

(B). $2x - 2$

(C). $2x - 4/x$

(D). $2x - 4$

Q16. If the probability of event A is 0.4 and event B is 0.3, and they are independent, what is the probability that both occur?

(A). 0.07

(B). 0.12

(C). 0.3

(D). 0.7

Q17. Solve for y in terms of x:

$4y + 2x = 10$

(A). $y = (5 - x)/2$

(B). $y = (5 - 2x)/4$

(C). $y = (10 - 2x)/4$

(D). $y = (2x - 10)/4$

Q18. Find the sum of the infinite geometric series with a first term of 8 and a common ratio of $1/4$.

(A). $32/3$

(B). $8/3$

(C). $24/3$

(D). 12

Q19. If $\sin \theta = 0.75$ for an acute angle θ, what is $\cos \theta$?

(A). 0.5

(B). 0.66

(C). 0.75

(D). 0.85

Q20. For the function $f(x) = x^3 - 2x$, find $f(-2)$.

(A). -4

(B). -6

(C). 4

(D). 6

Q21. Solve for x:

$5/(x + 1) = 1$

(A). 3

(B). 4

(C). 5

(D). 6

Q22. A cylinder has a radius of 3 and a height of 10. What is its volume?

(A). 30π

(B). 60π

(C). 90π

(D). 120π

ANSWER KEY READING & WRITING

Module 1 Answer Key

Passage 1 (Reading):
Q1. (B) Q2. (C) Q3. (A) Q4. (C)
Passage 2 (Reading): Q5. (B) Q6. (B) Q7. (A) Q8. (B)
Independent Grammar & Writing: Q9. (A) Q10. (C) Q11. (A) Q12. (A) Q13. (A) Q14. (A) Q15. (A) Q16. (B) Q17. (A) Q18. (B) Q19. (A) Q20. (A) Q21. (B) Q22. (A) Q23. (A) Q24. (A) Q25. (A) Q26. (A) Q27. (A)

Module 2 Answer Key

Passage 1 (Reading):
Q1. (B) Q2. (B) Q3. (A) Q4. (B) Q5. (B)
Passage 2 (Reading): Q6. (B) Q7. (B) Q8. (B) Q9. (B) Q10. (B)

Independent Grammar & Writing:
Q11. (A)
Q12. (A)
Q13. (A)
Q14. (A)
Q15. (A)
Q16. (A)
Q17. (A)
Q18. (C)
Q19. (B)
Q20. (C)
Q21. (A)
Q22. (A)
Q23. (A)
Q24. (A)
Q25. (A)
Q26. (A)
Q27. (A)

ANSWER KEY MATH

Module 1 Answer Key

Q1. (C)
Q2. (B)
Q3. (A)
Q4. (B)
Q5. (B)
Q6. (C)
Q7. (B)
Q8. (A)
Q9. (D)
Q10. (A)
Q11. (C)
Q12. (C)
Q13. (C)
Q14. (C)
Q15. (C)
Q16. (C)
Q17. (C)
Q18. (C)
Q19. (B)
Q20. (B)
Q21. (B)
Q22. (A)

Module 2 Answer Key

Q1. (A)
Q2. (C)
Q3. (A)
Q4. (B)
Q5. (B)
Q6. (A)
Q7. (A)
Q8. (C)
Q9. (A)
Q10. (A)
Q11. (B)
Q12. (C)
Q13. (B)
Q14. (A)
Q15. (A)
Q16. (B)
Q17. (A)
Q18. (A)
Q19. (B)
Q20. (A)
Q21. (B)
Q22. (C)

CHAPTER 20

FULL-LENGTH PRACTICE TEST 3

MODULE 1 – READING & WRITING

Passage 1 – "The Lost Library"

Read the passage below and then answer Questions Q1–Q4.

Hidden behind a crumbling façade in the heart of the city lies a forgotten repository of knowledge: the Lost Library. Dusty shelves once brimming with scholarship now stand silent beneath layers of neglect. Faded inscriptions and brittle manuscripts evoke the passion and intellect of generations past, inviting the curious to rediscover wisdom long sealed within its walls.

Liam, a dedicated archivist, discovered this relic while sifting through neglected city records. As he gingerly turned fragile pages, echoes of long-silenced voices seemed to whisper their stories. For Liam, the library was not merely a decaying building—it was a key to understanding lost traditions and the vibrant history of a community that once flourished.

Q1. What is the primary purpose of the passage?
(A). To describe the architectural design of an old building.
(B). To illustrate the historical significance and mystery of a forgotten library.
(C). To explain the methods of modern archival research.
(D). To compare different types of historical repositories.
Q2. Which detail best supports the idea that the library is shrouded in mystery?
(A). "Crumbling façade in the heart of the city."
(B). "Dusty shelves once brimming with scholarship now stand silent."
(C). "Faded inscriptions and brittle manuscripts evoke the passion and intellect of generations past."
(D). "Liam discovered this relic while sifting through neglected city records."
Q3. The word "repository" in the passage most nearly means:
(A). A storage place
(B). A decorative element
(C). A temporary shelter
(D). A public meeting space
Q4. Based on the passage, what can be inferred about Liam's attitude toward the library?
(A). He regards it as an outdated structure with little value.
(B). He is indifferent to its historical significance.
(C). He is deeply curious and sees it as a gateway to lost history.
(D). He intends to modernize it with new technology.

Passage 2 – "Beneath the Starlit Sky"

Read the passage below and answer Questions Q5–Q8.

Every summer evening, the town of Aurora transforms as residents gather in the central park under a vast, starlit sky. Families, friends, and neighbors come together while soft music drifts from a local quartet. Lanterns are released into the night, each one carrying a silent wish as they float upward amid constellations.

For many, this celebration is a cherished ritual—a moment to pause, to honor nature's quiet beauty, and to strengthen the bonds of community. The event, modest in scale yet rich in sentiment, exemplifies a shared reverence for the simple joys and the interconnectedness of life.

Q5. What is the main focus of the passage?
(A). To provide a detailed history of the town's park.
(B). To depict a seasonal celebration that unites the community under nature's beauty.
(C). To describe the technical aspects of lantern-making.
(D). To critique modern entertainment methods.
Q6. The term "starlit" in the passage most nearly means:
(A). Clouded
(B). Illuminated by stars

(C). Overcast
(D). Darkened
Q7. Which detail best supports the idea that the celebration fosters community unity?
(A). "Residents gather in the central park under a vast, starlit sky."
(B). "Soft music drifts from a local quartet."
(C). "Lanterns are released into the night, each one carrying a silent wish."
(D). "Families, friends, and neighbors come together."
Q8. What can be inferred about the town's attitude toward nature?
(A). They prefer urban life and avoid natural settings.
(B). They hold nature in high regard and celebrate its beauty.
(C). They view nature as chaotic and unpredictable.
(D). They are indifferent to natural phenomena.

Independent Grammar & Writing Questions (Module 1)

Answer Questions Q9–Q27.

Q9. Select the best revision for clarity:
"Due to the fact that the experiment failed, the team decided to cancel the project."
(A). Because the experiment failed, the team canceled the project.
(B). Owing to the experiment's failure, the team canceled the project.
(C). The experiment failed; therefore, the team decided to cancel the project.
(D). Since the experiment failed, the team decided that the project should be canceled.
Q10. Choose the sentence with correct punctuation:
(A). The principal however, announced the test results.
(B). The principal, however announced the test results.
(C). The principal, however, announced the test results.
(D). The principal however announced, the test results.
Q11. Identify the sentence with correct parallel structure:
(A). She enjoys reading, jogging, and to swim.
(B). She enjoys reading, jogging, and swimming.
(C). She enjoys to read, jogging, and swimming.
(D). She enjoys reading, to jog, and swimming.
Q12. Which sentence correctly revises the subject–verb agreement error?
(A). Each of the assignments have been reviewed.
(B). Each of the assignments has been reviewed.
(C). Each of the assignment have been reviewed.
(D). Each of the assignment has been reviewed.
Q13. Select the best revision for pronoun–antecedent agreement:
(A). Every student must bring his or her pencil to the test.
(B). Every student must bring their pencil to the test.
(C). All students must bring his pencil to the test.
(D). All students must bring their pencil to the test.
Q14. Choose the best revision to eliminate wordiness:
(A). In order to succeed in his career, he must work diligently.
(B). To succeed in his career, he must work diligently.
(C). For the purpose of succeeding in his career, he must work diligently.
(D). In order to be successful in his career, he must work diligently.
Q15. Select the best revision to correct the dangling modifier:
(A). After finishing the meal, we cleared the table.
(B). After finishing the meal, the table was cleared by us.
(C). After the meal was finished, clearing the table followed.
(D). After finishing the meal, clearing the table was done by us.
Q16. Which sentence is punctuated correctly with commas?
(A). My brother who is an avid reader loves historical novels.
(B). My brother, who is an avid reader loves historical novels.

(C). My brother, who is an avid reader, loves historical novels.
(D). My brother who is an avid reader, loves historical novels.
Q17. Identify the sentence that correctly employs a semicolon:
(A). The lecture was long, it covered multiple topics.
(B). The lecture was long; it covered multiple topics.
(C). The lecture was long: it covered multiple topics.
(D). The lecture was long it covered multiple topics.
Q18. Select the best revision to maintain verb tense consistency:
(A). She was writing her report when the phone rang.
(B). She was writing her report when the phone rings.
(C). She writes her report when the phone rang.
(D). She wrote her report when the phone rings.
Q19. Which sentence best improves clarity?
(A). The instructions provided by the teacher were confusing to the students.
(B). The teacher's instructions were confusing to the students.
(C). The instructions, which were provided by the teacher, confused the students.
(D). The confusing instructions were provided by the teacher to the students.
Q20. Select the sentence that best revises the error in parallelism:
(A). He enjoys hiking, biking, and swimming.
(B). He enjoys hiking, biking, and to swim.
(C). He enjoys to hike, to bike, and swimming.
(D). He enjoys hiking, to bike, and swimming.
Q21. Identify the sentence with correct modifier placement:
(A). Running quickly, Sarah crossed the finish line.
(B). Running quickly, the finish line was reached by Sarah.
(C). Sarah, running quickly, crossed the finish line.
(D). Crossing the finish line, Sarah was running quickly.
Q22. Which sentence uses a colon correctly?
(A). There is one rule in this contest: no cheating is allowed.
(B). There is one rule in this contest; no cheating is allowed.
(C). There is one rule in this contest, no cheating is allowed.
(D). There is one rule in this contest - no cheating is allowed.
Q23. Choose the best revision for conciseness:
(A). We are ready to begin the meeting.
(B). At this point in time, we are ready to begin the meeting.
(C). Currently, we are ready to begin the meeting.
(D). Right now, we are ready to begin the meeting.
Q24. Select the sentence that maintains consistency in point of view:
(A). If one wants to succeed, one must work hard.
(B). If one wants to succeed, you must work hard.
(C). If you want to succeed, one must work hard.
(D). If you want to succeed, you must work hard.
Q25. Identify the sentence that best revises an error in word choice:
(A). He was stunned by the news.
(B). He was literally stunned by the news.
(C). He was shocked by the news.
(D). He was exceedingly stunned by the news.
Q26. Choose the best revision to eliminate extraneous wording:
(A). Because it was raining, the match was postponed.
(B). Due to the fact that it was raining, the match was postponed.
(C). Owing to the rain, the match was postponed.
(D). In view of the rain, the match was postponed.
Q27. Select the best revision for clarity and conciseness:
(A). The solution to the problem is very simple.
(B). The solution to the problem is one that is very simple.

(C). The solution to the problem is simple.
(D). The solution to the problem is a simple one.

MODULE 2 – READING & WRITING

Passage 1 – "Voices of the Past: Reconstructing History"

Read the passage below and answer Questions Q1–Q5.

At the ancient site of Veritas, archaeologists have unearthed artifacts that challenge long-held historical narratives. Amid shards of pottery and fragmented inscriptions, researchers discovered symbols whose meanings remain elusive, prompting fresh debates among scholars. These findings suggest that the once–flourishing civilization of Veritas possessed intricate social structures and extensive trade networks. The painstaking work of these researchers not only offers a window into a bygone era but also calls into question the conventional methods by which history is reconstructed.

Through careful analysis and documentation, the team is reshaping our understanding of the past, illustrating that history is as much about interpretation as it is about discovery.

Q1. What is the primary purpose of the passage?
(A). To detail the daily routines of archaeologists.
(B). To explain how new discoveries challenge established historical narratives.
(C). To recount the complete history of the civilization of Veritas.
(D). To describe the physical appearance of ancient artifacts.
Q2. Which detail best supports the idea that the civilization of Veritas was complex?
(A). The presence of fragmented inscriptions.
(B). The suggestion of extensive trade networks and intricate social structures.
(C). The careful documentation by researchers.
(D). The elusive meaning of the discovered symbols.
Q3. The word "elusive" in the passage most nearly means:
(A). Difficult to interpret
(B). Easily understood
(C). Irrelevant
(D). Commonplace
Q4. What can be inferred about the archaeologists' approach?
(A). They rely solely on established theories.
(B). They work hastily without proper analysis.
(C). They are meticulous and open to revising historical assumptions.
(D). They disregard conflicting evidence.
Q5. Which statement best characterizes the tone of the passage?
(A). Dismissive and skeptical
(B). Analytical and inquisitive
(C). Nostalgic and sentimental
(D). Indifferent and casual

Passage 2 – "Digital Frontiers: The Future of Connection"

Read the passage below and answer Questions Q6–Q10.

In today's rapidly shifting digital landscape, virtual platforms have transformed the way people connect. Social media, video chats, and online communities have broken down traditional barriers of geography and culture, allowing instantaneous communication across the globe. Yet, this revolution is not without its challenges; concerns about privacy, misinformation, and the loss of face-to-face interaction persist. Despite these issues, many argue that the benefits of a digitally connected world—where ideas and voices circulate freely—far outweigh the drawbacks.

As technology continues to evolve, the future of communication appears poised to blend the digital with the personal, heralding an era in which virtual and physical interactions coexist in dynamic balance.

Q6. What is the main focus of the passage?
(A). To describe technical innovations in communication hardware.

(B). To examine the impact of digital platforms on global connectivity and interpersonal interaction.
(C). To argue against the use of digital media.
(D). To recount the history of the internet.
Q7. The term "transformed" in the passage most nearly means:
(A). Restricted
(B). Completely changed
(C). Slightly modified
(D). Disregarded
Q8. Which detail best highlights the potential negative effects of digital communication?
(A). The mention of privacy concerns, misinformation, and loss of face-to-face interaction.
(B). The breakdown of geographical barriers.
(C). The instantaneous nature of global communication.
(D). The circulation of ideas and voices.
Q9. What can be inferred about the author's perspective on digital connectivity?
(A). The author believes digital communication has only negative consequences.
(B). The author acknowledges both the challenges and benefits of digital connectivity.
(C). The author dismisses concerns about privacy and misinformation.
(D). The author thinks that digital platforms will soon become obsolete.
Q10. Which statement best encapsulates the tone of the passage?
(A). Alarmist and pessimistic
(B). Celebratory without reservation
(C). Balanced and forward-looking
(D). Cynical and dismissive

Independent Grammar & Writing Questions (Module 2)

Answer Questions Q11–Q27.

Q11. Select the best revision for clarity:
"After completing the project, the deadline was met by the team with impressive precision."
(A). After completing the project, the team met the deadline with impressive precision.
(B). After the project was completed, meeting the deadline was achieved impressively by the team.
(C). The team, having completed the project, impressively met the deadline.
(D). Completing the project, the deadline was impressively met by the team.
Q12. Choose the option that corrects the error in parallel structure:
"The candidate promised to improve healthcare, education, and to lower taxes."
(A). The candidate promised to improve healthcare, education, and lower taxes.
(B). The candidate promised to improve healthcare, to improve education, and lower taxes.
(C). The candidate promised improving healthcare, education, and lowering taxes.
(D). The candidate promised to improve healthcare, education, and the lowering of taxes.
Q13. Identify the sentence that correctly revises the subject–verb agreement error:
"Each of the proposals are being considered by the committee."
(A). Each of the proposals is being considered by the committee.
(B). Each of the proposals are considered by the committee.
(C). Every one of the proposals is being considered by the committee.
(D). Every one of the proposals are being considered by the committee.
Q14. Select the best revision for pronoun clarity:
"If a student forgets their notebook, the student should notify the teacher."
(A). If a student forgets his or her notebook, he or she should notify the teacher.
(B). If a student forgets a notebook, they should notify the teacher.
(C). If students forget their notebook, they should notify the teacher.
(D). If one forgets a notebook, that person should notify the teacher.
Q15. Choose the best revision to eliminate redundancy:
"In my opinion, I believe that the strategy will be successful."
(A). I believe that the strategy will be successful.
(B). In my opinion, the strategy will be successful.

(C). I believe the strategy will be successful.
(D). In my opinion, I think the strategy will be successful.
Q16. Select the best revision to correct the dangling modifier:
"While reviewing the manuscript, the errors were noted."
(A). While reviewing the manuscript, the editor noted the errors.
(B). While the manuscript was being reviewed, the errors were noted by the editor.
(C). The errors were noted while reviewing the manuscript.
(D). While reviewing the manuscript, noting errors was done by the editor.
Q17. Identify the sentence with proper comma usage:
(A). My cousin who lives in Paris is visiting this summer.
(B). My cousin, who lives in Paris, is visiting this summer.
(C). My cousin, who lives in Paris is visiting this summer.
(D). My cousin who lives in Paris, is visiting this summer.
Q18. Select the sentence that correctly uses a semicolon:
(A). The research was groundbreaking, it changed the field of study.
(B). The research was groundbreaking; it changed the field of study.
(C). The research was groundbreaking: it changed the field of study.
(D). The research was groundbreaking it changed the field of study.
Q19. Choose the best revision to ensure verb tense consistency:
"She writes her final draft last week and is now submitting it."
(A). She wrote her final draft last week and is now submitting it.
(B). She writes her final draft last week and submits it now.
(C). She wrote her final draft last week and submits it now.
(D). She writes her final draft and submitted it last week.
Q20. Identify the sentence that improves clarity:
"The instructions that were given by the professor confused many students."
(A). The professor's instructions confused many students.
(B). The instructions, given by the professor, confused many students.
(C). Many students were confused by the instructions that were given by the professor.
(D). Confusing instructions were given by the professor to many students.
Q21. Select the best revision for parallelism:
"She enjoys reading, writing, and to paint."
(A). She enjoys reading, writing, and painting.
(B). She enjoys to read, to write, and painting.
(C). She enjoys reading, to write, and to paint.
(D). She enjoys reading, writing, and the painting.
Q22. Choose the sentence with correct modifier placement:
"After proofreading the essay, errors were corrected by the teacher."
(A). After proofreading the essay, the teacher corrected errors.
(B). After proofreading, errors were corrected by the teacher in the essay.
(C). The teacher, after proofreading the essay, errors were corrected.
(D). Errors were corrected by the teacher after proofreading the essay.
Q23. Select the sentence that uses a colon correctly:
"There is one principle in this course ____ integrity above all else."
(A). There is one principle in this course: integrity above all else.
(B). There is one principle in this course; integrity above all else.
(C). There is one principle in this course, integrity above all else.
(D). There is one principle in this course - integrity above all else.
Q24. Choose the best revision for conciseness:
"At this point in time, we cannot determine the outcome."
(A). We cannot determine the outcome.
(B). Currently, we cannot determine the outcome.
(C). At present, we cannot determine the outcome.
(D). Right now, we cannot determine the outcome.

Q25. Select the sentence that best maintains consistency in point of view:
"If one aspires to excellence, you must put forth the effort."
(A). If one aspires to excellence, one must put forth the effort.
(B). If one aspires to excellence, you must put forth the effort.
(C). If you aspire to excellence, one must put forth the effort.
(D). If you aspire to excellence, you must put forth the effort.
Q26. Identify the sentence that best corrects an error in word choice:
"He was incredibly excited about the opportunity."
(A). He was extremely excited about the opportunity.
(B). He was literally excited about the opportunity.
(C). He was very excited about the opportunity.
(D). He was truly excited about the opportunity.
Q27. Select the best revision to eliminate extraneous words:
"Due to the fact that it was snowing, the game was postponed."
(A). Because it was snowing, the game was postponed.
(B). Since it was snowing, the game was postponed.
(C). Owing to snow, the game was postponed.
(D). As it was snowing, the game was postponed.

MATH MODULE 1

Q1. Solve for x:
$5x - 7 = 18$
(A). 4
(B). 5
(C). 6
(D). 7
Q2. If $f(x) = 4x - 3$, what is $f(3)$?
(A). 6
(B). 8
(C). 9
(D). 10
Q3. Simplify the expression:
$(6x^3) \div (3x)$
(A). $2x$
(B). $2x^2$
(C). $3x^2$
(D). $2x^3$
Q4. Solve for y:
$(3y)/4 = 12$
(A). 12
(B). 14
(C). 16
(D). 18
Q5. What is the slope of the line passing through the points (2, 3) and (6, 11)?
(A). 1
(B). 2
(C). 3
(D). 4
Q6. Solve the inequality:
$2x + 5 < 15$
(A). $x < 4$
(B). $x < 5$
(C). $x \leq 5$
(D). $x > 5$

Q7. If $7/x = 14$, what is x?
(A). 0.5
(B). 1
(C). 2
(D). 7

Q8. What is the area of a square with side length 8?
(A). 16
(B). 32
(C). 64
(D). 128

Q9. The ratio of boys to girls in a class is 3:4. If there are 18 boys, how many girls are there?
(A). 20
(B). 22
(C). 24
(D). 26

Q10. Expand and simplify:
$2(3x + 4) - x$
(A). $5x + 8$
(B). $5x - 8$
(C). $6x + 8$
(D). $3x + 8$

Q11. Solve for x:
$(x/5) - 3 = 2$
(A). 20
(B). 25
(C). 30
(D). 35

Q12. What is the value of $\sqrt{121}$?
(A). 10
(B). 11
(C). 12
(D). 13

Q13. A car travels 120 miles in 2.5 hours. What is its average speed (in mph)?
(A). 40
(B). 45
(C). 48
(D). 50

Q14. Solve the proportion:
$3/4 = x/12$
(A). 8
(B). 9
(C). 10
(D). 12

Q15. What is the solution set for the equation:
$2(x - 2) = 2x - 4$?
(A). $x = 2$
(B). $x = 0$
(C). All real numbers
(D). No solution

Q16. If $f(x) = x^2 - 1$, what is $f(0)$?
(A). 0
(B). 1
(C). -1
(D). -2

Q17. Solve the absolute value equation:

$|x - 1| = 4$

(A). $x = 5$ only

(B). $x = -3$ only

(C). $x = 5$ or $x = -3$

(D). $x = 3$ or $x = -5$

Q18. Find the solutions to the equation:

$x^2 - 9 = 0$

(A). $x = 3$

(B). $x = -3$

(C). $x = 3$ or $x = -3$

(D). $x = -3$ only

Q19. What is the area of a triangle with a base of 14 and a height of 5?

(A). 21

(B). 35

(C). 28

(D). 70

Q20. Simplify the expression (assume $x \neq -4$):

$(x^2 - 16) \div (x + 4)$

(A). $x - 4$

(B). $x + 4$

(C). $x^2 - 4$

(D). $x - 8$

Q21. Solve for x:

$(2/3)x + 1 = 5$

(A). 5

(B). 6

(C). 7

(D). 8

Q22. What is the distance between the points (0, 0) and (3, 4)?

(A). 3

(B). 4

(C). 5

(D). 6

MATH MODULE 2

Q1. Solve for x:

$3x^2 - 2x - 8 = 0$

(A). $x = 2$ or $x = -4/3$

(B). $x = -2$ or $x = 4/3$

(C). $x = 2$ or $x = -2$

(D). $x = 4/3$ or $x = -2$

Q2. If $f(x) = \sqrt{(5x + 20)}$, what is $f(0)$?

(A). $2\sqrt{5}$

(B). $\sqrt{20}$

(C). 4

(D). 5

Q3. Solve the system of equations:

$x + y = 7$

$x - y = 1$

(A). $x = 4, y = 3$

(B). $x = 3, y = 4$

(C). $x = 5, y = 2$

(D). $x = 2, y = 5$

Q4. Factor the quadratic:

$x^2 + 7x + 12$

(A). $(x + 2)(x + 6)$

(B). $(x + 3)(x + 4)$

(C). $(x + 1)(x + 12)$

(D). $(x + 4)^2$

Q5. If $g(x) = 3x^2 - 2x + 1$, what is $g(-2)$?

(A). 15

(B). 16

(C). 17

(D). 18

Q6. Simplify the radical expression:

$\sqrt{98} - 3\sqrt{2}$

(A). $2\sqrt{2}$

(B). $4\sqrt{2}$

(C). $5\sqrt{2}$

(D). $6\sqrt{2}$

Q7. For what value of x is the expression

$(x^2 - 25)/(x - 5)$

undefined?

(A). 5

(B). −5

(C). 25

(D). 0

Q8. Solve the inequality:

$2x^2 - 8 < 0$

(A). $x < -2$ or $x > 2$

(B). $-2 < x < 2$

(C). $-2 \leq x \leq 2$

(D). $x > -2$

Q9. Find the vertex of the parabola given by:

$y = -x^2 + 4x - 3$

(A). (2, 1)

(B). (2, −1)

(C). (1, 2)

(D). (−2, 1)

Q10. If $f(x) = (2x + 3)/(x - 1)$, what is $f(2)$?

(A). 4

(B). 5

(C). 6

(D). 7

Q11. A circle has an area of 49π. What is its radius?

(A). 6

(B). 7

(C). 8

(D). 9

Q12. Solve for x:

$\log_2(x) = 4$

(A). 8

(B). 12

(C). 16

(D). 32

Q13. If $h(x) = 1/(x + 2)$, what is $h(-1)$?

(A). −1

(B). 0

(C). 1
(D). 2

Q14. What is the sum of the first 7 terms of an arithmetic sequence with first term 3 and common difference 4?
(A). 100
(B). 105
(C). 110
(D). 115

Q15. Simplify the expression:
$(8x^2 - 32) \div (4x)$
(A). $2(x - 2)(x + 2)/x$
(B). $2x - 8$
(C). $2(x^2 - 4)/x$
(D). $(x - 2)(x + 2)/x$

Q16. If the probability of event A is 0.25 and the probability of event B is 0.4 (and they are independent), what is the probability that both occur?
(A). 0.1
(B). 0.65
(C). 0.25
(D). 0.4

Q17. Solve for y in terms of x:
$5y - 3x = 15$
(A). $y = 3 + (3/5)x$
(B). $y = 3x + 15$
(C). $y = (3x - 15)/5$
(D). $y = (15 - 3x)/5$

Q18. Find the sum of the infinite geometric series with first term 12 and common ratio 1/3.
(A). 16/3
(B). 18
(C). 20
(D). 24

Q19. If $\sin \theta = 0.8$ for an acute angle θ, what is $\cos \theta$?
(A). 0.4
(B). 0.5
(C). 0.6
(D). 0.8

Q20. For the function $f(x) = x^3 + x$, find $f(2)$.
(A). 8
(B). 10
(C). 12
(D). 14

Q21. Solve for x:
$7/(x - 2) = 7$
(A). 2
(B). 3
(C). 4
(D). 5

Q22. A rectangular prism has dimensions length = 5, width = 4, and height = 7. What is its volume?
(A). 120
(B). 130
(C). 140
(D). 150

ANSWER KEY READING & WRITING

Module 1 Answer Key

Passage 1 (Reading): Q1. (B) Q2. (C) Q3. (A) Q4. (C)
Passage 2 (Reading): Q5. (B) Q6. (B) Q7. (A) Q8. (B)
Independent Grammar & Writing: Q9. (A) Q10. (C) Q11. (B) Q12. (B) Q13. (A) Q14. (B) Q15. (A) Q16. (C) Q17. (B) Q18. (A) Q19. (B) Q20. (A) Q21. (A) Q22. (A) Q23. (A) Q24. (A) Q25. (A) Q26. (A) Q27. (A)

Module 2 Answer Key

Passage 1 (Reading): Q1. (B) Q2. (B) Q3. (A) Q4. (C) Q5. (B)
Passage 2 (Reading): Q6. (B) Q7. (B) Q8. (A) Q9. (B) Q10. (C)
Independent Grammar & Writing: Q11. (A) Q12. (A) Q13. (A) Q14. (A) Q15. (A) Q16. (A) Q17. (A)

Q18. (A)
Q19. (A)
Q20. (A)
Q21. (A)
Q22. (A)
Q23. (A)
Q24. (A)
Q25. (A)
Q26. (A)
Q27. (A)

ANSWER KEY MATH

Module 1 Answer Key

Q1. (B)
Q2. (C)
Q3. (B)
Q4. (C)
Q5. (B)
Q6. (B)
Q7. (A)
Q8. (C)
Q9. (C)
Q10. (A)
Q11. (B)
Q12. (B)
Q13. (C)
Q14. (B)
Q15. (C)
Q16. (C)
Q17. (C)
Q18. (C)
Q19. (B)
Q20. (A)
Q21. (B)
Q22. (C)

Module 2 Answer Key

Q1. (A)
Q2. (A)
Q3. (A)
Q4. (B)
Q5. (C)
Q6. (B)
Q7. (A)
Q8. (B)
Q9. (A)
Q10. (D)
Q11. (B)
Q12. (C)
Q13. (C)
Q14. (B)

Q15. (A)
Q16. (A)
Q17. (A)
Q18. (B)
Q19. (C)
Q20. (B)
Q21. (B)
Q22. (C)

Made in the USA
Las Vegas, NV
21 June 2025

23903907R00164